tear here

A Chronology of Shipwrecks

1200 B.C.E.: An ancient Phoenician ship, fully loaded with copper ingots and other commodities, sinks just off the shore of Uluburun, Turkey; its artifacts, which were recovered by archaeologists during the 1980s and 1990s, provide a wealth of historical information.

July 19, 1545: The Tudor warship *Mary Rose* sinks for no apparent reason while engaging French forces, killing more than 650 sailors and soldiers; Henry VIII, who named the ship after his sister, witnesses the event.

September 5, 1622: The 1622 Spanish Treasure Fleet is smashed by a powerful hurricane, which sinks eight of the 28 ships, including the treasure-laden ships *Atocha* and *Margarita*.

January 1686: The personal ship of French explorer Robert Cavalier, Sieur de LaSalle—the *Belle*—sinks in Matagorda Bay, Texas, stranding the explorer who is later murdered.

July 31, 1715: 1,200 die when 11 of 12 ships of Spain's 1715 Spanish Treasure Fleet sink during a massive hurricane off Florida's East Coast; though some treasure is salvaged, what remains inspired the modern era of treasure hunting that continues today.

1789: Mutineer leader Fletcher Christian orders the HMS *Bounty* burned and sunk in what has become known as Bounty Bay off Pitcairn Island in the Pacific Ocean.

August 28, 1791: The HMS *Pandora,* filled with arrested HMS *Bounty* mutineers, is smashed off Australia's northern coast, killing four mutineers and 31 crewmen.

September 11, 1857: Filled with California gold, the steamer SS *Central America* sinks in a hurricane, killing 426 men off the coast of North Carolina.

October 26, 1859: The steam and sail propelled *Royal Charter* is flung onto the rocky coast of Anglesey, Wales, where a hurricane smashes the ship in sight of shore killing 447 men, women, and children.

April 15, 1912: The RMS *Titanic* strikes an iceberg and quickly sinks, killing 1,517, shocking the world, and creating a scandal over a shortage of lifeboats on the liner.

May 7, 1915: A German U-boat's torpedo strikes the luxury liner *Lusitania* off Ireland's southeast coast, killing 1,198; American opinion is hardened against Germany.

May 27, 1941: The Nazi battleship *Bismarck,* struck by British torpedoes and gunfire, sinks in the Atlantic while attempting to return from a raid on Allied shipping during World War II; the event boosts British morale; nearly 2,100 German sailors are lost.

May 2, 1942: The British cruiser HMS *Edinburgh,* filled with Soviet gold bound for England, is scuttled after being damaged by Nazi torpedoes and surface ship gunfire north of Murmansk, Russia.

June 24, 1944: Imperial Japanese Navy submarine *I-52* is ambushed by a U.S. aircraft carrier in the South Atlantic and destroyed by a sound-chasing torpedo; an estimated 100 die aboard the submarine, carrying two tons of gold to Nazi Germany.

July 26, 1956: The Italian luxury liner *Andréa Doria* is impaled by the bow of the Swedish liner *Stockholm* and sinks; a total of 51 people are killed, although 1,660 are rescued from the *Andréa Doria*.

November 10, 1975: A storm lashing Lake Superior catches the iron ore carrier *Edmund Fitzgerald* in its grips, and the ship is mysteriously lost; the tragedy kills all 29 aboard; Gordon Lightfoot writes a hit song based upon the tragedy.

May 22, 1968: The nuclear attack submarine USS *Scorpion* is lost with all 99 hands in the Mid-Atlantic; eventually found, the *Scorpion*'s wreckage has yet to provide conclusive evidence as to the cause of its loss.

alpha
books

W9-CBT-259

Wealthy Wrecks

Some sunken ships are full of treasure and others are just plain old ships. Following are the richest wrecks discussed in this book. Beware of the estimates, because it is hard to determine how much sunken treasure is worth until it's all actually sold. The highest estimates, of each treasure are provided here. The actual value could be more or (unfortunately) less.

$1 billion: The SS *Central America's* September 11, 1857, lost while carrying a reputed 21 tons of gold from California makes it perhaps the richest wreck yet found. Since much of the gold is in pristine ingots and thousands of unissued coins, the gold is worth far more as collector's items—if buyers will pay the price. Priced for its gold alone, the find would be worth an estimated $172 million (which isn't too bad either). The latter figure is based upon a 1999 gold price of $256 per ounce.

$1 billion to $10 billion: The Spanish treasure ship *San Jose* had the misfortune of running into British warships off Columbia's coast on June 7, 1708, where a fortunate shot sent the ship to the bottom of the Atlantic. The ship has not only not been recovered, its location remains in question and its ownership is a matter of dispute. The amounts provided are estimates made as to the value of the treasure.

$20 million: This estimate is a very rough one for the amount of treasure recovered in contemporary times. The ships of the 1715 Spanish Treasure Fleet were carrying a reputed 14 million pesos worth of valuables, roughly seven times the amount carried aboard the *Atocha* and *Margarita* combined. Although some of the treasure was salvaged by Spain and others—including adventurers and pirates soon after the ships sank—much remained. It's estimated that $20 million in treasure was recovered from the various wrecks during the 1960s.

$400 million: The estimated cumulative value of silver, gold, emeralds, and jewelry aboard the Spanish treasure fleet ships *Atocha* and *Margarita* that sank in a hurricane while sailing as part of a 28-ship fleet on September 5, 1622. Between the two, they were carrying two million pesos worth of treasure by 1622 valuations. Famed treasure hunter Mel Fisher doggedly searched for these famous treasure ships for two decades.

$45 million: The 5.5 tons of gold carried aboard Britain's cruiser the HMS *Edinburgh* was being shipped by the Soviet Union's Joseph Stalin to pay for supplies during World War II. Although it was initially believed that another 4.5 tons of the yellow stuff was on the ship, this turned out to be just another treasure rumor.

$16 million: Well, for treasure hunters like us this just doesn't sound like very much, but it's today's price for two tons of pure gold carried aboard the *Royal Charter* when it was smashed against the rocks of Anglesey Island in Wales on October 26, 1859. If the treasure were found intact today (since most of it was in the form of bullion and coins) its value might be far greater since the items would be highly prized collectibles! Some of the gold is still being recovered, though much was allegedly picked up by inhabitants of the area. Like the SS *Central America,* the *Royal Charter* was bringing back miners and their gold from another gold rush—in Australia!

$16 million: Although the two tons of gold bullion aboard the World War II Japanese submarine *I-52* might be worth much more than this figure, as of the writing of this book it was still lying three miles beneath the Atlantic. If the gold bars—destined for Nazi Germany as payment for military technology— are recovered and sold to collectors, they could fetch many times more than their mere commodity price listed here.

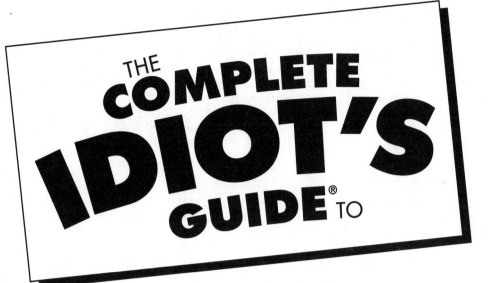

THE **COMPLETE IDIOT'S GUIDE**® TO

Sunken Ships and Treasures

by Stephen Johnson

alpha books

Macmillan USA, Inc.
201 West 103rd Street
Indianapolis, IN 46290

A Pearson Education Company

Copyright © 2000 by Stephen Johnson

All rights reserved. No part of this book shall be reproduced, stored in a retrieval system, or transmitted by any means, electronic, mechanical, photocopying, recording, or otherwise, without written permission from the publisher. No patent liability is assumed with respect to the use of the information contained herein. Although every precaution has been taken in the preparation of this book, the publisher and author assume no responsibility for errors or omissions. Neither is any liability assumed for damages resulting from the use of information contained herein. For information, address Alpha Books, 201 West 103rd Street, Indianapolis, IN 46290.

THE COMPLETE IDIOT'S GUIDE TO and Design are registered trademarks of Macmillan USA, Inc.

International Standard Book Number: 0-02-863231-1
Library of Congress Catalog Card Number: Available upon request.

03   02   01   00   4   3   2   1

Interpretation of the printing code: the rightmost number of the first series of numbers is the year of the book's printing; the rightmost number of the second series of numbers is the number of the book's printing. For example, a printing code of 00-1 shows that the first printing occurred in 2000.

Printed in the United States of America

Note: This publication contains the opinions and ideas of its author. It is intended to provide helpful and informative material on the subject matter covered. It is sold with the understanding that the author and publisher are not engaged in rendering professional services in the book. If the reader requires personal assistance or advice, a competent professional should be consulted.

The author and publisher specifically disclaim any responsibility for any liability, loss or risk, personal or otherwise, which is incurred as a consequence, directly or indirectly, of the use and application of any of the contents of this book.

Alpha Development Team

Publisher
Marie Butler-Knight

Editorial Director
Gary M. Krebs

Associate Managing Editor
Cari Shaw Fischer

Marketing Brand Manager
Felice Primeau

Acquisitions Editors
Amy Gordon
Randy Ladenheim-Gil

Development Editors
Phil Kitchel
Amy Zavatto

Assistant Editor
Georgette Blau

Production Team

Development Editor
Alana J. Morgan

Production Editors
Tammy Ahrens
Christy Wagner

Copy Editor
June Waldman

Cover Designer
Mike Freeland

Illustrator
Jody P. Schaeffer

Designer
Scott Cook and Amy Adams of DesignLab

Indexer
Brad Herriman

Layout/Proofreading
Angela Calvert
Mary Hunt

Contents at a Glance

Contents

Foreword

When Stephen Johnson called to tell me that he was going to try to pack the history of shipwreck exploration into one volume, my first thought was that he was either insane, a masochist—or both. Few subjects capture one's imagination with the intensity of shipwrecks and deep-ocean exploration and the lore of this field is filled with half-truths, blustery self-promotion, and outright fabrications. Separating truth from fiction is a monumental job—even for an experienced investigative reporter like Stephen. When I received the manuscript, I was frankly astounded by the detail and accuracy of his research. Through this book, you'll be given a peek into a mysterious universe—one to which only a handful of insiders or researchers were privy—until now.

Welcome to the world of maritime tragedies and triumphs: pirates and scalawags; and explorers and pioneers. These pages will introduce you to the excitement of exploration that first drew me in. Life holds few thrills like setting eyes on a shipwreck that has remained hidden for 2,500 years, or holding an artifact that was last held by a Spanish sailor 350 years earlier. I have not been disappointed in my quest for knowledge and adventure—and, I daresay—neither will you, as you experience these same adventures on the printed page.

What makes shipwrecks so fascinating? As you read this book, you'll discover each nautical tragedy features a host of twisting sub-plots—some even take place centuries after the shipwreck itself. While it is easy to think of a deep-ocean site in terms of riches for the lucky finder, the most valuable part of every shipwreck is the tale it tells.

It is estimated that there are at least 3,000,000 shipwrecks throughout the world. Each is a slice of history that captures a moment in time better than any photograph. This amazing submerged record of civilization and life at sea extends back in time to earliest man and captures the essence of every culture that has challenged Neptune's lair.

Technology today opens the way to the discovery of every shipwreck on the ocean floor. We conduct deep-ocean searches covering 60 square miles a day and find anything bigger than a 55-gallon drum. Working a half-mile mile deep is an everyday occurrence, and it is not unusual for us to find several shipwrecks in a good day's work. Many have no economic value, but archaeologists and historians can extract a fascinating story from each and every one.

So ... turn the page and dive into our world. You've got a first-class ticket to visit an amazing parallel universe, and you can do it from your favorite easy chair.

Greg Stemm, Tampa, Florida

Greg Stemm is a pioneer in deep-ocean shipwreck exploration and the co-founder of Odyssey Marine Exploration, a publicly traded company in the business of exploring deep-ocean shipwrecks. He directed the team that accomplished the world's first deep archaeological excavation, recovering 17,000 artifacts from a Spanish Galleon 1,500 feet deep—using only robotics.

He is currently president of the Professional Shipwreck Explorers Association, a UNESCO delegate to the Convention for the Protection of Underwater Cultural Heritage, a director of the World Entrepreneurs Organization, and past international president of Young Entrepreneurs Organization. Mr. Stemm has authored articles and lectured extensively on shipwreck exploration. He can be reached at www.shipwreck.net.

Introduction

Who can explain the fascination we all have with shipwrecks that litter the seas and waterways of the world? Some shipwrecks are older than 30 centuries, while others are relatively young, such as the *Titanic* lost in 1912. While you read this book, a boat, a ship, or some other watercraft is sinking somewhere. It's also highly likely that people are dying in these maritime mishaps. Sailing is serious business, and dead men tell no tales, which is why so many shipwrecks remain mysteries.

When ships are lost, especially large ones whose occupants lose their lives, public interest in these vessels is piqued. If officials are unable to explain why the ship sank, the ingredient of mystery is added to an already tragic situation. A thousand years ago we blamed sea monsters. Today, other speculation stirs the cauldron of the public psyche, turning everyone into a nautical sleuth with each producing his or her own theory.

Incredulity at the sinking of the so-called unsinkable *Titanic* was so great that people continue to devise theories about its loss. The same is true for the 1968 loss of the nuclear attack submarine USS *Scorpion* and for the more recent sinkings of massive bulk carriers that have simply disappeared. When something as expensive and complex as a ship sinks, it's often hard for people to believe that the sea can defeat technology and months of effort. Sometimes when these ships are found again weeks or years after they were lost, all the speculation begins anew.

These rediscovered maritime remains may contain ancient clay jars transported by Phoenician seafarers or the massive naval guns of the Nazi battleship *Bismarck*. Other ships, such as the galleons of the Spanish treasure fleet, have scattered their silver and gold along the jagged coral reefs that tore out their bellies during long-forgotten Caribbean hurricanes. When found, there is often a scramble by salvors and treasure hunters to turn tragedy into profit—a long and honorable custom of the sea bound by maritime law.

However, those who bring relics and artifacts to the surface are also hoisting controversy into the sunlight as public officials and historians argue against the "plunder" of wrecks for personal gain. Other critics go farther, saying people should take only pictures of some wrecks as a way of showing respect for the loss of life they might represent. Treasure hunting—which for decades seemed like a harmless and light-hearted pastime—is now under harsh criticism. Treasure-hunting legends like the late Mel Fisher are both revered and reviled.

Perhaps each one of us should ask ourselves why shipwrecks seem to have such a profound effect. Do we imagine ourselves lucky that fate did not place us aboard a ship broken by huge waves in a storm-tossed sea? Do we look in suppressed horror at what happened to those who did suffer such a fate? Does a primordial fear of the dangerous and mysterious sea coexist with an equally unquenchable urge to dare it with ships large and small?

Why is it that an airliner is considered little more than scrap metal after its shattered remains have told their tale to investigators? Perhaps it's because the modern conveyance of a jet airliner—built of high-technology materials and lightweight alloys—seems almost disposable, whereas a 1,000-foot cargo ship weighing thousands of tons seems like something that could not fall victim to the vicissitudes and capriciousness of nature. No one argues for an airliner to be left where it fell as a monument to its victims or as a tourist attraction.

Airliners are merely a means to travel from one place to another. On the other hand, a ship is imbued with the spirit of its crew. It is not only a mode of travel and transport, but also a home to those who live aboard it. Aside from being engineering marvels, ships are where meals are cooked and beds are made and people work every day. The ship and the crew live a symbiotic existence, depending on one another for survival.

Yet shipwrecks—hidden as they are beneath the unforgiving seas—gain a measure of respect and reverence accorded no other manmade object. Who isn't hushed into awed silence upon seeing the ghostly ships on the seafloor through the cameras of explorers like Robert Ballard or Jacques-Yves Cousteau?

The Complete Idiot's Guide to Sunken Ships and Treasures doesn't pretend to be a manual on how to hunt for treasure or how to sail your way through complex maritime law. But it does allow you to wade knee-deep into the world of sunken treasure ships and frightful maritime disasters during war and peace. It also provides a glimpse at the technology and history of ocean exploration that have provided a new era of shipwreck discovery.

Part 1, "Ghost Ships," sends you around the world for an overview of what is laying beneath the waves in the form of shipwrecks and opens the door for a peek at the pioneers of underwater discovery. Gain an understanding of how so many ships went from sailing proudly to sinking ignominiously only to find themselves the silent epicenters of controversy years later as their fate is debated between the treasure hunters and the historians.

Part 2, "The Many Pleasures of Sunken Treasures," takes you among the glimmering heaps of gold and the piles of emeralds of the treasure ships held in safekeeping by the depths. Learn why some spend years in an unsuccessful search for gold and discover how inventiveness has slowly made treasure hunting easier. If you've ever wondered where all that sunken treasure came from, you'll find the whole brutal and unhappy story here. And before even sticking your toe in the water to recover your sunken treasure, take a moment and read about the mine field that is now modern salvage law.

Part 3, "Shipwrecks: Oldies with Goodies," takes you on a journey into the past to some of the most fascinating shipwrecks ever to occur and to some of the incredible stories of how they were found and sometimes salvaged. Visit a 3,300-year-old wreck off the coast of Turkey that is still unlocking secrets to the past. Then sail on to learn why tons of treasure were torn from the innards of mortally wounded Spanish treasure ships in the seventeenth and eighteenth centuries. Witness the nineteenth-century deaths of the treasure ships SS *Central America* and the *Royal Charter,* which carried hundreds to watery graves after heroic struggles against hurricanes.

Part 4, "The Bigger They Are, the Harder They Fall," moves you to the sinking of some of the biggest and most famous ships. The luxury-liner disasters include the sinking of the *Titanic* and the *Andréa Doria* 44 years apart and the fearsome sinking of the *Lusitania* by a German torpedo in 1915. As you will see, more recent wrecks such as the 1975 loss of the Great Lakes iron ore carrier *Edmund Fitzgerald* still hold much fascination.

Part 5, "Sleeping Warriors," carries you through the oil-stained waters of naval warfare to look at a trio of maritime disasters involving warships. Learn about the unusual Japanese treasure submarine sunk in the Atlantic by the Americans in World War II and read the almost-forgotten story of a British cruiser that was torpedoed while carrying Soviet dictator Joseph Stalin's gold. The Cold War also left behind a legacy of shipwrecks including the mysterious 1968 loss of the nuclear submarine USS *Scorpion*.

Part 6, "Pirates and Other Treasure Hunters," introduces you to pirates who took treasure before it sank and to modern treasure-hunting legend Mel Fisher, who fought with attorneys instead of a cutlass to claim his booty from the waters around the Florida Keys.

Extras

In addition to being filled with chapters pertaining to virtually every issue surrounding shipwrecks and sunken treasure, *The Complete Idiot's Guide to Sunken Ships and Treasures* contains a glossary of terms related to seafaring, deep-ocean exploration, and salvage. You will also find a listing of shipwreck museums and underwater parks, a chronology of notable shipwrecks, and a comprehensive reading list for those wanting to go deeper into the subjects covered here. Along the way, the following boxes provide additional information:

Shiver Me Timbers

Learn things that may surprise you about shipwrecks, the undersea world, and the complexities of treasure hunting. This box is where you will also see some persistent myths dispelled.

Don't Go Overboard!

Warnings and hazards pertaining to the pitfalls of exploring sunken ships are found here. These sidebars include not only safety tips for budding underwater explorers but also warnings about legal pitfalls associated with treasure hunting and souvenir gathering.

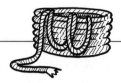

Know The Ropes

Explanations of specialized lore and technology encountered on the high seas (and beneath the seas) are here to make getting through the book smooth sailing. You can pick up tidbits on ways to spot sunken ships and the best ways to remove the silt that covers them.

Words To Treasure

Definitions to help you understand the difference between the "keel" of a ship and its "longitudinal bulkheads" are given in these boxes. You may not be an admiral after reading these definitions, but you'll certainly be less of a landlubber.

Special Thanks to the Technical Reviewer

The Complete Idiot's Guide to Sunken Ships and Treasures was reviewed by an expert who double-checked the accuracy of what you'll learn here, to help us ensure that this book gives you everything you need to know about sunken ships and treasures. Special thanks are extended to Angus Konstam.

Trademarks

All terms mentioned in this book that are known to be or are suspected of being trademarks or service marks have been appropriately capitalized. Alpha Books and Macmillan USA, Inc. cannot attest to the accuracy of this information. Use of a term in this book should not be regarded as affecting the validity of any trademark or service mark.

Part 1
Ghost Ships

Did you ever think of how many thousands and thousands of ships are lying beneath the oceans, lakes, and rivers of the world? How they got there and how they've been converted into legends is a fascinating story.

The history of undersea exploration has also become the story of shipwreck location and recovery with undersea pioneers learning how to dive deeper and stay longer, making more and more wrecks, particularly those at great depths, available for recovery. This technology has opened up the Titanic, Lusitania, *and numerous treasure ships to the efforts of salvors.*

Controversy stirs the waters around shipwrecks as archaeologists and historians argue for preservation and study while treasure hunters fight to keep recovered valuable treasure and artifacts. This part concludes with a look at the debate between the preservationists and the treasure hunters.

Chapter 1

Bound for Oblivion

In This Chapter

➤ The hidden world of shipwrecks

➤ Shipwreck mystery and mystique

➤ Shipwrecks: underwater time machines

➤ Life and death at sea

➤ How we talk about lost ships

➤ Learning from shipwrecks: what we learn from these ships

The sea is a dangerous place! Before airline disasters hypnotized the public, shipwrecks dominated disaster news. Hundreds of people went to sea in a capable ship only to disappear mysteriously, far at sea, or smashed by a storm against the shore for those on land to witness.

For thousands of years, ships simply disappeared and their wrecks found only by accident—if at all.

Think about this: Beneath every navigable body of water on earth lie the remains of wrecked ships large and small, ancient and modern. These include everything imaginable from magnificent ocean liners like the RMS *Titanic* and the *Andréa Doria* to massive cargo carriers such as the *Edmund Fitzgerald* and the wooden-hulled treasure galleons of the Spanish Empire.

Ships have always contained the industrial and human treasure of the societies that built them. Although the larger ones took years to build and represented national and international investment, they could sink in hours or only minutes. The best example of this irony is the fate of the RMS *Titanic*. Up to 4,000 workers worked two years and one month to build the ship. It sank only 160 minutes after striking an iceberg.

It was unfathomable to believe the merciless sea could swallow the ship in just a few hours or minutes. Believe it or not, some ships acquired fame, fans, and immense popularity only after their demise!

Along with the remains of the dead, the seafloor is littered with everything from fine china to World War II Jeeps. And yes—it's true—Spanish treasure still glimmers in dappled light amid Caribbean reefs.

Thanks to modern technology and a new breed of deep-sea explorers, we have been able to come within inches of famous wrecks like the *Titanic* as well as other ships that are thousands of years older than that great ship. We have become fascinated more than ever by these sunken relics and their artifacts that open the door to a forgotten past.

But the question remains: Why are we so fascinated? What is it about these mysterious wrecks that compels us to dive down and check them out?

There's only one thing more interesting than something new: It's something old that has eluded rediscovery. A beached ship is an eventual eyesore. Lose it under water, though, and it's mystique blossoms. We're fascinated by the treasures of Egyptian King Tutankhamen, not just for their opulence but because they were "lost" for centuries. The same is true of sunken ships and the historical treasures they carry.

Deep water is dark and foreboding. What it hides has entered another, more alien, and therefore more mysterious, realm. Who doesn't want to take a peek into the heart of that darkness? Once located with modern sonar—or sometimes by accident—these long-lost ships can be seen standing as mute, untouched monuments to the catastrophes that sent them to the bottom.

The Hidden World of Shipwrecks

Whether the surface of the sea is glass-smooth or churned into a wrathful tempest by storms, its timeless appearance belies what lurks below. Beneath the endless swells of the sea's surface, man has inadvertently decorated the impassive depths with tragedy. Far below the whitecaps, beyond the reach of sunlight, is a frightening tableau of destruction and disaster.

In Micronesia's Truk Lagoon, the skulls of World War II Japanese sailors stare accusingly at sport divers who visit the sunken ships upon which they died. Dozens of Japanese ships lie where they were sunk in 1944 by the U.S. Navy.

In the dark depths of the Irish Sea, the broken hulk of the liner RMS *Lusitania* is a silent reminder of the price paid by civilians in war. Her sinking by a World War I German U-boat's torpedo remains controversial.

The *Lusitania* is an unseen behemoth snagging the nets of unwary fishing boats dragging their nets across the granite seafloor upon which the doomed rests. The wreck also ensnarls the imaginations of those still debating why the ship sank so quickly and new theories are still emerging. The sea neither gives up her dead—or her secrets— easily.

Words To Treasure

Davy Jones's locker refers to both the bottom of the sea and the collective graveyard for all who have died at sea and were never found. Mariners of the past characterized Davy Jones as a soul-snatching devil.

And if you think modern navigational technology and ship construction have beaten the sea, think again. Though we no longer see the massive loss of life at sea that once was rife, it still claims lives. On average, two cargo ships sink each month, often killing those aboard. The bulk cargo carrier *Derbyshire,* lost in a typhoon on September 9, 1980, killed 42 crewmen and two of their wives. The ship now lies two and a half miles below the Pacific, southeast of Japan's southern home islands.

Like the *Lusitania,* the *Derbyshire's* loss soon became a mystery. Experts are still debating what sent the 900-foot ship to the bottom. Although little notice is now paid to these deadly disasters, *Davy Jones's locker* continues to be replenished on a regular basis.

The next time you're flying over the ocean, look down and imagine what's beneath the water along with fish, sputtering volcanoes, and mud. Don't let yourself believe that there's a lot of nothing! Scattered from the Atlantic to the Pacific are ships that have carried the products and people of civilizations past and present, as well as countless artifacts that tell the stories of these tragically fated individuals.

Skulking beneath the North Atlantic are the *Titanic* and *Andréa Doria.* A few miles beyond those are the wrecked longships that belonged to Leif Erickson's Viking fleet, which discovered North America. The *Lusitania,* shrouded with eerie fishing nets, is resigned to the muck off the Irish coast, where the ship was torpedoed during the second year of World War I.

As your 747 cruises over the Mediterranean, picture Phoenician and Roman ships, where they settled side by side, albeit in different centuries, after being dashed against rocks. Later, banking over the Indian Ocean, visualize the skeletons of Arab pirate *dhows* resting on the bottom their triangular *lateen* sails long since rotted away. Now you can go to sleep, knowing that you're safe in the air.

Sunken Objects of Desire

Believe it or not, many people think that there's something frightening about the hulk of a shipwreck beneath the dark water, guarding its dead and brooding over its waterlogged cargo. To salvage operators who lay claim to a recent shipwreck, the cargo and the valuable materials such as copper used in ship construction provide quick cash. While treasure is nice, it's seldom encountered in the real world of maritime affairs. Today's cargo ships carry cars, iron ore, grain, and electronic goods.

Older ships that would rate barely a sneer from a grizzled salvage diver have far more allure for the seeker of valuable artifacts, nautical archaeologists, and the average person. Old shipwrecks are repositories for items that haven't been seen for hundreds or thousands of years. Some of these items have immense historical importance while others are highly valuable artifacts such as a bronze pin from the infamous HMS *Bounty*.

Words To Treasure

A **dhow** is an Arab ship that's equipped with a unique triangular sail, called a **lateen**. The **junk**, which originated in Asia, was built around a pair of dug-out canoes lashed together to form twin watertight compartments 500 years before a similar design was employed by the West.

The prospect of finding something rare beneath the sea has an allure that affects adventurers and academics. Sport divers are willing to risk their lives for something as mundane as a plumbing fixture from the sunken luxury liner *Andréa Doria*. Undersea archaeologists spend up to two decades carefully excavating priceless historical treasures from a single ancient shipwreck.

The mere rumor of sunken treasure usually begins a stampede of treasure hunters who flock to a wreck site, scour the surrounding seafloor, and file lawsuits against one another. The words "silver" or "gold" can turn the most cautious Midwest business owner into the wildest-eyed treasure hunter around. The desire for sunken treasure and artifacts has grown so strong that virtually every government has passed tough laws to protect shipwrecks in their waters from plunder.

But for you and me, these sunken ships represent fascinating time capsules that promise a thrilling glimpse into history. Their existence is also a silent testament to a horrific event that was fatal to many on board.

To salvage experts like England's Keith Jessop and treasure hunters like America's Tommy Thompson, however, these ships represent challenges for innovative undersea entrepreneurs. For ocean explorers like Robert Ballard and undersea archaeologists like George Bass, the artifacts in the ocean represent years of recovery and research before they can be used for study and public exhibit. To the bottom feeders of artifact recovery—those who illegally plunder legally protected wrecks—these artifacts mean a fast buck in a thriving underground antiquities market.

Thanks to modern technology, we can view the awesome sight of gigantic wrecks like the Nazi battleship *Bismarck* through Robert Ballard's deep-water photography. We have also been able to view some of the rarest artifacts—such as the only known gold scarab in the world at Turkey's Bodrum Museum. The artifact dates back 3,400 years, and it might never have been available for public display if someone hadn't put it on a ship that later sank!

Shiver Me Timbers

George Bass, the founder of the Texas A&M Institute for Nautical Archaeology and considered one of the founders of underwater archaeology, supervised the excavation of the oldest known shipwreck. Although Robert Ballard (who found the *Titanic* and the *Bismarck*) and explorer Jacques–Yves Cousteau have participated in archaeological expeditions, neither are archaeologists. Nevertheless, in 1952, Cousteau and his team of divers helped excavate one of the oldest ships ever recovered, predating Bass's first undersea archaeological excavation by eight years.

Sea of Trouble

The history of humanity is tied closely to seafaring. Take this a little further, and you'll see that the history of seafaring is the history of shipwrecks, lost lives, and sunken cargo. Although it is true that such cargo sometimes includes fantastic treasures, most modern ships that sink tend to go down with ordinary things like iron ore, dishes, or fertilizer.

As technology advanced, ships became larger and more capable, a trend that probably began soon after the proverbial cave dweller straddled a log and paddled across a swollen creek. Man's escalating battle against the treachery of the seas has been fought with ships that have become bigger and more powerful. Nonetheless, they are still vulnerable to bad weather, uncharted rocks, and poor seamanship.

Even when looking at a modest-size ship, it's hard to believe that something so beautiful and seemingly strong could ever be lost. It's this impression that makes the sinking of great ocean liners like the *Titanic* or the *Andréa Doria* seem improbable, if not unbelievable. But sink they did and still do, with fatal regularity.

Some of the biggest ships built have become easy prey for the treacherous waters of the world. Their names are famous: *Bismarck, Edmund Fitzgerald,* and *Titanic.* Other ships that met tragic ends are little known. Some, like the ferry *Estonia* that sank in 1994, carried hundreds to their death, but it's a good bet you haven't heard of it. Circumstances, media attention, and even hit songs play a role in determining which lost ship becomes famous.

Well-known shipwrecks are often the focus of speculation if the cause of their sinking is never clearly established. The guessing game continues for famous ships such as the *Bismarck* and the *Titanic* and lesser-known tragedies such as the nuclear submarine USS *Scorpion.*

Shiver Me Timbers

From 1990 to 1997, a total of 99 bulk carriers—freighters and tankers—sank with the loss of 654 lives. Maritime safety organization representatives are appalled over the rising rates of modern shipping losses. The United Nation's International Maritime Organization has established new safety regulations for bulk carriers above a certain size to reduce safety problems. Are you surprised? Such tragedies are seldom, if ever, publicized by the news media. Inadequate training of crews and the aging of the world's fleet of ships are often blamed.

Damp Distinction

Why is it that some shipwrecks become famous and others remain unknown? The reasons are numerous and confusing. Some, like the *Titanic,* are famous because of the great toll or circumstances; in this case, 1,517 people died on April 15, 1912, during the ship's maiden voyage to America. Public outrage over the scandalous tragedy increased when it was learned that the ship had lifeboats for only half those aboard. Add to these elements the wealth of the famous passengers, and the event is riveting.

Don't Go Overboard!

Never say "never" when at sea, matey. A ship is a marriage of a buoyant structure and a variety of machinery that can suffer a failure or an accident. The *Titanic* was not exempt from these realities and neither is any other ship. Although it was believed that ships as impressive as the *Titanic* couldn't sink, more recent disasters have shown bigger and more modern ships are equally vulnerable.

The Big Fitz

The Great Lakes ore carrier *Edmund Fitzgerald* is mostly famous because singer Gordon Lightfoot wrote a hit song about the ship. Lightfoot called the *Fitzgerald* "the pride of the American side."

Affectionately dubbed "The Big Fitz" by local mariners, this popular ship was lost in a powerful storm on November 10, 1975, with 29 men on board. Although the *Edmund Fitzgerald* was the largest ship to sink in Lake Superior, it was far from the most deadly shipwreck on the Great Lakes, and its cargo was an unromantic load of iron ore. Some might say that those aboard the *Fitzgerald* were merely ordinary sailors, but the haunting song "Wreck of the *Edmund Fitzgerald*" connected millions emotionally to the fate of a ship little known outside the Great Lakes region.

Sink the Bismarck!

The German battleship *Bismarck* was sunk in a desperate Atlantic naval fight with British ships on May 27, 1941, and should be famous for having one of the largest casualty counts in naval warfare. However, it's remembered because it symbolized the seemingly invincible prowess of the German military, and also because of a rousing hit song, "Sink the *Bismarck*," recorded by Texas balladeer Johnny Horton, that reached number three on the charts in 1960. The song was inspired by a movie of the same name.

It took an airplane's torpedoes and 400 shells from British warships to completely cripple the *Bismarck* before the crew used explosives to sink her. At least 2,200 of the *Bismarck*'s crew died. What's remembered is not the number of sailors killed, but how satisfying it was for the beleaguered British to finally win a victory against Adolph Hitler's then-victorious war machine. Britain's prime minister Winston Churchill is said to have issued the simple order: "Sink the *Bismarck!*"

Fickle Finger of Fame

Does anyone remember the 852 people who died when the Baltic Sea ferry *Estonia* capsized and sank off Finland's coast on September 28, 1994? It's an event 72 years younger than the *Titanic* tragedy, but no one's made a Hollywood movie about it yet and few people can even recall the event!

It certainly was a tragedy in terms of human suffering, but for some reason it still didn't grab the public imagination or even serve as the basis of a TV movie. If you take the *Titanic*'s circumstances as a guide, the *Estonia* just didn't have the right dramatic elements to gain notoriety among America's news media—after all, it was just a rather unglamorous ferry, carrying only ordinary people on what was supposed to be an uneventful trip.

So what happened? The disaster occurred when tons of water poured through a huge bow door that had popped open. The ferry sank in 20 minutes, and only 138 people survived the catastrophe.

Don't Go Overboard!

Like the *Titanic,* testimony showed that the *Estonia* was not prepared for disaster. Survivors said the ferry's life preservers didn't fit and were hard to put on. Many said the life preservers were tied together. Learning the use and location of lifesaving equipment—even on a short voyage—is recommended even if not required by government regulations. If something doesn't look safe, find another boat.

Shipwreck Mystery and Mystique

Perhaps we're so interested in shipwrecks and tragedies at sea because the sea itself is so mysterious. It covers most of the planet and cleverly hides what's below. Because the sea has always presented so many riddles, people have used mythology to explain its hazards and the creatures that inhabit it. In past centuries, when mariners failed to return from the sea, survivors would use mythology to explain what happened. Those legends live on, even though we take them less seriously now.

Henry Wadsworth Longfellow best described our mixture of fear and fascination with the sea in his poem "Golden Legend."

> *The tales of that awful, pitiless sea,*
> *With all its terror and mystery,*
> *The dim, dark sea, so like unto death,*
> *That divides and yet unites humankind.*

Longfellow's imagery recalls not only the actual hazards of the sea but also the tales that man has spun about this sinister environment. Although it may have become a place of myth and legend, the sea also boasts real horrors such as huge waves and crushing storms. Before we came to understand the sea as well as we do today, people explained the mysterious tragedies as the work of sea monsters that devoured sailors, as well as *sirens* that lured sailors and their ships against the rocks.

One of hundreds of such tales is the classic Greek tale of *Scylla* and *Charybdis,* which were mythical maritime hazards in the straits between Italy and Sicily. Charybdis was a whirlpool that swallowed ships and sailors, and opposite this whirlpool was Scylla, a female monster with six heads. Those who sailed close to the whirlpool risked being sucked into the sea, and those who sailed too close to Scylla were eaten alive. A cave along those straits still bears the name Scylla. The hazards presented in this myth are often ascribed as the source of two popular phrases: "Between a rock and a hard place" and "Between the devil and the deep blue sea."

Words To Treasure

A **siren** is not the shrill howl of a police car or an air raid warning system, but a mythical, beautiful woman whose singing lured sailors to their deaths against rocks.

Even the landlubbers among us carry a lot of psychological baggage when it comes to the sea. After all, the sea can be a scary place! When it swallows a ship—especially huge, modern ships like the *Titanic* or the *Andréa Doria*—it reasserts its awesome power. These events mesmerize us. The 1956 sinking of the *Andréa Doria*—the first sinking televised worldwide—confirmed what we all knew: The sea will kill if it can.

Disastrous Guessing Game

As soon as it's realized that a ship has been lost at sea, everyone begins speculating as to the cause of the disaster. In the absence of any witnesses or evidence, speculation fills the vacuum. Even in modern times, when myths have been mostly supplanted by science, people come up with wild stories. Eventually, many of these stories are accepted and compete with the facts. While such stories often fill a need for those grieving a loss, they also fuel excitement over shipwrecks.

When the *Titanic* was lost, the public was truly shocked. The ship, which had been such a magnificent shipbuilding project, was widely believed to be "unsinkable." Of course, no ship is, but since the *Titanic* went down on its first voyage, killing more than 1,500 people, speculation as to the cause was inevitable. Despite the fact that everyone knew the ship struck an iceberg, many couldn't understand why the collision penetrated so many of the *Titanic*'s massive compartments. Recent finds indicate the steel was so brittle that it may have indeed cracked, contributing to her loss.

Nuclear Age Speculation

The most perplexing mystery of modern nautical times is the loss of the nuclear submarine USS *Scorpion* on May 21, 1968. Unaware of the tragedy, families stood in the driving rain waiting for the *Scorpion* and its 99 men to return, even though the ship had died a mysterious death in the Atlantic several days before.

Because so little is known about what destroyed the submarine, people have speculated endlessly as to the cause. Some investigators believe that the crew was taken prisoner and the submarine destroyed by the Soviet navy. Others believe the submarine was blown up by one of its own faulty torpedoes. The U.S. Navy has said it doesn't know conclusively what happened to the *Scorpion*. While it's obvious the *Scorpion* wasn't sunk by the Soviets, speculation continues.

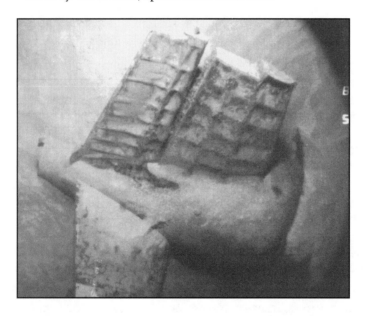

A ghostly image of the stern of the USS Scorpion *photographed 12,000 feet beneath the Atlantic, where it was lost without explanation.*
(Courtesy of the U.S. Navy)

It just shows that no matter how modern the age, playing the guessing game about what happened to lost ships is a fascinating pastime. Go back 3,000 years, and you may hear the loss of a ship being blamed on a sea monster. During the Cold War however, that sea monster became the Soviet navy.

Shiver Me Timbers

The Soviets continue to deny playing a role in the demise of the USS *Scorpion,* and the U.S. Navy long ago concluded the Soviets were nowhere near the submarine at the time of its loss. In a related story, however, one Soviet submarine was sunk when it collided with the American submarine USS *Tautog* in the North Pacific in 1970. The American crew listened as the Soviet submarine's hull imploded on its way to the seafloor. Damaged from the collision but still watertight, the *Tautog* crept home.

Shipwrecks: Underwater Time Machines

Although a sunken ship may appear unable of sailing another nautical mile, many shipwrecks still have one trip left in them—a voyage that can carry all of us back into era from which the ship came.

What if you opened a room that had been closed for 100 or even 500 years and found the room and its furnishings were completely untouched? It would be an amazing find and not dissimilar to shipwrecks discovered on the ocean floor. A key reason that shipwrecks appeal to many so strongly is that they are time machines to the past.

If something is abandoned on land, it won't be long before people have dismantled it and carried it away. Things on dry land are easy to see and get to. We count ourselves lucky when we find anything of value on the sidewalk or street, even if it's something as common as a coin. Sunken ships—with their treasures and cargo—are often invisible even if they lie only inches beneath the waves, hiding in the same hostile environment that claimed them.

Backward Glimpse

If a ship is lost at sea, it's held in a historical safe-deposit box—although a seriously wet one—and it is usually safe from tampering and plunder. Though deterioration occurs, portions of the wreck and its more durable artifacts can survive for hundreds of years.

Intact Chinese china recovered from 500-year-old wrecks often looks as new as the day it was made, since its smooth surface resists marine growth. The clock has literally stopped for these ships and for those who died. Untouched, these wrecks provide a priceless glimpse into the past.

Solemn Scenes

Over the past 40 years, technology has allowed us to explore the remains of sunken ships both large and small. The 1985 discovery of the *Titanic* was a famous event that triggered a tidal wave of interest in the "unsinkable" ocean liner.

The images taken of the shattered ship were breathtaking. On the seafloor were the shoes of those who had died after the ship's collision with an iceberg on April 14, 1912. Time had not erased even the smallest artifacts related to the *Titanic*'s demise, and entrepreneurs were quick to recognize the commercial value of such artifacts. Archaeologists, however, see these wrecks as road maps to the past that need to be carefully studied.

Don't Go Overboard!

The remains of any shipwreck more than 100 years old in U.S. coastal waters is considered a historical site, and its discovery should be reported to state authorities. It should not be plundered! It should not be touched without permission. Unrestrained treasure hunting could make you a criminal!

Life and Death at Sea

Lost at sea. The thought of it is enough to send a shiver up your spine! After all, it's only natural to believe that you'll meet your end on solid ground. What is probably more unnerving about dying at sea in a shipwreck is to think that your death also marks your simultaneous funeral. Your body is committed to the depths, never to be recovered.

The U.S. Navy has an official song dedicated to those whose who have died at sea. It is known simply as the "Navy Hymn" and recognizes the power of the ocean with solemn brevity:

> *Eternal Father, strong to save,*
> *Whose arm hath bound the restless wave,*
> *Who bidd'st the mighty ocean deep*
> *Its own appointed limits keep;*
> *Oh, hear us when we cry to Thee,*
> *For those in peril on the sea!*

Morbid Fascination

Fatal tragedy continues to fascinate us. Let's face it, we all like to gawk at car crashes, building fires, and even arguments between couples at restaurants. We can't help it. We're deeply fascinated by the misfortunes of others because we know that someday we, too, could be the victims. The more horrific the event, the more fascinated we are.

Paintings, early newspaper illustrations, and magazines found shipwrecks wonderful subjects. Renowned poets like Rudyard Kipling and Henry Wadsworth Longfellow wrote frightening and gloomy poetry about death at sea. It took a lot of imagination to make these scenes of people being killed and buried at the same time more horrible than they were.

Shiver Me Timbers

The *Titanic* was among the first ships to use wireless communications to call for help in a disaster. Instead of using SOS, it used the emergency call letters **CQD**. Such signals, when there was time to send them, meant ships would have some hope of help arriving. Wireless communication also meant the end of numerous sea mysteries because sinking ships were now able to notify anyone listening of their plight. The ship in distress would announce its position and answering ships would provide their own locations to establish when a rescue might be accomplished. Had the *Titanic* survivors not been rescued and if the ship's approximate position remained a mystery, the causes of the loss might still be unknown.

"SOS" was a signal adopted not because it meant "save our ship" but because the Morse code for the three letters of three dots, three dashes, and three dots seemed difficult to misinterpret. "CQD," the other early distress signal, was adopted since the code letters "CQ" had been applied to certain important telegraph messages on land. The "D" was added to indicate it was an urgent or "distress" message.

The Bad News

Imagine yourself in ancient Greece or China, waving goodbye to your friends as they depart for a journey across the water. When they fail to return as scheduled, you assume they were delayed. The horrible truth eventually becomes apparent—they will never return. You're never really sure what happened, since they couldn't send a radio message or pick up a telephone, so you create a myth to explain their disappearance. The mystery that surrounded voyages in the days before modern communication helped generate deeply rooted feelings about those lost at sea.

Those were the old days when it was often impossible to know why mariners who left on a good ship in fair weather didn't return. But don't kid yourself into thinking the bad old days are gone. Ships are still lost without a trace or a radio signal, despite modern technology. Sometimes we still have to use our imaginations to make sense out of what happened to a ship and an entire crew.

How We Talk About Lost Ships

Untold thousands have died at sea because of war, storms, and leaky ships, and a language grew up to describe the circumstances of those who never returned. At first, mariners who were late returning were considered "overdue." Soon after that, they were considered "missing." If they failed to return at all, they were then considered "lost," never to be heard from again. It's almost as if we can't make ourselves say that those poor people were drowned because of some terrible mishap.

Learning from Shipwrecks

Robert Ballard's discovery of the *Titanic* in 1985 laid to rest the belief that the liner had settled on the seafloor in a single piece. Though witnesses reported the *Titanic* went down bow first, raising its stern in the air before splitting in two, many believed the ship could be raised intact. Photographs have since proven that the ship did split in two and that its recovery, which was never more than an expensive pipe dream, was truly impossible.

Researchers have learned that many large ships break apart when they sink, and some even break apart before they sink. The cargo ship *Flare* snapped in two in Canada's Gulf of St. Lawrence on January 28, 1998, killing 21 crew members. Eerily, the bow of the ship continued to float past a handful of survivors until it finally sank. A deep submergence study of the lost USS *Scorpion* showed that it also split in two during its fall to the seafloor. Ships, just like falling airplanes, can tear themselves to pieces as they plummet.

Careful excavations of ancient wreck sites and the photographic expeditions of deep wrecks such as the *Bismarck* have yielded surprises and knowledge.

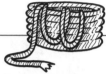

Know The Ropes

The U.S. Navy follows a very specific protocol when dealing with an overdue ship. If a vessel fails to arrive at an expected time, the ship is declared missing and an urgent search begins. If more time passes and the ship is not found, it is then declared lost. However, no mariner really believes the ship is unable to find its way. It's understood the ship is sunk, and its crew is most likely dead.

Sea Shell Shock

In June 1989, when Robert Ballard photographed the hull of the 50,000-ton battleship *Bismarck* 15,000 feet beneath the Atlantic, he was amazed to find the ship not only intact but also virtually devoid of shell holes. This evidence was confusing because it was believed that British warships had struck the *Bismarck* with up to 400 armor-piercing shells.

A close inspection of the *Bismarck* showed that many of the British shells had merely ricocheted off the massive warship's armor. Since much of her hull was buried in the mud, it was impossible to see all the potential damage. When Ballard returned with this information, a hot debate erupted over whether British gunnery sank the ship or the Germans—hoping to avoid British capture of the crippled *Bismarck*—had done the job themselves.

Ballard also discovered that the four massive turrets containing the *Bismarck's* eight 15-inch guns apparently fell out of their slots when the ship rolled upside down as it sank, leaving huge holes in the ship. Because the *Bismarck's* impact with the seafloor was so tremendous, explorers saw that it caused an underwater landslide when it hit the side of a submerged volcano.

Ready to Wear

After fighting a hurricane and flooding for 40 hours, the United States Mail Steamship *Central America* finally sank on September 12, 1857, killing 425 men and taking a fortune in California gold 8,000 feet beneath the Atlantic. After more than 130 years, the ship's unburied wood was eaten to nothing by wood-gobbling shipworms and bacteria, exposing its fabulously rich cargo of gold bars and freshly minted gold coins.

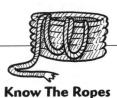

Know The Ropes

Textiles are among the rarest artifacts, since most are made from plant or animal fibers and are consumed either by insects or bacteria under ordinary conditions. Even clothing from the nineteenth century is relatively rare, since carpet beetles and a number of other vermin dine on natural fibers.

Although the sight of the gold on the seafloor was a treasure hunter's dream, another discovery was equally amazing—the intact clothing found in packed steamer trunks that were scattered about the wreck.

Carefully collected and preserved, items such as a white dress shirt and two morning robes were restored to virtually original condition. The state of the clothing was remarkable and provided researchers with superb examples of mid-nineteenth-century garments. To restore them to the best condition possible, the items had to be kept in seawater until they were returned to Ohio State University, where they were then freeze-dried to remove moisture and halt bacterial growth. The garments were then restored and preserved. Believe it or not, experts were even able to restore a readable copy of a novel entitled *Lady Lee's Widowhood* that was brought to the surface from one of the trunks!

The Least You Need to Know

➤ The seas and waterways of the world effectively hide sunken ships by the thousands to create a hidden world of artifacts and wreckage.

➤ Despite their impressive size and incredible cost, modern ships are still lost at sea, including the *Titanic*, which required 25 months and 4,000 workers to build.

➤ Some ships, like the *Titanic* and the *Edmund Fitzgerald*, became famous when they sank, but other, equally terrible sea disasters gained little notoriety.

➤ Mankind has traditionally used mythology to explain why ships failed to return from the sea, and people still play a guessing game to explain the mysterious loss of ships that seemed unsinkable.

➤ A ship that sinks in water deep enough to hide it is preserved from salvage, making it a potential source of historical knowledge for scientists hundreds or thousands of years later.

➤ The thought of death at sea has long haunted people as a particularly terrible thing, spawning gloomy poetry about the terrors of being lost without trace in the dark depths, and adding to the sea's dark mystique.

Underwater Sleuths

Although we continue to unravel questions about the biology, geology, and meteorology of the oceans, the general public seems to be more interested in what we've placed there by accident than what nature has done on purpose. With the discovery of the *Titanic* in 1985 by a joint French-American team 13,000 feet beneath the Atlantic, the public's hunger for the images and the stories of deep-water shipwrecks has steadily increased to fever pitch.

Though reaching shallow-water wrecks has long been easy, the once untouchable leviathans of the deep ocean have seized our imaginations. Even though the technology to locate these deep-sea mysteries has existed for more than 30 years, explorers and treasure hunters are only just now harnessing such innovations for the search of deep wrecks. Documentary filmmakers busily negotiate contracts with any interesting deep-sea shipwreck recovery operation to sate a hungry market. The shipwreck market is white hot, driven by our desire to see the ghost ships that have been hidden for so long.

But how did we start down the watery trail to these unfortunate wrecks, whose elusiveness may have been circumvented by technology and human curiosity? Who are the explorers that led us here, and what were their tools? Secure the hatches! We're going down for a look.

The First Deep-Sea Explorers

The first true deep-sea explorers were a rather unlikely pair. One was the wealthy engineering student Otis Barton, and the other was a curator of birds for the New York Zoological Society, William Beebe. Despite their different backgrounds, both men invented their own diving helmets and both were self-taught divers willing to risk everything for a glimpse of the ocean depths.

By the 1930s, military submarine crews had scarcely gone more than a few hundred feet underwater in their craft. Helmet divers were also limited to no more than the same depths due to decompression sickness caused by sea pressure. When Beebe began pondering what it would take to descend to such depths, few others were pondering the same challenge.

Beebe's interest in deep-sea exploration led him to write numerous articles on the subject. One of those articles caught the attention of Columbia University student Otis Barton, who had the same dream. Barton, whose grandfather had left him a generous inheritance, began trying to contact Beebe in 1926 with his own plans for a sphere that would allow two men to dive to great depths.

Deluged with numerous crackpot requests, Beebe ignored Barton until the student obtained an introduction through the help of a mutual friend. The bird curator was instantly impressed with Barton's elegantly simple design for a spherical pressure chamber raised and lowered by a winch. Barton's offer to use his inheritance to construct the diving chamber sweetened the deal.

The major obstacle facing Beebe and Barton was sea pressure that accumulated at the rate of .44 pounds per square inch for each foot of depth. This physical reality had long been a laughing matter to surface sailors who passed the time by submerging watertight metal containers so sea pressure could crush them. Beebe and Barton's conveyance into the deep would not only have to be incredibly strong but also capable of providing them fresh air and a way to see what they were risking their lives to view.

Words To Treasure

The word **bathysphere** is derived from the Greek word *bathy,* meaning "depth" and *sphere,* which describes its shape.

Heroes Under Pressure

Beebe and Barton risked being crushed by massive sea pressure to observe undiscovered sea life and were criticized by some scientists for their trouble. According to their critics, the observations were made too rapidly since their time under water was limited. Some scientists maintained that such brief observations were inadequate for the development of genuine scientific findings.

Although the two explorers proved that fish and other forms of sea life lived at great depths, other critics viewed their courageous accomplishment as nothing more than a dangerous stunt. Nevertheless, Barton and Beebe proved that humans could go deep into the sea, opening the door to excursions to the very bottom of the seas.

A Sinking Feeling

Funded by the National Geographic Society and the New York Zoological Society as well as Barton's inheritance, Beebe and Barton began testing the sphere and learned firsthand about the dangers of sea pressure. During an unmanned dive the bathysphere sprung a leak and partially filled with water. As the bolts were taken off one of the hatches, the water pressure inside shot one bolt across the deck with enough force to gouge a hole in a steel crane. On August 15, 1934, following nearly three years of tests and dives, Beebe and Barton reached 3,028 feet off Bermuda's Nonsuch Island, where Beebe had previously established a tropical research station. This depth greatly exceeded anything reached previously.

Know The Ropes

The bathysphere was a diving chamber made of $1\frac{1}{4}$-inch-thick cast steel. A trio of specially designed quartz viewing ports allowed the occupants to see out of the 54-inch-diameter chamber, and a heavy steel door was unbolted to allow entry. To help the explorers breathe, oxygen bottles were installed so the air could be replenished. Trays of chemicals removed excess moisture and deadly carbon dioxide. A steel cable reeled through a winch connected the occupants to the surface, and another waterproof line provided electricity and a telephone. Palm frond fans circulated the air inside the steel ball during the dives.

The exotic locale for these dangerous dives came about due to loan of the 14-acre Nonsuch Island to the New York Zoological Society in 1928 giving Beebe an inexpensive location to study all types of wildlife above and below the water. The risks were great and the technology strictly seat-of-the-pants but Beebe and Barton pulled it off.

This record depth would not be beaten until Barton, without Beebe, conducted a dive using a modified bathysphere in 1948 that allowed him to reach a depth of 4,500 feet.

Auguste Piccard: Top-to-Bottom Explorer

Although Auguste Piccard was considered to be an even more unlikely deep-ocean explorer than the birdman Beebe or his young sidekick Barton, Piccard's innovations ushered in the first deep dives on shipwrecks that used manned submersible craft. What is truly amazing is that this Swiss inventor began his career by designing and building high-altitude balloons for atmospheric research and ascended to a record altitude of 57,579 feet on August 18, 1934. He lowered his sights in 1937 by transferring technology he developed for ballooning to the design of a deep-submergence craft.

To accomplish his high-altitude feat, Piccard developed the first pressurized compartment to defeat the low pressure and the lack of oxygen encountered in the stratosphere. Piccard, feeling he had accomplished what he sought in high-altitude, decided to recycle his developments into a deep-submergence craft to allow him to conduct deep-ocean research. The result would be a craft that literally operated like a submerged balloon.

Down, Please

Piccard's deep-diving machine was a *bathyscaphe*. It operated much like a balloon to maintain its ability to descend and then ascend. Even though his submersible may have looked like a submarine, it was actually a large tank filled with buoyant gasoline that compressed under pressure. This technology enabled Piccard to provide more strength to the tank during its descent.

Words To Treasure

Bathyscaphe, in Greek, means "deep ship," which is hardly surprising since this invention carried its occupants farther down into the sea than any other had.

Thin and bookish, Piccard and his son Jacques descended to a record 10,330 feet in 1953, shattering Barton's 1948 record by nearly 6,000 feet.

To get this submersible to ascend, weights had to be dropped from the craft. Shedding weights remains a common, foolproof way to regain buoyancy for small submersible craft even today. Piccard understood the advantages of Otis Barton's design and created his own passenger compartment in a strong, pressure-resistant ball at the bottom of the craft.

The bathyscaphe deep-diving submersible designed by Swiss high-altitude researcher Auguste Piccard reached the ocean's deepest point of 35,800 feet in 1960. (Courtesy Archive Photos/ Popperfoto)

The bathyscaphe was not a true submarine since it was designed to essentially travel up and down to reach great depths. Unlike Beebe and Barton's bathysphere, Piccard's craft was equipped with batteries that powered small propellers to allow for some maneuvering. The propellers were mostly necessary to help the lumbering craft to counteract underwater currents. The bathyscaphe was incapable of cruising considerable distances. Although it could move through the water with small propellers, it was relatively unwieldy, though extremely reliable.

An Unbeatable Feat

Using his second design, Piccard was able to descend to 10,330 feet in 1953. In 1958, the U.S. Navy bought this model and named it the *Trieste*. Piccard's son and assistant Jacques made numerous dives aboard the *Trieste* for the Navy, including a record-breaking 35,800-foot dive in the Challenger Deep near Guam with Navy Lieutenant Don Walsh on January 23, 1960. The unwieldy submersible descended by virtue of gravity alone like a descending balloon and inadvertently struck the bottom so hard it damaged the craft! Luckily though, both men returned safely to the surface.

This was the first time anyone had reached such an incredible depth—and the last time the record will be broken—since there will be no deeper place on earth than the Mariana Trench.

Deep Detective Work

Ungainly, snail-slow, and big, Piccard's *Trieste* was no dolphin under the water and was described as not much more than a deep-sea elevator. Nevertheless, this craft was the first submersible ever used to investigate deep-sea shipwrecks. During its service in the Navy, the original *Trieste* and a newer version known as *Trieste II* were used to study the wreckage of two American nuclear submarines.

When the nuclear submarine USS *Thresher* sank and imploded on April 10, 1963, in 8,400 feet of water, the *Trieste* visited the wreck site after a lengthy search for the submarine. The newer *Trieste II* performed a similar grim reconnaissance mission in secret a year after the May 21, 1968, sinking of the nuclear submarine USS *Scorpion*.

Despite knowing generally where the *Thresher* was lost, it took four months of searching before the *Trieste* was able to recover identifiable wreckage from the submarine's debris field. Little was left of the 300-foot *Thresher* since its compartments had imploded, killing its crew instantly. The Navy's most advanced submarine sank below its crush depth after a small equipment cooling line carrying sea water ruptured and shorted out the nuclear reactor's control panel.

Those first voyages were the forerunners to the manned deep-sea excursions to wrecks like the *Titanic* and the *Bismarck*—explorations for which Robert Ballard has gained much fame. But we'll get to him a little later!

Jacques-Yves Cousteau: Explorer Extraordinaire

If you lived in the 1960s through the 1980s and occasionally walked by a television, you'd know the name Jacques-Yves Cousteau is synonymous with the ocean and its creatures. Though he also became identified with global environmental concerns, Cousteau believed that all things began and ended with the sea. His lifelong warning was simple and apocalyptic: "If the sea dies, everything dies."

Cousteau also opened the investigation of shallow-water wrecks and thought up the first agile, manned submersible for deepwater exploration.

Cousteau invented scuba diving with his development of the underwater breathing regulator in 1943, which he perfected under the noses of Nazi troops occupying his native France. He then went on to become an international force in making people aware of the role the oceans play in the lives of all living things.

Known as the Aqualung, Cousteau's invention would not only allow him to explore the oceans but provided badly needed funding for his efforts to do so.

Shiver Me Timbers

With the end of World War II, the French Navy didn't need explorers as much as it needed scuba divers who could locate and disarm hundreds of antiship mines left behind by the Nazis. Jacques-Yves Cousteau assembled and trained a team that developed diving techniques as they disabled mines using Cousteau's invention. Divers from this team formed the nucleus of the original group of divers with whom Cousteau began his undersea explorations.

Key to the Shallow Wrecks

Cousteau's Aqualung became the key for ordinary people and archaeologists to reach the shallow shipwrecks that littered hundreds of coastlines. This simple invention meant that explorers didn't have to hold their breath or walk about like astronauts with a hose connected to a bulky diving helmet. Despite its simplicity, the Aqualung was an amazingly helpful addition to the technological arsenal available to underwater explorers. Divers could now descend to a shipwreck much like a fish and glide freely while inspecting ships or recovering artifacts. Cousteau's device not only made working underwater easier but also made it less expensive because surface crews that were crucial for helmet divers were no longer necessary.

Lights, Camera, Dive!

If you want to gain recognition today as an undersea explorer or a famous discoverer of sunken ships like Robert Ballard, you have to get on television or at least appear on a talk show. Cousteau was way ahead of everyone in the public-awareness category. He became a self-taught filmmaker as soon as he began scuba diving so he could reveal the wonders of the undersea world to the rest of us. He won three Academy Awards including two for best documentary and one for best live-action short subject.

Shipwreck: The Movie

Long before the actual *Titanic* made its Hollywood debut in several feature films including the James Cameron film by the same name, Cousteau realized that a ship-wreck on the seafloor was something the public had never seen and was therefore an excellent subject for a film.

He knew where a sunken British steamship rested 60 feet underwater and made a film titled *Epaves* (the English title is *Wrecks*). This 1943 film showed scuba divers swimming across the deck of the sunken steamship. It was no Hollywood extrava-ganza, but it was a first. Even his simple, early films fascinated viewers and would later make people take Cousteau and his exploration propos-als seriously.

Making Exploration Pay

Cousteau learned early on that the only way to make ocean exploration pay was to sell movies and television documentaries about the efforts of his team. Here, again, Cousteau was a trailblazer for future explorers like Robert Ballard who needed media backing to fund expeditions. Though Otis Barton made movies from his bathysphere in the 1930s, he was not able to finance five decades of ocean exploration with his films, as did Cousteau.

Know The Ropes

It's now common for consortiums and explorers to negotiate television and publication rights for fascinating treasure- or wreck-hunting expedi-tions just as they would lease the use of equipment for the search. Sunken ships and their treasures are hot commodities. The public can't get enough of either. Selling the rights to their work is also an excellent way for treasure hunters and explorers to finance their expeditions.

An Archaeological First

While Cousteau was trying to get his underwater explorations off the ground and under the sea in the 1950s, he found himself selling the services of his divers to conduct archaeological dives on old shipwrecks in the bay at Marseilles. The 1952 excavation of the Grand-Congloué wrecks was done with a precision and delicacy not previously possible with the heavy, helmet diving equipment.

A large rock outcropping in Marseilles' bay, the Grand-Congloué was a bad dream come true for mariners who collided with it for centuries. Their ships, some dating back 2,000 years, litter the seafloor around the outcropping.

While he considered this work little more than salvage duty to pay the bills, Cousteau knew the real money lay in movies and documentaries. He would later publish a book on his expeditions and produce a film documentary on Spanish treasure fleet wrecks in the Caribbean.

Driving Down in Style

To submariners, moving through the ocean is "driving," not sailing. When Cousteau finally decided to design his own deep-diving submersible, he took this saying to heart and produced the coolest-looking sub on record. Of course, you would expect no less from the style-conscious French! Known as the "diving saucer," the futuristic craft looked more like a UFO than a submarine. Unfortunately, one of these graceful yellow craft was lost forever in 1958 when a cable lifting the empty submarine from the water snapped.

Undersea exploration pioneer Jacques-Yves Cousteau emerges from the two-man submersible diving saucer he designed. (Courtesy Archive Photos)

His submersible flew like an airplane beneath the sea and became another symbol for Cousteau's explorations and the model for future undersea exploration craft. The original diving saucer could descend to only 1,000 feet. While it couldn't reach the original depth of the *Alvin*'s 6,500 feet or the 35,000 feet reached by the cumbersome *Trieste*, Cousteau's saucer was incredibly agile.

In 1966, Westinghouse built the *Deepstar-4000* diving saucer based on Cousteau's design. (As the name implies, its diving depth was 4,000 feet, far deeper than the original model.)

This deeper-diving craft was used in 1971 by explorers who photographed rare species of fish on the floor of the Gulf of Mexico. Cousteau's design began a trend for small, deep-diving submersibles for research work.

Peering Into the Seas with Sonar

About the time Jacques-Yves Cousteau was putting the finishing touches on his Aqualung and turning people into temporary fish, Harold E. Edgerton—one of America's foremost scientific innovators—decided it was time someone figured out how to take a really good look through the water. His introduction to Jacques-Yves Cousteau in 1952 launched years of collaboration between the Frenchman and the Nebraskan.

Edgerton accompanied Cousteau on numerous exploration voyages. Early in their collaboration, Edgerton developed techniques for taking under-water images at great depths and invented a sound-activated device to trigger his cameras' strobe lights and shutters.

In fact, the good-natured Edgerton had invented the *stroboscope* and stroboscopic photography in 1931. Despite his roots in optical photography, Edgerton would soon realize that sound was the best way to make the deep sea transparent.

X-Ray Ears

Early *sonar* was only capable of locating objects floating between the surface and the seafloor. But Edgerton, a Massachusetts Institute of Technology professor, decided that sonar could become man's undersea eyes.

Edgerton set up the sonar system to operate side-ways so the reflected sound signal would reveal the contour of the seafloor and the objects upon it. This innovation provided stunning results and prompted Edgerton not only to refine the device but also to begin manufacturing side-scan sonar devices with several partners.

Words To Treasure

A **stroboscope** is a light designed to brilliantly flash at a high rate of speed to make moving or vibrating objects appear motionless and is often known as a "timing light." A stroboscopic photography flash provides powerful, repetitive flashes of light for photography in extreme low-light situations.

Words To Treasure

Sonar stands for "sound navigation and ranging."

Towed behind a ship near the seafloor, the sonar could scan an area of predetermined width. A wide search could produce an image of a large area and many objects could be immediately identified on the seafloor.

Modern side-scan sonars can be adjusted to cover a variety of swath widths with the narrower searches, providing a more detailed image of the seafloor. While conducting a preliminary search, a swath width of two kilometers might be advisable. Interesting, low-resolution returns may deserve a more detailed look with a swath width of only 50 meters.

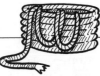

Know The Ropes

Sonar was developed following World War I by Britain and the United States as a way of using reflected sound waves to detect enemy submarines. A sound—called a "ping"—is generated, and its echo or reflection is then examined to show the location or even the shape of a submerged object.

Looking Back 400 Years

During the late 1960s, Edgerton became involved in one of the most ambitious shipwreck recoveries ever attempted when he used his side-scan sonar to confirm the location of the British warship *Mary Rose*. The ship had been submerged in some muck near Portsmouth, England, since 1545, when it sank with all its occupants.

When the quintessential Midwesterner helped the British determine conclusively that the site did, in fact, contain the *Mary Rose,* the discovery made side-scan sonar an official shipwreck-finding tool. Explorers now had a way not only for finding submerged wrecks but also for viewing them. Explorers could now enter a new age of undersea discovery that would include history's most fascinating shipwrecks in the deepest parts of the ocean.

A side-scan sonar image of a wrecked merchant ship in Chile's Valparaiso Harbor, taken using equipment produced by EdgeTech (scientist Harold Edgerton's company), plainly shows how technology has made the seas transparent. (Courtesy American Underwater Search & Survey, Ltd.)

Gearing Up for Going Down

By the 1960s, governments and navies wanted to know more about the oceans and began investing money in the deep-submergence-vehicle technology that would allow scientists to head for the seafloor and maneuver through the depths. At the same time, the era of unmanned towed camera sleds began, which allowed researchers to gather photographs on the seafloor without endangering themselves in a submersible.

Although Cousteau's original diving saucer was limited to diving only, these modern craft were squat-looking compared to Cousteau's graceful diving saucer. But form followed function, and these craft were capable of diving many times deeper than Cousteau's design. The *Alvin,* built in 1964 and designed by an aerospace engineer working for the General Mills cereal company for the Woods Hole Oceanographic Institute, was among the first to go into service. Its passenger chamber, like Barton's original diving chamber design, has the structurally strong shape of a sphere and is surrounded by a "skin" that gives it a submarine-like shape.

Know The Ropes

Deep-submergence vehicles are not considered full-duty submarines, since they must be transported to a dive site by another ship.

Bud Froehlich, who had designing high-altitude spy balloons produced by General Mills in the 1950s for the CIA, worked with Woods Hole official Allyn Vine to develop the submersible. The *Alvin*'s name is a contraction of Allyn Vine's own.

The little *Alvin* that is far smaller than the *Trieste* of Auguste Piccard, and the *Alvin*—which can now dive to 15,000 feet—achieved early fame for taking part in the search for a submerged hydrogen bomb on March 15, 1966. The bomb was lost off the Spanish coast for two months after a B-52 bomber collided with a refueling aircraft.

Although *Alvin* assisted in the search for the nuclear weapon, it was an unmanned sled used for recovering test torpedoes that actually snagged the parachute of the bomb and carried it to the surface.

The potentially cataclysmic accident occurred January 17, 1966, when a B-52 bomber collided in mid-air with a refueling aircraft off Spain's coast near the village of Palomares. While seven of 11 crewmen perished, four hydrogen bombs fell from the bomber. Three of the bombs were recovered fairly soon, although the ordinary high explosive in the two warheads detonated, spreading radiation over 558 acres of farmland.

The fourth bomb was finally found with the help of a Palomares villager who saw the bomb's parachute descend offshore. It was resting precariously on a steep cliff 2,250 feet beneath the surface.

One of the newest deep-submergence craft is Japan's *Shinkai-6500*—which is capable of diving to just over 21,000 feet—one of the most capable manned submersibles in use today. The *Shinkai-6500* entered service for the Japanese in 1989.

Unmanned Camera Sleds

Though seemingly crude compared to the deep-diving submersibles, towed camera sleds entered the undersea workforce in the 1960s. This device consisted of a steel frame with trim *vanes* to keep it level while it was pulled, submerged, through the water. Cameras bolted to the frame were able to blindly shoot hundred of pictures as the sled was towed back and forth over an area of interest. Of course, since the camera operators were working blind, sometimes they would end up with a picture of something interesting and sometimes they wouldn't!

Words To Treasure

A **vane** is a control surface found on missiles or objects towed underwater to provide stability during their travel and serve the same purpose as the feathered stabilizing vanes on the tail of an arrow.

Because of its repetitive nature, the process used for maneuvering these unmanned camera sleds, similar to the towing of a submerged side-scan sonar, soon came to be known as "mowing the lawn." Repetitious or not, though, this method was effective in locating sunken ships whose general location was known.

Newer sleds have both side-scan sonar and video camera eyes that allow operators to see where they're going so the devices can be "flown" rather than simply dragged. The cameras now are also able to send back both sonar and video images of what they're passing in "real time," or as it happens. This technology is a great improvement, as the older towed sleds couldn't reveal their discoveries until they were hauled from the deep and their film developed.

Robert Ballard used a camera-equipped sled named the *Argo* to locate the *Titanic* in 1985. Earlier camera sleds were used to locate the sunken nuclear submarines *Scorpion* and *Thresher*.

Row, Row, Row Your Robot

Words To Treasure

A **remotely operated vehicle (ROV)** is a device that can contain still or video cameras or sonar that is connected to the surface and controlled by a **tether** or **umbilical** that also can return images and information to the operators on the surface.

With further advances in technology at their disposal, scientists are now touting the capabilities of deep-diving, *remotely operated vehicles (ROV)*. Connected to the surface by a cable known as an *umbilical* or *tether* towing cable and a power supply, these remotely operated vehicles can be lowered into the depths to perform many different operations, from locating objects on the bottom of the seafloor to actually picking up items and bringing them back.

For their work, these remotely operated vehicles can also be equipped with sonar, video cameras, manipulator arms, and even suction devices for lifting. These systems can perform many of the functions that divers now do, only at far greater depths and without the safety risks.

Far from looking like humanoid robots that you've probably seen in science-fiction movies, these remotely operated vehicles look more like massive boxes that are covered with tools and cameras. And they can reach almost unlimited depths. A model used by the U.S. Navy, known as *CURV III*, can dive to 20,000 feet.

With the use of scuba equipment, people can safely dive to around 130 feet using caution, but professional divers using advanced techniques and decompression chambers can dive to 1,000 feet. The risks at the lower depths are considerable.

Modern Technology Meets Sunken Artifacts

Explorers like Beebe and Otis opened the door to the deep ocean, and years later, scientists demonstrated the promise of remotely piloted vehicles and robots. All the while, entrepreneurs were paying attention. Their eyes were on fabulous treasures long denied *salvors* because of the great depths that hid the lost cargo.

Sledding to Treasure

Ohio engineer Tommy Thompson believed that he could use robots on a high-technology expedition to retrieve, from two miles beneath the Atlantic, the billion-dollar golden treasure trove amid the wreckage of the steamship SS *Central America*. The ship was carrying a vast shipment of gold from the California gold rush when it was lost in a hurricane on September 12, 1857.

Words To Treasure

A **salvor** is someone other than the member of a ship's crew who helps save or salvage a ship or its cargo.

After raising $10 million from 161 investors, Thompson's Columbus-America Discovery Group set about finding the *Central America* using side-scan sonar on a towed sled. The search was just as frustrating for him as it had been for deep-sea explorers in earlier decades, but in 1986 the *Central America* was finally found.

Mechanical Prospector

Thompson and his associates then created specifications for their own remotely operated vehicle that could not only lift gold bars but also vacuum gold dust from the seafloor. The remotely operated vehicle was also equipped to encase stacks of gold coins in silicone gel for retrieval.

During a highly secret operation in 1989, Thompson's remotely operated vehicle—called *Nemo*—recovered hundreds of millions of dollars in gold from the *Central America* wreck. If you're picturing the *Nemo* as nothing more than a toy robot, don't be fooled! This remote-operated gold digger was actually a car-size box of gizmos!

Robert Ballard: Finder of Lost Ships

Robert Ballard has combined the skills of a scientist with modern search technology to become known as one of the world's premier finder of lost ships.

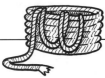

Know The Ropes

Researchers like Robert Ballard began to acquire deep-diving tools in the early 1960s with the development of the *Alvin* three-person submarine in 1964 and the *Aluminaut* built in 1966. The Aluminaut was built by Reynolds Aluminum Company and could carry a crew of six to a 15,000-foot depth. It is now retired. The U.S. Navy's *Sea Cliff* submarine, which can dive to 20,000 feet, has been given to Woods Hole Oceanographic Institute in Massachusetts, which also operates the *Alvin.* Such submersibles are expensive to maintain and operate, and the Navy's gift is a way to save taxpayer's money.

Words To Treasure

A **hydrothermal vent** is one through which magma or water superheated by molten lava is forced to the surface.

Though explorers traditionally wow the public by finding things never before seen, Ballard has stunned the world by finding things once seen by humans but then lost for decades—sunken ships. Once an obscure deep-ocean geologist working with the Woods Hole Oceanographic Institute, Ballard was consumed by the dream of tracking down and finding the *Titanic,* the world's greatest lost ship—but more about that later!

The trophies to Ballard's undersea sleuthing need little introduction. He's bagged the *Titanic* (1985), the German battleship *Bismarck* (1989), and American and Japanese warships that were sunk in the dark Pacific waters north of Guadalcanal Island (1992). Ballard has now become a household name—something that few scientists other than physicist Albert Einstein have achieved—and all of these efforts have been brought to the public by popular documentaries.

Groundwork for Discovery

As a geologist, Ballard spent years surveying the seafloor in various deep-submergence vessels and was one of a handful of scientists who discovered deep-ocean *hydrothermal vents* in 1977. These vents were openings along the Mid-Atlantic Ridge that spewed a scalding mineral soup into the icy seas. Ballard also discovered a multitude of sea creatures living around the scalding openings in total darkness! Because there is no light, these creatures live off hydrogen sulfide instead of oxygen.

For days in the early 1980s, Ballard lived 2,000 feet beneath the Atlantic aboard the Navy's nuclear-powered, research submersible *NR-1.* It was crawling along the bottom to prove that the seafloor could serve as a battlefield. Ballard is believed to have spent more time in the deep sea than almost any other civilian scientist.

A Titanic Dream

A well-respected oceanographer and geologist, Ballard long dreamed of locating the legendary *Titanic,* a somewhat fanciful aspiration for someone doing other complex work. Ballard, however, had been bitten by the shipwreck-hunting bug. As a youth he had read *A Night to Remember* by Walter Lord about the *Titanic*'s fateful sinking and had remained spellbound by the event. He waited for the day when the technology and circumstance would allow him to locate the queen of the lost ships.

Ballard was overjoyed in 1973 to learn that the American deep-diving submersible *Alvin* was being upgraded to dive down to 15,000 feet. He knew it would allow the possibility of actually visiting the *Titanic,* which lay in an area no deeper than 13,000 feet. Though he would first use the remotely controlled camera sled *Argo* to visit the *Titanic,* Ballard would eventually dive on the *Alvin* to see the legendary wreck with his own eyes.

The Right Circumstances

By 1982, Ballard convinced the Navy to allow him to develop an unmanned towed camera sled that could observe and photograph the seafloor for long periods. Its other—more secret—purpose would be to provide a way of finding and examining lost nuclear submarines. Dubbed the *Argo,* the sled would be equipped with sonar to allow it to search the seafloor along with a trio of video cameras. These cameras were enhanced with technology to penetrate the blackness of the sea.

Though early towed camera sleds look like an uncompleted weekend project (since they're little more than a steel frame packed with cameras and sonar), the *Argo* was different. It could "see" with its cameras as it traveled along the pitch-black seafloor and transmit those images to monitors on the research ship. This technique allowed technicians to "fly" the *Argo* with confidence, whereas an obstruction could wreck a "blind" sled.

Shiver Me Timbers

Towed camera sleds equipped with side-scan sonar are used not only by the Navy but also by private industry. With pipelines and offshore oil operations requiring undersea "eyes," such sleds are often used for inspections and photographic work. Remotely operated vehicles can then be used to retrieve items or make repairs. NASA has tested at least one remotely operated vehicle to recover the reusable solid rocket motors jettisoned from the space shuttle during launch, thus eliminating risks to divers.

Older towed instrument sleds were simply programmed to take pictures as they were towed across the bottom. The film was later developed, and researchers hoped they accidentally got a photograph of something. This method is a little like wearing a blindfold while you hang your video camera out your window to randomly record whatever goes by. Ballard knew the Navy needed a better system.

Titanic *Found!*

The Navy ordered Ballard to use the *Argo* for a 1985 photographic survey of the wreckage of the nuclear submarine USS *Scorpion* that lies in nearly 13,000 feet of water. After filming the *Scorpion* wreck site, Ballard was granted permission to test the Navy-owned system in his search for the *Titanic*.

The *Argo,* towed in a slow precise pattern over the *Titanic*'s suspected wreck site, eventually spotted the liner's wreckage with low-light cameras. The process is painstaking, since the ship's location must be carefully plotted before the sled is moved through a precise pattern so the same area is not searched twice.

The first things spotted by the cameras were lighter types of debris. Ballard's team used the *Argo* to follow that trail until one of the *Titanic*'s massive boilers came into view. Jubilation erupted aboard the research ship when Ballard and his team made their discovery in the early hours of September 1, 1985.

Ballard's dream of visiting the *Titanic* in person had been realized, but the scientist has now become a champion of remotely operated vehicles for deep-sea research and exploration. Such vehicles are less expensive than deep-submergence vehicles like France's manned *Nautile* since they don't need to provide a pressure-proof life-support chamber for humans. A maneuverable unmanned vehicle that can send real-time images back to an operator is capable of performing reconnaissance, photography, and artifact collection just like a manned submersible that must also contain a costly pressure-proof life-support system for occupants.

Shiver Me Timbers

Although the news media went into a feeding frenzy over Ballard's announcement about the *Titanic*'s discovery, nothing was said for years about the secret mission to the *Scorpion* site weeks before. The submarine mysteriously sank with all hands on May 21, 1968. Ballard had also been ordered to look for any additional evidence as to the sinking of the submarine that carried 99 men to their deaths and to measure the escape of any radiation from the *Scorpion*'s two nuclear torpedoes or nuclear reactor. That shipwreck remains a mystery.

The Limelight

Ballard's fame gained him the recognition previously afforded to undersea explorer Jacques-Yves Cousteau. Ballard soon found himself in demand to take part in documentaries and returned to the *Titanic* in July 1986 for a series of manned dives on the wreck using the *Alvin*.

Ballard would also use *Jason Junior,* a small, ROV that could be guided into small spaces on the *Titanic* through commands transmitted by fiber-optic cable. The ROV was part of the Navy project Ballard oversaw during the development of the *Argo*. Though *Jason Junior* was plagued with problems, the expedition was a success, as it brought back thousands of high-quality color images of the *Titanic*.

Stepping Into Cousteau's Flippers

By April 1989 the famous Ballard was busy with a pair of expeditions. Initially, Ballard sailed to the Mediterranean where his team had located a 2,000-year-old Roman ship the year before. His team intended to do an archaeological survey and recover objects with a newly developed remotely operated vehicle named *Jason,* a larger version of the *Jason Junior*.

Using the full-sized *Jason* ROV, Ballard intended to raise artifacts from the 2,000-foot depth where the Roman ship lay. The operation was known as the Jason Project (after the ROV and the mythical Greek seafarer) and would televise the expedition's findings live to North American museums whose auditoriums were filled with students.

His second expedition would be to the German battleship *Bismarck* that had been sunk in a vicious sea battle with British warships on May 27, 1941. Sponsored by Turner Broadcasting System and the National Geographic Society, Ballard was under a huge amount of pressure to perform, since he had failed to locate the *Bismarck* in 1988. This time, however, the undersea geologist-turned-explorer was successful in locating the Nazi warship, thus raising his own profile even higher in the eyes of the public.

Flooded with Discoveries

As of February 1998, Ballard was intending to turn his sonar gaze to the Black Sea, where deep, oxygen-free waters may have preserved a 7,000-year-old civilization that could have been wiped out by the great flood mentioned in the Old Testament—the very same flood for which Noah built his Ark.

Although Ballard doubts that the Ark itself will be found, he hopes to determine whether melting glaciers at the end of the last Ice Age could have played a role in flooding much of the world 7,000 years ago.

The Least You Need to Know

➤ Although many scientists believed nothing lived deep in the ocean, naturalist William Beebe and adventurer Otis Barton proved otherwise when they descended to a record 3,028 feet into the Atlantic in 1934, thereby inaugurating deep-ocean research.

➤ The deepest submerged point in the world of 35,800 feet was reached in 1960 by the deep-submergence vessel *Trieste*.

➤ Undersea explorer Jacques-Yves Cousteau opened up undersea exploration to the common person, and his filmmaking efforts blazed a path for other media-savvy ocean explorers like Robert Ballard.

➤ The important development of side-scan sonar made it possible to obtain images of the seafloor using reflected sound waves and led to the discovery of famous shipwrecks that would have otherwise been nearly impossible to locate.

➤ The development of towed camera sleds followed by remotely operated vehicles that could send back instant images of the seafloor have become so capable and cost effective they are often used instead of manned submersibles like the *Alvin* that visited the *Titanic*.

➤ Side-scan sonar technology combined with highly capable remotely operated, deep-diving vehicles has opened a new door to deep-ocean wreck recovery demonstrated during the late 1980s by Tommy Thompson's Columbus-America Discovery Group's recovery of massive amounts of gold from the SS *Central America* off the East Coast.

Chapter 3

So Many Wrecks, So Little Time

In This Chapter

➤ Wrecks from (A)egean to (Z)uider Zee

➤ Enemies of the ship: war, weather, and worms

➤ Historical shipwrecks: gone but not forgotten

➤ Florida's Gold Coast

➤ How many shipwrecks are there?

➤ Skeleton coasts: the final ports of call

Seafaring's roots are almost as long as recorded time itself, dating back more than 10,000 years. While the use of boats for near-shore fishing and on inland waterways goes back nearly 9,000 years in Europe, archaeological finds make it clear that societies preferred floating to walking when conducting commerce with distant trading partners.

The early, small boats evolved into ocean-crossing galleons that gave way to seagoing behemoths like the immense supertankers now slaking the world's petroleum thirst.

The hazards posed by sea travel form the historical connection between all ships and all mariners. The loss of the ill-fated RMS *Titanic* shows that no ship is truly "unsinkable"—even in relatively modern times. Any ship is prone to slipping beneath the waves if it challenges the sea long enough. Some estimates claim that half of all ships built have become wrecks due to weather, war, or navigational error.

Hence the tales of men pitting themselves against storm-tossed oceans are breathtaking, frightening, and irresistible. Even the ships and their gracefully functional designs often serve as the subjects of great painters and illustrators. The marriage of beautiful ships and salty seafarers created a timeless alliance against maritime hazards. In the days of the wooden-hulled vessels, it was said of the sailors that they were "iron men in wooden ships"—necessarily tougher than even the ships they sailed.

A wrecked car in a front yard is an eyesore. Add water, and a shipwreck on the seabed is a thing of tragic, mysterious beauty.

Wrecks from (A)egean to (Z)uider Zee

Imagine what America would look like if every automobile that broke down was left where it died, sulking alongside highways or in parking lots. Eventually, nations like America would be awash in derelict cars.

Now think about the countless boats and ships that have sailed the gulfs, bays, seas, and oceans for nearly 100 centuries. When accidents or violence claims them, they have nowhere to go but down, and there's usually no compelling reason to retrieve them. The oceans have become a massive dumping ground. Here and there wrecks are poking above the water near shore, but most are hidden from view.

Welcome to King Neptune's dark, cold, but extremely large and well-stocked junkyard. Any location that humans have sailed to or from on a regular basis is littered with ships. The only time most wrecked ships are raised is if they have financial or historical value or if they're blocking a navigable waterway.

Viking Wrecks

If you want to talk about unusual shipwrecks in unexpected places, then you want to discuss the Vikings. They were the wild men of Europe, heading everywhere their largest boats, known as *drakkars*, and smaller ones known as *Knorrs*, would carry them to conduct raids of conquest. These Norsemen stole anything that wasn't nailed down, including humans and religious artifacts (both of which were sold for a tidy profit). The Vikings' famous raids—known as *strandhogg*—carried them to wreck and ruin most everyone else. As a result of these raids, the Norsemen made Ireland a Viking state and they roved as far as the Middle East.

Since it was a sign of exalted position in Viking society to be buried in a Viking boat, many examples of these boats have actually been found on land. An amazing number were also preserved in near-perfect condition where they had been left in the chilly waters of Scandinavia. From the eighth to the eleventh centuries,

Words To Treasure

A **drakkar** is the name given to long, narrow raiding ships powered by both sail and oars. **Knorrs** were wider and more stable and therefore used for long voyages by Vikings in their wide-ranging raids over much of the world. Drakkars were also known as **longships**.

the Vikings left wrecked ships from the North Sea to the Mediterranean with stops in Newfoundland, Russia, and Iraq.

Despite considerable maritime skills, Erik the Red saw 10 of his 25 Viking longboats sink during a voyage across the frightening North Atlantic from Iceland to Greenland in 983 B.C.E. It just goes to show that losing a good portion of your fleet was the accepted cost of doing business in the old days.

The Scandinavian Vikings sailed from the New World to the Middle East conducting raids. Many of their ancient ships were well-preserved and can be seen today in museums.

Spain's High Price

Renaissance Spain learned a thing or two about the cost of doing maritime business. The Spanish treasure fleets that fell victim to storms in the Pacific and Atlantic oceans are responsible for the current "treasure" ship craze. In the process of fighting their way home, they added whole new sunken graveyards to the map.

Sailing between the fifteenth and early nineteenth centuries, many of these treasure-laden ships—like others of the period—sank. Maps show Spanish wrecks proliferating around the Florida Keys, Cuba, and the Dominican Republic. Still others lie off the coasts of Colombia, South Texas, Mexico, and the Philippines. Silver reals, *cobs,* and gold ingots, along with plundered New World gems and jewelry, are still awaiting persistent and lucky treasure hunters near the remnants of ships that carried them.

Although most of the estimated 13,000 Spanish treasure ships made it back to Spain from the New World, enough of them sank along the way to fill minds of treasure hunters with visions of wealth. These wrecks alone have created a cottage industry in treasure hunting, though some offer only cultural artifacts. Nonetheless, the discovery of these wrecks and others like the *Titanic* has generated new interest among the public, prospective salvors, moviemakers, and sport divers.

Words To Treasure

A **cob** was a Spanish coin crudely cut from a thin strip of silver that was then trimmed and stamped by hand, most likely by Indian labor.

Words To Treasure

To **strike** on a sailing ship doesn't mean a work stoppage, but the lowering of a sail or flag. The **mainsail** is the main sail of the ship and became one word because sailors don't have a long time to chat. The **topsail** is the smaller sail at the top of a mast. A ship that **foundered** is one that sank.

High and Dry Wrecks

Not all rediscovered ships are as big and famous as the *Titanic*. And not all were underwater. One of the most fascinating ships to be located and preserved also

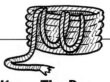

Know The Ropes

Tropical cyclone is a generic term describing the three classes of storms in the Atlantic: depressions, storms, and hurricanes—with the hurricane being the most powerful. In the Pacific, hurricanes are referred to as typhoons. A cyclone becomes classified as a hurricane when its winds reach 74 mph, but hurricanes can generate winds of more than 160 mph, and these storm systems can also be hundreds of miles wide.

happens to be one of the oldest. But this ship never did sink—in fact, it was found in the desert near an Egyptian pyramid!

The 4,500-year-old sailing ship is 145 feet long and was excavated near the pyramid of King Khufu of Egypt—also referred to as Cheops. Khufu, who ordered construction of the Great Pyramid of Giza, also called for the burial of five ships for his use in the afterlife. This idea has undoubtedly crossed the minds of more than a few dedicated fishermen unable to say goodbye to their bass boats!

Thanks to the efforts of tomb robbers—whom some might call "pioneering treasure hunters"—only three empty, boat-shaped pits were found along with part of one ship discovered in 1954. Archaeologists hit pay dirt in 1987, when they found a complete ship. The royal ship of Khufu has been restored and today resides in a glass case near Khufu's pyramid. It is one of the most well-preserved ships in the world—even if it never sailed anywhere!

A sinking tanker endangered by a hurricane during World War II has water rushing over its decks after it has been run aground. (Courtesy National Archives)

Enemies of the Ship: War, Weather, and Worms

Though some try to generate intrigue and mystery to explain the loss of ships, the causes are usually quite mundane. Sometimes the reason for a ship's loss seems silly, though the results can be catastrophic and fatal. Warfare is a well-known cause for shipwrecks, but storms and worms may have done just as much damage.

Storms may be the biggest traditional cause of ship losses, although poor seamanship and bad maintenance may exacerbate a storm's effects. In the days when a weather report was what a sailor could see with his own eyes, there were few clues to warn mariners that a storm was approaching.

For thousands of years, sailing ships were not as large or stable as the massive ships of today with their mighty engines. Lacking the ability to sail against powerful rolling seas and gale-force winds, the ships often ended up dashed against the shoreline where they grounded or were tossed about in the open seas until they *foundered*. To make matters worse, sailing ships often had to *strike* their *mainsails* and *topsails*—their only means to propulsion—so they wouldn't be blown completely over.

If the winds were too powerful and blew a ship toward treacherous coastal rocks, a captain might order the ship anchored to hold her steady. If that failed, he might resort to ordering the masts cut down to further reduce wind resistance. If the ship still appeared to be heading for grounding, the last resort might be to lighten the ship by releasing the anchors and dumping cannons or cargo. Lightening the load would give the ship a shallower draft, meaning it would ride higher in the water, and allow it to come closer to shore. When these orders came down, it was usually a pretty good indication that the ship was about to become another shipwreck.

Don't Go Overboard!

Only the largest ships should ever attempt to "ride out" a hurricane or any strong storm if they can't sail out of its path. Smaller craft are always advised to weather a hurricane in a protective harbor.

Words To Treasure

A **galleon** was a relatively large ship during the period that it was used from the fifteenth to seventeenth centuries and possessed a trio of masts and two or more decks. Though closely identified as a Spanish ship, it was used by many European nations.

The Biggest Blow

The heavy volume of Spanish treasure fleet traffic in the Caribbean and Gulf of Mexico, combined with the area's attractiveness as a hurricane bull's eye, meant a sobering number of treasure-ship wrecks. The National Hurricane Center has compiled a list of 467 *tropical cyclones* that slammed through these regions since 1492, and each storm claimed more than 25 lives.

Many sunken Spanish treasure ships in the Caribbean, the Gulf of Mexico, and off America's East Coast were the result of such storms. The power of these weather systems is immense. As many as 12,000 people died when a hurricane struck the Texas coastal city of Galveston in 1900, and a six-day storm in October 1780 killed an estimated 22,000 on Barbados and nearby islands.

Think about being aboard a tossing Spanish *galleon* with water crashing down on the deck as a 100-mph winds blow you toward a submerged reef. Once you hit the reef the ship will sink, leaving only the mast protruding above the whitecaps. Your only chance at survival was to swim ashore through massive waves knowing few ever made it. Those were truly the good old days, eh, matey? If you hear about a sunken ship found near the shore, you can be assured it was probably driven there by some sort of storm.

A satellite image of Hurricane Gilbert, which struck the Caribbean and Gulf of Mexico in September 1988, causing massive damage.
(Courtesy National Weather Service)

Shiver Me Timbers

On one of his expeditions, Christopher Columbus arrived at Hispaniola on June 29, 1502, and warned Don Nicholas De Ovando (an official who had previously sent Columbus back to Spain in chains) that storm conditions were brewing. Ovando refused to allow Columbus permission to enter the Santo Domingo harbor and departed that night with a fleet headed for Spain. Ovando and 500 hands died in the storm when most of the fleet was lost. The only ship to make it to Spain was one carrying Columbus's assets.

Too Close for Comfort

As strange as it seems, a large percentage of ships were not lost in the middle of the ocean but near shore and often within sight of land. Maps pinpointing shipwrecks reveal that tragedies occurred precisely because ships were too close to shore and were *grounded* or holed by jagged coral reefs or rocky coastlines.

When a hurricane flung the British clipper *Royal Charter* toward the rocky shore of Anglesey Island off Wales in 1859, the proximity to land and shallow water actually sunk the ship. Ships far out at sea successfully endured the frightening storm. Hundreds died within shouting distance of the coast that served as the anvil against which the *Royal Charter* was smashed.

Even Christopher Columbus's flagship, the *Santa Maria,* was lost when it struck a reef near the Dominican Republic. His sailors had chafed at the seemingly endless trip across the Atlantic Ocean only to see their ship sink near land.

Conqueror Worm

In the days of wood-hulled ships, one of the biggest dangers to their buoyancy was something that sounds silly: *shipworms*. These ugly guys are mollusks capable of boring into the wood of hulls. Though not insects, they're akin to seagoing termites and capable of turning a ship's hull into a leaking shadow of its former sturdy self. The worst of these was the *teredo,* which was found in warmer waters and gobbled away at Christopher Columbus's ships.

To protect ships from organisms such as shipworms, marine architects began experimenting with hull sheathing of all sorts, including lead and copper. Even some ancient ships bear antiworm *cladding.*

Despite the beauty and tradition of wood, it's little wonder that the ship builders of today prefer steel, fiberglass, and Kevlar for ships that need to last with minimal maintenance. When old shipwrecks are found, the only portion of the wood remaining is that buried by sand and mud. An interesting side note though is that we have no confirmed reports of shipworms attacking the wooden prosthesis or "peg legs" often ascribed to pirates and sea captains.

Words To Treasure

A ship is considered **grounded** when it has been pushed or piloted into shallow water, causing it to stick on mud or rocks. A **stranding** is considered more serious but is basically the same. Some ships can't be recovered without damaging the vessel. Often, the cost of doing so is not worth the value of the vessel being saved.

Words To Treasure

Shipworms, also known by their Latin name *teredo,* plague wooden-hulled ships, boring into the wood and devouring it. Some shipbuilders cover wooden hulls with **cladding** made from sheets of copper to prevent shipworm damage.

Shiver Me Timbers

The USS *Constitution,* known reverently as "Old Ironsides" and still afloat after 200 years, is constructed of large, strong pieces of American oak, using a robust design. Wooden planks thick enough to deflect British cannon fire gave the ship its nickname. While it possessed copper sheathing to protect its hull from marine organisms like shipworms, it never sported an ounce of iron armor.

Misfortunes of War

Water covers most of the Earth's surface, and man has done a good job of losing ships anywhere possible. Aside from shipwreck sites being clumped around new and old port cities, wrecks also mainly litter major shipping routes. Wars have played the biggest role in distributing wrecks in exotic, out-of-the-way places.

The global nature of World War II meant military ships were sunk in far-flung places that seldom saw anything larger than a dug-out boat. Formerly unknown islands and locales lay claim to some of the most fascinating undersea graveyards in the world.

These wartime wrecks lie scattered from Truk Lagoon in the Federated States of Micronesia in the western Pacific to the frigid waters of the "Murmansk run." This route, which ran through the North Sea to the Barents Sea port of Murmansk in northern Russia, was used by Allied ships ferrying war material to the Soviet Union port by the same name. The bottom of the North Atlantic is littered with the hulks of Nazi U-boats that share a cold bed with thousands of merchant ship victims.

Fortunes of War

A very few of those military ships turned out to be treasure ships, but some warships bearing gold bullion and other forms of currency were lost during the maelstrom of World War II. A notable example is the British cruiser HMS *Edinburgh* that sank north of the then-Soviet port of Murmansk while carrying 4.5 tons of gold belonging to the Soviet and British governments. (Before rushing out to learn how to dive to 800 feet while wearing a heated dry suit, please note that most of that gold has already been recovered.) This extraordinary story is discussed in Chapter 23, "Cold, Cold Cache."

War created another odd treasure-ship wreck in the Philippines when a ship loaded with 15 million pesos of that nation's silver reserves was scuttled near Corregidor Island to keep it out of the hands of invading Japanese. Though most of the fortune has been recovered, an estimated one million silver pesos remain unfound.

A Heavy Toll

If the term "mass production" could be applied to the production of shipwrecks, then that certainly occurred during World War II when ships were sunk as fast as they were built!

The German *Kriegsmarine* U-boat campaign sank 5,150 Allied warships in operations that ranged from the Atlantic to the Mediterranean and even to the Pacific. The unsung heroes of the U.S. Navy's submarine fleet sank another 1,950 ships during its campaign against the Japanese. Keep in mind, however, that even more ships were lost during the war that lasted from 1939 to 1945.

During World War II—the last era of large-scale naval warfare—ships weren't just sunk by other surface vessels and subs. Ships also fell victim to mines, bombing, depth charges, and torpedoes dropped from the air. Military wreck sites around the world have become premiere diving locales. Nevertheless, most nations consider their sunken warships official gravesites, and souvenir hunting is often illegal.

Recycled Ships

It became almost commonplace between the fifteenth and nineteenth centuries for European nations to settle disputes with naval battles. Unlike twentieth-century warfare that efficiently converted proud warships into a valued scuba-diving destinations, previous battles often saw protracted fights that resulted in ships being captured.

Words To Treasure

Kriegsmarine is the German word for its World War II navy. Literally translated, the word means "war navy."

Don't Go Overboard!

The U.S. government considers the removal or possession of any item from a sunken American warship that has not been stricken from its list of active ships a crime—no matter the wreck's location or age.

Shiver Me Timbers

Prior to the 1800s and the development of more lethal armaments, navy forces often went to sea with the intention of capturing intact military ships for their own use. Sailors also wanted to wrest valuable cargoes or treasure from enemy ships. Captured ships such as these were termed **prize ships** because many countries gave their warship captains a percentage of the recovered spoils.

Despite the advent of gunpowder and naval gunnery by the fifteenth century, it wasn't easy to sink even a wood-hulled warship with the poorly performing weapons. This factor forced many combatants to pass close to one another not only for cannon broadsides but also so that sailors and infantry could pepper an enemy ship with musket fire before boarding the opposing vessel.

Plenty of naval battles were settled with hand-to-hand combat. Legendary American Naval officer John Paul Jones captured 10 ships this way during his Revolutionary War raids in Britain's home waters. Capturing vessels meant robbing the sea (at least temporarily) of a few more sunken ships.

Gone but Not Forgotten

It's an ill wind that blows nobody good, according to the old proverb, just ask Kublai Khan. His massive invasion fleet was intended to conquer Japan but instead became the largest collection of shipwrecks in history. As the Mongol leader who ruled China, in 1274 Khan saw typhoons wreck one of the fleets he sent to invade Japan. The son of the brilliant but cruel Genghis Khan, Kublai Khan figured lightning couldn't strike twice in the same place. He decided it was time to mount another invasion to show Japan who was boss in thirteenth-century Asian politics. Khan spared nothing for the invasion—readying thousands of ships and more than 150,000 Korean, Chinese, and Mongol troops for the biggest invasion up to that point in history.

What Khan and company faced was a highly trained and motivated Japanese force that was as large or larger than Khan's own. The Japanese met the invaders at Hakata Bay on Kyushu, Japan's southernmost major island. Here, the defenders fought Khan's troops to a standstill. The Japanese presented such a strong challenge that Khan's generals ordered the troops back on the ships to avoid a counterattack while planning their next move overnight. This turned out to be the worst possible move.

Words To Treasure

During World War II a desperate Japan believed it could turn back the American advance by organizing **Kamikaze** pilots, a force of suicide pilots, to crash their explosive-packed aircraft into enemy warships. The pilots were considered to be Japan's human version of the **Divine Wind**. Unfortunately for them, their efforts failed to save them from defeat, although the kamikaze pilots did cause terrible damage to American naval forces.

Two-Time Loser

Sadly for junior, the second invasion only served to add a new phrase to the Japanese language while subtracting several thousand Chinese junks from Khan's navy. That's right: It stormed again! A cyclone struck Khan's seaborne force when it was north of Kyushu, sinking 4,000 junks and drowning 100,000 soldiers. That day—August 15, 1281—inspired the Japanese to name the cyclone "Kami Kaze" or *"Divine Wind."*

Though it's possible that some of Kublai Khan's ships carried currency, the junks undoubtedly carried mostly weaponry and commonplace artifacts. What survived these past 700 years underwater would be of immense historic value to researchers and of extraordinary value to collectors. Amazingly enough, there doesn't seem to be any record of large-scale attempts to salvage Khan's invasion fleet! Japan, however, secured the treasure it really wanted—the Japanese never again saw their homeland invaded.

The Way to San Jose

Considering the uncertainty of the treasure-hunting game, finding a billion-dollar treasure 1,000 feet below the Atlantic and not being able to touch it might be considered just another day at the wreck site.

This is precisely the situation that occurred when a treasure-hunting consortium named Sea Search Armada, Inc., located what they believed was the fabulously rich Spanish treasure ship *San Jose* and found themselves challenged for possession by Columbia, in whose waters it lies. The legal challenge stunted their efforts after they spent $10 million conducting the search. Unfortunately for treasure hunters, virtually every major treasure find in recent years has been accompanied by extensive litigation, a reality in this discovery as well.

The discovery of the Spanish treasure ship *San Jose* was a dream come true for investors in Sea Search Armada's efforts to locate the long-forgotten war galleon, since it had been carrying a treasure with a value estimated between $1 billion and $10 billion. After studying archival records and conducting a survey of the seabed, Sea Search Armada, Inc., of Seattle finally located the Spanish ship off Columbia's Caribbean coast.

Loaded with gold, silver, and gems from Colombia, the *San Jose* and 16 other ships of a Spanish treasure fleet encountered the sails of four British warships on June 7, 1708. During the ensuing battle, nearly 200 cannon shots were exchanged until a lucky cannon shot detonated the *San Jose*'s powder magazine with a terrific explosion.

The ship was covered in smoke and flame momentarily before sinking, and fewer than a dozen souls survived the explosion that saddened no one more than the British commodore, Charles Wager. As commander of the British force, Wager's capture of the ship could have made him a very rich man!

Unfortunately for Wager, the *San Jose* slammed to the seabed near Colombia's 12-mile territorial limit, a zone established by the United Nations treaty that also includes a 200-mile Economic Exclusionary Zone. Nations can lay claim to anything of value in the waters within these boundaries. The San Jose lay there undisturbed and almost forgotten until the detective work of the Sea Search Armada found what it believed was the wreck site.

Don't Go Overboard!

Because many ships were wrecked when their hulls were penetrated by unyielding coral reefs, much treasure hunting is conducted around these complex and environmentally sensitive formations. Treasure hunters are urged to not damage coral, since the reefs play an important role in promoting sea life. Many countries, including the United States, protect their reef systems with stringent laws.

Here Comes the Judge

Ownership of the treasure became an issue ensnarled in Colombia's judicial system. The courts ruled initially that Sea Search Armada had ownership of 50 percent of the treasure, while Colombian government lawyers argued that Sea Search Armada is entitled to only 5 percent of the find. The latest wrinkle has Colombia disputing whether the wreck is at the location specified by Sea Search Armada.

Had the treasure been at that location where Sea Search Armada claimed it was, an environmental issue would have arisen: Much of the 300-year-old treasure would have been encrusted inside a coral reef. Removing the coral to obtain the treasure would damage the fragile reef. As has been the case for much of the twentieth century, treasure—like success—has a thousand fathers.

Sea Search Armada, Inc., subsequently evolved into IOTA, a new treasure-hunting consortium that was searching for Spanish treasure ships in the Pacific.

Florida's Gold Coast

The Sunshine State hasn't always lived up to its name in the minds of the mariners who found themselves and their ships smashed against its shores by hurricanes and lesser storms. Believe it or not, more shipwrecks may lie off the coast of America's peninsular state than the coastline of any other!

Why, you ask, is Florida so lucky? First, Florida has 1,350 miles of coastline and forms the eastern boundary of the Gulf of Mexico. Only the massive state of Alaska has more shoreline than Florida with 6,639 miles. In addition, Florida lies in the path of the hurricane traffic that regularly sweeps through the region. Finally, and perhaps most important, a huge volume of maritime traffic has sailed near its shores.

Know The Ropes

The **Gulf Stream** is a powerful ocean current that goes by several different names as it runs from the equator north along the western Atlantic. Sailing in this current is highly beneficial, since it carries ships along at a faster clip. Mariners traveling from the Americas to Europe use the Gulf Stream whenever possible.

Treasure Fleet Playground

Since it's true that any coastal area can boast shipwrecks, you might be wondering why Florida is the one that is characterized as having a "Gold Coast."

Well, from 1520 to 1740 Spanish treasure ships plied the 90-mile-wide Straits of Florida separating Key West from Cuba. Thus Spanish ships returning from the New World ended up in a small geographical area, since it was in Havana that these treasure fleets assembled and prepared for their return with New World riches. When these fleets departed Havana for Spain, they did so by hitching a ride on the Gulf Stream northward up Florida's coast.

The Gulf Stream moved north along what is now America's East Coast and gave sailing ships a helpful push for their return trip to Europe.

When you add into the mix the vicious hurricanes that blow through this area six months of each year, you have the recipe for sunken treasure—and plenty of it! Ships pinned against the Florida coast were lucky if they were able to survive at all.

Famed Treasure Trio

Historians, archaeologists, and treasure hunters are still trying to locate all the treasure ships that were lost around Florida, but one particular triumvirate of shattered treasure fleets stands out. These ships are now known only by the years in which they were lost: the 1622, 1715, and 1733 Treasure Fleets. Hurricanes sank some or all of the ships in each fleet, and their wrecks lie from Key West in the south to the eastern coast of Florida.

One of the most famous of all treasure ships is the *Atocha,* part of the 1622 Treasure Fleet discovered in 1985 by treasure hunter Mel Fisher in the Florida Keys. Even today silver and gold are being brought up from that wreck. Ten wrecks of the decimated 1715 Treasure Fleet have been located along a 45-mile stretch of southern Florida. Likewise, the 1733 Treasure Fleet was also lost in the Florida Keys when a hurricane sank all but one of a dozen or more major ships. So the next time you're beachcombing or snorkeling around Florida's southern waters, keep a sharp watch! Who knows what you might find!

How Many Shipwrecks Are There?

Since humans have been going to sea for more than 10,000 years, there's no way of knowing exactly how many ships have been launched or how many ended up as shipwrecks.

Although maritime records have been accumulated throughout history, such records are fragmented—and in the case of ancient records—completely lost if they ever existed at all. What might amaze you is that, even during fairly modern times, shipping losses were not always considered worth recording. Although Spain's bureaucrats kept track of their treasure fleet losses, a comprehensive listing of ship losses didn't come into being until maritime insurer Lloyd's of London began the Lloyd's Registry in 1734.

Nevertheless, enough information is available to make it clear that there are a lot more ships rotting and rusting beneath the water than you might suspect. And don't forget that shipping losses have also occurred in lakes and rivers! So, let's look at some of the numbers we do have to get an idea of just how many wrecks are sleeping below the surface.

It's All in the Numbers!

The eastern coast of Britain alone may have as many as 8,200 wrecks, with some dating back to 43 A.D. Some areas have as many as 44 wrecks per mile of coastline! Although ships were lost at random along the coast, this averages about one wreck for every 120 feet of shoreline. One of these graveyard areas includes the Scilly Isles, which indicates—at least for mariners—that there is nothing silly at all about Britain's coast. There may be from 25,000 to 100,000 wrecks around the British Isles.

As many as 10,000 ships insured by British companies may have been lost during a single five-year period in the mid-1800s while conducting trade around the world.

Freshwater Wrecks

The unforgiving briny ocean isn't the only place you can lose a ship. This fact is something easy to forget when talking about shipwrecks. Inland lakes and rivers are also filled with thousands of ship and boat wrecks.

One example of this phenomenon is the Great Lakes, which comprise the largest system of freshwater lakes in the world. Navigating these miniature seas is comparable to sailing across the open ocean. The weather can be horrifying, the waves tall, and the visibility often close to zero. Unless you're a denizen of the Great Lakes region or are deeply knowledgeable about maritime issues, you'll be surprised at the number of shipwrecks that have occurred on these five lakes.

Don't Go Overboard!

While sitting on your houseboat on a peaceful lake thankful you're not on the dangerous briny deep, it's best to remember that thousands of ships and boats have been lost in every waterway from the Mississippi River to the Great Lakes. An average of 6,500 Americans drown each year with many deaths occurring in fresh water. Of these drowning deaths, 2,000 are children up to age 19.

One dedicated researcher spent 11 years compiling the history of each known Great Lakes shipwreck. David Swayze found more than 3,700, with the earliest dating back to 1697. Needless to say there are more—including the sunken craft of Native Americans. We shouldn't forget that these five massive lakes also bore the transport of people and cargo long before Europeans ever arrived.

Shiver Me Timbers

While fighting 90-mph winds and 25-foot waves the night of November 10, 1975, the *Edmund Fitzgerald* suddenly disappeared from radarscopes as it approached White Fish Point on Lake Superior. "Big Fitz" was the largest vessel ever lost on the Great Lakes.

The massive amount of heavy industry in the Great Lakes region, including the auto and steel industries, required prodigious shipments of raw materials in specially built bulk carriers. One such carrier was the *Edmund Fitzgerald,* which we cover in more detail in Chapter 21, "Wreck of the *Edmund Fitzgerald*." Built in 1958, it is perhaps the most famous ship ever lost on the Great Lakes.

Wartime Tolls

During World War II, submarines sank at least 8,000 ships alone as the belligerents attempted to destroy not only one another's naval forces but also their merchant shipping. But this number still doesn't take into account the thousands of ships and submarines sunk by surface warships, mines, and accidents. In World War I, it's estimated that the German Imperial Navy sank 5,000 ships with its U-boats.

With these incomplete numbers quickly approaching 30,000, it's easy to see that the total number of ship skeletons beneath the world's navigable waters is probably many times more than this figure.

Skeleton Coasts: The Final Ports of Call

The prose surrounding ships and shipwrecks often gets a shade dramatic; hence the tendency for various coastal areas to inherit frightening names, marking them as graveyards for ships. Virtually every country with a coastline has areas considered hazardous to shipping. Because thousands of shipwrecks dot Great Britain's coastal waters, it's surprising that the entire coast of England hasn't been given a scary name!

However, one pair of coastlines has become famous as the sites for numerous ship sinkings. Oddly enough, they face each other from opposites sides of the Atlantic. One is known by the dramatic name Graveyard of the Atlantic; the other is simply called the Skeleton Coast.

A Very Grave Place

The Graveyard of the Atlantic lies along the eastern side of North Carolina's Outer Banks, a region swept regularly by storms. Ships moving along this area are often slammed by all sorts of storms—never mind the dreaded hurricanes, which are the most powerful storms to strike North America. Countless ships lie in this "graveyard," but the most famous is a warship, the experimental ironclad USS *Monitor*.

Unable to tolerate rough seas, the *Monitor* foundered 16 miles southeast of Cape Hatteras on December 31, 1862—just 11 months after the ship was launched and nine months after its famous naval battle with the Confederate warship *Merrimack*. Although the battle may have ended in a

Don't Go Overboard!

The USS *Monitor*'s wreck site was established as a National Marine Sanctuary, and the dive to the wreckage is considered dangerous because of the depth and the state of the *Monitor*'s debris. Since it's federally protected, a federal representative must accompany divers. Some artifact recovery is allowed but only when the objects retrieved might be otherwise lost and then they must be handed over to the federal government.

draw, the Atlantic storm that swamped the *Monitor* won hands down. In fact, 16 of her hands went down with her as she sank. The *Monitor* now lies in 230 feet of water under the care of the National Oceanic and Atmospheric Agency, as well as the U.S. Coast Guard. Plans are being made by the federal government to raise portions of the ship that are deteriorating faster than expected.

The World's Loneliest Cemetery

Perhaps the most frightening of all nautical graveyards is the 400-mile stretch of forbidding coastline along the southwest coast of Africa known as the Skeleton Coast. Just a photograph of this coastline presents a chilling scene—a windswept sea crashes against a narrow ribbon of sand beyond which lies the barrenness of the inhospitable Namib Desert. The desert stretches for hundreds of miles inland, so the Skeleton Coast is literally in the middle of nowhere.

Those lucky enough to survive a wreck here have no town to walk to, no water to drink, and nothing to eat. Rusting hulks of cargo ships dot this coastline whose name stands not only for the skeletons of the ships that met their fate here but also for the bleached bones of their occupants.

Hundreds of ships, big and small, have been shoved by powerful winds against what is one of the most desolate places in the world. Running along the coast of Namibia toward the country's border with South Africa, this coast is one of the most remote and desolate places on earth.

As a result, Skeleton Coast has become a natural tourist destination for those who want to see the rusting hulks of ships like that of the merchant ship *Edouard Bohlen* that was thrown ashore in 1909.

A sailboat that has been thrown upon the beach of Africa's Skeleton Coast now sits in one of the loneliest places in the world.
(Copyright Helmar Rudolph)

The Least You Need to Know

➤ Sailors were considered tougher than the ships they sailed because of the hazards that threatened wood-hulled ships.

➤ Egyptian leader Khufu ordered construction of the Great Pyramid at Giza as his tomb 4,500 years ago including the burial of five ships for use in his afterlife, of which two have been excavated to be the oldest surviving ships ever recovered.

➤ Mariners gave different names to different sections of the Gulf Stream, the current sailors use to help propel their ships.

➤ Spanish treasure fleets badly damaged or destroyed by tropical storms are known by the years in which they sailed.

➤ War is one of the greatest contributors to Davy Jones' locker, with 8,000 ships sunk in World War II by submarines alone. This figure excludes hundreds of others sunk by aircraft, mines, and other surface ships.

➤ Florida's coastal waters are reputed to have more shipwrecks than any other location in the United States due to its large coastline, a traditionally high volume of maritime traffic, and its history of powerful hurricanes.

Chapter 4

Legacy or Loot?

In This Chapter

➤ Profit vs. knowledge: salvors vs. archaeologists

➤ Giving history a lift: raising England's *Mary Rose*

➤ Growing cooperation between treasure hunters and archaeologists

➤ Federally protected American shipwrecks

Perhaps the basic wildness of the sea makes it natural to consider anything that's lost in the water or that washes ashore as your property when you find it. After all, would you think about asking anyone's permission before prying a rusted pocketknife from the sand at the water's edge? Of course not!

So you can understand what happened when divers located valuable wreck sites over the years and thought nothing of making off with dinnerware, munitions, or anything else that looked as if it would be fun or profitable to own. The attitude toward any shipwreck, especially one that seemed to have no claims upon it, has traditionally been one of "finders keepers." In some circumstances, salvage law has said the same thing since the finder of the wreck can be granted permission to recover a ship and its cargo.

During the past 40 years, however, it's become more obvious that a large part of human history is locked within the remains of sunken ships. With the mass marketing of scuba equipment since the early 1950s, ordinary people could reach thousands of wrecks in clear waters for sightseeing or souvenir hunting. This pastime horrified archaeologists and historians, who realized that their keys to the past were being removed one at a time. Within a few years, many wrecks had been picked clean!

Another issue close to the hearts of warship sailors and professional mariners involves the symbolism behind each sunken ship, particularly those lost in war or violent storms. These wrecks often represent a gravesite for men and women who never had a proper burial ashore.

Dr. Robert Ballard's discovery of the RMS *Titanic* wreck in 1985 added fuel to the growing controversy over the correct treatment of wreck sites. Although Ballard and his team subsequently opposed disturbing the *Titanic's* wreckage or artifacts, others have done so. What some call *plundering* is at the center of a growing argument over the ownership and sanctity of historically important shipwrecks.

Words To Treasure

To **plunder** a wrecked ship of its artifacts is to remove them fraudulently or without proper permission. The ill-gotten gains themselves are also known as plunder, another word for booty.

Ballard, along with most governments and the community of marine archaeologists, believes that nautical sites should be properly studied and preserved for the good of the public. On the other side of this argument, however, are the entrepreneurs whose ability to raise capital has helped them to raise artifacts and treasure from some of the deepest wrecks. The efforts of these for-profit expeditions have been criticized as tasteless and garish—if not merely disrespectful of the dead.

Negative public and judicial responses to indiscriminate recovery of wrecks has prompted a growing number of treasure hunters to enlist the aid of archaeologists to help properly excavate, catalog, and recover artifacts. While some consider this move nothing more than window dressing to deflect criticism, the entrepreneurs argue that the slender resources of academia's archaeologists are unequal to the task of recovering and preserving artifacts that deteriorate daily.

This controversy is far from over.

Souvenir Ships or Sacred Sites?

Profit and history aside, the fact that many shipwrecks involved the loss of life often instills sense of reverence about them. The newer the shipwreck, the stronger this feeling. It's little wonder that the sinking of the *Titanic* with its loss of 1,517 souls less than 100 years ago has generated emotional responses.

The September 1, 1985, discovery of the RMS *Titanic* meant the world finally knew the location of history's most famous shipwreck. Unseen for 73 years, the factual liner had reached fable status owing to the horrific end of its maiden voyage. Scientist and former Navy officer Robert Ballard located the ship with the assistance of the French Research Institute for the Exploration of the Sea—commonly referred to as IFREMER.

Ballard made another expedition to the *Titanic* in 1986 and brought back photographs and video images but left everything physical where it was. For Ballard, the wreck was a gravesite, and in its own way, sacred, so he left only a commemorative plaque on the deck to mark his visit.

Shiver Me Timbers

The sanctity of nautical gravesites runs deep. In the Cold War's oddest scene, a 1974 sea burial was held for six Soviet submariners aboard the CIA spy ship *Glomar Explorer.* The dead Soviet sailors were crew members of Soviet submarine *K–129* that sank accidentally in 1968. Their remains were inside a portion of the submarine that had been grabbed from 16,000 feet beneath the Pacific with the help of *Glomar's* giant mechanical claw. Eccentric billionaire Howard Hughes, an ardent anticommunist and lover of intrigue, had built the ship with CIA money.

No Rest for the Weary

For all of Ballard's protests, the *Titanic* was still not left in peace. Another expedition mounted in 1987 by Titanic Ventures, Inc.—now known as RMS Titanic, Inc.—used IFREMER's deep-submergence craft *Nautile* to bring up hundreds of artifacts from 12,000 feet below the surface of the Atlantic. The first of these artifacts was a banged up silver serving tray. A crystal wine decanter was later recovered and taken to a U.S. District Court in Norfolk, Virginia, where RMS Titanic, Inc., produced it as evidence to arrest, or claim, the *Titanic.*

Would you believe that the boss of this for-profit expedition was actually a former car dealer and entrepreneur from Connecticut? It's true, and his name is George Tulloch. Praised by some and lambasted by others, Tulloch organized several expeditions to pluck thousands of objects from the *Titanic*'s debris field. For this, Tulloch received a torrent of criticism. He persisted and has won key legal battles to establish RMS Titanic, Inc.'s claim to the wreck.

Recovering Expenses

To cover the cost of the expedition, RMS Titanic, Inc., has sold actual lumps of coal taken from the liner and replicas of other items raised from the deep. The liner, for all its magnificence, was far from being a treasure ship. But its notoriety and fame—boosted in no small measure by the 1998 movie *Titanic*—made the doomed liner the world's largest celebrity. Her early twentieth-century fixtures, passenger belongings, and even the humble anthracite from her coal bunkers have acquired value.

A piece of this hot-selling coal, a commodity that seems akin to the Pet Rock of the late 1970s, can be had for as little as $14.99. Yes, it comes with a certificate of authenticity. And should the historic significance of the coal wear off, it could at the very least be used to generate heat, which is advantageous. Really, what could you do with an out-of-favor Pet Rock?

Tulloch has also assembled a traveling, international exhibition of *Titanic* artifacts including a 20-ton hunk of the ship's hull that was recovered in 1998. Those wishing to see these artifacts must purchase tickets, thereby giving Tulloch one more source of income to continue his expeditions.

Shiver Me Timbers

Tulloch's RMS Titanic, Inc., was salvor-in-possession of not only the *Titanic* but also its image. Tulloch and his group have made legal history by gaining ownership of the image of an object. A federal judge in Norfolk, Virginia, ruled that RMS Titanic, Inc., had the right to disallow anyone from photographing or diving on the wreck without its permission. This ruling outraged many, and at least one shocked observer said that the ruling was like making it illegal to look at the Empire State Building! However, a federal appeals court ruled in 1999 that the public can visit and photograph the wreck site.

Profit vs. Knowledge: Salvors vs. Archaeologists

Nautical archaeologists and treasure hunters are alike in that they both want to discover old shipwrecks and submerged artifacts. However, they often behave differently after the find is made.

Archaeologists carefully place a *grid* over their excavation, mapping the location of even the smallest objects. They also note the condition of items found and study their origins and construction. Then they have to subject the artifacts they have recovered to detailed tests. These tests can help them to gather additional clues that the average treasure hunter wouldn't be concerned with. The smallest object might be cast aside by a treasure hunter but end up being the most valuable find—historically—to the archaeologist who is trying to understand something about people who died 3,000 years ago.

Treasure hunters, on the other hand, have bills to pay and things to do, like moving to the next valuable shipwreck. They've been sweating under the sun and shivering under the water looking for treasure for years. Many have found treasure only to spend it looking for more. It can be a desperate existence—even after finding a huge treasure.

Famous Florida treasure hunter Mel Fisher, who discovered the Spanish treasure ship *Atocha* (see Chapter 11, "Rich Disaster: Wreck of the 1622 Treasure Fleet," for more on this story) and its millions in silver and gold in the mid-1980s, was once so broke he bought groceries with Spanish pieces of eight recovered from the wreck. Like most treasure hunters, Fisher was often just one step ahead of creditors during his expeditions. However, Fisher's persistence paid off with the discovery of two fabulously rich Spanish shipwrecks in the 1980s. At the time of his death following a long battle with cancer in December 1998, Fisher was a wealthy man.

Faced with astronomically high operating costs of the incredibly difficult job of searching for ship-wrecks, treasure hunters are under terrific pressure to succeed. Knowing that a victorious search can be plagued with legal problems puts treasure hunters under even more pressure when they successfully locate a wreck. Famed treasure hunter and author Robert F. Marx found a fortune in silver around the wreck of the Spanish galleon *Maravilla,* which was sunk off the Bahamas in 1656. He dutifully turned the gold over to authorities only to find himself in a long-term legal snarl. Eventually, Spain turned up claiming some of the treasure.

Words To Treasure

A **grid** placed over a shipwreck is usually made up of sections of plastic pipe, and it allows archaeologists to map where each item was found. This mapping helps researchers understand how the ship was constructed and how its cargo was loaded. Knowing the position of various items can also tell researchers how the items were used. Such care provides a full idea of the ship and its role in history.

Perpetual Public Treasures

Academics and students, on the other hand, are usually happy to be poor doing something they love—historical detective work. With grants from foundations and benefactors, academic types will work tirelessly on a shoestring budget until the job is complete or the money runs out, whichever comes first! Whatever historical objects or actual treasures make it to the surface are then catalogued, studied, and turned over to whatever government they belong to.

These objects are usually available for study, and if the find is spectacular enough, the objects frequently end up in specially built museums. This is exactly what happened to the Swedish warship *Vasa* three centuries after its August 10, 1628, sinking in Stockholm's harbor. Thousands of proud Swedes turned out to watch the unveiling of this artifact.

So what happened to the *Vasa?* Well, its maiden voyage turned into a horrifying event. A sudden but light wind tipped the ship twice, causing it to take on water through its open cannon ports. After drinking a fatal overdose of water, the *Vasa* quickly sank, killing as many as 50 on board.

Discovered in 1956 by Swedish navy divers and recovered in 1961, the *Vasa* was subsequently restored and rebuilt. The warship, which is in a miraculous state of preservation, is now in its own museum, which has become an internationally re-nowned tourist attraction.

Twice-Hidden Treasures

Treasure hunters claim that no one enjoys the spoils of a wreck that simply lies on the seabed, and distinguished nautical archaeologist George Bass agrees—but for different reasons. Bass says the careful recovery of a wreck and its artifacts can provide a tourist destination that is culturally profitable for the visitor and financially profitable for the host community. Selling artifacts to private collectors—the goal of the treasure hunter—sometimes means they are lost for a second time—first in the water and then inside vaults and mansions. However, some complain that artifacts sometimes disappear into dusty storage at universities and museums, never to be seen again.

Wetter Is Better

Despite the "little brother" status of marine archaeology next to the old man of terrestrial archaeology, a number of important antiquities have been found in better condition at submerged sites than on land. Unfortunately for archaeologists, the better-financed treasure-hunting expeditions are purchasing an ever-increasing level of wreck-finding technology. The threat to possible archaeological sites is clear and worrisome to archaeologists.

The Tender Touch

Fortune hunting, according to scientists like Robert Ballard and archaeologists like George Bass, is often a slash-and-burn technique, since time spent over a wreck is so costly; in fact, it is often counted by the minute. In the past, explosives, vegetation-damaging silt blowers, and crowbars have been the tools of treasure hunters in a hurry.

Shiver Me Timbers

The gold-bearing wreck of the liner *Egypt* that sank in 1922 in 400 feet of water was blasted with 11,000 pounds of high explosives until the room containing the gold bullion was ripped open. A huge claw was dropped into the hole to wrench the gold from the interior of the ship. The operation was completed in 1932, only two years after the *Egypt's* discovery off the coast of Brittany, France. Virtually all of the gold, valued at $1.5 million in 1932, was recovered. The present-day value of the *Egypt's* gold is estimated to be $22 million. Unscrupulous treasure hunters have used similar techniques on historically important shipwrecks.

Giving History a Lift: Raising England's *Mary Rose*

The sixteenth-century English warship *Mary Rose* (see Chapter 14, "A Rose Blossoms Again," for more about *Mary*) has gone from wreck to recognition, but it took time and money in equally large helpings.

The rediscovery, survey, and raising of the English warship *Mary Rose* was a challenge to those who had nursed the project since the mid-1960s. It took from 1965 until 1971 to confirm the *Mary Rose*'s location and still another 11 years to survey and catalog the wreck site. The remnants of the ship's hull were not even raised until October 11, 1982. It took from 1965 to 1971 just to confirm its location in the muck of Portsmouth Harbor on Britain's east coast.

Shiver Me Timbers

King Henry VIII's favorite ship, the *Mary Rose,* sank July 19, 1545, as it maneuvered to do battle with French invaders in Portsmouth Harbor. As many as 700 sailors, soldiers, and archers died aboard the ship when it leaned over too far and sank. Only around 40 aboard managed to escape. Like the Swedish ship *Vasa* that sank 123 years later, this ship's structural instability caused the disaster. Also like the *Vasa,* water was allowed to come in through the *Mary Rose*'s open cannon ports.

Few people have as much reverence for their military history as the Britons do, so you shouldn't be surprised to know that when it came time to recover the remains of one of the country's most tragic shipwrecks, it was to be done with care and respect.

Money Matters

However, the project—like most archaeological excavations—was tough to finance. The *Mary Rose* Committee, which later became the *Mary Rose* Trust, was looking for funding just as much as it was searching for the ship. Eventually, the high and the mighty of Britain climbed aboard to support the effort.

His Royal Highness Prince Charles, who dove on the wreck in 1975, became president of the *Mary Rose* Trust in 1979 and gave the effort a tremendous public relations boost. The raising of the *Mary Rose* became a global media event when a considerable segment of its hull was lifted to the surface of Portsmouth Harbor 437 years after sinking.

Had there been gold bullion and silver ingots heavy in her hold, British warships would have been needed to guard the site 24 hours a day to fend off treasure hunters.

But, with little more than rotted wood, scattered artifacts, and the bones of its dead to attract entrepreneurs, the *Mary Rose* was destined to be lonely.

Preservation: The Unending Task

Bringing up the artifacts and the remains of the ship was light duty next to the years of restoration and preservation work that had to be accomplished. It's not unusual for archaeologists to create a year's worth of preservation work for every month of underwater recovery, and this was definitely the case with the *Mary Rose*.

From 1982, when the ship was raised, until 1994, its timbers were sprayed with chilled water. Now the remnants of the hull are sprayed with polyethylene glycol, a water-soluble wax that strengthens and preserves the wood. This process will continue for at least the next 16 years. Even though the expense of preserving the 450-year-old ship will undoubtedly outweigh its financial value, this type of work is necessary to keep the ship and her artifacts available for future generations.

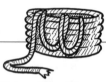

Know The Ropes

The recovery of very old wood artifacts presents complicated problems to archaeologists. If the wood should dry out, it would warp and crack beyond recognition. When wooden artifacts are brought to the surface, they must often be kept wet until the wood can be chemically treated to prevent disintegration.

The *Mary Rose* sits inside its own museum and preservation center at Her Majesty's Naval Base, in Portsmouth, England. Because money is still a concern for those looking after the *Mary Rose,* fund-raising efforts continue. Were the ship in private hands, the urge to sell off the collected artifacts might be too strong to resist, especially considering the expense of caring for them. But maintaining all the artifacts in a single place is crucial to their study by experts and is one of the primary goals of archaeologists.

It's little wonder that so many historically valuable shipwrecks await excavation. It's hard for many nations struggling with the human needs of their populations to focus on archaeology.

Growing Cooperation Between Treasure Hunters and Archaeologists

No matter how angry treasure hunters and archaeologists may be with one another, it's interesting to note the seeming contradictions when it comes to recognizing a wreck for historical value.

Many states and countries allow ordinary maritime salvage laws to govern the recovery of ships and artifacts on wrecks less than 100 years old. However, wrecks that are older may require governmental permission for exploration or salvage. Treasure hunters strongly believe that wrecks and their artifacts are being allowed to deteriorate while awaiting an excavation that will never come.

Archaeologists shoot back that wrecks have survived for hundreds of years and that much of the cargo, particularly glass and earthenware, are almost impervious to deterioration. Time seems to be at the center of the dispute: The archaeologists want to reach back into time in a careful, scientific way, whereas treasure hunters are businesspeople in a hurry to beat the competition to a promising wreck.

The Golden Rule

There does seem to be an interesting degree of hypocrisy in determining which ship is inviolate and which can be cut open with underwater welding torches and then salvaged. Take the case of the HMS *Edinburgh,* whose life and death are more fully discussed in Chapter 23, "Cold, Cold Cache."

Sunk with millions in Soviet gold paid to Great Britain during World War II, the *Edinburgh* was first attacked by a German U-boat and then by German aircraft. Damaged and in danger of being captured, it was sunk by the British themselves off what was then the Soviet coast. By the late 1970s, the thought of putting this gold in their respective treasuries looked inviting to both the British and the Soviets.

Although the British government considered the ship an official war grave, a salvage firm was allowed to burn its way inside the armored warship and retrieve the gold when its recovery technique promised to do the least amount of damage. It seemed that the living (with expenses) took precedence over the dead (whose accounts were settled).

Nonetheless, the pot is still boiling with treasure hunters arguing that they're the only ones who will invest in locating many sunken ships while archaeologists warn of the destruction of sites that could better explain the past.

Conscientious Plunder?

Oddly, treasure hunters and archaeologists may be a bit harder to tell apart if the current trend continues. Treasure hunters, coming under increasing legal and media attack for tearing into wrecks, are now taking a more measured approach. Well-heeled treasure-hunting enterprises are even hiring archaeologists to assist them with their work!

R. Duncan Mathewson III, an archaeologist with impressive credentials, once worked for the Florida treasure-hunting legend Mel Fisher. Mathewson surveyed wreck sites, cataloged artifacts, and sometimes argued with his boss in an attempt to prevent the sale of a historically valuable item. Mathewson and other academics who have grasped the proverbial bloody paw of the treasure hunter find themselves sometimes ignored and ostracized by nonprofit archaeology.

Shiver Me Timbers

The rancor that once existed between some archaeologists and treasure hunters may evaporate for good if treasure salvors follow the example of "commercial exploration" firm Odyssey Marine Exploration in Tampa, Florida. Odyssey applies careful archaeological methods to the recovery of historical artifacts (and treasure) in the deep ocean. The firm's careful 1991 excavation of a seventeenth-century Spanish shipwreck off the Florida Keys was praised by university archaeologists, and the firm plans to cooperate with universities on future projects.

Archaeological Nemesis

The late Mel Fisher—irrepressible treasure hunter and champion of free enterprise—while going full-steam ahead in locating ships, wasn't making many friends among classically trained archaeologists. He engendered even more rancor when he successfully weathered federal legal challenges to his ownership of the booty. The inventor of a device that helps blow away sand from the seabed at an enormous rate, Fisher also managed to upset environmentalists when the federal government sued him for destroying sea grass in the Florida Keys National Marine Sanctuary.

He became a treasure-hunting David fighting the Goliath of the federal government when he successfully opposed federal attempts to strip him of silver and gold recovered from the *Atocha,* one of Florida's richest Spanish wrecks. Eventually, Fisher became the poster boy for treasure hunters whom preservationists love to hate.

Fisher smiled through it all. At the time of his death in 1998, he was under investigation for supposedly selling faked Spanish treasure—an allegation Fisher first dismissed as ridiculous. Dying, Fisher made an agreement with the government to reimburse anyone who could prove they were sold fake coins. Fisher's personal saying about the ups and downs of treasure hunting has become a rallying cry for his fellow hunters: "Today's the day!"

Don't Go Overboard!

As of 1997, Florida state law prohibited anyone from defacing or removing any archaeological specimen on state land or within the boundaries of a landmark zone. Such vandalism is worth a year in jail and a $1,000 fine. Dig into one of these sites or attempt to sell an artifact belonging to the state, and you could become an antiquity yourself by sitting in jail for up to 10 years.

Federally Protected American Shipwrecks

Every American warship lost at sea, or in any other body of water, remains protected by law, and the defacing or plunder of any of these ships is illegal. Even Confederate warships sunk during the Civil War are now the property of the government. Some have become emotionally symbolic, while others have acquired extreme historical value.

When Japanese bombs struck the battleship USS *Arizona* in Pearl Harbor's *Battleship Row* on December 7, 1941, a massive staccato of explosions rocked that huge ship and killed 1,117 men. Perhaps more than anything else, that scene, which was captured on film, galvanized many Americans in their grim determination to avenge the attack.

The *Arizona* was shattered beyond use; its tall superstructure was cut away so that nothing showed above the water. Only the ship's shattered hull was left to lie on the bottom. Nevertheless, its equipment and guns were salvaged and put on other ships readied for combat.

Words To Treasure

Battleship Row was the name given to an anchorage of massive concrete moorings at the U.S. Naval Base at Pearl Harbor where the battleships of the Pacific Fleet would essentially park. These battleships were prime targets for the Japanese attack.

The *Arizona* instantly became a symbol of America's failure to be prepared and a sad reminder of those who died as a result of the Japanese sneak attack. On May 30, 1962, a memorial was dedicated over the *Arizona* wreck site. In 1965 the *Arizona* was deemed a national historic landmark. It lives on fully protected by stringent federal laws.

Look but Don't Touch

Dishes, silverware, and hundreds of other objects litter the site of the *Arizona*. Lying in 38 feet of water, it would be a dream excursion for diving enthusiasts, but only official diving expeditions for the government have been allowed. The remains of nearly 1,000 men are believed to be inside the wreckage visited by thousands of tourists—and mourners—yearly. Despite time, Americans are still deeply reverential toward the *Arizona*. The wreck is a haunting and solemn memorial, encrusted with marine growth and visible to those above.

Civil War Wrecks

While perhaps the best-known of America's warship gravesites, the *Arizona* is just one of many American (and Confederate) fighting ships scattered around the world under not only the water but also the protection of the federal government.

The recent discovery of the Civil War submarine *H. L. Hunley* has added yet another warship to those the government intends to protect—and possibly recover. The *Hunley* was a Confederate submarine that destroyed the USS *Housatonic* off Charleston, South Carolina, on the night of February 17, 1864.

Using an explosive charge attached to a harpoon-like device, the *Hunley* impaled the *Housatonic* and then backed away before detonating the explosive with the yank of a lanyard. The *Hunley* did not return from the scene of the battle and was lost with all hands.

Shiver Me Timbers

The *H. L. Hunley,* named after its main financial backer, actually sank a total of four times, killing 30 men—including Hunley. It sank twice when swamped by swells and a third time when a valve could not be closed—this incident killed Hunley himself. All the same, it was raised three times and put back into service. The last sinking is the still-mysterious loss of the *Hunley* following its attack on the *Housatonic.*

Hunting for the Hunley

Located in 1995 by an expedition led by adventure novelist Clive Cussler, the *Hunley* find sparked a battle over the early submarine's ownership. Despite a rash of claims, which always seems to follow the discovery of a historical ship, the General Services Administration (GSA) still had title to all abandoned Confederate military property. The GSA then transferred ownership of the *Hunley*'s wreckage to the U.S. Navy.

Cussler, who never intended to profit from his find by the retrieval of artifacts or the raising of the *Hunley,* kept the location secret until he was assured the site would be protected. A dispute arose when F. Lee Spence, senior editor of *Wreck Diver* magazine, claimed he originally located the *Hunley*'s approximate wreck site but did not confirm it with a dive. Spence has since only asked that his contribution be recognized. Cussler's organization, the National Underwater and Marine Agency, was able to locate and then confirm that the wreck was the *Hunley.*

The *Hunley*'s design was so unique and advanced for its time that its historic significance can't be overstated. Nor, learned Cussler, could its financial value. After locating the Hunley's site, he began to hear rumors that collectors were willing to pay tens of thousands of dollars for the ship's artifacts. Cussler's secrecy was undoubtedly well-advised.

Shiver Me Timbers

The federal government has determined the *Hunley* is a good candidate for recovery. Various organizations are raising money to pay for the salvage and restoration. The 7.5-ton submarine was 39.5 feet long and was propelled by a crank turned by as many as eight men sitting across from one another. The *Hunley* would be the first Confederate warship ever raised and restored.

Far from Home: CSS Alabama

Far from home but not forgotten, the Confederate warship CSS *Alabama* lies in 200 feet of water off Cherbourg, France. Discovered in 1984 by a French minesweeping vessel, the *Alabama*'s identity was confirmed by French Navy Capt. Max Guerout who dived to the wreck, and the United States was notified of its location. To protect the wreck in foreign waters, the United States reached a landmark 1989 agreement with France, recognizing the site's historic significance while agreeing to international cooperation in researching the site. The U.S. Navy granted permission to the Association CSS *Alabama* to operate archaeological investigations of the wreck site.

Distant Showdown

The *Alabama* took part in a little-known segment of the Civil War in which Confederate warships prowled the oceans to sink Union ships. The *Alabama*—a *sloop-of-war*—took 60 prize ships valued at $6 million before meeting its fate at the hands of the Union warship USS *Kearsarge*.

In a sea battle off France's Cherbourg coast, the USS Kearsarge *is depicted sinking the Confederate raiding sloop* Alabama *as its crew abandons the doomed vessel. (Courtesy of the Mariner's Museum)*

The *Alabama* had entered the French port of Cherbourg where Captain Ralph Semmes sought permission to refit and overhaul his ship. The *Kearsarge,* which was hot on the trail of Confederate sea raiders, arrived soon after to sit offshore. On June 19, 1864, the *Alabama* came out to meet the *Kearsarge.*

Words To Treasure

A **sloop** was a low-profile ship with a short bowsprit or prow. This type of ship was used often on the American Great Lakes and remains a popular design for yachting.

Because the *Alabama* was supplied with inferior gunpowder that degraded its gunnery, the ship fell victim to the excellent gunnery of the *Kearsarge.* After much maneuvering between the two ships, the *Kearsarge's* gunners landed numerous hits on the *Alabama,* which was eventually reduced to a smoking wreck. With no other options, Captain Semmes surrendered his crew to the *Kearsarge.* The *Alabama* then slipped beneath the waves into obscurity.

The Least You Need to Know

➤ Shipwrecks and their valuable artifacts have created friction between treasure hunters and those who want to see such wrecks treated as hallowed memorials to those who died at sea.

➤ Treasure hunters must turn a profit, and their hasty methods of recovering artifacts and treasure are horrifying to archaeologists who want to carefully study and preserve clues to the past.

➤ The *H. L. Hunley* sank three times—killing crew members each time—before it was finally lost for good with all hands during the sinking of the USS *Housatonic* on February 17, 1864.

➤ The Confederate war sloop *Alabama* was at a terrific military disadvantage because the gunpowder for its naval guns was inferior, which is one reason that the *Alabama* was unable to defeat the USS *Kearsarge* off the coast of France on June 19, 1864.

➤ The capricious nature of treasure hunting leaves those involved in the game wealthy one day and broke the next, which explains why treasure hunter Mel Fisher once had to buy groceries with recovered Spanish pieces of eight.

➤ Pioneer marine archaeologist George Bass knew nothing about scuba diving when he agreed to excavate his first submerged shipwreck off the coast of Turkey in 1960.

Part 2
The Many Pleasures of Sunken Treasures

Although the term "shipwreck" seems synonymous with "sunken treasure," the number of sunken treasure ships compared to ordinary shipwrecks is exceedingly tiny. However, untouched treasure ships still lie on the seafloor, and Part 2 discusses their existence.

Although wealth seems to be lying around waiting to be scooped up, locating a shipwreck is extremely difficult, even when its approximate location is already known. This part reveals the problems associated with finding shipwrecks and describes the technology developed to overcome them, including the use of crude diving bells and Jacques-Yves Cousteau's role in developing scuba equipment.

Part 2 also discusses the New World origins of the treasures carried aboard the most famous and numerous treasure ships—those belonging to the Spanish Empire. The complexities of maritime law and the fact that finders are not necessarily always keepers is covered at the end of this part.

Treasure Hunting's Soggy History

Unlike most enterprises, the job of visiting shipwrecks—whether for fun or profit—is an endeavor in which one starts at the top and works his way to the bottom. The water can be clear or murky, dangerously cold or pleasantly warm. Sea life can thrill or threaten, and, of course, sea pressure increases the deeper you go. Go down 10 feet and your ears pop; get down to 3,000 feet, and even the hulls of nuclear submarines implode.

When diving meant sucking in your breath and plunging in, submerged salvage work was a brief experience. As a result, it required many dives. At least 300 years before the birth of Christ, humans were attempting to devise ways to dive deeper and longer.

Technology for extended underwater activities may have progressed slowly, but people were working on shallow portions of the seabed earlier than most might think. The driving force behind the most important innovations was nothing less than the need to recover valuables lost by sunken ships or, if possible, the ships themselves.

Jump on in, the water's fine!

Original Sunken-Treasure Hunters

If mountain climbing has been justified with the phrase "because it's there," then those who dive upon sunken ships do so "because it's under there." Humanity has a long history underwater. Before there were wrecks to explore, people pinched their nostrils and dove for dinner. According to some social anthropologists, some tribes should be referred to as hunters, gatherers, and divers.

Prior to the advent of large-capacity sailing ships, a valuable treasure known as amber was already tempting people to dive—or at least wade—for treasure 13,000 years ago. If you've seen the movie *Jurassic Park,* you'd know that this ancient material encases extinct insects and animals. That's not Hollywood hype, folks; it's fact!

Somewhere between a mineral and a gem, amber was plentiful in the waters of the Baltic Sea, where it lay in the offshore sand. The hardened globules had oozed from extinct conifers to become one of the first materials used for decoration.

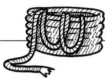

Know The Ropes

Those who searched for amber in the northern climes, such as the Baltic Sea region, dressed for warmth and used nets and poles. The material is abundant in the Baltic and is often found on the beach after powerful storms have churned the seafloor.

Early Treasure-Hunting Restrictions

Amber was once so valuable that it was illegal to gather it along the Baltic Sea. Leaning over and picking up a hunk of the stuff actually meant a death sentence in the thirteenth century! The Teutonic knights who ruled the Baltic Sea area monopolized the amber trade.

But even before the Teutonic knights were in control, the Roman Empire's desire for amber prompted it to use Baltic slaves to recover the precious material. It was often a cargo aboard the ships of the Phoenicians and the Romans. Many of these ships never made it to port, so goodly amounts of amber are still awaiting archaeologists and treasure hunters to gather it from the seabed for the last time.

The Greek Divers

Warm, clear waters have always prompted people to hold their breath and dive for what's below. Even if there's nothing at the bottom of a swimming pool but a penny, there's a natural urge to dive for it. Ancient people were no different, especially when the stakes were far more valuable.

The Greek poet Oppian, who lived in the second century B.C.E., wrote extensively about diving activity in the warm seas around Greece. His description of Greek sponge divers embracing stones for a faster plummet to the seabed is frightening. The divers slammed into the bottom, wrote Oppian, where they quickly hacked at sponges with a curved knife. When their lungs were about to burst, they tugged a rope signaling helpers to snatch them upward. As you might imagine, any delay in this choreography meant death.

From Sponges to Statues

It's only natural that Greece's famous divers should end up discovering the treasures scattered about the Mediterranean region as they looked for less exciting things like sponges.

In 1900, Greek sponge divers recovered one of the most famous submerged bronze statues ever found. This statue, called *Antikythera Youth,* was found off the Greek island of Antikythera. It's one of many antiquities located accidentally by divers, though many similar treasures remain unknown, since their recovery was never reported to authorities.

New World Divers

On the other side of the globe, the Spanish were impressed with the diving abilities of the Indians of the New World, who often reached 100-foot depths in search of pearl-bearing oysters. Unfortunately, these death-defying deeds would also be rewarded with death. The Spanish soon organized pearl fisheries and put the Indians to work generating more treasure for Spain.

Like most colonial enterprises involving Spanish use of the Indians, the treatment of the native peoples was harsh and unhealthy. These *free divers* were often forced to work from dawn until dark, and many died not only from dangerous conditions but also from European diseases.

When Spanish treasure ships were lost and strong bodies were needed for the salvage efforts, Indian divers were often pressed into service with little regard for their safety. The Spaniards cared not a whit about the sharks when the Indians were doing the swimming.

Words To Treasure

A **free diver** is someone who swims beneath the surface of the water without devices to assist in breathing. Obviously, the Native Americans pressed into service for diving in the New World were far from free.

Salvage: As Old as the First Shipwreck

When money's involved, the sky (or the seafloor) is the limit. As soon as ships laden with valuables started to sink, people began to organize treasure-hunting and salvage operations.

When the greedy Perseus, King of Macedonia, suffered a military reversal fighting the Romans in 169 B.C.E., he reputedly ordered a substantial amount of his treasure dumped into Lake Lydias to avoid its capture. To hide the location, he murdered everyone who took part in the dumping. Remember, these were the days before presidential impeachment hearings. When the coast was clear, Perseus sent his divers to recover the treasure.

Shiver Me Timbers

Perseus, who was at war with the Romans at the peak of their military strength, eventually saw his army defeated. He was imprisoned in Italy until his death in 165 B.C.E. He was the last Macedonian king.

Early Salvage Law

With the vast amount of trade in the Mediterranean stretching back centuries before the birth of Christ, Roman, Greek, and Phoenician ships were beginning to litter the sea bottom in large numbers. Some carried copper and foodstuffs, but others carried precious items well worth the risk of drowning, at least in the minds of salvors.

By the third century, with so many going headfirst into the lucrative salvage business, the Greeks found it necessary to establish laws governing salvage. These rules established what portion of the recovered goods went to the diver.

Know The Ropes

Salvage divers who recovered sunken goods or treasure from one cubit of depth (roughly 18 inches) were granted $^1/_{10}$ of its value, according to Greek law of the time. Those who made deeper recoveries gained a higher percentage of the reward. The recovery of treasure deeper than eight cubits earned the diver half of what was returned to the surface. The rest of the salvage proceeds went to the owner of the sunken cargo. If the owner was absent (or perhaps lost with the ship), the owner's share went to the government. Yes, some things never change.

Legendary Salvor

In ancient days, if you wanted to recover treasure, you'd better find a Greek diver for the job. One Greek salvage expert was so good that his efforts for both salvaging—and sinking—ships passed into legend. Famous for his skills, Scyllias was sought out by the Persians to recover treasure sunk off Pelion on Greece's west-central coast during the fifth-century Persian Wars.

Scyllias did as he was asked and also managed to obtain a share of the salvaged treasure for his own use. Perhaps too valuable to spare, Scyllias was kept with the Persian fleet. The Greek historian Herodotus wrote that when Scyllias learned his Persian captors were about to attack his own countrymen, he escaped from the ship upon which he was held. He either swam or rowed a boat to Greek forces at Artemisium to warn of the attack.

The information provided by Scyllias was invaluable, allowing the Greeks to effectively fight the Persian fleet. Scyllias remains a hero today, even if some of his deeds are overblown. Scyllias should have been a busy man after the Persian Wars, since hundreds of ships were lost during the fighting.

Shiver Me Timbers

Much of what Scyllias accomplished was told and retold before Herodotus wrote it down, roughly 50 years after the Persian Wars ended. One account has Scyllias escaping from the Persians by swimming submerged with his daughter Cyane for a distance of nine miles. The accounts also have them breathing through reeds to avoid surfacing. Other legends have Scyllias cutting anchor ropes of Persian ships after his escape. Who knows? However, it appears Scyllias was real, and Persia certainly waged a prolonged war against the Greeks.

Beachcombers Clean Up

Less than enthusiastic about hugging a big rock and heading for the bottom of dark waters for treasure? Well, landlubbers do have a treasure-hunting option: beachcombing. No need to get in over your head with this hobby!

But, let's face facts. If you want to find actual Spanish treasure on a beach in the United States, you're going to have to go to Florida, California, or even the southeast Texas coast. Despite legends to the contrary, there's just not a lot of sunken treasure on the average beach. And Florida's about the only place where beachcombers have found such treasures. Then again, you never know where you're going to find something interesting.

Helpful Storms

Storms are the bane of mariners and the cause of most Spanish treasure fleet shipwrecks; however, bad weather can also dredge up coins and artifacts lying just below the surface and deposit them on the beach. You have to move quickly, though, since another storm can hide everything that was revealed the week before.

One lucky beachcomber made a spectacular discovery along Colored Beach in Florida near the wrecks of the 1715 Spanish Treasure Fleet: a magnificent bumblebee with wings fashioned out of gold. Its body is an emerald believed to be Colombian.

A Beach of Silver

Homebuilder Kip Wagner looked like the very picture of a 1950s postwar building contractor. With his white T-shirt and chino trousers, he would walk along the

Atlantic coast near his home in Sebastian, Florida, looking for Spanish coins. His strolls soon netted him a pile of silver coins with none marked newer than 1715. But he never quit looking—or finding—the occasional Spanish coin.

Early Technology

In Wagner's early days of beachcombing, sleek, lightweight metal detectors had not yet been developed. The only devices available were war-surplus mine detectors that were bulky, heavy, and olive drab. This $15 item from an army-navy store became Wagner's tool.

From the late 1940s until the mid-1950s, Wagner had found hundreds of coins on the beach. But his attitude about treasure hunting changed when he heard about the loss of the 1715 Treasure Fleet and how its survivors came ashore to await rescue. The fleet's 11 ships had been packed with treasure from Asia and the New World.

A Silver Trail

With his metal detector, Wagner moved inland and found an iron nail and a cannon-ball. He began digging at that location and soon discovered a diamond ring. He deduced that this site was the camp where the survivors gathered after the wreck.

Looking toward the rolling surf, Wagner decided to have someone fly him over the shallow waters just offshore. Hanging from the door of a light plane chugging at the edge of its stall speed, Wagner saw the shadow of a wreck site. In 1960, he formed one of the first American treasure-hunting consortiums and became the first big-time treasure hunter.

One of the partners in Wagner's venture, U.S. Air Force Lt. Col. Harry Cannon, dove to the sight in August 1960 and found a huge wedge of silver. More wedges came up, and Wagner's hunch was vindicated in the richest possible way.

Wagner, who proclaimed himself a millionaire after his discoveries, was still wearing his trademark white T-shirt when photographed by *National Geographic* magazine in the 1960s. Wagner died in 1972.

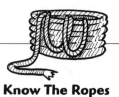

Know The Ropes

An excellent method of spotting a sunken ship in relatively shallow clear water is to fly above the suspected wreck site. Although really old ships decay, they can leave a telltale outline on the seafloor.

Waterlogged Eye Patches: Pirate Salvors

Pirates, as a rule, were a horrible bunch of people, really. Though I discuss their character flaws further in Part 6, "Pirates and Other Treasure Hunters," let's just say they were the scum of the Earth, as well as of the sea. Their desire for plunder, booty, swag, and treasure seemed matched only by their lust for murder, rape, and random cruelty.

When you visualize payday for a pirate, it's the day he's pressing his cutlass to the throat of a terrified woman on the heaving deck of a captured ship. But some days were just another day at the office, especially when the pirates decided they would become salvors of sunken treasure. And this happened at least once in a very big way.

The same wrecked Spanish Treasure Fleet of 1715 located 230 years later by Kip Wagner was the target of another group of treasure hunters shortly after it was lost. These salvors included some of the cruelest pirates of the Caribbean.

A Culture of Plunder

By the beginning of the eighteenth century, it was getting a bit difficult to tell the pirates from the legitimate navies involved in the confusing maritime warfare conducted by European nations. The lust for treasure had become so ridiculous that it became British Royal Navy policy to capture treasure ships on the high seas.

When a pair of British naval officers failed to pursue Spanish treasure ships off Cartagena, Colombia, following a battle in 1708, the officers were given courts-martial. Said their commander, Sir Charles Wager, "A man who will not fight for treasure will not fight for anything."

With nations infected with treasure fever, it's no surprise that pirates were craving ill-gotten booty; after all, they fought for treasure and nothing more.

The Richest Prize

Spain's 13-year War of Spanish Succession had created a demand for New World treasure while simultaneously delaying its shipment to Europe. At war's end in 1713, Spain ordered as much silver as possible sent home.

Treasure from Asia and the Americas was stuffed into 11 ships in Havana Harbor in the summer of 1715. Wind caught the sails of the ships, and they glided toward the Gulf Stream and home. But this party was about to end as quickly as it began.

The traditional enemy of the treasure fleets—a hurricane—caught the ships as they moved north along Florida's East Coast. They were driven into shallow water, and all 500 souls aboard died when the ships sank.

Good News for Pirates

British officials and their former pirate employees, including *privateer* Henry Jennings, knew about the wealth of the wrecked Spanish fleet. Jennings subsequently assembled a 300-man force to raid the Spanish salvage efforts taking place near what is now Vero Beach, Florida. By this time, Jennings was an outright but enterprising sea robber.

This murderous entrepreneur decided to raid the Spanish salvage camp near the wrecks. His amphibious assault was exquisitely executed, and the Spanish were routed. At least 350,000 pieces of

Words To Treasure

A **privateer** was a captain with his own warship who received government permission to destroy and capture ships belonging to that nation's enemies. Privateers who operated without permission were pirates.

eight were snatched along with a Spanish ship riding at anchor. This event, which carried ugly consequences for America's East Coast, is examined more fully in Chapter 26, "The Rudest Treasure Hunters."

Once the word got out, every other pirate in the region joined the hunt. Many would grab local Indian divers and press them into service recovering the treasure scattered about the wrecked ships. In those days, the hulls of the 1715 Treasure Ships still jutted above the surface of the shallow water, making them easy to find.

Know The Ropes

To discourage anyone from finding the wrecked ships that Spain had lost in shallow water, Spanish salvage crews often set the decks afire. The masts and the superstructure would then burn until reaching the water, making the wrecks far less visible. What wood was not burned or buried by mud was eventually eaten by shipworms, effectively hiding the wrecks from treasure hunters for hundreds of years.

Years of Plunder

For years, official Spanish expeditions and those launched by pirates swarmed over the wreck sites and plundered what remained. There was no talk of treating the shipwrecks as memorials to the dead or perhaps establishing a protected site for tourism as would be done today. Had anyone recommended such to the pirates or Spanish officials at the time, it's interesting to consider how the idea would have been received.

The whole scene became distasteful to one governor of colonial Virginia, Alexander Spotswood. He would later say the pirates were little more than "a bunch of profligate fellows returning constantly to the wreck sites like dogs to their vomit." Unlike the governors of other American colonies, Spotswood was no friend of the pirate.

A Treasure-Salvaging Adventurer

A man who would later become the governor of Massachusetts Bay Colony and conduct business with pirates while holding office perhaps set the precedent for the foreign plunder of Spanish shipwrecks by adventurers.

Nearly 20 years before the feeding frenzy among the wrecks of 1715, a man who came uncomfortably close to being a pirate himself obtained a title from Britain for his role in recovering substantial treasure from a sunken Spanish treasure ship. Known as an adventurer, William Phips was coarse, brutal, and uneducated. He was also capable of finding and influencing people of means. On top of it all, Phips was one lucky guy.

Having walked from Maine to Boston as a youth, Phips married the widow of a shipbuilder and was soon at the helm of a trading sloop, making stops in the West Indies. There he heard talk of Spanish shipwrecks containing treasure and eventually convinced Britain's King Charles II to provide a warship and 95 sailors for an expedition. Phips set out in 1684 to find his fortune.

The expedition was a bust, and the sailors, sick of both the fruitless treasure hunting and the roughshod Phips, became mutinous. Phips fired them all and picked up a new crew at Port Royal, Jamaica. After more searching, Phips also called it quits and returned to Britain. When the heavy-handed Phips arrived empty-handed, British royalty washed its hands of him.

Shiver Me Timbers

Port Royal, Jamaica, was literally "sin city," having become an official haven for pirates and privateers employed by the British. By the late seventeenth century, more than one fourth of the 4,000 Europeans in Port Royal were pirates. It served as a protective harbor for merchant ships and pirate vessels. It was also a place for pirates to spend their booty on liquor and prostitutes. On June 7, 1693, about 60 percent of the city sank beneath the water when an earthquake shook the island. At the time of the disaster, Port Royal was a bigger and more important city than Boston.

Luck at Last

Back in England, the persuasive Phips formed an investment consortium and was off on a second expedition in 1687. Miraculously, Phips's two-ship fleet located and plundered the Spanish shipwreck *Concepción* that sank 46 years earlier off the north coast of Hispaniola. Phips used divers who were described as either Native Americans or African slaves to recover the treasure 40 feet below the surface.

Distrustful of a diving bell brought to the wreck, the divers refused to use it and held the traditional stones to carry them rapidly to their work. Phips's expedition recovered 37,538 pounds of silver coins, 2,755 pounds of silver ingots, and 25 pounds of gold. The British court granted Phips 16,000 English pounds as well as a knighthood. King James II took the royal cut of 20,000 English pounds.

The Least You Need to Know

➤ William Phips walked from Maine to Boston as a young carpenter with no formal schooling before becoming an adventurer and salvor of sunken Spanish treasure.

➤ Free divers that William Phips pressed into service during his treasure expedition were unwilling to use a diving bell during the recovery of the treasure from the Spanish treasure ship *Concepción* near Hispaniola.

➤ Scyllias, the famous Greek diver who recovered Persian treasure in the fifth century, is credited with swimming nine miles underwater.

➤ The War of Spanish Succession was the result of royal politics affecting the balance of power in eighteenth-century Europe.

➤ Treasure-hunting pioneer Kip Wagner's first metal detector was a U.S. Army surplus model purchased for $15.

➤ Perseus, the last king of Macedonia, reputedly sank his own royal treasure during a retreat from the Romans in 169 B.C.E. and later used divers for its recovery.

Sunken Treasure Is Hard to Find!

Finding sunken ships is hard work!

Think about it! Stand alongside a supertanker, and it just doesn't seem like you can lose something that big. But don't kid yourself. The 852-foot RMS *Titanic* eluded detection for 73 years. You don't have to be Jacques-Yves Cousteau to know there's a lot of water on the planet and that much of it is extremely deep.

You've heard the old saying "It's like finding a needle in a haystack." Well, that's easy next to finding a submerged shipwreck. Finding a ship, and the objects that have spilled out of it, is an even bigger challenge for a lot of reasons.

First, water covers 70 percent of the Earth's surface, and 97 percent of that water is concentrated in the world's oceans. Consider that the average depth of the four oceans is 13,124 feet, and you'll see that playing hide-and-seek with a lost ship is a daunting proposition.

Don't Go Overboard!

Sea pressure in salt water increases at the rate of .44 pounds per foot of depth. If a ship is 10,000 feet below the surface, it is subjected to 4,400 pounds of pressure per square inch. Though their diving depths are secret, military submarines probably can't go much below 2,000 feet. Expensive, specially designed deep-submergence submarines are required to deal with deeper depths.

How Deep Is Deep?

If the average ocean depths don't impress you, then take a moment and consider the deepest portions of the various oceans:

➤ Challenger Deep in the Mariana Trench, Pacific Ocean: 36,200 feet

➤ Puerto Rico Trench, Atlantic Ocean: 28,374 feet

➤ Java Trench, Indian Ocean: 25,344 feet

➤ Eurasia Basin, Arctic Ocean: 17,881 feet

These numbers prove how easy it would be to hide all 29,028 feet of Mount Everest in the Mariana Trench! The tallest mountain in the continental United States is Mount Whitney in California, and it would fit easily in the Arctic Ocean's relatively shallow Eurasia Basin. Mount Whitney is 14,494 feet in elevation.

Hiding Places Galore!

Although some portions of the seafloor are flat and smooth, much is not. The bottom of the sea can be as rugged as the Rocky Mountains. Imagine looking for something beneath a huge expanse of water. It is three miles down inside a tiny valley, which is inside a huge mountain range bigger than the Rocky Mountains. Now, you're three miles above towing a camera sled attached to the end of six-mile cable trying to find the ship. Talk about flying blind! Think about that the next time you scratch your head over how long it took to find the *Titanic*.

Words To Treasure

An **ocean trench** is not a ditch dug to shelter soldiers from enemy fire, but a natural geologic formation that is akin to a deep valley or gorge on land.

If you could drain the oceans, you would see a seascape more rugged and spectacular than any landscape (minus the trees, of course). Nothing demonstrates this fact better than the Hawaiian Islands. In reality, they are simply the small, visible tips of huge volcanoes that have moved upward from the depths of the Pacific. So if that's just the tip, imagine what's underneath!

Unlike most shipwrecks, the *Titanic* managed to sink to nearly 13,000 feet in one of the deeper areas of the Atlantic. It lies on the Grand Banks off Newfoundland, a seafloor plateau looking toward the Mid-Atlantic Ridge.

Shiver Me Timbers

The Mid-Atlantic Ridge runs from north to south in the Atlantic and is part of the mid-oceanic ridge that snakes beneath all the world's oceans. The segment in the Pacific is the East-Pacific Rise. The Mid-Atlantic Ridge is a massive split that was created through volcanic activity. This volcanic activity not only created a split in the seafloor but also generates new seafloor both west and east of the split. This process is thought to be capable of creating a new Atlantic seafloor every 150 million years. The center of the ridge is 25 miles wide and a mile deep. Lose a ship here and consider it gone for good!

The Sea Keeps Its Secrets

The *Titanic* is beneath 13,000 feet of water, which is more than two miles straight down. Confusion over the *Titanic*'s precise location kept well-equipped *Titanic* hunters, like the late Texas oilman Jack Grimm, unsuccessfully busy for years.

Finding the *Titanic* took the newest technical know-how of France and the United States. The arsenal hefted by the searchers included not only side-scan sonar, satellite positioning systems, and computers, but also much patience and a lot of detective work.

Nature's Disappearing Act

Most ships go down close to shore in relatively shallow water, so you might wonder why these ships can be so hard to find. Well, consider this: As soon as a ship is beneath the water, the sea begins a natural process of camouflage.

Coral, sea creatures, and even the currents do their work with the assistance of sediments washed to the sea by rivers and streams. Marine life attaches to the ship and its spilled cargo and begins to grow there, giving the wreck the texture and appearance of the seabed, while silt is slowly deposited on the wreck in a process called *deposition*. Depending on the currents and the amount of silt moved, ships can be buried 25 feet below the seafloor over a period of several hundred years.

Know The Ropes

The **deposition** of silt upon the seafloor occurs at different rates around the world and can be measured with a high degree of accuracy. The amount of silt covering an object can reveal how long something has been submerged. Each region has its own average deposition, so location also needs to be taken into account to properly calculate how long something has been under the waters.

Though many ships leave debris fields when they sink, it is also important to know that the sea begins to camouflage these items quickly. Coral growth, plant life, and sea anemones can encrust an item from a sinking ship in a tropical region quite rapidly. A sixteenth-century bronze cannon may look like nothing more than the rest of the scenery by the time a twentieth-century scuba diver shows up to look around.

Murky or dark water can hide a ship in water just a few feet deep and a few feet from shore for hundreds of years even when records exist of its location. Such conditions conspired to hide famous French explorer LaSalle's ship *La Belle* for more than 300 years inside south Texas's Matagorda Bay!

Even massive steel ships have only a limited amount of time before rust robs them of their structural strength and collapses them under their own terrific weight. Experts theorize that the *Titanic* may have only a few more decades before it, too, begins to collapse into the mud.

A Big Haystack

Despite the best technology, the general area of a shipwreck must be known before a realistic search can be conducted. The seas provide too big a haystack for random searches. Just consider the task of searching a patch of ocean the size of a small New England state for a ship!

Robert Ballard found the *Titanic* by using a sled containing towed cameras because the liner's position had been reported during its sinking. Although that position wasn't precise, it gave searchers a 75-square-mile box in which to do a preliminary search using side-scan sonar. The *Bismarck*'s site, a 150-square-mile area, was a more difficult challenge, though that ship, too, was eventually located.

One of the most challenging shipwreck searches ever was the hunt for the nuclear submarine USS *Scorpion* that was lost without anyone's knowledge. It disappeared mysteriously in May 1968 with all 99 of her crew while returning to the United States from the Mediterranean.

The submarine would have remained lost forever inside a mid-Atlantic mountain range had a trio of underwater listening stations not heard the submarine breaking apart May 21, 1968. Those sounds allowed Navy scientists and mathematicians to determine the sub's location within 200 feet. Even then, it took months of towing a camera sled shooting thousands of photographs of the seafloor to actually find the sub's wreckage 12,000 feet below.

Often, as was the case with the *Titanic,* a ship's final position is uncertain. This confusion makes the watery search zone too big and the needle—despite its seemingly large size—very, very hard to find.

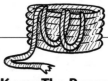

Know The Ropes

Ships lost closer to shore face a more rapid process of being covered by silt carried to the sea by erosion. In surf or strong tidal zones near shore, ships are covered up like driftwood on the beach. The action of waves washing over an object move the object and wriggle it deeper into the sand.

Old-Fashioned Wreck Hunting

For hundreds of years, salvors looking for wrecks that didn't have a telltale mast protruding from the waves used a number of techniques, most of which were pretty simple.

If a wreck were presumed to be in a certain area, salvage crews would drag *grapnels* or anchors along the bottom to snag the ship or some of its cargo. This process could take a long time and might produce false results. If something were snagged, a diver would go over the side to investigate. He might find a ship, or he might just find a large rock.

This process was time-consuming and undoubtedly frustrating. Without an eyewitness to a sinking, finding a ship in this manner was hopeless. Without precise coordinates, the haystack is just too big.

Words To Treasure

Despite the many arguments over this word, a **grapnel** is essentially the same thing as a grappling hook. Both have an iron or steel shaft with flukes for catching and holding things. A grapnel is also a small anchor.

An Underwater Egypt

The discovery and the salvage of the British liner *Egypt*'s gold treasure is an example of a mid-1930s salvage expedition that used a combination of old techniques and new technology. Such modern devices as armored diving suits (which were developed in the 1920s and brought back in the 1960s) were used along with the dragging method and a little magic. However, the technology eventually worked better than the magic.

Mostly, what finally located the *Egypt* and its treasure was tenacity, innovation, and brute force.

Shiver Me Timbers

In a strange coincidence paralleling the loss of the *Andréa Doria* 34 years later, the *Egypt* was struck by a cargo ship whose specially reinforced bow allowed it to break through ice during winter runs in northern climes. The merchant ship *Stockholm* that struck the *Andréa Doria* also had a bow reinforced for ice. Both ships were stabbed from the side and both incidents occurred in fog. However, the *Andréa Doria*'s collision occurred at night and the *Egypt*'s in daylight.

The sinking of the *Egypt* occurred on May 19, 1922, in foggy daytime weather, when its hull was badly punctured in a collision with a French freighter called the *Seine*. Although the other ship didn't sink, the *Egypt* did. Within 20 minutes it had settled to the bottom 400 feet below, drowning 71 crewmembers and 15 passengers.

The Deepest Salvage

The *Egypt's* great depth would have ordinarily ended the salvage effort before it began, since salvage diving was limited to around 150 feet of depth during the 1920s. However, the *Egypt* was carrying the one thing that will make people spend money, risk their lives, and use new technology—treasure!

Swedish engineer Peter Sandberg had received permission to salvage the *Egypt* in 1925. The maritime insurer Lloyd's of London owned the *Egypt* since it had insured the liner and its cargo. Sandberg mounted an expedition but failed to locate the wreckage on his own from 1925 to 1927. The year before Sandberg began his quest, an entrepreneurial Italian attorney named Giovani Quaglia began his own salvage business named Sorima, which was short for Societa Ricuperi Marittimi (or Society for Maritime Recovery).

Shiver Me Timbers

Shrewdly anticipating a growing need for oil around the world, Giovani Quaglia quit the practice of law following World War I to become the first Italian to buy and operate a tanker fleet. Quaglia then decided to begin his own salvage business and quickly developed a reputation for making use of technical innovations.

The Price Is Right

Containing 10 tons of silver and five tons of gold, the *Egypt* was begging to be salvaged no matter what was required, so Sandberg gambled on Quaglia's company Sorima. Like Robert Ballard who found the *Titanic* and the *Bismarck*, Quaglia attempted to narrow down the location of the sinking by studying radio messages. He eventually determined that the *Egypt* was located within a 60-square-mile area.

Quaglia and his tough-looking crew, which included an inventive diver named Alberto Gianni, began looking for the *Egypt* in 1928. They were prepared to exploit every possible resource—including the paranormal! During the two years they hunted for the *Egypt's* location, Quaglia tried everything from consulting a monk who claimed to have extra sensory perception to using an early magnetometer to measure the presence of ferrous metals such as steel.

Eventually, Quaglia found the *Egypt* the way ships had been found for hundreds of years: He dragged a 6,000-foot long cable suspended 25 feet off the seafloor between two ships. The cable, which was kept buoyant with floats, was dragged for 13 months until it finally snagged on the massive bulk of the *Egypt* lying nearly 400 feet beneath the Atlantic. After the cable snapped, it was hauled back aboard. The *Egypt*'s telltale white paint had scraped off on the cable, telling the salvors that they had finally found the ship in its pitch dark, high-pressure grave.

High-Pressure Work

After the *Egypt*'s discovery in 1930, Quaglia and his tough crew of salvors had to leave the site to conduct a salvage operation of an American munitions ship named the SS *Florence*. The ship they were removing munitions from exploded, sinking Quaglia's salvage ship and killing nine members of his crew.

Shiver Me Timbers

When stormy winter weather in 1930 made salvage efforts too dangerous, Quaglia's salvage ship *Artiglio* was dispatched to what was believed to be less hazardous duty: removing ammunition from a wrecked ship. The munitions exploded, sinking the *Artiglio* and killing several of its crewmembers.

A new ship was obtained and Quaglia, the risk taker, and his fellow salvors returned to the *Egypt* for the deepest salvage up to that time. They defeated the sea pressure and the risks of decompression sickness by first using state-of-the-art robot-like diving suits. These hard-shell suits had movable arms and legs and grasping clamps that the diver could manipulate. Though these suits were useful, they still weren't agile enough to allow the divers to get into the compartment of the ship where the treasure was stacked three decks below.

A New Technique

When Quaglia and his crew returned to the wreck of the *Egypt* in 1930, they had to solve the puzzle of how to get through three decks of the ship and bring out the gold. It was time for more brute force. Quaglia and Sandberg hit on another idea—use *high explosives* to clear a path to the treasure room and then wrench the gold and silver free with a giant, mechanical claw, or "grab." So much for subtlety. Time was (and still is) money.

Diver Alberto Gianni designed a pressure-proof observation chamber so he could direct the deployment of the grab. The chamber was pretty simple, really, just a tube with four view ports set around its top, but he was also supplied with air and a telephone that allowed him to communicate with the surface.

The grab was a huge circular claw that was lowered to the wreck and could be used to snatch away debris and eventually, treasure. Gianni would descend to the wreck site and direct the claw to place explosive charges and to winch away the resulting debris. Months of blasting followed until a path was finally cleared to the precious cargo.

The crew recovered its first gold bullion from the *Egypt* on June 22, 1933. The effort was something of a media event at the time, since it was the deepest salvage ever attempted. At one point, while winching too aggressively, a salvage ship almost capsized under the strain of the submerged load. The team finished its job in 1935 and came away with $1.5 million in gold and silver on behalf of Lloyd's of London.

Know The Ropes

High explosives refers to a class of explosives that release a higher rate of energy during a much briefer explosion, making them valuable for cutting through steel. TNT is an example of a high explosive. These explosives "cut" steel, whereas slower bursting explosives are better at crumbling rock.

Accidental Encounters of the Rich Kind

Ships, sunken treasure, and wonderful artifacts have long been discovered by happenstance. A fisherman above a shoal south of Jamaica in 1906 peered into the crystalline water beneath his boat and saw something shimmering on the submerged reef. After making a few dives, the fisherman collected a half dozen gold bars and a stack of gold coins—all of it Spanish treasure spilled from the wreck of a ship whose name is lost to history.

News of this accidental find turned everyone within earshot into an adventurer, but the reef was to surrender no more treasure to those who were actively looking for it. Only one poor fisherman caught his limit on San Pedro Shoals, 130 miles south of Jamaica.

Don't Go Overboard!

A **shoal** is an area of shallow water caused by a sandbar or a coral reef. Unwary mariners who collide with shoals just below the water may find themselves aground or fighting to stay afloat should their craft suffer hull damage. Modern sonar equipment can warn a mariner of shallows that can ground or puncture a boat, but sailors in times past had to keep a constant lookout for uncharted shoals, since they can sometimes be found far from land.

Knee-Deep in Gold

The Cayman Islands south of Cuba are well-known for the accidental treasure discovery of 58 gold coins in 1900. The inadvertent treasure hunter was Captain James

Foster, who found the gold while wading in shallow water near the islands. "It is easier to find coins off Cayman Island than it is to find seashells," Foster told a Boston newspaper. All were minted in 1735 and sold for $7,000.

Dredging Up the Past

If Greek sponge divers and vacationers can find wonderful antiquities and anglers can find their own golden opportunities, then Virginia's oyster gatherers are not about to be left out. In the mid-1930s, a crew dredging for oysters in the York River located what turned out to be a pair of British warships left over from Earl Lord Cornwallis's 1781 fight at Yorktown.

It's well-known that many British warships ended up on the bottom of the York River. The French defeated Cornwallis's supporting fleet, and Cornwallis was forced to scuttle 13 vessels that faced capture. Many of the artifacts recovered during an expedition that lasted from 1934 to 1935 remain in the collection of the Mariner's Museum in Newport News, Virginia.

Net Proceeds

To date, the waters off Louisiana may just be the luckiest source of accidental finds, since two extraordinarily rich Spanish treasure ships were snagged in the nets of different fishing trawlers 14 years apart.

The most recent accidental find occurred on August 2, 1993, as the trawler *Mistake* was attempting to net *butterfish* in the Gulf of Mexico. On that ordinary summer day, 50 miles off Louisiana's coast, something snagged the boat's net. Even before retrieving the net, Captain Jerry Murphy scowled at the damage he knew had been done to his equipment. His mood changed when he watched in amazement at what fell out of the net. Banging to the deck in large clumps were hundreds of Spanish coins.

Murphy called his partner, Jim Reahard, and stammered out the news. Their next call was to well-known maritime attorney David Paul Horan who swore them to secrecy until he could arrive and help them navigate the legal shoals of claiming the wreck. What they had discovered on the flat floor of the Gulf of Mexico was the wreck site of the *Cazador*, a Spanish treasure ship that had disappeared without a trace in January 1784.

Words To Treasure

Butterfish acquired their name not because they're a pale yellow color, but because of a slimy mucus coating that makes them soft to the touch—like buttah!

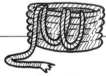

Know The Ropes

Although it could have been thrashed by a local squall, the *Cazador* was in water hundreds of feet deep, far from reefs that would have served as an anvil for hammering winds. Far from shore, the *Cazador* could have ridden out the storm. However, many things can kill a ship. It could have fallen victim to a shipboard fire that detonated its powder magazine, or it could have suffered a hull failure.

Solving a 200-Year-Old Mystery

When the *Cazador* failed to dock in New Orleans by January, 11, 1784, the Spanish searched for the ship and its crew. Although some have assumed the ship was done in by a major storm, National Hurricane Center research indicates only one major storm occurred in the region that year, and it struck six months after the loss of the *Cazador*. Besides, as any Gulf of Mexico mariner knows, hurricanes quit blowing through the Western Hemisphere by November 30 and don't resume until June 1.

Words To Treasure

A **magazine** on a warship is not something to read, but a specially constructed vault where ammunition for its guns is stored.

An Amazing Sight

A camera lowered to the wreck during clear conditions revealed a most amazing sight. With most of the ship's wood completely eaten away by shipworms, the *Cazador*'s treasure lay alone in a bed of ooze 270 feet beneath the surface. The stack of coins was 30 feet long, 15 feet wide, and nearly one foot high. This display of wealth would have been a sobering sight for even the most jaded treasure hunter!

A pile of Spanish coins known as pieces of eight that were recovered from the Spanish treasure ship Cazador *in the Gulf of Mexico.*
(Copyright Grumpy Partnership)

The depth of the wreck meant that only extremely skilled divers using specialized techniques could descend to the *Cazador*. The initial dive was conducted using "technical divers" who were breathing special mixes of gases to avoid *the bends*—the crippling or fatal effects of *decompression sickness*.

It would seem the *Cazador*'s skipper was above reproach. So important was the delivery of the treasure to Louisiana that Spanish officials handpicked trusted mariner Gabriel de Campos y Pineda to captain the warship from Mexico to Louisiana. The Spanish, after nearly 300 years of losing treasure ships at the most inopportune times, eventually accepted the *Cazador*'s disappearance as another unexplained tragedy.

Spanish authorities listed the ship as missing when it failed to reach New Orleans after departing from Vera Cruz, Mexico. Its cargo was 450,000 silver coins for Spain's economically anemic Louisiana colony.

El Nuevo Constanté

It's said that commercial fishermen armed with massive nets may be the greatest lost ship finders in the world, and it could be true considering another treasure ship discovery in the Gulf of Mexico.

Curtis Blume was a shrimper who plied his trade netting the decapod crustaceans the Gulf of Mexico is famous for. Piloting his boat, *Lady Barbara,* Blume's fields were the murky waters off Louisiana's coast. It was just another winter day in 1979 when his shrimp net dragged three copper ingots into the sunlight from a depth of 18 feet.

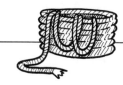

Know The Ropes

Decompression sickness—also called **the bends**—results from nitrogen rapidly bubbling out of body tissue when a person ascends too quickly from underwater. Sea pressure forces the nitrogen into the body fluids like carbonation into a soft drink. A rapid ascent doesn't allow this nitrogen to fizz out gradually, resulting in swelling in the joints and other, possibly lethal, symptoms. This condition is called the bends, since it makes people walk in a stooped position until the nitrogen exits the tissues. The deeper you dive and the longer you remain submerged, the longer the decompression period.

Unsure of what he had, Blume showed the ingots to fellow shrimper Steve Smith. Using a dredge, the two men returned to the location and brought up not only more copper but also silver ingots and gold coinage. Knowing the state of Louisiana would lay claim to such an important archaeological find, the men reported the presence of the wreck to authorities.

Constant Adversity

After piecing together the puzzle, researchers decided the wreck was *El Nuevo Constanté* (the *New Constant*), which was lost, along with another ship, around September 1, 1766, on the Louisiana coast. *El Nuevo Constanté* had been heavily loaded for a return voyage to Spain and was carrying several thousand copper ingots known as "pigs." It was also a treasure ship and, thus, was loaded with 5,000 pesos' worth of gold and silver ingots weighing 160 pounds.

The British-built galleon had been under Spanish ownership since 1764 and was commanded by Julian Antonio de Urcullu. Though the ship had been in Vera Cruz since February of 1766, a series of delays prevented it from sailing until August 21 with a fleet of five other ships. Apparently, Spain never seemed to learn to pay attention to the weather patterns, as this sailing schedule put the fleet at sea near the middle of the region's six-month hurricane season.

Shiver Me Timbers

The National Hurricane Center's records indicate that a storm struck what is now Galveston, Texas, on September 4, 1766. The timing indicates that this storm is the one that struck the *El Nuevo Constanté*. At Galveston Island, the hurricane flung five other Spanish treasure ships onto the beaches and wrecked a sixth offshore. All occupants of the ships that beached on Galveston Island were saved, along with their cargoes.

By September 1 all six ships had been caught in a huge storm. *El Nuevo Constanté* and another ship, *Corazon de Jesus,* were driven by powerful winds into the shallows along the Louisiana coast in separate locations. The others were scattered by the winds.

Cashing In

With four partners, Blume established the Free Enterprise Salvage Company and bargained with the state of Louisiana over the artifacts and the treasure of *El Nuevo Constanté*. The deal that was struck allowed the state to pay for the archaeological cataloging of the site while Blume's salvage company paid for the actual recovery.

Words To Treasure

Bullion is the production of ingots of any precious metal, including silver and gold, in which quantity is valued for shipment and storage. **Specie** is a term for coined money.

Louisiana would keep 25 percent of the artifacts and treasure found, with Free Enterprise Salvage and its members keeping the remainder. What came out of the wreck site was great for the state and for Blume—the intact lower portion of the hull, 80 pounds of silver ingots, and 50 pounds of gold. The total estimated value of the *bullion* and *specie* was a half-million dollars.

As for de Urcullu and the survivors of the 1766 storm, they made their way ashore near what is now Cameron, Louisiana. Urcullu ordered that a small boat be sent to seek help from the Spanish settlement of Balize. This town was also on Louisiana's coast, but 170 miles west of where they were marooned. A month later they were rescued when two ships arrived from Balize. Those aboard the *Corazon de Jesus* (*Heart of Jesus*) were also rescued at the site of their wreck 50 miles west of Urcullu's ship.

A Divining Moment

Locating a completely submerged shipwreck may be only a phone call away if you follow the example of some treasure hunters and ship salvors. Extra sensory perception, psychic powers, and dowsing rods have all been used by those desperate to find ships, gold mines, and oil.

Even Giovani Quaglia tried a *dowsing* rod (along with his divine, divining monk) during his long and difficult search for the *Egypt*. These devices—so simple that a crude one can be made out of a wire coat hanger—have been around for thousands of years.

If you only want the very best, pick up a treasure-hunting magazine or get on the Internet and order a factory-made dowsing rod. Many have precision ball bearings for extra sensitivity a pistol-type dowel grip and a horizontal rod at the top. After you get the dowsing rod, take a walk or get on your boat. When the rod moves, maybe you've found something (or maybe you haven't).

If you're the traditional sort, use a forked stick and hold the two ends as awkwardly as possible (with the backs of your hands facing each other). Go to a suspected shipwreck site. If the forked dowser points down or if the horizontal rod on the store-bought model swings a bit, it's time to put on your wet suit!

Science gave up on divination via dowsing long ago. Though many swear *at* the method, thousands more still swear *by* it.

Words To Treasure

Dowsing is the use of a divining rod that some claim is directed by energy collected by the person holding the device.

Don't Go Overboard!

Sir William Barrett, of the Royal College in Dublin, attempted to conduct a study of paranormal powers by founding the Society for Physical Research in 1882. After studying dowsing, Barrett concluded, "... few subjects appear to be as unworthy of serious notice and so utterly beneath scientific investigation as that of the divining rod."

The Least You Need to Know

➤ Giovanni Quaglia gave up his job as an attorney to become the first salvor to recover items from a deep-water shipwreck.

➤ The Pacific Ocean, on average, is slightly deeper than the Atlantic Ocean.

➤ *El Nuevo Constanté* was a British ship before it was purchased by Spanish buyers; two years later it was wrecked on Louisiana's coast in the hurricane of 1766.

➤ Volcanic and geologic activities along the center of the Mid-Atlantic Ridge produce new rock at a pace that replaces the Atlantic seafloor every 150 million years.

➤ Butterfish are not yellow. But they are squishy and mushy to the touch because of their heavy mucus coating, which—amazingly—doesn't seem to bother people who consider the fish a good dish.

➤ The salvage ship *Artiglio* was blown up while its divers were removing explosives from a wrecked ship in 1930; many divers and crew members were killed in the explosion. Ironically, the ship had stopped work on the *Egypt* salvage operation because heavy winter weather made the site too dangerous.

Chapter 7

A Breath of Fresh Air

In This Chapter

➤ Deep-thinking inventors

➤ Diving bells ring up riches

➤ Scuba: now everyone's a treasure hunter

➤ How low can they go?

Although most shipwrecks occur in *littoral* waters, a fair number have actually been thrown up on beaches where they might remain for many years. I don't know about you, but for me the term *shipwreck* always seems to bring that type of scene to mind.

But those beached wrecks don't hold much mystery, since you can climb aboard, walk around it, and sometimes even go inside for a look. The wrecks that hold the greatest amount of mystery are always those that we can't see, the ones that are beneath the water, even if only by a few inches.

The newfound excitement surrounding old shipwrecks has been prompted not so much by the fact that we knew magnificent liners like the *Titanic* or the *Lusitania* were below the waves, but because we've been able to locate and see them up close. Photographs and films by explorers have revealed them to us in all their ghostly underwater appearance. The sight of them in their gloomy submerged graves contrasts eerily to their past magnificence.

It seems that with today's technology, virtually no shipwreck can escape detection, or even the removal of its objects. It should be no surprise that the investigation of shipwrecks and their treasures has long been a force driving the development of diving and deep-submergence technology. It's interesting to note that the first hard hats of the industrial revolution were helmet divers.

When equipment was developed that enabled people to walk in shallow regions of the sea, the primary purpose of such innovations became the discovery of shipwrecks and recovery of their artifacts.

Deep-Thinking Inventors

Those with really gigantic hairstyles may have inherited the moniker "helmet head," but that nickname historically belongs to a man whose love for animals moved him and his brother to develop the first successful diving apparatus.

John Deane was an inventive rebel without a pause. Around 1820 in Whitstable, England, the muscular Deane watched in horror as a neighbor's horse-filled barn caught fire. Spotting a suit of armor through the door of a nearby farmhouse, Deane—on the spot—invented a lifesaver.

Words To Treasure

Littoral waters are those that exist near shore and extend out where the water's depth reaches 200 feet.

Grabbing the helmet, Deane ordered that a hose pumping water on the fire instead be used to pump air to the helmet. Looking like an astronaut in a badly funded space program, he rushed into the flaming barn. Sustained by the fresh air, Deane led the horses to safety amid the cheers of bystanders.

By 1823, Deane's older brother Charles Anthony Deane patented a refinement of John's emergency concept as a breathing apparatus for firefighters. John, however, saw their future heading in another direction—straight down.

A Well-Dressed Diver

Not long after the barn fire, the Deanes fabricated a diving helmet fitted with glass viewing ports. Using the same water pump that had failed to extinguish the barn blaze, the Deanes again pumped air to their invention. John Deane took a test plunge but discovered that having an air-filled float on his head made him completely unstable while submerged. The addition of lead weights to his feet gave Deane the stability he needed, and the device was patented. The outfit became known as "diving dress."

A Clean Sweep

Lightheaded and heavy footed in his new diving suit, John Deane began a career as a *sweeper,* a salvor who recovers valuable anchors and anchor chains lost by ships. John and Charles Deane then went on to conduct some of the most astonishing salvage feats and discoveries of shipwrecks during the nineteenth century.

The Deanes even located and salvaged naval guns and other artifacts from the wreck of the ill-fated warship *Mary Rose,* which sank near Portsmouth on July 19, 1545, a wreck that wasn't located again for another 140 years. Their four-year expedition is revisited along with a full account of the *Mary Rose* catastrophe and subsequent recovery in Chapter 14, "A Rose Blossoms Again."

An early 1900s helmet diver stands beside a member of the diving crew while demonstrating a telephone communication system. The equipment has changed little since its invention in the 1830s. (Courtesy of the Mariner's Museum)

Another famous shipwreck inspected by John Deane was the *Royal George* that sank rather ingloriously at her Spithead moorings on August 29, 1782. The Deanes' salvage firm began diving on the wreck in 1832, 50 years after the sinking. Suffering from an unseen structural failure in its hull, the *Royal George* sat lower in the water as supplies were loaded for its departure on the day of the sinking.

Finally, when it was heavy with provisions, the ship suddenly rolled over as high-pressure air blew through the passageways—indicating that water was rushing into the hull. The ship then righted itself to sit upright in the mud with its masts protruding above the water.

A Better "Dress"

Other inventors made improvements to the Deanes' design. One such modification bolted the helmet to the top of the suit worn by the diver,

Know The Ropes

With iron becoming the favored material for guns by the 1830s, the 108 cannons aboard the *Royal George* had little military value, since most were made of brass. The brass, on the other hand, had a high salvage value as a raw material.

and this adaptation became the model that helmet divers would use for the next 150 years. The helmet developed by the Deanes simply rested on the head of the diver by virtue of its weight.

For the first time, salvage workers could enter the depths, remain as long as their stamina allowed, and conduct serious work. Ships that had defied recovery could now be repaired underwater and refloated. Ships still afloat could receive repairs below their waterlines by helmet divers, precluding costly visits to *dry docks*.

The Deanes' diving helmet definitely had its drawbacks. The divers had to move slowly because of the heavy weights that compensated for the helmet's buoyancy, and the helmet's small viewing ports restricted visibility. Swimming gracefully like a free diver was impossible, since the head could never be lower than the body. The helmet was really little more than an air-filled bucket whose life-giving contents could spill out very easily.

Almost as amazing as the longevity of Charles and John Deane's invention is the length of John Deane's career underwater. At nearly 60, he was still diving beneath the frigid waters near Russia's Crimean peninsula to salvage items from ships sunk during the Crimean War.

Understanding Shipwreck Curiosity

John and Charles Deane understood public interest in shipwrecks, and that prompted them to commission exquisitely detailed and highly accurate watercolor paintings of items retrieved from various ships. Paintings of the cannons recovered from the *Mary Rose* faithfully reproduced even their discoloration. Today those paintings stand on their own as beautiful works of art.

When better-equipped searchers found other lost ships 155 years later, cameras and the nautical artists would also be part of their teams. Letting the public in on the magnificence of their finds ensures research funding, television deals, and fame. Actual footage of the massive wreck of the *Titanic* provides the initial scene in the 1998 hit movie.

Know The Ropes

The diving rig designed by John and Charles Deane became known as the **open diving dress,** since the helmet was not attached to the suit worn by the diver. The weighted helmet, if pointed downward, could spill its air and drown the diver. Later diving ensembles connected the helmet to a waterproof suit, making it impossible for the helmet to fall off. This modification also allowed the diver to lean over if necessary.

Words To Treasure

A **dry dock** is an enclosed space at shipyards where water is pumped out so a moored ship is left high and dry on blocks to allow repairs.

Diving Bells Ring Up Recoveries

Engineers use the term *elegant* when discussing a solution to a problem that is simple, complete, and flawless. The *diving bell,* in lieu of more complex technology, was a very elegant concept in its own way.

The premise of a diving bell was simple: Upturn a glass jar, push it mouth down into the water, and the pressure of the air keeps out the water. Do the same with a larger enclosure, and you have a diving bell. Diving bells enabled humans to work beneath the water for centuries. Though the diving bells provided a respite for divers, their work periods were still limited by how long they could hold their breath.

Diving bells must be heavy enough to remain stable and then weighted at their base so they're not prone to tipping upwards, since they're filled with air. Often seats are provided inside the bells for several people. Sometimes the bells can be located so close to the seafloor that divers can stand on the sand while taking a break.

When the rough-and-tumble adventurer William Phips employed divers in his 1687 expedition to recover the sunken Spanish ship *Concepción* off Hispaniola, he used a diving bell shaped more like a square box equipped with a seat and viewing windows. Unfortunately, all of his forethought was to be for nothing, as his divers—who are thought to be Native Americans or Africans—didn't want to use his device.

A Long History

Diving bells go far back into antiquity, so figuring out who invented the first one could be a bit hard, although we do know that the earliest were undoubtedly made of wood. However, a most unlikely inventor designed one of the first advanced diving bells in the late seventeenth century.

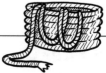

Know The Ropes

Gaining support for expensive underwater operations means mastering not only undersea skills but also public relations. John and Charles Deane recognized this factor intuitively and put the drawings of artifacts to use by making them available to King William IV of England. Their efforts as amateur historians who recognized the value of their finds beyond fiscal concerns may seem unusual for salvors, but others in the nineteenth-century British salvage industry kept similar records.

Words To Treasure

Diving bells get their names from their shape, which are often bell-like. At times, actual bells were used for underwater work because of their weight and design.

English astronomer Edmond Halley, who was ordinarily preoccupied with heavenly affairs—yup, as in Halley's comet!—turned his attention to deeper matters in the 1690s. He designed an elaborate diving bell that allowed divers to work underwater for up to two hours. Made from timbers covered with lead, the bell was supplied with fresh air from lead-lined containers. Divers performing salvage on the seafloor in rudimentary helmets sucked air from hoses that led back to the bell.

Whatever their drawbacks, the bells undoubtedly saved the lives of numerous divers who might not have had the stamina to return to the surface after some unexpected exertion. Halley's bell became a sensation when it allowed divers to spend a total of two hours underwater at 50 feet of depth. Among the prime treasures the diving bells were used to recover were expensive naval guns from ships lost at sea.

Alexander the Great's Dive

To the historically uninitiated, his name might sound like that of a World Wrestling Federation champion, but Alexander the Great was one ancient leader who lived up to his name and is said to have counted diving in the sea and using a diving bell as one of his interests.

This king of Macedonia was a rare national leader who was also a heck of a general. He conquered all of his neighbors and founded Alexandria, Egypt, where he died in 323 B.C.E. He figures in here because this ruthless and brilliant king is reputed to have used a diving bell for excursions into the depths.

Alexander's alleged dive has been discussed throughout history, and the story circulated as far as India, where his armies once marched. Several artistic renderings of the dive still exist. Macedonia, and most of the Hellenic world, was a maritime region dependent on the sea for food and trade. It's not surprising, then, that a Hellenic leader would express an interest in such an excursion.

What makes this claim even more interesting is that Aristotle was once Alexander's boyhood tutor. Aristotle was extremely familiar with diving bells and how they operated. He wrote of them in the fourth century B.C.E.: "They enable the divers to respire equally well by letting down a cauldron; for this does not fill with water, but retains the air, for it is forced down straight into the water."

Don't Go Overboard!

Though a diving bell provides a haven of breathable air for divers, the supply is not endless, since air contains only a limited amount of oxygen. Divers who remained inside a submerged diving bell too long could pass out or die. Older diving bells lacking a fresh-air supply must have their air recharged by raising them again to the surface.

Shiver Me Timbers

While Alexander may or may not have descended into the ocean in a diving bell, he certainly did some strange things. Because other fabled military leaders had marched across the inhospitable southern desert of Iran, Alexander did the same thing in 326 B.C.E. after conquering much of what is now India. Many died during the pointless trek. He later believed he would become a god.

Scuba: Now Everyone's a Treasure Hunter

What exactly is it with the French and swimming underwater? Everyone knows about French navy officer, ocean explorer, and Aqualung inventor Jacques-Yves Cousteau. The famed Cousteau and his less well-known partner, engineer Emile Gagnan, invented a breathing valve that allowed the development of modern scuba equipment.

After helmet diving was perfected in Britain in the early nineteenth century, a passel of French innovators spent the next 120 years enabling humans to become creatures of the sea. People needed some way to dive deeper, stay longer, and move faster, and the French were fascinated with this challenge. France was, after all, a coastal and a maritime nation with a great deal of interest in the sea.

The French inventors wanted divers to have more freedom underwater. A bulky rubberized canvas suit, 90 pounds of lead weight, and a bronze helmet were fine for raising wrecked ships and building submerged piers, but there had to be a better way. The French got right on it.

Famous French Frogmen

At almost the same time that John and Charles Deane were developing their diving helmet, a Frenchman named Lemaire d'Angerville came up with a self-contained breathing device for use underwater. The 1828 invention allowed divers to breathe from a leather bag strapped to their chests. While not completely practical, it was a step in the right direction.

Precisely 30 years after the appearance of the Deanes' diving helmet, Benoît Rouquayrol and Auguste Denayrouze perfected their compressed-air diving system. (Try saying those names with a diving regulator in your mouth!)

By 1865 the system made it possible for a person to remain 30 feet underwater for a half hour. A compressor from above recharged the system's air tank with a hose connecting the diver to the surface. The apparatus worked and seemed to have promise for those needing to go underwater for work or pleasure, but it did not become an instant, much less a slow, success.

The nifty invention was so modernistic for the time that it apparently caught the fancy of French (yes, French!) science-fiction master Jules Verne. The writer incorporated the Rouquayrol-Denayrouze system in his masterpiece *20,000 Leagues Under the Sea*. In it, Verne's submariners use the diving equipment to swim outside the *Nautilus*, his fictional submarine.

Know The Ropes

The Rouquayrol-Denayrouze diving device was limited because the technology of the period did not allow production of lightweight, high-pressure air tanks. This system had to be constantly refilled from above, though a valve in the diver's mouth allowed the diver to breath fresh air without a bulky helmet.

Shiver Me Timbers

The USS *Nautilus* was the first American nuclear-powered submarine and was commissioned into active service on September 30, 1954. While perhaps only a coincidence, its name was the same as that of Jules Verne's fictional submarine, *Nautilus,* whose mysterious and unlimited power source seemingly predicted nuclear propulsion. The real *Nautilus* is a dockside exhibit at the Submarine Force Museum in Groton, Connecticut.

Despite these early setbacks, more inventive Frenchmen were ready to step up to the plate. In 1926 French navy commandant Yves le Prieur developed a system using strong, high-pressure air cylinders and a mouthpiece. Unfortunately, the mouthpiece lacked a regulated circuit, so air escaped from the mouthpiece whether the diver was breathing or not. This wholesale loss of air greatly limited the time that could be spent underwater.

A commander in the French navy developed rubber swim fins in the 1930s to provide submerged swimmers with more propulsion. Now all that was needed was for a few more Frenchmen to enter the scene.

The Jacques of a Lifetime

Jacques-Yves Cousteau was a French naval officer who was to be the next in a long line of French undersea innovators. He was living in France during an unhappy time—the World War II Nazi occupation—but he wasn't about to ignore the challenge of turning men into frogmen despite the fact that he was busy supporting a family while playing a role of a spy.

Having become obsessed with the mysteries and the promise of the sea during the late 1930s, the naval officer had involved himself with research into making it possible for man to dive unrestricted to the sea depths for purposes of exploration and discovery.

In 1942 he went to Paris to find an engineer to help him with a technical roadblock. Cousteau had been working to develop a device that would regulate the flow of

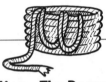

Know The Ropes

The **demand breathing regulator** was necessary for prolonged diving. It had to provide air only when the diver needed it. Other systems were wasteful in that they spewed air constantly even when the diver didn't need it.

Words To Treasure

Scuba stands for self-contained, underwater breathing apparatus. The term is applied to any self-sufficient diving system.

compressed air so a diver could breathe naturally underwater. Brushing past the despised Nazis who controlled the city, the French navy officer met with engineer Emile Gagnan to explain his predicament.

Gagnan listened and then tossed Cousteau a plastic device he (Gagnan) had recently designed to deliver propane gas to automobile engines in the gasoline-starved nation. The device was then being converted to deliver anesthesia gas to surgical patients. The valve met Cousteau's requirement so perfectly that a workable demand breathing regulator was built within weeks.

A World of Frogmen

At the end of World War II, the Cousteau-Gagnan Aqualung was marketed and became an immediate success. For the first time, ordinary people with a minimal amount of training could do what helmet divers had done for years—go into the sea and have a good look around. With the Aqualung, divers could actually swim lithely about the water without dragging a bulky air hose behind them.

The main attraction of scuba gear was that divers no longer required support crews laboring to provide air from a boat above. Helmet divers looked fearsome in their gear, but they were at the mercy of their assistants not only to receive air but also to be reeled back to safety. The heavy diving suits were replaced with little more than a weight belt and air tanks. The innovation freed divers to stay submerged for relatively long periods at depths of up to 130 feet.

Vulnerable Wrecks

Now even amateur divers could explore the depths and the wrecks in them. During the 1950s, many shallow shipwreck sites in accessible areas were picked clean by sport divers, using Cousteau's Aqualung. No one thought much about this activity at the time, since picking up souvenirs on the seafloor seemed innocent enough.

Although the threat to antiquities soon became obvious, the damage was partially outweighed by the benefits, since Cousteau's Aqualung also made nautical archaeology possible. Helmet diving made such delicate and demanding work nearly impossible, but scuba equipment was a different matter, since it could basically turn archaeologists into fish.

By the 1950s, university professors who had once trifled with the curse of the mummy's tomb in Egypt's desert would be elbowing sharks out of the way of historic shipwrecks.

Cousteau's invention and his love of the sea were combined in a massive archaeological undertaking in 1952 when he and his team of divers helped

Words To Treasure

Grand-Congloué is the name of a large rock in the Bay of Marseilles against which many ships may have been smashed to cause their loss.

excavate a site where two ancient trading ships sank atop each other 100 years apart. The ships were lost in the Bay of Marseilles in Southern France.

At first historians believed that only one ship was wrecked at the spot. But after 25 years of study, researchers realized that there were actually two. One wreck is a Greco-Roman ship that sank in the second century B.C.E., and the other is a Roman wreck lost in the first century B.C.E. Hundreds of artifacts were located under the watchful eye of archaeologists. The wrecks are known as Grand-Congloué 1 and 2.

How Low Can They Go?

In the 50 years since the use of Cousteau-Gagnan Aqualung became widespread, divers have been able to go anywhere they please as long as it isn't much deeper than 130 feet or in waters strictly controlled by the military. The only other limitations on where divers explore and how long they can stay are related to physiological restrictions.

With new diving techniques, scuba divers willing to take extra training and use new techniques may be able to dive to 1,000 feet. These divers are usually referred to as *technical divers,* since they must breathe a mixture of gases different from ordinary air. These techniques make a greater number of wrecks available to souvenir-hunting divers and raise the hackles of preservationists who want to keep such sites intact.

Deadly Treasures

At issue is whether the depths and the shipwrecks cloaking them will continue to claim new victims. The problem is pressure. The deeper divers go, the more wrecks they can reach, but also the greater the pressures their bodies must endure.

In fact, the lure of deep shipwrecks has resulted in liners like the *Andréa Doria* being the scene of deaths decades after the accident that killed 51 and sent the ship to the bottom. The unique hazards of diving upon the *Andréa Doria* are examined in Chapter 19, "Amazing Rescue: The *Andréa Doria,*" which focuses on the life and death of the stricken liner. But what is important to know now is that the ship is still adding to its death toll. In 1998, three divers perished while diving to the *Andréa Doria,* 240 feet beneath the Atlantic.

Words To Treasure

Technical divers are sometimes known as **Trimix** divers, since they alter the mixture of oxygen, nitrogen, and sometimes helium they breathe to allow deeper diving.

Don't Go Overboard!

Unknown to those whose only diving experience is in a really large bathtub, diving is a physiologically demanding and complex sport. Its participants are required to master considerable technical knowledge and obtain certifications before being allowed to dive. Superb equipment is needed, and no one is supposed to dive alone. Failing to master the necessary skills can often mean death.

Deepening Concerns

Regardless of the danger, divers can't seem to resist regularly descending 240 feet to inspect the wreck of the once-magnificent Italian liner. The wreck is considered a premier diving excursion for scuba enthusiasts around the world. Without restrictions on the removal of artifacts on the wreck, many divers have helped themselves to everything from statues to plumbing fixtures.

We already know that as more wrecks are discovered and rediscovered in deep water, divers will lay claim to souvenirs, but sometimes the wrecks themselves will lay claim to the divers.

As more divers go deeper to visit the wrecks, many divers' organizations are expressing concern about the safety of technical diving while wondering whether the wrecks are worth the risk. Critics have accused the technical divers of plundering artifacts and turning nautical gravesites into weekend larks. Archaeologists can only worry, as even more artifacts from ships new and old become accessible to souvenir hunters.

The Least You Need to Know

➤ Diving helmet coinventor John Deane liked horses enough to risk his life by dashing into a burning barn wearing a helmet from a suit of armor to which air was being pumped—a lifesaving device he had invented on the spot!

➤ To save money, the British government managed its own flawed and dangerous salvage operation of the Tudor-period warship *Mary Rose*.

➤ British astronomer Edmond Halley invented the first advanced diving bell in the 1690s, but these devices have been in existence in one way or another for so long that we don't know who invented the very first one.

➤ Jacques-Yves Cousteau operated as a spy for France during World War II at the same time he was working to develop the breathing regulator that made modern scuba diving possible.

➤ Despite their extensive skills as technical, or Trimix divers, three such explorers perished in 1998 while descending to view the wreckage of the *Andréa Doria* in 240 feet of water.

➤ Jules Verne incorporated the Rouquayrol-Denayrouze diving system invented in 1865 into his science-fiction classic *20,000 Leagues Under the Sea*.

Chapter 8

Inches from Millions

In This Chapter

➤ Clearing the underwater fog

➤ Metal detectors: not just for geeks

➤ Don't get mad; get MAD!

➤ Helpful fish stories

➤ Knowledge by the galleon

If there's one thing that will get undersea archaeologists, treasure hunters, and plain old sport divers underwater, it's a sunken ship. If you find it, they will come. The trouble is that finding it initially is a tough challenge, though one made easier through the years with advancing technology.

Once you've finally located your dream wreck, simply being able to see what you're doing in rough currents and silty conditions is nearly impossible. And the work that needs to be done on shipwrecks is often tedious and demanding. While sport divers want to go deeper and stay longer to enjoy sunken ships, particularly those that have been seen by very few others, archaeologists want to delicately map, catalog, sketch, and eventually recover the secrets of the past.

Sunken-treasure hunters, however, are another matter entirely. They are entrepreners, not historians. Traditionally, their goals have been fundamentally simple: Find a wreck, recover anything of value, and move on. End of story. They have to "shrink" the seas with research and technology to find a quarry that is often hidden to someone just looking at the surface of the sea above a wreck site. For divers to perform any type of real work on a wreck, they needed innovations.

But how do they do their work? We know that the sea is a vast area that hides many secrets, but somehow these guys have managed to get the ocean to unlock some of its treasure chests. Want to find out how these clever seekers have gone about searching? Then read on!

Words To Treasure

Mel Fisher's **mailbox** is a pair of steel pipes crooked like elbows mounted side by side, which can be lowered to direct a boat's **prop wash**—the rush of water produced by its propeller—to clear sand and silt.

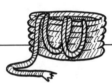

Know The Ropes

Another device that divers and salvors use when working on a sandy or silted seafloor is called an airlift, which is somewhat like a special vacuum cleaner! A long pipe connected to surface pumps draws up loose silt and moves it overhead so that it can be carried away. It can also allow debris being sucked away to be examined for artifacts. One disadvantage, however, is that the airlift does not clear debris nearly as quickly as the mailbox does. The airlift can be a delicate excavation tool whereas the forceful mailbox contraptions can damage buried objects.

Clearing the Underwater Fog

Mel Fisher was the epitome of the American treasure hunter. Imbued with irrepressible optimism and a ready smile, he would say to anyone around, "Today's the day!" even though most days weren't.

As romantic as sunken-treasure hunting seems, it's hard, dangerous work hampered by one of the most elemental things on earth—dirt. We've already talked about deposition and how some regions of water cover sunken objects at different rates, so we know what they're dealing with. This accumulated silt is the treasure hunter's nemesis. Not only can it completely camouflage what you're looking for, but if it gets stirred up underwater, it's a blinding fog.

Inventing a Better Mailbox

Fisher had a reason to be such an unfailing optimist—he had a trick up his sleeve that could make tons of that nasty search-blinding silt disappear.

When Fisher and treasure hunter Kip Wagner became partners in the 1960s, Fisher began working the hulks of the wealthy 1715 Treasure Fleet along a 50-mile stretch of tidal surf off Vero Beach, Florida. Being so close to shore meant that wave action was constantly churning up clouds of silt that drastically reduced visibility.

Blinded by this submerged dust storm, Fisher and his divers realized they might be passing within inches of a gold bar or a pile of silver coins and never know it. With the help of Fay Feild, a fellow treasure hunter and electronics expert, Fisher developed an elegantly simple device to solve the problem: the *mailbox*. The men decided to blow the swirling silt away with the salvage boat's twin propellers. This would be done by using a pair of elbow-shaped steel tubes that were lowered over the back of the boat.

Special Delivery

Mel's invention worked even better than expected, since it not only blew away the clouds of silt but also removed sand from the seafloor. Once the boat was firmly anchored, the elbow-shaped tubes were lowered over the boat's propellers, and the engines were turned on. Clear water would rush down the tubes, displacing the swirling silt. To Fisher's amazement, the force of the water also began scouring sand off the seafloor, exposing artifacts. This accidental benefit ushered in a new era of sunken-treasure hunting.

The big tubes looked like a pair of cylindrical mailboxes, so the contraption was christened the "mailbox," a name that has stuck with it for the past 35 years. The device—depending on the size of a boat's propellers and the speed at which they were turned—could blast huge holes through centuries of accumulated silt.

Fan Mail

Before there was a mailbox, divers depended on a variety of methods for removing silt. Even with new technology, one of the original methods—called fanning—is still in use. Fanning involves sweeping one's hand rapidly near the seafloor. This movement creates turbulence that forces the silt and sand away from the object in question.

The technique is fast (for a small area) and does not remove tons of sand, as Mel's mailboxes do, but fanning is cheap, easy, and delicate. It's also an extremely good method for sport divers who want to look at something without causing damage to a fragile form of sea life or an object that has survived centuries underwater.

Though ecologically sound and genteel, this method of removing silt is not for the business-oriented treasure hunter who is paying for labor and equipment by the hour.

Shiver Me Timbers

Mel Fisher's treasure-hunting team found itself in hot water in 1992 when the U.S. government filed a lawsuit claiming that Fisher and his company, Salvors, Inc., had bored nearly 100 holes in the sandy beds of sea grasses surrounding the Florida Keys. The government said Fisher's mailbox was the culprit. The craters were created along a mile-long stretch in the Florida Keys National Marine Sanctuary.

After Mel Fisher proved the effectiveness of mailboxes, other treasure hunters have had their own mailboxes constructed and mounted on their boats. Seeing a boat with two huge crooked pipes mounted on the stern is a good indication that you're looking at a treasure-hunting vessel.

Get to the Rock Bottom of Treasure

Gold and silver are heavy and tend to sink in silt or mud. Over the years divers have discovered that the extremely heavy gold items will actually migrate to the hardpan, or the hard bottom of the seafloor beneath the silt, which can be as deep as 25 feet!

Those seeking artifacts and treasures never cease to be amazed that what they're looking for seems to be able to hide itself in nooks and crannies in the hardpan or among coral clusters. Divers once had to dig with shovels or use explosives to clear away tons of silt to reach the hardpan. But of course, when you're using such aggressive measures, you never know what other damage you could be causing. The mailbox provided a relatively cheap and safe solution to a problem that had long bedeviled treasure hunters in shallow waters.

Metal Detectors: Not Just for Geeks

Metal detecting has long been a hobby not just in the United States but around the world, although you'll probably find more interesting things if you use a metal detector in really old countries like Britain or Greece instead of in the New World! In older countries the coins you find could be anything from freshly minted change to something going back before the time of Christ.

Go to any accessible American shoreline, and you'll probably see someone with a metal detector. Often, it's an older person equipped with a sensible hat for the sun and a trowel for excavating an interesting "hit." While most folks will come up with quarters, wristwatches, and automobile lug nuts, it's still an enjoyable exercise. Unfortunately, your chances of finding a Roman coin on the beaches of Coney Island or San Diego are slimmer than the thong on a bikini!

But don't think metal detecting is just for nerds wearing Bermuda shorts, black socks, and dress shoes. Today's metal detectors are precise, reliable instruments that can accurately tell you what's under your feet. The detectors are so reliable that they have found their own place in the professional treasure hunter's underwater arsenal.

You have to admit that metal detectors really must be darned effective at locating ancient coins and artifacts, since at least one country has banned their use on protected lands without written government permission!

Know The Ropes

The law specifying the requirement for permission prior to using a metal detector on lands containing scheduled ancient monuments (SAMs) was enacted in 1979. If this measure sounds a little harsh to Americans who chafe under ordinary speed limits, the British government is probably justified in taking the view that if people find something, they will dig it up and most likely keep it. Obviously, antiquities found on public lands should be retained for the benefit of the general public. Some British counties have more than 900 such SAMs, so watch your step.

Great Britain requires anyone seeking to use a metal detector at one of the country's scheduled ancient monuments (SAMs) to have written permission in hand at the time.

Fishing with Fisher

Metal detecting, like most technical innovations, grew out of an attempt to accomplish something completely unrelated. It seems that another guy named Fisher has had a serious impact on treasure hunting.

Gerhard Fisher was hired in the 1920s to develop equipment that would allow pilots to navigate with the use of radio signals. This equipment, which later became a standard item on aircraft, can pick up virtually any radio signal and follow it to its point of origin, giving the pilots a way to find airports in bad weather. In the seat-of-the-pants flying days of the late 1920s, this information was a godsend for pilots. It would also prove to be a boon to treasure hunters operating closer to the ground.

Though Fisher (Gerhard, not Mel) was successful in his task, he realized that the radio-direction-finding system was occasionally plagued with errors. These inaccurate readings were caused by metal buildings or by mineral deposits in the earth. The radio-direction-finding gear was inadvertently acting as a metal and mineral detector. Fisher was able to understand this problem and took steps to compensate for the variations so pilots wouldn't crash into mountains or otherwise end their flights on a down note.

The scientist then took the time to understand the science behind these meddlesome signals and recycled these findings into the development of the earliest metal detection devices. His firm, Fisher Research Laboratory, began producing metal detectors in 1931 and remains in business to this day.

Getting the Signal

Minerals that are buried, or dissolved in water, return a signal to a metal detector as easily as metallic objects. Both materials can serve as transmitters by interfering with electronic waves produced by the detector. Because minerals are present in soils to varying degrees, one challenge facing manufacturers of metal detectors is to filter out their electronic returns. In recent decades, these efforts have paid off, making the detectors more sensitive than ever.

Words To Treasure

An **electromagnetic field** is an area of energy containing both electrical and magnetic components. The passage of electricity through a conductive material will produce an electromagnetic field as will an ordinary magnet.

A Different Kind of Mine

The familiarity most people have with metal detectors dates back to World War II, when Allied forces found themselves tiptoeing through millions of mines laid down by German troops in North Africa and Europe.

Known as mine detectors, these devices consisted of a pole that contained an electro-magnetic coil on the end. Soldiers would have the electronics of the device in a back-pack or slung over their shoulder. Audio signals picked up by the detectors would be transmitted through earphones to the operator.

Following World War II, just about everything left over was sold to the public, and treasure hunters immediately saw the value in buying GI mine detectors. Except for becoming lighter in weight and more advanced electronically, the metal detectors of today are essentially the same. Headphones are still used (especially to block out other noises such as pounding surf), and the more compact devices of today look basically similar to the wartime models.

Shiver Me Timbers

The Nazi war machine realized mines with metallic components were easily found by Allied metal detectors. New mines with wooden containers were introduced to make it hard for advancing soldiers to detect the weapons. Some mines are now made completely out of plastic and can be detected only with chemical sensors that sniff out the explosive inside.

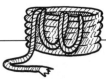

Know The Ropes

Many people who never go scuba diving purchase rugged, waterproof watches, because they block out moisture and tend to be relatively long-lasting. The same rule of thumb applies to metal detectors, since they are often used on the beach or the rain. Water-resistant or water-proof models are preferable, since detectors, like ships, sometimes sink unexpectedly. If buying a detector, shop competitively, read reviews, and get the best price.

Treasure-hunting legend Kip Wagner decided he needed help locating silver and gold while still an amateur beachcomber in the 1950s. His first metal detector was a military surplus model from World War II. This just goes to show that big-time treasure hunters appreciate the value of anything that helps them "see" beneath the sand.

Detecting the Right Detector

Anyone who is a qualified scuba diver wants to expand his or her activities while underwater, and many have taken up metal detecting on the seafloor because companies now make waterproof detectors. In the old days of scuba diving, folks waterproofed their own cameras and detectors, but now you can have anything made for you—for a price!

Because water is a good conductor of sound and because many detectors have systems with small speakers to announce alerts, divers don't have to wear earphones.

If you're swimming above a 2,000-pound bronze cannon, you'll hear the sound sooner than you would if the signal were carried through the air, since sound travels faster through water than air.

Although metal detectors are waterproof, it's always a good idea to read the specifications of your own model to ensure that you don't exceed its depth rating. Not only is water a good conductor of sound, but water—and especially salt water—is a good conductor of electricity. Keeping water out of your expensive metal detector is crucial.

Not all metal detectors are created equal. *Pulse-induction* models emit short bursts of electromagnetic energy up to thousands of times a second. These devices then read the electromagnetic feedback from buried metals while ignoring mineral signal returns. While this type of detector has shortcomings, it is highly effective in salt water, which can contain problematical amounts of dissolved minerals.

The *very low frequency transmitter receiver* units can ignore electronic returns from small pieces of metal refuse, thereby eliminating some pointless digging. However, this technology fares less well when used in salt water, since suspended minerals frequently create false signals. Skip the house payment and buy one of each!

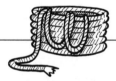

Words To Treasure

Pulse-induction metal detectors work better in salt water and areas where high levels of minerals exist in the ground. They manage to discriminate against accepting those minerals as metallic returns. **Very low frequency transmitter receiver** units can ignore useless pieces of metallic refuse and are recommended for fresh water or dry land prospecting.

Don't Get Mad; Get MAD!

It seems that if it weren't for war, treasure hunters wouldn't have any fun—or efficient—search tools to play with. Yup, you guessed it; yet another treasure-hunting toy has emerged from the warehouse of war.

During the very dark days of World War II, desperate experts in the British and American navies wanted a foolproof way to detect Nazi submarines. The German U-boats were on the verge of starving the Britons out of the war by sinking merchant ships that were carrying food to their island nation. Sonar (which became a superb shipwreck finder after a solid career as ship wrecker) had difficulty tracking U-boats just below the surface. Knowing that, crafty U-boat commanders often wallowed there in wait.

Know The Ropes

MADs can tell treasure hunters where iron and steel items are located. However, their usefulness can be partially negated if heavy deposits of iron ore in the seafloor cause a disruption in the magnetic field, making the searchers believe they've found a ship. The earth has its own general magnetic field. Disruption of this field by ferrous or iron metals including steel can be measured.

113

The answer to finding Nazi U-boats that outsmarted sonar was at the technology firm Texas Instruments, a company that had been involved in another treasure hunt—the search for the black gold of oil. One geophysical research tool the company developed was a *magnetic anomaly detector*—called MAD—that could determine the geological structure of the earth by flying the instrument overhead to measure differences in the earth's electromagnetic field. Magnetic anomaly detectors are also known as magnetometers.

When World War II started, the U.S. Navy wanted to mount these devices on airplanes and blimps to locate German U-boats. Because the steel hulls of the U-boats would disrupt the ordinary magnetic field generated by the earth, this "anomaly" was detectable by the equipment.

Shiver Me Timbers

Though MAD could find submarines, the technology was still in its infancy and required the pilots to fly as close to the water as 300 feet during long patrols to pick up a good reading. Treasure hunters, who were usually trolling the devices in boats, had no trouble staying close to the water! Although the early devices didn't differentiate a steel bucket from a Spanish galleon's iron fixture, they were still effective.

War and Pieces of Eight

After World War II, treasure hunters were eager to exploit any available technology and were strongly attracted by the magnetic possibilities of war-surplus MAD systems. For years, Mel Fisher bought newer and newer models of MAD devices as the Navy disposed of them. The first ones he purchased came from scrapped antisubmarine aircraft.

While darned good at locating deposits of iron or steel in shallow depths, MADs were useless as gold or silver detectors. Those materials had no affect on the magnetic field. If you're looking for an iron cannon or a steel-hulled ship, a MAD is great, but if valuable bronze, brass, or gold artifacts are even just an inch beneath the surface, your MAD might as well be a pine log hooked to a wire.

Operator Error

Treasure hunter Robert Marx used a MAD—but without success—while hunting for the Spanish treasure ship *Nuestra Senora de las Maravillas*. The ship was lost in 1656 in the straits between Florida and the Bahamas and was carrying five million pesos in silver when it went down. Though partially salvaged by the Spanish and others during the intervening years, much of the treasure remained on the seafloor. Little did Marx know that he had actually been over the wreck for months.

Even though his MAD was indicating that there was iron on the seafloor, Marx dismissed the reading, believing that it came from another shipwreck nearby. Despite his best efforts, Marx located the wreck by accidentally pulling up ship ballast stones on his anchor. His boat had been sitting right over the wreck off and on for months! So much for technology!

Shiver Me Timbers

Amazingly, the *Maravillas* was not lost because of a hurricane, which is exactly what took down most of the Spanish treasure ships that foolishly sailed between the June-to-November storm season. The *Maravillas* and another ship collided because of poor seamanship, smashing a hole in its hull. The *Maravillas*'s captain intentionally grounded his ship on a reef in hopes of keeping it above water, but winds pushed the ship off its perch, sinking it in 50 feet of water. Almost everyone on board perished. A priest who survived wrote an account of the wreck and his survival. This story was crucial in helping Robert Marx locate the ship.

Modern MADs are sleek, missile-shaped devices that can be towed in the water behind a boat to provide readings that indicate the presence of iron-based objects. While good at finding the general area of a wreck, metal detectors are recommended for smaller artifacts such as jewelry.

Helpful Fish Stories

If you want to be the first one on your block to locate a lost shipwreck or bring home several million dollars in sunken Spanish treasure, you better get on speaking terms with commercial fishermen and the locals of areas where ships are known to have been stranded or sunk.

Surprisingly, some people could care less about a shipwreck near their village or home. Having heard about a wreck their entire lives, they acknowledge its location but lack the curiosity or perhaps the skills to investigate.

Hooked on Treasure

The complaints of fishermen tired of snagged lines near Portsmouth, England, accurately guided diving helmet inventor and master salvor John Deane to the remnants of the *Mary Rose* during his 1830s investigation of that 300-year-old hulk.

After finding a pair of cannon at the shipwreck, Deane wrote Britain's Royal Board of Ordnance, detailing how he came to explore the site in June 1836 and giving full credit to the exasperated fishermen:

> *Honble. Gentlemen,*
>
> *With Humble reference to the Ancient Gun refered to in your letter dated 22nd June 1836 we most respectfully beg leave to state to your Honble. Board that it was recovered thro' the instigation of 5 poor fishermen, who had frequently got their lines etc entangled in something, but could not find out what it was.*
>
> *John Deane*

Deane and his partner William Edwards agreed to share with the fishermen a portion of whatever salvage fees came their way, since they had stumbled upon the wreck. This arrangement would have doubled the fishermen's catch, since they mostly wanted the troublesome wreck out of their way.

Shiver Me Timbers

John Deane and William Edwards were eager for the salvage contract but hesitant to set a firm price, knowing the difficulty and uncertainties of the project. Impatient English government officials decided they would not deal with such prima donnas. Announcing that they would do the job for "one-fiftieth" of what the professionals would have charged, they cobbled together an incompetent fiasco. Inexperienced divers were fired left and right, explosive charges failed to work, and tragically, a young British army corporal with no diving experience drowned on his second dive to the wreck on May 20, 1838.

Net Profits

If anyone knows the seafloor, it's the fishermen who have *seined* vast stretches of water ranging from shallow bays to deep oceans. They know where unidentified objects have snagged and torn their nets and often have interesting stories to tell about objects dragged from the seafloor. Most treasure hunters, no matter their stature as finders of treasure, place a great deal of stock in the knowledge of local fishing-boat captains and crews.

And don't forget, the richest shipwrecks found in the Gulf of Mexico were accidentally discovered by fishermen.

When fishing-boat Captain Jerry Murphy hauled up Spanish coins in his fishing net in the Gulf of Mexico in 1993, he did what any red-blooded American entrepreneur would do: He called his partner and salvaged the treasure himself under state supervision! In 1973, Curtis Blume netted copper ingots from the Spanish ship *El Nuevo Constanté*. It was also a treasure ship that yielded thousands of silver coins. Like Murphy, Blume claimed his share of the find.

Ho-Hum, Another Shipwreck

Sometimes, folks just don't care about a shipwreck because familiarity breeds boredom. Unlike the fishermen upset with the *Mary Rose,* locals in coastal communities are sometimes so inured to a wreck's existence that they no longer pay it any mind.

Words To Treasure

To **seine** is to drag a fishing net supported by floats at the top and weighted along its bottom edge for the purpose of catching fish, or an occasional shipwreck.

Treasure hunter Robert Marx, intrigued by the mural of a ship inside a church, asked the local priest what the mural represented. The mural, said the priest, was donated to the church decades before by shipwreck survivors of that very vessel to thank the local residents for their help. When Marx asked where the ship sank, the priest nonchalantly pointed to a spot a stone's throw from shore. Everyone in the village knew about it, but no one considered the ship or its cargo of any importance. Marx had made another discovery.

Knowledge by the Galleon

French ocean explorer Jacques-Yves Cousteau believed that a little homework never hurt anyone when it came to tracking down elusive shipwrecks. When searching for wreck sites, one of the first things Cousteau did was to study nautical charts for the reefs and obstacles most likely to mortally wound ships. A dive near these submerged obstacles most often revealed shipwrecks.

Dangerous locations with historically high amounts of maritime traffic invariably have plenty of sunken ships nearby. The moral here is that knowledge of local conditions and common sense are worth their weight in gold when trying to determine the location of a wreck.

There is no quick, easy, and cheap way to find a shipwreck whose location is not already public knowledge. The road to such information is likely to be over rough and confusing seas, but there are places where one can start the search.

Nautical Detective Work

Those who have decided to make the big score by searching out shipwrecks loaded with treasure should probably invest a ton of research for every ounce of actual diving.

Don't count on the fabled treasure map or a helpful tip from a crusty, one-eyed mariner sporting a parrot on his shoulder. This is going to take some work!

Potential treasure hunters need to learn some basics. First, knowing how to read a nautical chart is crucial, as is gaining general knowledge about currents and seafloor conditions for the area you're interested in.

If you're merely looking for ships sunk during the past 100 or 200 years, a great deal of documentation is available through various insurance companies and from nautical charts that indicate shallow wrecks.

Your next stop will be various archives located throughout the world. One of the most important is maintained by Lloyd's Register, which has inspected the condition of ships for more than 200 years. A separate firm, the insurance company Lloyd's of London, has also compiled the names of ships lost that were insured by the firm. Their documentation and publications cost money. There is no free lunch in the shipwreck or sunken-treasure business.

Words To Treasure

Procesal is a form of Spanish writing that is curiously devoid of punctuation and therefore difficult to read. It is used extensively in the Archive of the Indies on official documents related to Spanish treasure fleet ships from the early 1500s until the 1800s.

The Hulls of Knowledge

For Spanish treasure fleet enthusiasts, there is only one place for serious researchers. It is the Archive of the Indies in Seville, which houses massive stacks of antiquated documents detailing Spain's New World experiences. Unfortunately, knowledge of antiquated Spanish and an ability to decipher an ornate script known as *procesal* are necessities. The claim by some that the fifteenth- through nineteenth-century writings are a breeze to read is heavily disputed by researchers.

Shiver Me Timbers

Treasure hunters had feverishly sought the *Atocha* for years but were looking in the wrong place until historian Eugene Lyon identified the Florida Keys island closest to the *Atocha's* wreck site. Following the 1622 wreck, the island had been renamed in honor of Marquis de Cadereita, who salvaged some of the treasure the following year. Searchers had been thrown off by 100 miles by assuming the island's original name was correct. Is anyone confused? Well, don't feel bad, so were the treasure hunters.

Documentation from this archive allowed history instructor and history doctoral candidate Eugene Lyon to provide treasure hunter Mel Fisher with crucial information regarding the location of the fabulously wealthy treasure ship *Atocha*.

The Least You Need to Know

➤ When beachcomber Kip Wagner began to get serious about treasure hunting, the first metal detector he bought was a war-surplus model.

➤ The development of metal detectors was rooted in an attempt to enable pilots to use ordinary radio broadcasts to determine their direction of travel during bad weather.

➤ The Wehrmacht, which was the name of the German army in World War II, planted millions of land mines, forcing Allied soldiers to use metal detectors in order to locate them.

➤ Sound travels much faster in water than it does through the air because water is far denser than air.

➤ Magnetic anomaly detectors—MADs—were invented in Texas for the geophysical exploration efforts of the oil industry.

➤ Although finding a sunken ship is a tough accomplishment, divers were often unable to see through a cloud of silt to explore the wreck until the invention of a device called the "mailbox" that blew away the cloudy water.

Chapter 9

Fish Scales of Justice: Modern Salvage Law

In This Chapter

➤ Who owns what

➤ Arresting a ship

➤ Deep wrecks: whose law applies?

➤ The *Titanic:* no peeking

➤ The government's wrecks

It's time to turn off *Baywatch,* get up from the sofa, and claim your shipwreck. Sure, an avalanche of potato chip crumbs will irk the cat at your feet, but you've got to get moving. Your competitors are ready to pounce on your treasure ship, and time is running short!

Run out to the garage and make sure your side-scan sonar and camera-equipped, remotely operated vehicle are ready for loading aboard your 120-foot search-and-recovery ship. All the while, Mel Fisher's voice is in your ear repeating softly, "Today's the day!"

As your ship pushes for the open ocean and the briny sea breeze slaps your face, you're suddenly seized with a horrifying realization—you forgot to pick up your lawyer, Marvin Sharktooth, Esq.

Stop the boat!

Forget the crushing pressure of the deep ocean; if you don't know your way around an admiralty court or how to claim legal rights to a shipwreck, you're going to be in for a worse fate than that of the passengers and crew of the sunken ship you're hunting for.

Admiralty law, which encompasses *salvage law,* is a very specialized area, but one that deserves study from the hunters of sunken ships and submerged treasure. Federal and state laws govern who owns what underwater. Some ships, like warships, are completely untouchable to salvors and divers.

Many sunken civilian ships are actually "owned" by people, corporations, or federal and state governments. At one time, you were not even supposed to take pictures of the RMS *Titanic* without the permission of its owner! (Yes, a corporation has been made trustee of the *Titanic.*)

Recovering artifacts from a shipwreck means you have to do three things: Find it, claim it, and "work it," as the old salvors say. Technology has made finding and working the wreck the easiest parts. Unfortunately, finding yourself locked in a legal battle with insurance companies, state governments, other treasure hunters, and even your own partner can actually consume more time and money than the search and recovery itself.

Don't Go Overboard!

Before spending a penny searching for a valuable shipwreck, invest in legal and historical research on your prospective shipwreck prey. It's imperative that you ensure it is not protected from tampering by federal or state laws and does not lie in waters where a state or nation can lay claim to the ship automatically. Finding a ship and recovering its treasure may mean you'll simply be turning it over to a bureaucrat on your way to jail. Under new laws, some wrecks cannot be salvaged unless the salvor can show that the original owner, or an insurance company that paid a claim on the sunken ship, has officially abandoned the wreck. Salvaging a wreck owned by someone else could result in either criminal charges or civil litigation.

Although salvage was once the domain of crusty old sea dogs with rusting ships and tough-as-nails helmet divers, the times have changed. Thanks to great advances in diving equipment and technology, these mysterious wrecks are more accessible than ever before. Scuba equipment made shallow-water wrecks accessible to sport divers by the 1950s, and high-technology search-and-recovery techniques have recently made deeper wrecks ripe for picking. Unfortunately for the would-be treasure hunter, the result of all this advanced technology is the now-inevitable and complex legal wrangling over who controls the wrecks and treasures that no one ever thought would be found.

Newer legislation has given states control over shipwrecks in some cases, but the legal waters are still murky. States have waged legal battles against shipwreck recovery operations to halt often-successful attempts by treasure hunters to claim wrecks under traditional salvage law. The archaeologists are angry, the treasure hunters are angry, and even the sport divers are angry.

So perhaps you need a general understanding of the complex—and sometimes contradictory—world of salvage law before you claim your shipwreck. Flick that potato chip off your miffed cat's head and ponder the weird world of salvage law before heading back out into those choppy legal waters.

Who Owns What

When a ship is built, it's owned by whoever paid for it, so determining who owns a new, fully operable ship is easy. Trying to understand who owns a ship that is abandoned, damaged, or adrift without a crew is a bit more complicated.

Since virtually every ship is insured, the sinking or grounding of a vessel means an insurer is usually obligated to reimburse the owner for the loss. If an insurer does pay a claim for the loss, then the wreck and cargo go to the insurer. This is why virtually all ships lost in the past 100 years are essentially owned by someone, somewhere, and it's often an insurance company that holds the claim.

If a ship is determined to be officially *abandoned*, in the legal language of salvage, then federal law says it belongs to the state in whose waters it rests. A ship that has simply sunk and has not been located for salvage or recovery is not necessarily an "abandoned" ship. The owners may simply not know where the ship is, or they may lack the technology to find it. Federal judicial decisions have held that abandonment must be an overt act. But what does all this mean to you, the potential treasure hunter? Basically, it means that you can't claim a wrecked ship just because its owner can't find it. In this case, the early bird doesn't necessarily get the worm!

Words To Treasure

An **abandoned wreck** is one whose owners have actively indicated that they have no interest in. **Salvage** actually refers to the saving of a damaged or grounded ship by a **salvor,** someone who voluntarily saves the ship or its cargo.

A Piece of the Wreck

An insurance company, such as the famous Lloyd's of London, that has gained title to a ship can sign a contract with a salvor to either raise a sunken ship or recover anything of value from the wreck. A salvage firm can also buy the wreck outright and own it until it decides to officially abandon it. However, under a standard salvage contract, salvors earn a percentage of the value of what they recover. It's a tough business, since salvors must often cover their own expenses from their profit. This type of arrangement is known as the "no cure, no pay" agreement.

Let's take an example: Although Lloyd's could have sold the liner *Egypt* when it sank off the French coast in 1922 with gold and silver aboard, the insurer instead contracted with Swedish engineer Peter Sandberg in 1925 to recover the liner's treasure. Sandberg eventually turned to the Italian salvage firm called Sorima to find and recover the treasure. Part of the deal was for the group to be paid a percentage of the value of what was recovered. The gold and silver recovery wasn't completed until 1935.

Wrecks can be bought and sold just like used cars as long as they have value. Most wrecks are sold by insurance companies, but a secondhand market has developed in which salvors sometimes sell a wreck to another salvor.

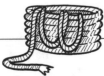

Know The Ropes

Working in the salvage business is tough and sometimes physically and financially dangerous. The no cure, no pay agreement often struck between salvors and the owners of ships in trouble means that there must be a "cure"—that is, the rescue of a ship and its cargo—or there is simply no pay.

Words To Treasure

LOF, or Lloyd's Open Form, was the first standardized contract for salvage and has been used since 1892—with the latest revisions made in 1995.

Expensive Help

The true meaning of *salvage* is the assistance given to a ship that saves the vessel, its cargo, or its passengers. They can be threatened by anything: collision, fire, grounding, or attack. If the damaged ship accepts help that is successful, the salvor—whether it's the captain of a supertanker or someone in an inner tube—is entitled to a "reward" for his or her efforts.

Since no one is able to easily pass documents back and forth on the high seas between a helpful ship and one that's burning out of control, the issue of compensation sometimes has to wait to be resolved until after the emergency. The amount of money paid to a salvor is based on many things, including the determination that the salvor's efforts provided a "useful result" and the value of the ship and cargo saved.

After the fire is out, or the grounded ship has been pulled into deeper water and refloated, the issues of salvage reward are usually settled by attorneys representing the salvor and the ship's insurance company. These matters can always land in an admiralty court if the parties disagree on how much the salvage assistance was worth, especially since the insurer of a boat usually pays for the salvage.

When a contract is signed, it's usually a standard salvage contract known as *Lloyd's Open Form,* or *LOF.* It was developed by the maritime insurance firm in 1892 and had gone through nine revisions by 1995.

Worldwide Rules

Because shipping occurs in international waters, the International Convention on Salvage has formulated a lot of basic guidelines for fair salvage practices. These guidelines set out general rules for salvage and attempt to gain voluntary compliance from shipping firms. The provisions are in the form of a treaty that other nations can agree to follow.

A code of ethics, which asks salvors to seek additional help if necessary, has also been established. Although it may seem obvious that more help would be a good thing if the conditions were bad enough, seeking help could also force the original salvor to split the reward for preserving another ship. Thus the purpose of the code of ethics is to preclude a salvor from refusing assistance to the detriment of the ship being saved.

Oil and Water

In the good old days of shipwrecks when the worst pollutants carried by ships were dirty sailors, no one thought much about the damage caused by a ship's cargo. Now ships are carrying millions of gallons of oil, and environmental damage can be massive. To help protect the environment, the LOF salvage agreement includes provisions in which a salvor can receive pay for helping a troubled ship even if the salvage efforts only reduce the pollution hazard without saving the ship and its cargo.

In the old days, salvors were fearful of poking the nose of their ship into a situation that meant only expense without profit. Society's unwillingness to endure environmental damage has prompted insurers to pay for efforts that mitigate the spills of oil or other pollutants.

Arresting a Ship

If a wrecked ship and its cargo aren't owned by anyone and it hasn't been designated as a historical site, you might have a wreck you can claim as your own through a process known as "arrest." Now, don't get too excited and start wondering how you're going to handcuff a 900-foot oil tanker or read the rights to a bulk cargo carrier. *Arrest* in this situation means to halt others from salvaging a wreck by order of an admiralty court prior to a salvage firm gaining what amounts to a trusteeship over the wreck.

Words To Treasure

Arresting a ship is a bit different than arresting a person since the legal maneuver merely halts any activity regarding the ship providing a prospective salvor a chance to be placed in control of a ship.

Shiver Me Timbers

Any claim or lawsuit pertaining to salvage or admiralty law falls within the jurisdiction of the U.S. district courts. Although there's not an official "admiralty court" in the United States, lawsuits and other matters pertaining to maritime law are heard by U.S. federal judges. State district courts are set up within individual states to try civil and criminal cases under state law. If an admiralty suit is filed regarding an oceangoing ship, it is with a federal court and usually in the closest coastal city.

But first you have to find the ship in question and bring proof that you've located it and have the ability to recover either the ship or any valuables aboard. When George

Tulloch and his organization claimed the *Titanic,* they did so in a Norfolk, Virginia, federal courtroom. To prove they had been to the *Titanic,* they brought back a crystal wine decanter plucked from 12,000 feet beneath the Atlantic. When the Columbus-America Discovery Group, which found the SS *Central America* off North Carolina, wanted to claim its ship, the group flew a lump of coal to the same courthouse.

If a federal judge thinks you've worked hard enough to bring back an artifact, you'll most likely be named salvor-in-possession of the wreck.

The Case of the Central America

When engineer Tommy Thompson organized the Columbus-America Discovery Group in the mid-1980s to search for the SS *Central America* and its tons of gold off North Carolina's coast, he was well aware of the legal challenges that always erupt when someone finds a serious treasure.

After finally locating the *Central America*'s treasure on September 11, 1988, Thompson had an airplane fly by and snag a lump of the *Central America*'s coal so it could be taken to an admiralty court—the U.S. district court in Norfolk, Virginia. Thompson and his team were allowed to arrest the *Central America*'s wreck by order of the judge, but that didn't end the matter.

Lawsuits were filed by 39 insurance companies—as well as by other treasure hunters—that were all claiming the gold. Hundreds of millions in gold was at stake, and all parties had dollar signs in their eyes. Almost all the suits were thrown out, and only a handful of insurance companies were successful. And even then, they were only granted a fraction of the treasure. Although Columbus-America had been successful at finding and recovering the treasure, the organization spent nearly six years in court before it officially owned the treasure that its members had fought so hard to find.

Don't Go Overboard!

The U.S. Coast Guard, which knows a thing or two about rescuing people at sea, has stern advice for the operators of ships large and small: There's no substitute for maintenance and knowledge. A salvage crew or the Coast Guard may not be able to arrive in the nick of time if a ship endangers itself. A ship's owner or insurer may end up spending like a sailor to save the ship from an avoidable accident.

Everyday "Treasure" Ships

Ships are arrested every day in the United States, but they're not usually classic treasure ships. Some are still afloat, abandoned by their owners with unpaid crews at ports around the country. Sometimes they're recent shipwrecks with valuable machinery and cargo on board. Sailors who have been left high and dry without their wages will often stay with a ship so they can make a claim against its cargo and equipment.

Full-time salvors actually operate boats and equipment in high-traffic port areas around the clock. Their sole business is to help ships and pleasure craft in trouble and thereby obtain salvage fees. When your sailboat runs aground, these salvors are much like seagoing wrecker drivers; they can tow you off a rocky shoal or help you fix your damaged boat.

However, don't expect a flat $50 towing fee! More often than not, they charge the old-fashioned way according to the laws of salvage—a percentage of the value of the ship and cargo saved by their efforts. So make sure you have good insurance! The salvage of a grounded $42,000 sailboat off New Jersey's coast in 1995 resulted in the award of a $9,000 salvage fee to the salvor by a federal judge.

Safer Seas

It's estimated there may be as many as 50,000 shipwrecks in and near the United States. Some of these ships are rowboats and others are U.S. Navy cruisers. For those who don't know it already, America is a maritime nation. We have thrived by shipping products back and forth across the oceans. Thousands of sea voyages start or end at dozens of ports on the East, West, and Gulf Coasts.

The same is true for many other nations around the world, but an interesting and reassuring phenomenon is occurring: Fewer ships are sinking! Tougher ships, more reliable engines, superb communications, and unerring electronic navigation aides like the Global Positioning System mean that fewer ships are getting into trouble.

This is good news for everyone except the salvors. Although an average of $1 billion worth of property has been salvaged yearly since 1978, some reports indicate the amount of salvaged cargo and shipping rescued is dropping drastically. Industry analysts say the value of cargo salvaged in 1995 dropped to $500 million.

An Arresting Controversy

Easily the most controversial claim to be filed under American salvage law involved the Spanish slave ship *Amistad* that grounded on Montauk Point on Long Island, New York. The ship contained 53 Africans who had been kidnapped from West Africa and taken to Cuba where they were sold into slavery. After boarding the *Amistad* for a trip to another part of Cuba, the slaves revolted and killed all but the two Spaniards who had purchased them. Instead of sailing the Africans home, the Spaniards sailed the *Amistad* to New York.

A pair of U.S. Navy officers aboard a survey ship named the *Washington* found the grounded *Amistad* and took it into custody. At the same time, two civilians ashore had captured the Africans who had gone to look for water. Both groups sought to "arrest" the Africans as salvaged "cargo." The Naval officers and the two civilians filed competing claims to take possession of the slaves.

The federal courts ruled that the Africans were free men despite arguments from the government that a treaty with Spain forced the United States to return them. The Supreme Court eventually heard the case and ruled that the Africans should be returned to their homes at government expense.

Shiver Me Timbers

At one point during the protracted legal battle to determine the fate of the Africans, the U.S. government made an argument that only an attorney could have conjured. The Africans, argued the government's lawyers, had commanded a slave ship at the time it grounded and were therefore in violation of New York law prohibiting slave trade! The Supreme Court of the United States said this argument was ridiculous. However, *Washington* officers Thomas Gedney and Richard Meade were granted a percentage of the nonhuman cargo of the *Amistad* as a salvors reward.

Deep Wrecks: Whose Law Applies?

You know, things were pretty simple around the admiralty court in days gone by. If a ship holed itself on rocks in 30 feet of water, ownership of the wreck was established and a salvage company was contracted to refloat the ship and the cargo. Even when a ship completely sank in water not exceeding 100 feet or so, the same process was followed and rugged helmet divers went down and recovered the propellers, the cargo, and other items of value.

Deep wrecks? Pshaw on that, matey. In the old days, a ship deeper than 100 feet or so was Davy Jones's concern and not that of Judge Justice J. Justice of a U.S. district court. Not anymore, though; time and technology have changed everything.

A Shallow Tradition

For about 4,000 years, the term *salvageable shipwreck* referred to any sunken vessel that could be reached by wading into the surf or by diving with nothing more than a deep breath. If a ship was in water deeper than 50 or 100 feet, it no longer existed to salvors for all practical purposes.

The invention of helmet diving in the 1830s finally made possible the lengthy exploration of sunken ships. Sustained by air pumped from the surface, these helmet divers were able to efficiently recover items from such wrecks. Almost all of these wrecks were near shore and were found either because their masts were sticking out of the water or because a fisherman's net was caught on the wreck. Sometimes wrecks could be seen through extremely clear water, but even these were sometimes inaccessible due to their depth.

Since shallow-water wrecks were almost always in the territorial waters of one nation or another, there was little question about whose court had jurisdiction over a sunken ship.

Shiver Me Timbers

One of the first famous shipwrecks to be investigated and partially salvaged through the use of diving equipment was the English warship *Mary Rose,* which sank on July 19, 1545, near Portsmouth, England, killing nearly 700 aboard. Helmet diving inventors John and Charles Deane were also early salvage experts, and they recovered 23 cannons from the wreck's site, along with human remains. However, the work was still too difficult with the equipment of the time, and the effort was eventually abandoned.

International Waters

Until the advent of deep-submergence craft, remotely operated vehicles, and side-scan sonar, there was just no reliable way to locate and visit shipwrecks that were more than a few hundred feet underwater. Understandably, salvors weren't rushing to the admiralty court to wake up the judge and make their claim on ships sunk 14,000 feet in the middle of the Atlantic. Not only could they not get down there, they couldn't even find the ships!

By the 1950s, however, the situation began to change with the development of side-scan sonar and miniature submarines. The value of these tools was improved by the development of underwater robots and camera sleds in the 1960s. This technology (which had mostly been the domain of the offshore oil industry and the U.S. Navy) became well-known to the public during the 1980s, thanks mostly to the discovery of the RMS *Titanic* by Woods Hole Oceanographic Institute scientist Robert Ballard.

Ballard did not arrest the *Titanic* during the original expedition that found the ship with sonar and remotely operated camera sleds. Nor did he claim the ship after a subsequent trip in 1986 during which he dove to the wrecked liner on the deep-submergence craft known as *Alvin.* Ballard maintained that the ship should remain unmolested as a memorial to those who died at the time of her sinking.

Know The Ropes

Titanic discoverer Robert Ballard has consistently asked that only photographs be taken from the wreck of the *Titanic* and said it was never his intention to arrest the *Titanic* for personal gain. He has also expressed outrage at the stripping of artifacts from what he believes is a gravesite. Others point out that the *Titanic* and many of its artifacts are simply melting away because of corrosion and bacterial infestation and that recovery will save *Titanic* items for future generations.

Out of Their Depth?

Although salvors have traditionally had the ability to claim an abandoned wreck in international waters, doing so has been relatively rare for two reasons: No one has been able to find most of the deep-water wrecks, and shipwrecks frequently occur near shore.

The 1981 salvage of Soviet gold from the British cruiser HMS *Edinburgh* in 800 feet of water in the Barents Sea stands as one of the deepest salvage operations to date using divers. Though the ship was in international waters, the British and Soviet governments approved the salvage beforehand, greatly reducing the legal hassles the salvage consortium would have endured.

However, it's the use of deep-diving submersibles and remotely operated vehicles that has shaken up the world of salvage law the most. Courts now consider granting ownership to wrecks that are hundreds of miles into international waters. Although these claims are granted, some argue that one country can't apply its law to an area hundreds of miles outside its own territory.

The *Titanic:* No Peeking!

When former auto dealer George Tulloch helped assemble Titanic Ventures, Inc., he did so intending to obtain ownership of the *Titanic*. Since Ballard's discovery of the ship two years earlier, no one had returned to arrest it in an admiralty court.

Tulloch's group located the *Titanic* in 1987. Using a manned deep-diving submarine, the Titanic Ventures, Inc., consortium gathered 1,800 objects from the wreck and its debris field. Since a French team recovered those items, they were returned to France, where they were preserved until their ownership could be established. French law required public notification about the recovered objects in case others might want to claim them.

By the time this requirement was being met, an expedition consortium named Marex-Titanic, Inc., led by treasure hunters Jack Grimm and James Kollar, arrived at the wreck site in September 1992 to begin recovering artifacts. This endeavor sparked a legal battle between Marex-Titanic and Titanic Ventures, which later became RMS Titanic, Inc.

Words To Treasure

The **salvor-in-possession** of a wreck is essentially a trustee entitled to the wreck and all of its artifacts and equipment at the discretion of an admiralty court.

Long Arm of the Law

Judge J. Calvitt Clarke, speaking for the U.S. District Court in Norfolk, Virginia, halted Grimm and Kollar's expedition in mid-ocean. Clarke took this action because the Norfolk district court was already in possession of artifacts that Tulloch's group had recovered.

The *Titanic* was arrested, and RMS Titanic, Inc., was later named *salvor-in-possession* of the liner. Kollar and

Grimm were thwarted in their attempts to retrieve artifacts and lay claim to the ship. Despite a sea of other legal claims, including one from an insurance company challenging RMS Titanic, Inc.'s bid to obtain rights to the wreck, Clarke made RMS Titanic, Inc. salvor-in-possession in June 1994.

No Pictures, Please

An unusual salvage law precedent regarding the *Titanic* was set by Judge Clarke of the U.S. District Court in Norfolk, but later was struck down. In June 1998, Clarke ruled that a British sight-seeing group could not visit the *Titanic* wreck site in submersibles on a photography exhibition. Clarke's ruling was based on an effort to prevent the unauthorized pillaging of the liner and its debris field. It held that anyone descending to the site might be tempted by the huge debris field to recover items belonging to RMS Titanic, Inc. This decision was heavily criticized, since it went beyond simply denying a nonsalvor the opportunity to collect artifacts.

However, a fifth U.S. Circuit Court of Appeals ruling in April 1999 reversed Clarke's ruling that had expanded RMS Titanic, Inc.'s salvor rights to include images of the ship. The federal appeals court held that RMS Titanic, Inc., owned the liner but said granting it exclusive rights to the ship's image was counter to the intent of international salvage law. The decision held that such rights would encourage a salvor to leave a wreck intact rather than recover its artifacts and equipment.

Soon after Clarke signed his order prohibiting anyone but RMS Titanic, Inc., from descending to the wreck, European and Australian tourists were already visiting the *Titanic*. They descended nearly 12,000 feet to stare at the wreck through the portholes of a deep-diving submarine. Each sightseer paid around $32,500 to visit the liner 1,000 miles away from Clarke's court. No action was taken against the tour organizers.

The Government's Wrecks

While some maintain the government is a wreck, none can dispute that the U.S. government owns a lot of wrecked ships. For all practical purposes, the U.S. Navy never relinquishes control of a sunken warship. In fact, anything that the government loses underwater—including airplanes and crashed dirigibles—is protected!

The law is pretty plain on the salvaging of artifacts from sunken U.S. Navy warships. If you swim down to a sunken Navy warship and take a souvenir, you're in violation of federal law. You could be fined, you could go to jail, or both. Don't think Uncle Sam is the only spoilsport on this subject, since virtually every navy in the world has rules prohibiting this very type of activity.

However, having a law and enforcing it are two entirely different matters. Although U.S. law states that warships remain the property of the U.S. government forever, it might be hard to enforce that law if a foreign nation plunders a U.S. Navy ship in international waters.

The Unfortunate Mr. Steinmetz

Richard Steinmetz was not a treasure hunter, but an antique dealer, who found himself in some very hot water with the U.S. government. For years he had owned the bell from the Confederate warship *Alabama*. The commerce raider was sunk on June 19, 1864, in the unlikely waters off the French coast, following a battle with the Union warship *Kearsarge*.

A British diver descended to the wreck in 1937 and brought back the *Alabama*'s bell, which would later sit in an English pub for years before Steinmetz purchased it. Then one day there was a knock at Steinmetz's door, and federal agents came in to seize the bell. Steinmetz was never even reimbursed by the federal government for the seizure. The law held that because the bell was always U.S. property, he had never had ownership of the item.

In a 1992 lawsuit between the United States and Steinmetz, the ailing antique dealer lost and was told by the federal courts that although the court sympathized with him, the bell had to go back to the U.S. Navy.

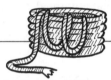

Know The Ropes

Possessing something that's determined to be stolen property unknowingly is no defense against it being seized, and items wrongfully taken from protected shipwrecks are no exception. Even though you might purchase an item believing it was honestly acquired, you will have to return it to the government or the rightful owner of a wreck if it's discovered in your possession.

Abandoned Shipwreck Act

In 1988, the federal government passed a law making it a bit clearer who owned what when it came to shipwrecks lying within America's territorial waters. This law came about to protect historical wrecks. The Abandoned Shipwreck Act essentially gave the states the title to any abandoned shipwrecks within their submerged lands, excluding military ships. The act includes wrecks that are up to three miles from a state's shoreline.

Shiver Me Timbers

The Abandoned Shipwreck Act has had a profound effect on salvage operations in state waters, since a prospective salvor must now prove that a wreck is not abandoned in order to take control of it from the state. However, this situation is a strange one, since salvors have traditionally tried to prove that a wreck is abandoned to clear the way for their salvage efforts. Proving the wreck is not abandoned usually requires that a salvor locate documentation that an insurer paid a claim on the shipwreck in question.

However, wrecks that have not been abandoned, meaning those that still belonged to someone, cannot be owned by the states. When Deep Sea Research, Inc., located the steamship *Brother Jonathan* that sank in 1865 off California's coast, the company had to prove in federal court that the wreck was not abandoned and was successful in doing so. Deep Sea Research, Inc., located records showing that an insurance company had paid claims on the wreck.

California unsuccessfully argued the wreck located off its coast was abandoned so that it could lay claim to the wreck under the Abandoned Shipwreck Act. The federal court said no to this argument, and the Supreme Court of the United States upheld the lower court's decision.

When it comes to salvage law, a good rule of thumb to keep in mind is that the finders are not always the keepers.

The Least You Need to Know

➤ Often, maritime insurance companies own shipwrecks, if they have paid a claim on the loss of the ship and its cargo.

➤ Shipwrecks, like any other commodity with value, can be bought and sold by insurance companies, salvors, or anyone else who holds title to the wreck.

➤ Because laws pertaining to maritime trade are covered under federal statutes or laws, the maritime cases are heard in ordinary U.S. district courts.

➤ Safer ships and better navigational tools are putting a crimp into the earnings of salvage firms, since there are far fewer shipwrecks than there once were.

➤ The famous slave ship *Amistad* was the subject of a successful salvage claim by the two U.S. Navy officers who were granted a portion of the cargo aboard the ship as a salvage reward but were denied ownership of the slaves.

➤ Legal claims filed for the ownership of deep-water wrecks is a recent phenomenon, since these wrecks were beyond reach before the perfection of side-scan sonar and deep-diving vehicles until recently.

Part 3
Shipwrecks: Oldies with Goodies

Shipwrecks have been a part of man's seafaring history since the sinking of the first crude canoe. In Part 3 you'll learn about one of the oldest shipwrecks ever located and recovered at Uluburun, Turkey, and the painstaking process involved in this mission.

You'll also read the horrifying stories of storm-smashed Spanish treasure fleets and of the terrible loss of life—and treasure—during the seventeenth and eighteenth-centuries.

This part concludes with accounts of the loss and recovery of the sixteenth-century warship Mary Rose *and the amazing recovery of the nineteenth-century treasure ship* SS Central America.

Chapter 10

The Oldest Wreck

In This Chapter

➤ The Uluburun wreck: history's oldest

➤ A cargo of clues answers Bronze Age questions

➤ A decade of underwater archaeology at Uluburun

➤ Unraveling the origins of the Uluburun wreck

A practical-minded landlubber seeing the decayed and buried remnants of a sunken and ancient shipwreck will jump to the conclusion that its sailing days are long gone. With its timbers eaten to nothing and silt covering its submerged fragments, the ship is not much more than a scattering of debris. How wrong this person would be!

An ancient ship, that is little more than a pile of fractured pottery and waterlogged splinters, may have one more voyage left, and it might be the most incredible trip it ever made! A trained archaeologist assisted by historians and modern technology can convert the wreckage of a forgotten ship into a vessel that can cross centuries to reveal information about the time from which it came, whether it was 300 years ago or 3,000.

Ancient shipwrecks, the cargo, and artifacts they carry provide us a stepping stone that links the near-mythical past to our present reality. While they sometimes carry treasure, even something as mundane as a writing tablet can provide answers to baffling questions about a people and their history.

The wreck of just such a merchant ship at Uluburun near Kas, Turkey, happened when its hold was full of trading goods and the items of everyday life. It remained untouched for thousands of years, protected by water no deeper than half the length of a football field. Its secrets are only now being revealed.

Don't Go Overboard!

Although the famous *Titanic* sank far out in the Atlantic in 12,000 feet of water, most ships meet their demise near shore on rocky shorelines. Storms and poor navigation can quickly put a ship "on the rocks," ending its useful life. The wrecked remains of ships are often clustered around shorelines or rocky outcroppings like the Grand-Congloué in Marseilles's bay. The Uluburun wreck was likely one of these ships since it was lost very close to shore. Although it might be comforting to see the shoreline while sailing, experienced sailors know that keeping plenty of distance between ship and shore is advisable.

It was no *Titanic;* but then again, it wouldn't have held much interest to archaeologists if it were. The Uluburun wreck is, for the time being, the oldest shipwreck ever discovered. While museums and libraries are filled with accounts and artifacts from the early 1900s—the time of the *Titanic*—relatively little is left to inform us about the ships that sailed the Mediterranean and the people who piloted them more than 3,000 years ago.

The ship's origins, its life, and its final chapter are mysteries that have been slowly unraveled during nearly two decades of underwater archaeology. It's time to pull on that neoprene wetsuit and dive into the past!

The Uluburun Wreck: History's Oldest

Don't be too impressed by the amount of time that archaeologists and sport divers spend underwater until you consider that Mediterranean sponge divers work on the seafloor day in and day out all year long. With this in mind, it shouldn't be too much of a surprise that such divers have been the ones to find some of the region's most stunning and historically important artifacts. It was during just such a "day at the office" when Turkish sponge diver Mehmet Cakir stumbled across an ancient ship in 1982.

Cakir had descended to 150 feet to look for sponges along a steep underwater wall descending sharply from the bank of Uluburun, a finger of land protruding into the Mediterranean from Turkey's southwest coast. The name "Uluburun," roughly translated, means "Big Nose" cape.

What Cakir saw was like nothing he had seen before—the remnants of a wrecked ship so old that most of its hull had disappeared, leaving behind much of its cargo of ceramic jars, copper oxhide ingots, and disk-shaped glass "bun" ingots. Many of these things clung to the steep submerged wall that may, in itself, have ended the sailing days of the ship.

Historical Crossroad

Cakir's report was soon investigated by divers from Turkey's Museum of Underwater Archaeology in Bodrum. Initial examinations of the site showed that the wreck was at least 3,300 years old and that the ship had originally sailed during 1200 B.C.E.

It was the oldest shipwreck ever found and promised not only to yield artifacts never before seen but also—perhaps—to answer questions about the ancient world in which it had once traveled. In its day, the ship had moved from port to port, picking up and delivering goods, until it met its end on the barren and rocky shores of Uluburun.

Because the ship sank a mere 100 yards from the shore, the crew may have been able to swim to safety following the event that sent the ship beneath the waves. However, no one knows exactly how the ship ended up dashed against the rocks of Uluburun's steep coast or what really became of its crew.

Its loss occurred a century before the legendary Trojan War and probably during the same century that the "boy king" Tutankhamun took his place upon Egypt's throne for his 10-year reign. Between 100 and 200 years after the ship sank, the extraordinary Mycaenean Greek civilization was destroyed by causes that historians still do not understand.

All the while, the wreck of Uluburun napped. Its remains had hung precariously on the steep ledge since the time when the pharaohs ruled Egypt and bronze was the leading material for the production of weapons and exquisite works of art.

Shiver Me Timbers

Much of the cargo of the wreck at Uluburun consisted of copper oxhide ingots along with a brittle material that was identified as almost pure tin. These two metals, when combined, formed bronze, one of man's first alloys. This material preceded the use of iron for weapons. Bronze was hard, highly resistant to corrosion, and considered extremely valuable. Its components of copper and tin were extremely marketable items, akin to exotic raw materials used in today's computer processing chips. As such, they were used as payment for debts or to buy favor from leaders in the Mediterranean region. The ratio of copper to tin aboard the wreck was 10 to 1, the same ratio for making bronze. For these reasons and others we know that the wreck of Uluburun occurred during what was known as the Bronze Age.

A Cargo of Clues Answers Bronze Age Questions

Some ships are huge like the *Titanic,* which was nearly three football fields long, while others are far smaller. But, when it comes to shipwrecks for archaeologists and historians, size doesn't always matter. What is important, however, is whether the wreck contains clues to the past that can answer questions about the way people lived, worked, interacted, and thought.

The wreck at Uluburun is a mere 50-feet long, and the ship could have been of the Canaanite design that was common at the time. The boat may have been manned by Phoenicians who lived along what are now the coastal regions of Syria, Lebanon, and Palestine. From studying the wreck, we know that the vessel was not a speedy, rowed galley for war, but a trading ship designed to operate under the propulsion provided by the wind in its sails.

Hard-Working Ship

This flat-bottom ship appeared to have had a spacious hold that was capable of carrying tons of goods to and from various ports. Valuable items such as bronze weapons were stored in the stern of the ship, while the larger sections of the hold contained large jars filled with aromatic resins and pottery. In the center of the hold were stone anchors, ingots of copper, and various other goods.

It is thought that this ship had a single mast and a rudder controlled by a helmsman on a slightly elevated stern (that's the poop deck to you old salts!). The ship most likely also had a wicker fence running around the perimeter of its hull to serve as a splashguard against pesky waves in rough weather. This fence may have also served a secondary purpose of keeping sailors from being tossed overboard too easily!

Piecing Together a Shipbuilding Puzzle

The wood recovered from the hull of the Uluburun wreck is the largest amount of material to be recovered from such an old wreck. At first, scientists thought it was fir, but later analysis showed that the wood was cedar. Cedar is a superior form of lumber for hull planking, since it is able to stand up to saltwater immersion far better than many other woods.

Keeping in mind that iron and steel ships were more than 3,000 years in the future when the one that sank near Uluburun was built, ancient ship builders obviously used the best materials they had available. Cedar is a strong wood that could be easily shaped with the crude, hand-powered tools of the time.

The cedar planking for the hull of this ship was assembled using a mortise and tenon construction

Words To Treasure

Before modern sawmills provided precut lumber, carpenters and shipwrights made use of **adzes,** which are long-handled tools with a highly sharpened, curved blade for shaping large pieces of wood.

method, which did not rely on nails or any other type of metal fasteners. Planks were shaped with an *adze*—a curved chisel with a handle for shaping wood—and then assembled. This same type of construction was being practiced on Greek and Roman ships a thousand years later, which just goes to show that this construction concept was well proven.

A Decade of Underwater Archaeology at Uluburun

By 1984, archaeologists with the Institute for Nautical Archaeology at Texas A&M University had cobbled together the required funding and grants for an expedition to the site. This team, along with Turkey's Bodrum museum staff, would begin 11 years of exploration, excavation, and restoration.

The leader of the effort was George Bass, who pioneered the use of established archaeological techniques under water with the excavation of a wreck off Cape Gelidonya, Turkey, in 1960. Bass was also founder of the Institute for Nautical Archaeology. Disinterested in scratching in the dirt for fragments of pottery on terrestrial digs (that's "land" digs to you biology majors), Bass was drawn to underwater archaeology because so much of what was found submerged had remained intact.

For 11 years the team led by Bass returned to Uluburun to uncover the secrets of the wreck. Such work is painstakingly slow and precise. The site must be photographed, surveyed, mapped, and then carefully recovered. Turkish law requires each object brought up in Turkish waters to remain in that country, so foreign archaeologists like Bass can take only drawings, photographs, and notes with them when they leave.

An Old Hand

Bass was no stranger to underwater archaeology's hazards and had become famous among *National Geographic* magazine readers and other underwater archaeologists. During his career, he oversaw the development of diving safety innovations and techniques to make the investigations of ancient wrecks faster and more accurate. He had also supervised the first full underwater archaeological excavation of a submerged shipwreck in 1960 at Cape Gelidonya, Turkey.

As a diver, Bass knew how tedious it was to emerge from a deepwater wreck below 130 feet and hang on a rope for as long as 40 minutes while dangerous nitrogen bubbles percolated safely out of the bloodstream. Consequently, he introduced suspended chambers to underwater archaeology so divers could relax and decompress comfortably without wearing scuba equipment.

Knowing that divers might also need an air-filled refuge while on the bottom, Bass employed a clear plastic-domed stand containing a spare oxygen tank and a telephone. Those needing an emergency supply of air, or even just a rest, could retreat to what became known as the "telephone booth."

Uplifting Innovations

Divers working underwater were able to move things that would be tremendously heavy on land thanks to their relative buoyancy, but even under these conditions divers needed a helping hand. So divers used air and balloons as assistants. Heavy-duty lift balloons with cables attached were hooked to heavy objects and then filled with air from extra scuba tanks. The balloons then rose carrying the artifacts to the surface.

Since using a cable to haul items to the surface would complicate the operation by requiring more boats and equipment, balloons could provide an incredibly simple way to lift and move great loads.

Deeply Tedious

During the 11 years that volunteers, archaeologists, and others worked on the wreck of Uluburun, 22,413 dives were necessary to map and recover the artifacts. (Many of these dives were no more than 20 minutes long because the depths involved.) The site, which tumbled down the underwater cliff for hundreds of feet, was carefully scoured by divers, but it took many trips! Often they would use their bare hands to fan away the sand to reveal fragile objects.

Simply finding something meant that even more work had begun. A month of artifact recovery translated into years of preservation work as the objects were cleaned and restored.

Words To Treasure

Dendrochronology may be easier to say than to explain. Simply saying it's the counting of the rings of a tree to determine age is far too simplistic. Climatic conditions may halt a tree's growth one year and then cause a tree to grow several rings the next. Dendrochronology also allows scientists to determine when severe weather conditions or volcanic eruptions occurred, based on a complex examination of the rings of the wood being studied. This dating technique is considered highly accurate.

After the recovery and restoration of an artifact, skilled artists were needed to draw the recovered objects, much as they have since English helmet salvager John Deane commissioned such works in the 1830s while recovering artifacts from the *Mary Rose*. A complete record of the artifacts is compiled for future study by others seeking answers to historical riddles.

How About a Date?

Buried amid the stone anchors, copper and tin ingots, and sand were very unglamorous chunks of firewood that may have provided the exact time of the ship's loss. Using the science of *dendrochronology* to study the rings of the firewood, scientists were able to estimate the year of the ship's sinking at 1316 B.C.E.

Using the firewood as a date marker is more accurate than using the intact parts of the ship, since the ship itself could have been built many years before its loss. Firewood, being a consumable, would probably not last more than a single voyage. Although other artifacts can provide ways of allowing archaeologists to guess the ship's age, this method is among the best.

Deep and Dangerous Duty

As the wooden hull of the Uluburun wreck rotted away, part of its cargo clung to the steep embankment, while other portions of it slid or fell another 30 feet down a steep underwater cliff. The divers excavating the wreck often went barefooted during the excavation for a surer foothold to make sure they didn't lose their footing and drop valuable artifacts into the deeper and darker water below.

Had a diver slipped from the steep cliff, striking something during the fall wouldn't have been as much of a problem as the increased pressure at the greater depths. Below 130 feet of depth, the pressure drives nitrogen into the diver's tissues and bloodstream; that can bubble out if the diver ascends too fast to allow the decompression of the ordinarily harmless gas. At deeper depths, nitrogen narcosis occurs. This condition makes divers feel as if they've had six margaritas too many and can fatally impair their judgment.

The High Price of Safety

Although the seemingly simple replacement of nitrogen with helium in the divers' breathing mix would have reduced some of those problems, the higher cost was too much for the expedition. As it was, Bass and his teams were already trying to make ends meet by using volunteers and getting donations from such organizations as the National Geographic Society and the National Science Foundation. Bass's lack of funds stands in stark contrast to highly publicized treasure expeditions that seem to have unlimited capital from investors lured by treasure wrecks.

Free enterprise and the public's desire for a glimpse of lost luxury liners generates enough money to allow the hire of hugely expensive deep-submergence vehicles. Although the discovery of twentieth-century ships is interesting, they can explain far less to us than much older wrecks. Unfortunately for archaeologists trying to investigate centuries-old wrecks, newer ones have been attracting much of the funding and interest during recent years.

Unraveling the Origins of the Uluburun Wreck

Archaeologists and historians originally believed that the seagoing merchants of the Mediterranean were the Mycenaean Greeks and that ships as old as the Uluburun wreck belonged to them. This theory makes sense, since the Greeks—of course—inhabited Greece and developed a powerful civilization that many others—including the seemingly all-powerful Romans—revered.

Words To Treasure

Phoenicia is the extremely old Greek word for a segment of the coastal portion of Syria and Palestine. It became a trading and manufacturing center as early as 2000 B.C.E.

Bass now believes the Uluburun wreck was manned by people who came from the greatest group of merchants and seafarers the ancient world ever saw—the Phoenicians. This loosely organized grouping of peoples inhabited the regions that today are called Syria, Lebanon, and Egypt. While they were manufacturers and business operators of the highest order, they never seemed to be able to unite to resist the pressures of larger powers.

As a result, they relied on their entrepreneurial skills to pay off any conquerors that threatened them. Since they were superb craftsmen, mariners, and businesspeople—sometimes referred to as Canaanites—the Phoenicians used checkbook diplomacy to keep things running smoothly.

Historical Treasure

While a shipwreck like the one that punched the "Big Nose" and sank thousands of years ago can be expected to produce amazing historical nuggets, gold or other highly valuable objects are generally not anticipated. Amazingly, the Uluburun wreck produced both at the same time.

A gold scarab found in the wreck, which may have been in a barrel of discarded valuable metals, was inscribed with the name of Nefertiti, the wife of Pharaoh Akhenaten who came to power in 1380 B.C.E. Although scarabs were considered important good luck charms in Egypt and were carried by many, finding a gold one is incredibly rare.

A golden scarab engraved with the name of the Egyptian queen Nefertiti found on the Uluburun wreck was in a scrap barrel destined for recycling more than 3,000 years ago.
(Copyright Institute of Nautical Archaeology)

The legendarily beautiful Nefertiti had mysteriously disappeared 12 years into her husband's reign, 50 years prior to the ship's loss. This interval would have been long enough for the magic of that scarab to wear off, making it scrap. Nevertheless, things must have been rosy at the time the gold scarab was engraved, since its inscription indicated Nefertiti was a co-ruler with her husband.

The presence of the Egyptian scarab hints that the wreck may have Egyptian origins, though nothing can be stated for certain. Other evidence, including a Canaanite sword, indicates that the ship was Phoenician. However, the discovery of a Mycenaean (Greek) sword also revealed that the crew may have been a multinational group—much like the crew found on today's merchant ships.

A Golden Cup Brimming with Mystery

The mysterious discovery of a pure gold chalice amid the wreckage of the ship astounded the archaeologists working to recover the wreck. Archaeologists are more accustomed to seeing decayed timbers, bronze objects, and clay jars coming up from the seafloor. The rich cargo of metals and the gold cup prompted Bass to remark, "This is no tramp steamer we're dealing with." No one has yet been able to trace the cup's origin, but it may have belonged to someone of high rank.

Surprisingly, a commonplace Mycenaean Greek clay cup found right next to the gold one proved of more historical value, since its shape reveals that it was probably made near the end of the reign of Pharaoh Amenhotep III, whose 38-year reign over Egypt ended in 1379 B.C.E. All in all, it's pretty interesting to tie all the loose historical ends together by using the debris from a shipwreck, but more mysteries were still to be solved by the Uluburun wreck.

Know The Ropes

An archaeologist is like a detective working with centuries-old clues like the gold chalice at the Uluburun wreck. Archaeologists can usually compare the design, construction, and materials used in an artifact with similar items whose origins have been ascertained. The mystery chalice, that bears no inscriptions or engraving, is simply a pair of cones fitted at their narrow ends with three rivets. Its gold material, while rare, provides fewer clues to its origins than would a piece of pottery made from clay. Such a valuable item is also mystifying since the presumably rough-and-tumble crew of the ship would not have been using such a delicate item as dinnerware. The case continues!

Where Were They Going?

The origins of the ship may have been Phoenician, and it may have been performing the age-old work of carrying goods to one port and returning home with goods from another. The Uluburun wreck was carrying 10 tons of Cypriot copper and was possibly heading west at the time of its loss, since Cyprus was east of where the ship went down. This account can be inferred from looking at the items recovered from the wreck.

Its cargo also suggests that the ship had made the rounds of the Mediterranean. The hold of the ship contained ostrich shells that were to be sold as containers, hippopotamus teeth, and Egyptian ebony. An advertisement for merchant seamen of the period could have accurately promised "Join the Bronze Age merchant fleet and see the ancient world!"

Words To Treasure

Terebinth is an aromatic resin produced by a variety of pistachio tree and was once heavily used in the ancient Mediterranean region to provide scents to various perfumes.

The ship was also carrying a full ton of the then-popular incense *terebinth*, which is made from the resin of a pistachio tree. (After metals, in fact, terebinth was the most plentiful commodity on the ship.) The resin, most often collected in Syria and Turkey, had many uses in perfumes and other concoctions, and its presence gives us another indication the ship was heading west at the time of its sinking. (The terebinth, despite the passage of 3,300 years, retains its sharp odor.)

A Home Run with Homer

Homer, who wrote the *Iliad* around 800 B.C.E. about the Greek heroes who fought the Trojan War 400 years before, had mentioned that the ships of his time carried brushwood onboard, and this statement has puzzled generations of historians and archaeologists. But the Uluburun wreck was soon to solve another mystery.

Bass believes the springy clumps of twigs and brush were packed into the holds of this boat, and others like it, to protect the hulls from damage by its cargo, especially the hard and heavy copper ingots. Since we're talking archaeology and ancient history here, there are, of course, people who disagree with Bass's interpretation, but it does seem that those twigs may have been the "packing peanuts" of antiquity.

Homer's descriptions of the construction of ships during the twelfth century B.C.E. (about 100 years from the time of the Uluburun wreck) also precisely matches the construction of the ship wrecked off Turkey's coast.

The discovery of the Uluburun wreck may have opened a new debate about the date traditionally set as the time that Homer composed the *Iliad* (somewhere in the eighth or ninth century B.C.E.). Most historians believe that since the Phoenicians—about whom Homer writes—began their wide-ranging seafaring in the eighth century, Homer must have lived around that time. Other scholars maintain that Homer lived during the time of the legendary Trojan War in the twelfth century B.C.E.

Small Artifacts Equal Big Discoveries

To archaeologists, the wreck at Uluburun represented a massive loss to whomever owned the ship's cargo. Its value for the age was extraordinary, and it apparently sank while fully loaded with a cargo that may have belonged to a royal family. Even with such a large and valuable cargo, however, the small items found in the wreck have been the most interesting to scientists.

The bun-shaped ingots of cobalt blue glass found on the ship are the earliest known examples of such raw materials. They originated from the Syrian-Palestinian coast, where Phoenicia existed. Ingots of this type were probably melted down and used by artisans in the production of vases and containers.

The diptych, or a writing tablet with two wooden covers connected with ivory hinges, found at the Uluburun site may be the world's oldest book. The "pages" consisted of beeswax plates that were written upon with a sharp stylus. Of course, it wasn't just lying on the ground intact, but was instead pieced together from numerous fragments of wood and ivory found in the wreck.

Shiver Me Timbers

Homer made a sole reference to a writing tablet in the *Iliad*. In Homer's words, "... he sent him to Lycia and gave him baneful signs in a folding tablet." The tablet of Uluburun was so small that it could fit in the palm of a man's hand, but it was indeed a folding tablet. However, no diptych had ever been found dating back as far as the Bronze Age about which Homer wrote. Not surprisingly, the wax had long since deteriorated.

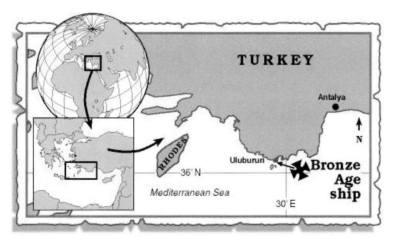

A map of the wreck site off the coast of Uluburun, Turkey.
(Drawn by Ken Ellis)

The Least You Need to Know

➤ The Bronze Age shipwreck near Uluburun ended its life as many shipwrecks have done throughout history—by most likely being smashed against the shore by a storm or due to poor seamanship.

➤ Bronze, that was usually composed of 10 percent tin and 90 percent copper, is highly resistant to corrosion, and its wide use between 3500 B.C.E. and 1000 B.C.E. gave the name "Bronze Age" to that period.

➤ The 50-foot-long Uluburun wreck is an example of how ancient ships were constructed using carpentry techniques with little or no use of metal fasteners.

➤ Divers mapping and excavating the Uluburun wreck had to dive so deep that many of their dives were limited to less than 20 minutes, necessitating 22,413 dives during the 11-year recovery project.

➤ A unique and baffling gold cup located in the wreck contains no clues to help researchers understand its origins or age, though the origin of a less-expensive cup found nearby was quickly determined.

➤ Homer's epic poem the *Iliad* provides insight into Mediterranean culture during the twelfth century B.C.E. However, there is some scholarly controversy over exactly when the blind poet lived partially due to evidence recovered in the Uluburun wreck.

Chapter 11

Rich Disaster: Wreck of the 1622 Treasure Fleet

In This Chapter

➤ Spain's 1622 Treasure Fleet

➤ Sailing toward destruction

➤ Spain attempts to salvage its fortune

➤ Mel Fisher's search for the *Atocha* and *Margarita*

➤ The *Atocha*'s deadly curse

➤ Finding the treasure

For hundreds of years, Spain shipped silver and gold plundered from the New World back across the Atlantic in convoys of ships known as the treasure fleet. If these ships—which congregated for protection from attack—ran afoul of hurricanes, they often sank collectively.

Ships that sank during this period ended up in one of two boats, so to speak. Some were quickly located and stripped of their treasure, while others were never located or, if found, were too inaccessible for recovery. When the latter sank anywhere near Florida, they became the prize targets of twentieth-century treasure hunters.

On September 5, 1622, a treasure fleet whose cargo was desperately needed by the Spanish monarchy collided with a hurricane just one day after sailing out of Havana, Cuba. Of the eight lost among that 28-ship fleet, at least three of them were treasure ships, with two sharing a total of two million pesos in silver and gold.

Of these three treasure ships, Spanish officials were able to immediately relieve one ship of its treasure, while a second, the *Santa Margarita,* was only partially salvaged. The third was located but defeated the efforts of enslaved divers to penetrate its hold and recover the treasure inside. This ship was the legendary *Atocha.*

For centuries, the name of the *Atocha* has been both battle cry and prayer for anyone wishing to strike it rich as a hunter of sunken treasure—particularly since the *Atocha's* treasure is believed to be worth several hundred million dollars today!

The destruction of the 1622 fleet was a terrible economic blow to Spain, but it was a tale that faded over time until a treasure-hunting renaissance emerged in South Florida in the 1960s.

Eventually, the 1622 disaster would become synonymous with the irrepressibly optimistic treasure hunter Mel Fisher who, like the *Atocha,* would end up in the eye of the storm, though his was a storm of both criticism and worship. The seemingly cursed treasure fleet would touch his own family with death as Fisher fought for years to unravel the secret of the *Atocha's* hiding place.

The story of the 1622 Treasure Fleet's destruction is a tale of greed, tragedy, and bittersweet triumph. So say your prayers, make sure your own treasures are stowed, and come aboard for the fatal voyage of the *Atocha* and its sister ships.

Know The Ropes

The massive amount of goods and treasure shipped by Spain from the Caribbean across the Atlantic was a tempting target for other European powers who seemed constantly at war with one another. If invading another country seemed too costly, capturing its ships was a less expensive option. Spain made itself a target for such maritime pilfering by operating a fleet of floating armored cars for several centuries. Although the capture of a treasure ship was a dream of many a captain, success was relatively rare.

Spain's 1622 Treasure Fleet

The Spain of the early seventeenth century was the premiere power of Europe, since that nation had built much of its economic and military capabilities from the economic rape of the Americas.

With the death of colonialism in the past 100 years, and the ascendancy of highly competitive industrialism, it can be hard—if not impossible—for us to imagine a nation basing its wealth on what it could plunder from weaker peoples. Still, that's just what Spain did. And the Spanish did it on a much grander scale than just about anyone else.

Spain shipped so much treasure in the 1500s that pirates and foreign navies were attempting to rob heavily armed Spanish treasure ships. And there was no shortage of targets, since the treasure ships bobbed like corks along the Gulf Stream toward the bottomless pit of Spain's inept fiscal policies.

By 1618, Europe's Thirty Years' War had begun and Spain eventually found itself drawn in as a combatant. Its monarchy desperately needed the New World treasure to foot the bill. The nation's debts were high, its currency was weak, and its needs were many. Spain demanded another delivery of New World treasure, and fast!

With everyone needing money, from Spain's monarchy to the merchants who had sold goods in the New World and awaited their silver, the heat was on to turn the ships around and get them back to Spain as soon as possible. But would they make it in time?

Deadly Delays

And so it began. The Tierra Firme Fleet, which delivered goods and picked up slave-mined silver and gold at South American ports, was late. It had been delayed in Spain and arrived in the New World island of Dominica in May 1622, putting it weeks behind schedule. This fleet would be known as the 1622 Treasure Fleet—so named after the year it sailed—and its primary purpose was to return to Spain with all the riches it could carry.

Defending the rear of this treasure fleet was *Nuestra Senora de Atocha,* a 20-gun guard ship. Owing to the *Atocha's* placement in the column of ships, it was referred to as the *Almiranta,* while the ship leading the convoy, *Nuestra Senora de La Candelariá* was the *Capitana.*

Shiver Me Timbers

The *Atocha* started its maritime career in a halting fashion. Built in Havana as a 500-ton guard galleon, the *Atocha* was 110 feet long and considered among the most powerful warships of the day. However, shipbuilder Captain Alonso Ferrera was unable to finish the *Atocha* on time, finally delivering the vessel a year behind schedule on August 16, 1620. On its first voyage to Spain, the main mast proved faulty and was replaced. After arriving safely in Spain in late 1620, the ship then sprang serious leaks in its bow, forcing the ship into port for lengthy repairs. By early 1622, the *Atocha* was ready to become the *Almiranta,* or the guard ship, at the rear of the 1622 Treasure Fleet when it sailed for the New World.

The Tierra Firme Fleet sailed first to Cartagena and then on to Portobello on May 24. Here the ship would encounter yet another delay when it was learned that the expected treasure had not yet arrived at Portobello from Panama City, 50 miles distant. The *Atocha* would have to sit at anchor for more than a month.

Don Lope Diaz de Armendariz, Marquis de Cadereita (you can take a breath now), was the commander of the Guard Fleet. He arrived in Portobello with his warships and was hopping mad when he learned that the treasure hadn't yet arrived from Panama City. He angrily ordered the Spanish president of Panama to get cracking, get the treasure, and get it to Portobello. The Marquis knew that hurricane season was approaching and that any more delays could mean destruction of the fleet.

Nonetheless, it wasn't until July 22, 1622, that the *Atocha* hauled up its anchor after a stop in Panama to pick up 12 tons of tobacco and more treasure at still another port. And it wasn't until August 22, 1622, that the Tierra Firme Fleet and the Guard Fleet made it to Havana, where the ships would be provisioned and prepared for the return to Spain. More gold and silver was crammed into the *Atocha*'s hold. A surviving manifest shows that the ship was carrying treasure worth one million pesos, including silver, gold, and tons of other goods.

Although estimates vary widely and wildly, the cumulative treasure of the *Atocha* and *Margarita,* including gold, silver, and gems, has been placed at between $200 million and $400 million.

An old drawing depicts the Spanish treasure ship Nuestra Senora de Atocha *as it would have appeared around the time of its loss in a hurricane in 1622.*
(Courtesy of the Mariner's Museum)

Hurricane Alley

As last-minute preparations were made to load cargo and prepare the 28 ships of the treasure fleet for its return, Spanish officials found themselves standing in the dead center of the hurricane season. The Marquis de Cadereita remained worried about the weather and called a meeting to discuss the wisdom of leaving Cuba during hurricane season.

Though neither the Spaniards nor anyone else at the time understood the nature of the storms, these dangerous weather patterns initially formed off the West Coast of Africa and moved westward across the Atlantic. As they neared the Americas, they became powerful storms and invariably headed straight for the heart of the Caribbean. The one that would smash into the 1622 Treasure Fleet was being born even as Cadereita held his meeting in Havana.

Weather or Not to Sail

Cadereita's discussion soon became an argument as officials 3,000 miles from Spain weighed the risk of colliding with a hurricane against the order to deliver the badly needed treasure without delay. Their alternative was to wait a month or two until the hurricane season slipped away.

Shiver Me Timbers

If you can conceive of the government of the U.S. making a profit off every foreign business venture executed by businesspeople, you'll have an idea of the racket developed by the Spanish monarchy. Spain's spendthrift royalty took a piece of every transaction in the New World by restricting all trade with its colonies to an agency controlled by the monarchy. It also taxed all the silver and gold mined in the Americas, while holding a monopoly on tobacco imports to Europe. Spain had allowed itself to become dependent on treasure and restrictive trade policies and found itself desperate for the arrival of the treasure. With the monarchy's hand in everyone's pocket, it's little wonder that ordinary Spaniards returning from the New World became premiere smugglers of gold and silver to avoid the royal tax bite.

Spain, with out-turned pockets, waited anxiously for the gold. Merchants wanted to be paid, creditors needed their money, and the Spanish monarchy wanted to continue the expensive pomp and ceremony for which it was famous.

Money talked loudly during this period of Spain's financial crisis, and the decision was to sail. (Is anyone surprised?)

Hurry Up and Wait

The rather silly notion that the alignment of the planets and moon had a profound effect on the earth's weather may have been the final straw for the waiting fleet. The Guard Fleet's chief pilot, Lorenzo Vernal, recommended waiting another week because the current alignment of the earth, moon, and sun would cause terrible weather disruptions in the meantime.

The Marquis de Cadereita agreed to wait, and another week went by before the order was given to sail. The fleet was now due to leave Havana on September 4, 1622.

Know The Ropes

Before many of the world's mysteries were unraveled, sailors had to rely on a lot of superstition to help them find their way around the seas. Even as late as the eighteenth century, mariners were still carrying frogs as navigational devices. (It was believed by some that a frog placed on the deck would hop toward land!) Magnetic compasses didn't come into use until Mediterranean mariners began carrying them in the twelfth century.

Know The Ropes

To **tack** is to turn a sailing ship.

When a deck is **awash**, it's not in the process of being cleaned, but is either riding so low in the water or being struck by seas so rough that seawater washes across its main deck.

Sailing Toward Destruction

A month and a half behind schedule, the 28 ships of the treasure fleet unfurled their flags and glided out of Havana harbor. The *Atocha*, being the *Almiranta*, fell in at the rear of the convoy. The route called for the ships to head north first, rather than directly east toward Spain. They needed the powerful nudge of the Gulf Stream to propel them back to Spain, and the best place to hop aboard this invisible ship-mover was near the Florida Keys that trailed from the southern tip of Florida's peninsula.

Rough Weather

As dusk settled over the ships, they were roughly 30 miles northeast of Havana. It was then that the command was given for the ships to *tack* to the north. Looking to the southeast, the sailors saw a wall of thick clouds rising from the horizon far into the sky.

The ships sailed throughout the night, and the next morning found themselves facing a wind blowing against the direction of the Gulf Stream. The wind created strong wave conditions that made sailing a rough experience, to say the least. At worst, large waves piled up by the wind could swamp or shatter ships.

By the morning of September 5, 1622, sailors aboard the *Atocha* and other ships were struggling to reduce the amount of sailcloth catching the wind. The daylight shriveled to near-darkness as the skies became completely overcast. Powerful winds began to batter the fleet, and sailors secured every opening on their ships.

Ten-foot waves put the deck of the *Atocha awash* as she fought the waves piled up by the wind that was running head-on into the easterly pushing waters of the Gulf Stream.

Time to Pray

Aboard the *Santa Margarita,* heavy with her one million pesos of treasure, conditions had become so bad that the priests began hearing the confessions of the terrified crew. Meanwhile, in the crowded decks below, passengers were sobbing and shrieking as they were thrown about. Both the *Atocha* and the *Margarita* were loaded not only with cargo but also with passengers returning to Spain.

The *Margarita*'s captain, Bernardino de Lugo, went into the ship's dark lower decks where the people were huddled and wailing. He called for quiet and told them a priest would soon be there to hear their confessions. One priest, in the middle of praying and hearing confessions, fell over dead from an apparent heart attack, cheating the roiling sea out of claiming him as a victim.

Similar scenes were repeated on the *Atocha,* where Spanish Catholics knelt before a small statue of the namesake of the *Atocha,* Our Lady of Atocha, one of Spain's most revered sites, where the Virgin Mary is said to have appeared.

Shoved into the Shallows

The silvermaster of the Margarita, Gutierre de Espinosa, decided that things had gotten out of hand and prepared for the worst. With the help of an assistant, he took part of his own personal silver treasure and placed it in a sea chest that he secured with ropes.

The wind, which had been blowing from the north, now began to blow from the southeast. This wind struck the rear of the fleet, driving the helpless ships toward the reefs of the Dry Tortugas and the Marquesas Keys, islands at the southwestern tip of the Florida Keys. Grounding now became the threat to the *Atocha;* the *Margarita;* a third treasure ship, the galleon *Rosario;* and five other ships. The remaining 20 ships of the fleet had already cleared the shoals and were sailing into open water and safety.

By the morning light of September 6, 1622, those aboard the ships saw 15-foot waves pounding their craft. The wave action was so powerful that the troughs revealed the sharp and unyielding coral reef below.

Hopeless Fight

The sailors knew it was only a matter of time before they were thrown against a reef in shallow waters, so orders were given for the ships to begin dropping their anchors in hopes of holding the boat still in the wild seas.

The anchors fell to the bottom, snagged a hold, and then either snapped against the heavy wave action or were simply pulled along if they failed to obtain a purchase on the seabed. The *Rosario* ran aground and was battered by the waves, as were some of the other small boats. Roughly 50 miles east of these ships, the rudderless *Margarita* and the *Atocha* were heaved by huge waves toward shallow water.

Don't Go Overboard!

Life at sea during the seventeenth century was rough, but bad weather had the potential to make it deadly. Atlantic hurricanes killed thousands aboard Spanish treasure fleet ships through the centuries. Sailors kept an eye on weather conditions to determine if they should delay sailing or change course to avoid a "blow" (that's storm to you landlubbers). However, weather forecasting was usually based upon what you could see, and there was seldom any advance warning of stormy weather.

The *Atocha* found itself lifted by a massive wave, and as the ship headed down into the wave's trough, its bow slammed into a reef exposed by the waves. The collision smashed a hole in the bow, and the *Atocha* rapidly sank, leaving only its mast above the water. There was a wild scramble to get out of the holds, but for nearly everyone aboard, it was too late.

To this very mast clung five survivors of the wreck—three seamen and two black slaves. The ship's 48 passengers, an infantry company with its 13-year-old flag bearer, and the rest of its crew, were drowned. By the time the *Atocha* had settled in 55 feet of water, 260 people had died. The *Margarita* was wrecked in shallower waters, and 68 of those aboard survived. In all, 550 people died in the wrecks near the Dry Tortugas.

As ships sailed in to look for survivors, a crewman aboard the frigate *Santa Catalina* spied something floating in the water. When the ship got closer, the sailors saw that that the floating object was a sea chest. Opening it, they found the clothing and treasure of the *Margarita*'s drowned silvermaster, Gutierre de Espinosa.

Spain Attempts to Salvage Its Fortune

As other ships sailed in to rescue the survivors of the disaster, the remainder of the treasure fleet made its way back to Havana, where a somber conference was held at the behest of the Marquis de Cadereita. Once again the question was debated: to sail or not to sail? Some argued for an immediate return to Spain to deliver what was left of the treasure, though two million pesos from various ships now lay on the seafloor. Both the Marquis and Gaspar de Vargas, a navigator with 15 voyages to the New World, argued for the fleet's immediate return to Spain.

Other pilots insisted that the rough seas had damaged the ships and that repairs were necessary. To cross the Atlantic in wounded ships would invite even more trouble, they warned. When Juan de Lara Moran, the commander of the Tierra Firme fleet, spoke, he sided with the pilots.

Saving What's Left

Moran believed a salvage effort had to be mounted to recover the sunken treasure before Spain's numerous enemies (which included much of Europe) were able to locate the wrecks and steal the Spanish treasure. Case closed. Moran's logic was inescapable to the officials who had already lost tons of treasure to poor decisions and delay. Vargas was ordered to command an expedition and head for the wreck sites to recover the treasure.

The Official Treasure Hunt

Real estate people know that location is important, but if you're looking for a sunken ship, knowing the precise location is absolutely necessary or failure will be your only reward. Fortunately, Bartolome Lopez, captain of the *Santa Catalina* that had recovered the *Margarita*'s silvermaster's trunk, arrived with information as to the *Atocha*'s location.

Vargas, a tough man of action, was already on his way to the wreck site by September 16, 1622, when Lopez's information arrived. Lopez was then sent to catch up with Vargas at sea to guide him to the *Atocha*. Once there, Vargas sent divers down to the wreck, where they were unsuccessful in breaking open the closed hatches of the ship.

Vargas was unable to locate the *Margarita*, but he found the *Rosario's* survivors on Loggerhead Key and rescued them. Continuing on, he then located their ship with its decks protruding from the water. He burned the ship to expose its cargo below and recovered virtually everything in its hold, including the silver and gold.

Shiver Me Timbers

The *Rosario's* sailors and passengers were lucky because their ship managed to make its way over the reef and into the shallow waters of Loggerhead Key relatively intact when it grounded. Because the ship settled with its decks above water, those aboard were not thrown into the churning surf to drown and were eventually able to make it to shore.

Another Storm

As fate would have it, on October 5 a storm that was more destructive than the first struck the salvage fleet, forcing Vargas and his band to anchor their ships and seek refuge on Loggerhead Key. As survivors and sailors weathered the storm, violent seas tore the *Atocha* apart, scattering its wreckage across a wide area of the seafloor. The *Atocha* and its massive fortune were now fully lost and would remain so for nearly 400 years.

Vargas continued to search for the again-lost *Atocha* through January 1623, but the wreck now eluded him despite the use of grapnel anchors dragged along the bottom. Bad weather forced a halt in the operations, but Vargas returned in February.

A National Emergency

With the loss of the *Atocha* and the *Margarita*, and with the word out that other treasure ships had also sunk, the Spanish monarchy faced an economic crisis. Vargas was given anything he needed to recover the treasure. Even the Marquis de Cadereita came to inspect the operation in the Florida Keys.

On August 6, 1623, Vargas said he believed the treasure of the *Atocha* and the *Margarita* was irretrievably lost, buried by sand that had sifted over their remains. After nearly a year of work and the expenditure of 100,000 pesos, Spanish officials admitted failure.

Shiver Me Timbers

The visit by the Marquis de Cadereita set into motion a seemingly minor chain of events that would have a drastic effect on future treasure hunters seeking the *Atocha*. The islands around which they were working were renamed Cayos del Marques, or "the Keys of the Marquis," in honor of his visit. This nomenclature would confuse those searching for the treasure in the twentieth century, since many were looking for the treasure based on the original names of the islands. Historian and Spanish shipwreck researcher Eugene Lyon unraveled this mystery and pointed the way to the initial discovery of *Atocha* artifacts in 1973 and the discovery of the bulk of the ship's treasure in 1985.

One More Try

Francisco Nunez Melian was a salvage master and entrepreneur who obtained a contract in 1624 to salvage the *Margarita* and *Atocha* wrecks. A resident of Havana, Melian used his numerous political connections to obtain the agreement, and his would be the first private venture to seek the 1622 treasure.

After four years of searching, Melian's slave Juan Banon burst to the water's surface and announced he'd found something. Holding a sizable stone to pull him to the bottom once again, Banon sucked in his breath and plunged downward. When he resurfaced, he was cradling a silver ingot that looked like a blackened loaf of bread.

For his part in the drama, Banon received his freedom, something that Melian had promised to the first diver who discovered the *Margarita*'s treasure. Melian eventually recovered more than 300 silver ingots from the wreck but was later accused of stealing the treasure. He was tried and acquitted of this charge and unsuccessfully sought the *Atocha*'s treasure in 1643. Melian died in 1644.

Mel Fisher's Search for the *Atocha* and *Margarita*

For the next 300 years, the *Atocha*'s shattered remains hid from a world that had largely forgotten her tragic story and her amazing treasure. But a winding road would lead a former California chicken farmer who was also an American scuba diving pioneer to renew the search for the *Atocha* that had thwarted Melian.

Near the end of the 1940s, Fisher became fascinated by sunken treasure after taking up the sport of skin diving near Tampa, Florida. In 1950 he moved to Torrance, California, to start a chicken ranch with his father but eventually started one of the world's first scuba equipment shops.

By 1963 Fisher had moved to Florida to take part in the Real 8 treasure partnership headed by pioneer treasure hunter Kip Wagner. Wagner had recovered some of the treasure from the wrecked 1715 Treasure Fleet off Florida's Vero Beach. Fisher successfully recovered even more treasure from the 1715 wreck sites, but eventually turned his attention to the *Atocha* and *Margarita* wrecks.

The Key to the Keys

By 1969, Fisher had established a friendship with history doctoral candidate Eugene Lyon, who was leaving for Spain for a year's study at the Archives of the Indies in Seville. While there, Lyon discovered a sheaf of records titled "Accounts of Francisco Nunez Melian," the Spanish salvor who recovered some of the *Margarita*'s treasure and who failed to find that of the *Atocha*.

Lyon realized that the *Margarita* had been salvaged near an island bearing two different names, depending on the ages of the maps he was studying. The same island bore the names Keys of the Matecumbe and Marquesas Keys. Lyon deduced that the islands had been renamed after the Marquis de Cadereita visited the salvage operation nearly 350 years earlier.

Payday

Fisher now began to search the general area of the Marquesas Keys, as the islands were named on the map. Using a *magnetometer,* Fisher and his team searched the east side of the islands until, in 1971, Lyon found another letter indicating the *Atocha* and the *Margarita* were to the west of the Marquesas Keys. The search then moved to that side of the island.

By July 1973, Fisher's 14-year-old son Kane Fisher and another diver, Mike Schneidelbach, had found three gold bars in a hole dug by a "mailbox" mounted at the rear of their search boat (remember the mailbox from Chapter 8, "Inches from Millions"?). On July 9, 1973, Lyon matched the numbers on one of the bars to the *Atocha*'s treasure manifest. It had been loaded at Cartagena months before the *Atocha*'s demise.

Words To Treasure

A **magnetometer** is essentially the same device as a magnetic anomaly detector. Both are used to sense the deviations in the earth's magnetic field caused by the iron or steel contained in sunken ships.

The Margarita

Although much of the *Margarita*'s treasure had been heavily salvaged, Fisher hired a crew to search for the ship as the hunt for the *Atocha* continued. By April 1980, gold bars were being discovered, and by the fall of 1981 divers had recovered 118 pounds of gold bullion, 180 feet of gold chains, and 56 gold coins known as doubloons. Along with the treasure, Fisher's divers also located a 23-foot section of the *Margarita*'s hull, cannon, and dozens of other artifacts.

Shiver Me Timbers

Although it's easy to jump to the incorrect conclusion that treasure ships were mostly filled with gold, the truth is that silver comprised the bulk of Spanish treasure. **Doubloons,** which were gold coins, were far rarer than the silver **real** coin carried by Spanish treasure ships, though more often mentioned in movies and fiction. Although many don't immediately recognize the term "real," most of us have heard of "doubloons," despite their relative scarcity.

The *Atocha's* Deadly Curse

Although 260 perished aboard the *Atocha* on September 6, 1622, the treasure-filled wreck was not through dealing out misery. In 1973, Nicki Littlehales, the 12-year-old son of *National Geographic* photographer Bates Littlehales, died when he was sucked into the prop-powered silt blowers at the back of one of Mel Fisher's boats during search operations.

This terrible event would not be the last tragedy to strike Fisher's search team. Another deadly accident would befall his group, known as Treasure Salvors, Inc., at the moment of their victory. After nearly five years of searching for the *Atocha's* cannon—which would indicate where the bulk of the ship's treasure might be—they had finally achieved success. As in the case of *El Cazador* being snagged by the nets of the fishing boat *"Mistake,"* the event occurred more by accident than by skill. However, that success was not without a price.

Brief Happiness

On July 13, 1975, Mel Fisher's son Dirk Fisher dove to check the anchors of the search boat *Northwind* and nearly bumped into a pile of cannon. An organized search was conducted, and two piles of bronze cannon were located and recovered. Locating the cannon was a major breakthrough for the team. Eventually, nine of the bronze guns were brought to the surface.

Although tracking down the remainder of the *Atocha's* treasure would take another decade, Fisher and his divers were ecstatic, believing that success was at hand.

Tragedy Strikes

At 5:30 A.M. on July 19, 1975, some aboard Fisher's river tug the *Northwind* realized it was listing and discovered that a leaking toilet valve was shipping water into the tug and causing a dangerous tilt. As those aboard worked to correct the leak, they realized that a faulty fuel valve had failed to redistribute fuel in the *Northwind*'s tanks, adding to the imbalance. With little warning, the tug capsized. Of the 11 aboard, three died—including Fisher's son Dirk Fisher; Dirk's wife, Angel; and fellow diver Rick Gage.

Shiver Me Timbers

The *Northwind* was a river tug that was long past its best days. It was one of the primary search vessels fitted with the mailbox blowers at the rear to clear silt from the bottom. Cramped, dirty, and rusty, the *Northwind* housed 10 search team members at the time it sank, as well as *National Geographic* photographer Don Kincaid (who had discovered an eight-foot-long gold chain as a treasure diver for Fisher four years before). One aboard was Donny Jonas, who was trapped inside the capsized tug. In pitch darkness, he yelled in vain for help until a floating flashlight miraculously bumped into him. With the light, Jonas was able to find his way out of the water-filled tug to safety. Fisher sold the tug to salvors while it was still submerged and never again used his other river tug, named the *Southwind*.

Finding the Treasure

A decade after his son's death, Mel Fisher and his Treasure Salvors team were still zigzagging west of the Marquesas Keys searching for "hits" on their iron-sensing magnetometer. On July 19, 1985, the magnetometer revealed the presence of iron below. A diver's reconnaissance confirmed the presence of a small swivel gun.

More divers descended to discover a trail of *ballast stones* that led to the huge pile of *ballast* that marked the final resting place of the *Atocha*. The ship had carried 20 tons of *ballast* stones to counterbalance the weight of her superstructure and masts. Now that the worms had eaten the wood, only stones and treasure were left.

Words To Treasure

Ballast is the weight placed in the lowest part of a ship to provide stability. **Ballast stones** were once the preferred method of providing this extra weight.

Fisher had triumphed after a 16-year search. He had spent hundreds of thousands of dollars, lost his son and daughter-in-law in an accident, and found an estimated $400 million in silver and gold.

A map of the wreck site of the Atocha.
(Drawn by Ken Ellis)

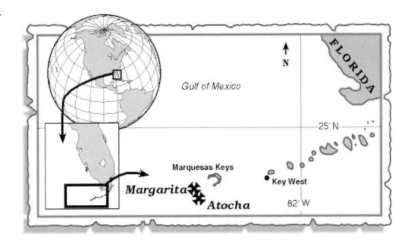

The Least You Need to Know

➤ Delays caused the 1622 Treasure Fleet to sail during the height of the hurricane season, sealing the fate of eight ships that were sunk and killing 550.

➤ The *Atocha,* built in Cuba but delivered a year behind schedule, was plagued with problems, including a faulty mast and a leaking hull.

➤ Most of the passengers aboard the *Atocha* and the *Margarita* were huddled below the decks of their respective ships when they sank.

➤ Of the 28 ships in the 1622 Treasure Fleet, 20 made it to safety while the remaining eight sank around the Florida Keys.

➤ When the surviving ships of the treasure fleet limped back to Havana, a heated argument erupted over whether the fleet should immediately sail to Spain.

➤ The sinking of Mel Fisher's search ship *Northwind* killed Mel Fisher's son Dirk Fisher; Dirk's wife, Angel Fisher; and diver Rick Gage.

Chapter 12

The *Belle* of the Bay

One of the most prolific (and eccentric) European explorers to explore the New World was Robert Cavelier, Sieur de La Salle, who began his amazing expeditions 170 years after the Italian navigator Christopher Columbus made his way to the Caribbean.

Although famous for claiming vast stretches of the North American continent for France, the deadly unraveling of his accidental expedition in Texas was his most tragic exploration. The reason La Salle concerns us here is that his ill-fated search for the mouth of the Mississippi left one of the most interesting shipwrecks ever recovered—as well as another that is still being sought.

Besides, when it comes right down to it, the story behind the shipwreck is a good yarn. La Salle's maritime expedition to the Gulf of Mexico in 1684 ended with an Indian massacre of settlers and his own murder by mutineers. Among other things, the reason for these disasters can be traced to the loss of two ships supporting the expedition—*La Belle* and *Amiable*.

If you wanted to explore the New World 300 years ago, you needed at least three things: two really good ships and a third for a spare. When La Salle's expedition lost its last ship, *La Belle,* the group found itself marooned. The explorers not only lacked supplies but also had no way to get word back to civilization when things got bad. Which they did, very quickly.

La Salle's personality wasn't a big help either. Paranoid, hot-tempered, autocratic, remote, gloomy, and prone to long depressive spells, the explorer would snap out of his emotional doldrums and launch an impressive string of discoveries.

So far, only *La Belle* has been located and recovered. This wreck is particularly unusual in that it's the oldest French colonial wreck recovered in America, and it still retains 20 percent of its original hull timbers. It has yielded an astonishing amount of information, including the skull and partially preserved brain of a French crewman who died when the ship was lost.

When the wreck was found, Texas decided not to leave it in the muck and murk of Matagorda Bay for yet another 300 years and recovered the ship in a unique operation. Archaeologists are now reconstructing a frightening picture of what actually happened to the ship and its explorers.

So grab your snuffbox and load your flintlock pistols! We're going in for a close look at a seventeenth-century French exploration tragedy.

La Salle Did It All

To understand the significance of the wreck of *La Belle,* we're going to have to understand the complex, slightly odd, and unyieldingly rigid man who was Robert Cavelier, Sieur de La Salle. Born in Rouen, France, on November 21, 1643, La Salle was educated by Catholic Jesuit priests and was a priest himself until a desire to explore outstripped his patience for religious bureaucracy.

La Salle raised eyebrows among his highly disciplined Jesuit superiors by boldly telling them he wanted to be sent to China. Instead, the would-be wanderer was ordered to study theology. Undaunted, La Salle wasted no time in resigning his clerical duties.

An Explorer Is Born

To call La Salle restless might be a bit of an understatement. He dreamed of travel and read the popular accounts of Jesuit priests preaching to the Indians of Canada, an enterprise loaded with obvious hazards. These accounts, combined with La Salle's innate urge to travel, prompted him to move to Canada, where he began to farm, which was about the only way to make a franc in the wilds of North America. But La Salle's foray into agriculture gave him time to become a premiere woodsman.

In no time at all, La Salle had become a *coureur de bois,* French for "wood runner," which was used to describe a European who learned how to navigate the forests and survive the Canadian wilderness. He established four forts and opened up large areas to trade with the Indians for their highly desired furs that were prized in Europe.

Mississippi Mandarin?

La Salle originally thought that the Mississippi River would take him to the Pacific Ocean, but he soon realized that the river ran instead to the Gulf of Mexico.

After a series of expeditions that carried him by boat across the Great Lakes from 1671 to 1681, La Salle eventually traveled down the Mississippi River to Louisiana but was unable to determine precisely where the Mississippi entered the Gulf of Mexico. Once there, however, he claimed that massive Midwestern American watershed for France. Not a bad day's work!

Shiver Me Timbers

The Spanish, for all their familiarity with the Caribbean and the Gulf of Mexico, were remarkably ignorant of the river of opportunity the Mississippi represented. It was a waterway that ran all the way north to what is now the border between Minnesota and Canada. The Spaniards, despite their maritime skills and eagerness to conquer new lands, seemed mostly interested in silver and gold. Acquiring vast new territories for farming and logging held little interest for the nation that "discovered" the New World. The French, on the other hand, had made their fortunes fishing, farming, and trapping and were more interested in claiming new lands.

La Salle then decided it was time to get out on the deepwater and have a look at America from the south, which he considered the best way to map the coastline and pinpoint the Mississippi from the Gulf of Mexico. La Salle wanted to gain support from the French King, Louis XIV, for this expedition.

Royal Support

Louis XIV was famous for not granting many people an audience, but he was so infected with enthusiasm for exploring America that he did agree to see La Salle. The explorer pleaded his case for establishing a base on the Gulf of Mexico at the mouth of the Mississippi. He salted his pitch with how such a fort could thwart Spanish efforts in the area.

Louis XIV bought into the idea, although La Salle cooled his heels for a long while before hearing he had been granted the backing of the king. The explorer was granted four ships, 100 soldiers, and nearly 200 colonists. His exploration force would contain a total of 320 people. As some suspected at the time, the whole mission was poorly thought out because the difficulty of spotting the Mississippi along Louisiana's marshy and confusing coastline was not foreseen.

Moody Leader and a Motley Crew

Despite his zeal and success at exploration, La Salle was no leader of men. Though he was brilliant and fair when dealing with Native American peoples, he turned off just about everyone else. And if he wasn't simply making people uncomfortable, he was openly despised. Henri Joutel, an old acquaintance of La Salle's, wrote, "When Monsieur de La Salle is among us, joy is often banished." Joutel would be a loyal follower of La Salle during the explorer's ill-fated expedition.

Many of those who served under him hated his silly, overly proper behavior. (He once refused to allow a marriage in the wilds of Texas between two French colonists because they were of unequal social rank.) His aloofness didn't play well on the frontier, where tempers ran hot and disputes were often settled with violence.

Making things even worse for the brooding explorer was the caliber of his soldiers. Minister Jean-Baptiste Seignelay commented that they were "no more than children and men of little use." Seasoned and disciplined professional soldiers might endure a thorny, remote leader, but the combination of amateur soldiers and unfit leadership was a sure recipe for disaster. As we'll see, his sailors weren't much better.

Assembling the Fleet

La Salle's fleet was nothing like the impressive array of ships that the Spanish sailed during the heyday of their treasure fleet operations. Expeditions were expensive, and explorers—like Columbus and La Salle—took whatever they could get.

La Salle's "fleet" included:

➤ *Joly:* A 36-gun warship

➤ *La Belle:* A small, six-gun *frigate*

➤ *Amiable:* A 300-ton store ship

➤ *St. Francoise:* A 30-ton *ketch* (which would carry food only as far as Santo Domingo)

Words To Treasure

A **ketch** is a relatively small sailing vessel with a main mast at the front and a smaller one at the rear. A **frigate** is a fast, small warship that is a step down from the larger "ship of the line," which is what the *Joly* was with its heavier armament.

The fleet, its settlers, and its half-baked sailors and soldiers left France to find the Mississippi by way of the Gulf of Mexico on July 24, 1664. However, the trip began only after a long series of petty arguments—started by La Salle, of course—with the small flotilla's naval commander, Captain de Beaujeu.

La Salle wanted to know where and what his officers would be eating during the voyage. Beaujeu, a professional sailor, told La Salle he could care less and later wrote, "Almost everyone believes he is unbalanced."

La Salle Was No Columbus

La Salle was given command over the route they would take while looking for the river, while de Beaujeu was given command of the Atlantic crossing. Since they could never agree, they eventually quit talking altogether.

Soon after the flotilla reached the Caribbean, pirates seized the *St. Francoise* with its crucial provisions, and many of those aboard the remaining ships became ill. Provisions were in short supply until the boats arrived in Santo Domingo, where whatever was for sale was outlandishly expensive.

With both of the expedition's leaders—La Salle and Beaujeu—not talking and supplies in short supply, things were really looking good for this expedition!

River! What River?

During his pitch to Louis XIV, La Salle admitted that it might be tough to find the mouth of the Mississippi, since it was camouflaged by southern Louisiana's famous coastal marshlands. Truer words were never spoken.

After finally leaving Santo Domingo, the small convoy headed west, sailing as close to the shore as possible while looking in vain for the Mississippi River's mouth. The flat land and dense coastal underbrush camouflaged the massive river's mouth that pours into the Gulf of Mexico through five fingers at the end of the Mississippi Delta.

Goodbye Mississippi; Hello Cannibals

Heading west along Louisiana's southern coast, La Salle apparently decided to turn southward and follow the Texas coastline for several hundred miles—without realizing how completely lost he was. Eventually, La Salle realized his error and landed along what is now the coast of south Texas. Little did he realize that the Indians of Texas had not yet been subdued by Spanish conquistadors, unlike the tribes enslaved by the Spaniards in Mexico.

Shiver Me Timbers

The Karankawa Indians of Texas were composed of five tribes of extremely tough and fearsome people who lived both along the shore and inland and eventually became known for their courage and brutality in the face of European encroachment. The level of cannibalism said to be practiced by the Karankawas is disputed and may have only been symbolic, but the tattooed, seven-foot tall Indians were frightful and fearless. Their unwillingness to accept European and American settlers resulted in their being exterminated by the mid-1800s.

Among the numerous Indian groups in Texas, one of the toughest was the tall, coastal-dwelling Karankawas. It's believed that they practiced ritual cannibalism on the bodies of their slain or captured enemies.

Texas Wrecks

Having gone 400 miles past the Mississippi River, La Salle and his group now faced the flat, sandy coastline of Texas. By January 17, 1685, water supplies were running low and La Salle decided to risk a landing in Matagorda Bay, Texas (80 miles north of what is now Corpus Christi). Henri Joutel, La Salle's loyal friend and the captain of one of his sailing vessels, managed to bring the *Joly* safely ashore.

La Salle, following in another boat, decided that the *Amiable* and *La Belle* should also enter the bay, even though it was sheltered by a barrier island and jaggedly sharp shoals of oyster shells.

Alcohol and Water Don't Mix

A man known only as Captain Aigron was in command of the *Amiable,* and his odd demeanor was blamed on the alcohol he was known to consume in large quantities. He refused to allow the pilot to guide his entry into the bay and began to sail the ship into the anchorage.

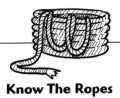

Know The Ropes

Traveling by ship to an unexplored region of the world presents a nearly insurmountable problem when it comes time to pull over and go ashore. Ships need to get close to shore without getting into water that is too shallow. They must pick their way carefully through an unfamiliar coastline to find a place to drop anchor without getting stranded on a sandbar or completely wrecking the boat.

La Salle was pensively watching this drama when he heard shouts and realized that his band was being attacked by Indians—who had in fact had already captured some of his men. La Salle charged the Indians, halted the attack, and demanded to go to their village. Unfortunately, a shot rang out. While it managed to frighten the attacking Indians, it also signaled the worst possible news to La Salle—the *Amiable* was sinking.

A drunken Captain Aigron had run the *Amiable* aground, which tore open the ship's hull and allowed 12 months' worth of supplies to spill into the bay. Although the axes and wine were saved, the bulk of the supplies was lost.

La Salle and his companions immediately built a fort along the mouth of a river, using materials salvaged from the *Amiable.* Christened Fort St. Louis, it would be their unhealthy haven as many died of disease, snakebites, and bad water. Nevertheless, the sight of the still-afloat *La Belle* reassured them that at least someone could go for help if it were needed.

Bye-Bye, La Belle

By mid-March, Beaujeu reasoned that it was time for him to return to France with the warship *Joly* and offered to take anyone unwilling to remain at the settlement. He left with those not willing to enjoy the wilds of Texas, leaving only 180 people behind.

The final tragedy struck in January 1686 when *La Belle* ran aground and sank while under the command of its skipper, who had been out searching for fresh water. La Salle was told the skipper of *La Belle* had been drunk at the time of the sinking. Some conflicting reports have *La Belle* sinking because of a storm, although Texas's vicious hurricane season ends in October and doesn't start again until June.

Murder and Mayhem

The settlers had by now developed a deep hatred of La Salle. He had been exploring for 11 months after their arrival in their coastal hellhole, and their last ship was gone, but all he seemed to care about was more exploration.

Shiver Me Timbers

Although the loss of *La Belle* has been blamed on either a drunken boat captain or on a strong wind that blew it onto hull-splitting oyster shell shoals, the incident did occur in January, months before the June start of the hurricane season. Even though winter storms known as "Blue Northers" or "Texas Northers" pack potent winds through southeast Texas and could have been the kind of storm that sunk *La Belle,* the strongest Texas Norther generally has only half the velocity of a hurricane.

Unfazed, La Salle took a select group of men and headed northward to look for the Mississippi River. While La Salle was away, a pair of mutinous expedition members went on a killing spree near what is now Navasota, Texas, murdering two of their companions.

When La Salle arrived to investigate on March 19, 1687, he, too, was murdered. In early May 1687, the two mutineers were also shot in a showdown with other members of the band. The survivors of the group trudged on to the Arkansas River, where two Frenchmen had built a house to await La Salle's arrival.

Massacre

Made curious by the wrecks of the *Amiable* and *La Belle,* Spanish soldiers arrived at Fort St. Louis on April 22, 1689, to find the half-eaten bodies of the French settlers in their wrecked encampment, the obvious victims of a Karankawa attack. However, details of this tragedy are sketchy. Only 12 people are known to have survived the expedition.

Looking for *La Belle*

Barto Arnold, an archaeologist for the state of Texas, began searching for *La Belle* in 1978. During the search, he located about 24 wrecks in the seemingly peaceful Matagorda Bay, but none of these was La Salle's ship.

Amazingly, the 12-mile-wide bay, which seldom exceeds 18 feet in depth, is home to as many as 300 wrecks. These include the *Amiable* (which remains lost) and Confederate Civil War blockade-runners that braved the treacherous shoals of the bay to avoid the Union navy that once patrolled the Texas coast.

La Belle's Magnetic Personality

Arnold tried again in June 1995, using a *magnetometer* over likely *La Belle* wreck sites. This device is designed to locate iron objects interfering with the Earth's magnetic field. Arnold, who is now with the Institute of Nautical Archaeology at Texas A&M University, dragged the device back and forth across the bay during the summer of 1995.

As luck would have it, the first location Arnold selected as the most probable wreck site of *La Belle* turned out to be the spot where the ship had lain for 309 years beneath 12 feet of water. Student archaeologists from across America volunteered on what was considered a premiere archaeological project. Each day they would enter the muddy water and dig with their hands. Florida State University archaeology student Chuck Meide located a 793-pound bronze cannon that confirmed the wreck was *La Belle*.

The incredibly well-preserved remains of La Salle's personal ship La Belle *as seen from above the cofferdam built to hold back the waters of Matagorda Bay, Texas, to allow the ship's recovery. (Courtesy of the Texas Historical Commission)*

A Dam Good Answer

With *La Belle*'s identity confirmed, more than $4 million in state funding and donations were provided for her excavation. Arnold's group decided to build a *cofferdam* around the remains of the 50-foot boat so archaeologists could see what they were doing. Without a way to keep the murky water away from the wreck site, the divers would have had to recover the wreck by touch!

Shiver Me Timbers

Sunken ships are often excavated by divers, but the recovery of the *La Belle* and its artifacts was done with the use of a **cofferdam.** This structure was built around the submerged ship before water was pumped out of the enclosure to allow archaeologists to study and retrieve the ship and its contents. Cofferdams are seldom used for the study of shipwrecks, but one was previously employed by the U.S. Navy in Havana Harbor in 1911 to study why the battleship USS *Maine* exploded and sank on February 15, 1898.

Volunteers and state archaeologists were amazed to find the bottom section of *La Belle* intact in the mud with barrels, coiled rope, and artifacts still lying as they had been neatly stowed more than 300 years earlier. A grim discovery was the skeleton of a sailor lying atop mud-covered ropes in the bow of the ship.

Sitting amid the waters of Matagorda Bay, Texas, a cofferdam enclosed by a roof holds back the water to allow the excavation of La Belle, *which sank in January 1686. (Courtesy of the Texas Historical Commission)*

The Face of the Past

The French sailor may have been killed during the grounding that sank *La Belle,* or he may have died of thirst, since the ship was short of water at the time of its loss. Unfortunately, we may never know for sure exactly how he died.

What is known is that part of the sailor's brain matter remained intact inside the skull. The skull was taken to the Scottish Rite Hospital for Children in Dallas, where it was subjected to a three-dimensional imaging analysis. A company in Arlington, Texas, subsequently used this image to create a plastic replica of the skull.

Dr. Denis Lee, a professor of medical and biological illustration at the University of Michigan, used this replica to reconstruct the man's face. This endeavor may be the first time such a reconstruction has ever been performed on the remains of a historical shipwreck victim. The skull is now being kept at the Texas A&M University Conservation Lab.

Shiver Me Timbers

The reconstruction of the facial features based on a three-dimensional model of someone's skull is often used to help identify crime victims whose skeletal remains have been found. Clay is molded over the plastic skull model according to actual tissue thickness while following the contours of the face. The process can be quite accurate. (DNA has also been extracted from the remains of the French sailor in hopes that his relatives in France might someday be located be using sophisticated blood tests.)

La Belle: *A Well-Preserved Wreck*

La Belle's hull timbers were disassembled and are now being preserved and readied for reassembly and eventual exhibition. Wave action, shipworms, and bacteria were responsible for the wearing away of the upper part of *La Belle*'s structure.

The approximate construction date of the ship, which was given to La Salle by Louis XIV as part of his exploration agreement, may have been determined using several sources of information. Spaniards who saw the wreck of *La Belle* protruding from the shallow waters soon after it sank described its appearance as that of a new ship. French shipbuilding records indicated a ship named *Belle* was built in 1683. Also, inscriptions on cannon recovered from *La Belle* reveal that they were not built before 1684.

A Treasure of Artifacts

La Belle was not a treasure ship in the financial sense, although her artifacts, if sold on the private market, could have fetched a handsome price. It's believed that divers may have taken some of the boat's small *swivel guns* during the intervening years, but they have never been found.

Heavy Historical Artillery

During the excavation that was conducted between September 1996 and April 1997, almost one million individual artifacts were recovered, including three incredibly ornate bronze cannon, a jar of mercury, leather shoes, a ruby ring, and wooden casks containing muskets.

The identity of the ship was also confirmed by the decoration on the bronze cannon (which was remarkably well preserved thanks to the corrosion-resistant qualities of bronze). The decoration was the symbol of the Count of Vormandois, Louis XIV's illegitimate son who was made grand admiral of the French navy at the ripe old age of two. (He served until he was a doddering 16 years old.) His tenure ended in 1683, providing additional proof the ship was La Salle's.

The sediment in Matagorda Bay played a major role in preserving the items buried beneath it. Organic materials such as wood deteriorate much more quickly in warmer climates like that of south Texas, but the presence of a wooden bowl in the wreckage is testament to the unusual quality of *La Belle's* cache of artifacts. The nature of the mud sealed up *La Belle* and her artifacts quite nicely.

Words To Treasure

A **swivel gun** is a small-caliber cannon mounted on the railing of a ship on a pedestal, which can be maneuvered quickly and fired at close-range targets such as small boats or members of boarding parties.

A Long Conservation Process

A long period of restoration and conservation is now required to preserve the objects recovered from *La Belle*. Texas Historical Commission officials predict that it may be 2003 before these items can be placed on display. In the meantime, officials have established a Web site that provides photographs of the archaeological project and details about the artifacts (http://www.thc.state.tx.us/belle/; see Appendix B, "Deepen Your Knowledge," for more information).

A map of the location of the wreck site of La Belle. *(Drawn by Ken Ellis)*

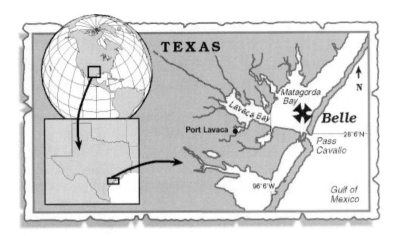

The Least You Need to Know

➤ La Salle was a woodsman and explorer who traveled on ships during his far-reaching journeys, but he was not a trained sailor.

➤ The confusion about how La Salle's ship *La Belle* ended up being smashed on an oyster shell shoal may never be resolved. Some observers blame the weather; others believe that the ship's captain was drunk at the time.

➤ French King Louis XIV enthusiastically supported La Salle's expedition to locate the Mississippi River's mouth from the south by traveling along the Gulf of Mexico.

➤ *La Belle* was only about 50 feet long and was primarily a supply ship for La Salle, although he used it for exploring the waters around Matagorda Bay, where he deposited his settlers after mistakenly passing by the Mississippi River.

➤ The *Amiable,* the other support ship used by La Salle in the expedition that accidentally landed him in Texas, was also lost in Matagorda Bay and has not yet been found despite the efforts of archaeologists to locate the ship, which was larger than *La Belle.*

➤ A cofferdam similar to the one used in the excavation of *La Belle* was used in 1911 to expose the battleship USS *Maine,* which mysteriously exploded in Havana Harbor in 1898.

Chapter 13

Wedding Bells and Death Knells

In This Chapter

➤ The 1715 Treasure Fleet

➤ Hurricane!

➤ Salvaging Spain's treasure

➤ Treasure regulation

➤ Tourist attraction

There's nothing easier to remember than a jingle. Advertising people figured that out a long time ago and—by the way—so did sailors! Over time they developed a seabag full of instructional ditties. One has made the rounds of the Caribbean region for years about the ship-killing hurricane season that lasts from June through October:

> *June, too soon;*
> *July, stand by;*
> *August, come they must;*
> *September, remember;*
> *October, all over*

Unfortunately, the Spanish officials in charge of launching treasure fleets across the Atlantic tended to ignore the advice of the lowest-ranking deck swab who ever lashed himself to a mast during a storm: If you wait too late, it will be too late.

Then again, a vagabond seaman didn't have to answer to the king of Spain when millions of pesos in treasure didn't arrive to pay royal debts.

Although Spanish officials should have learned their lesson after the hurricane-season loss of the 1622 Treasure-Fleet (you remember Chapter 11, "Rich Disaster: Wreck of the 1622 Treasure Fleet"), the 1715 Treasure Fleet was to become yet another victim of Spanish haste to move riches to Europe as quickly as possible.

Already delayed in various ports (sound familiar?), the fleet endured its final fatal holdup when Spain's King Philip V ordered it to wait for delivery of the New World jewelry desired by his newest wife.

That's right, Spain got down on its knees when it needed gold and silver in the worst way and once again begged Mother Nature to rob it blind with a hurricane. The 1715 Treasure Fleet, hauling 14 million pesos in treasure, was to be one of Spain's richest sacrifices on the altars of avarice, bad fiscal policy, and wishful thinking. By comparison, the 1622 Treasure Fleet disaster was a drop in the bailing bucket since only two million pesos in treasure were lost during that event.

Old enough to know better but unable to change, Spain found itself in another fiscal bind, but this time risked two years' worth of treasure when it allowed 12 ships to depart Havana during hurricane season. Only one ship would survive, while the rest were smashed against Florida's south-central coast. With the retrospective view of nearly 300 years, we might say: "Well, it's only money."

When the 1715 Treasure Fleet disaster occurred, people sort of half expected to drown when they were sailing, but it was still quite awful. The disaster's casualty total came unhappily close to the number of people lost when the *Titanic* sank. It ranks right up there as one of the greatest losses of human life at sea, with 1,200 people drowned.

Besides cutting a hole in Spain's moneybags, the 1715 disaster spurred a number of events that included a rash of piracy, as pirates plundered not only the wrecks but the Spanish who were attempting to rightfully salvage their country's treasure. By the late seventeenth century, a "golden age" of piracy had dawned in the Caribbean and Atlantic. (We'll touch upon that in detail in Chapter 26, "The Rudest Treasure Hunters.")

Another side effect of the tragedy was the birth of America's treasure-hunting culture that created a simmering warfare between entrepreneurs and archaeologists. By the 1960s, excitement over the silver and gold recovered from the wrecks touched off a fever that still shows no sign of cooling.

And through it all, people are still picking up coins along the stretch of beach where the disaster occurred.

Know The Ropes

When the *Titanic* sank in glass-smooth seas on April 21, 1912, a total of 1,517 people died. The shortage of lifeboats aboard the liner was the primary cause of the fatalities. Those who perished in the 1715 Treasure Fleet disaster drowned in violently stormy seas. Lifeboats would not have helped, since they would have instantly capsized in the wild waves created by a hurricane.

The wind is beginning to howl and the seas are building, so let's trim our sails, batten our hatches, and hope for the best as we retrace the tragedy of one of the costliest maritime disasters.

Double Your Money: The 1715 Treasure Fleet

On average, a pair of treasure fleets would sail to the New World each year, carrying goods and passengers to the Americas. It was hazardous and slow, but the return trip made the venture worthwhile for Spain, since those ships brought back the treasure that was the cornerstone of its economy.

One fleet would sail to South American ports, while another would go to Mexico, and both would empty their holds of trade goods to make room for treasure. Still, even these two fleets per year were scarcely enough to keep up with Spain's demands. Delays, sunken ships, and pirate raids were more than just problems; they were serious threats to Spain's well-being as a nation.

A complex series of events increased the amount of treasure to be sent home to Spain in 1715, since a long war had made the seas too risky for regular treasure transport. Although Indian slaves kept digging for silver, gold, and emeralds, steady shipments to Spain had been impossible for several years.

War and Other Problems

We talked briefly about this era in Chapter 5, "Treasure Hunting's Soggy History." The War of Succession disrupted Europe and pitted everyone against everyone else for about 13 years. The War ended with a treaty signing in 1713, and Spain decided it was time to turn on the spigot that poured silver and gold into its coffers.

Shiver Me Timbers

The 1715 Treasure Fleet's massive wealth was extremely unusual, since New World silver production had been slipping for years. On average, the amount of silver shipped was generally 10 times that of the gold transported. Silver production peaked in 1600 at Spain's richest silver mine in Potosí, Bolivia, and declined thereafter. The extraordinary amount of silver aboard the fleet meant that the sinking of the 1715 Treasure Fleet would be the largest single loss of treasure experienced by Spain during the 300 years of treasure fleet operations.

Silver production had been on the decline for several reasons, not the least of which was the high mortality rate of the Indians who were enslaved by the Spanish to work the mines and handle the toxic silver-processing operations. However, with production humming along and few ships to carry the treasure home, the biggest treasure shipment in years was now waiting to sail.

Fashion Victims

King Philip V was Spain's wimpy monarch who ascended to the throne in 1700. When his first wife died in 1714, Phil became betrothed to a tough, power-hungry Italian woman named Elizabeth Farnese, duchess of Palma.

When Farnese refused to consummate the marriage until she received her choice of New World jewelry, Phil jumped into inaction by ordering the fleet to wait for the jewels to be made. This decision, along with other delays, may have actually been a death sentence to the roughly 1,200 who died when the fleet sailed smack into a hurricane in the second month of the hurricane season.

Not until the divorce of Donald and Ivana Trump 276 years later would the price of love be so high.

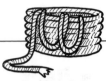

Know The Ropes

Philip V wasn't the only guy trying to keep his wife in new silk underwear while he wore last year's pair. The expense of meeting the fashion demands of wives in eighteenth-century Spain grew so great that the number of marriages in Spain declined, as frugal men avoided getting hitched. It was even proposed that women wear a modest national uniform to reduce extravagant clothing costs borne by husbands. This suggestion was considered the best way to entice men back into matrimony.

Hurry Up and Wait

The Tierra Firme (Mainland) Fleet, which had completed its mission of picking up treasure in South American ports, had waited four months in Havana for the arrival of the Nueva Espana (New Spain) Fleet from Mexico. The five ships of the Nueva Espana Fleet had been delayed by—among other things—the wait for eight chests of jewels for Philip V's manipulative new wife.

The head of the Mainland Fleet, General Don Antonio de Echeverz y Zubiza, and New Spain Fleet commander, General Don Juan Esteban de Ubilla, both knew time was critical. Upon the arrival of Ubilla's fleet in Havana, it still had to be provisioned for the two-month return journey. So let's do the math: If the hurricane season started in June, and the ships would not be ready to sail until July 24—well, I'm sure you get the picture!

Assembling the Fleet

Echeverz and Ubilla found their 11-ship convoy augmented by the French ship *Grifón*, under the command of Antonio Darié. The Spanish generals both commanded large fighting ships termed *Capitanas* and had the firepower of two smaller *Almirantas*, which would guard the rear of the convoy.

Although these four ships carried the lion's share of the irreplaceable treasure and firepower, the smaller ships were also armed. Altogether, the fleet carried 200 cannon.

The smaller ships in this fleet included *pataches* (reconnaissance ships); *naos* (cargo ships); and *resfuerzas* (resupply ships).

The ships were packed to the *gunwales* with fresh fruit and vegetables and live animals for slaughter. Jars filled with water were crammed in every available nook—indeed, some were even hung off the mast!

Every ship's master looked toward the eastern horizon for signs of stormy weather. What stared back was a blue sky and the slightest wisp of a single cloud. Although a reassuring sight, everyone knew this calm picture could change in 24 hours.

Words To Treasure

Gunwales are the top level of a ship's main deck, where cannons were originally placed. A ship "loaded to the gunwales" was extremely full.

Setting Sail

The eight chests of jewels belonging to the duchess of Palma were stowed in Ubilla's own cabin aboard his warship. They contained such items as a heart inlaid with more than 100 pearls, a massive emerald ring, and a rosary of polished coral.

The day of the fleet's departure was a joyous occasion as small boats skirted across the harbor and people hung out pennants recognizing the event. The passengers eventually filed aboard the ships for their two months at sea. Soon the people and their baggage were stored. It was July 24, 1715. Unfortunately, the travelers had only seven days left to live.

Ubilla and Echeverz maneuvered their ships out of Havana's harbor and sailed north to jump on the liquid conveyor belt of the Gulf Stream just south of the Florida Keys. Interestingly enough, they would be traveling in roughly the same direction as the ill-fated 1622 Treasure Fleet.

The idea of hopping into the Gulf Stream was that its current would help propel the ships through the Florida Straits and up the eastern coast of America at speeds of up to nine knots, if all went well. Of course, it didn't.

No Luxury Liners Here

Crowded, filthy, and reeking, the ships of the 1715 Treasure Fleet would have shocked even the poorest immigrant in the lowest hold of the White Star Line's RMS *Titanic*. Passengers not traveling first class aboard one of the ships in a Spanish treasure fleet were crowded below the decks in reeking compartments in near darkness.

As the voyage progressed, the food became foul, and maggots wriggled in the meals that were served to the hapless passengers. On the bright side, sweetened chocolate drinks were usually provided. This concoction was an ironic treat to have aboard the treasure ships, since conquistador Hernán Cortés had discovered chocolate while he was wrecking the Aztec Empire in search of treasure.

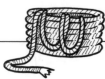

Know The Ropes

Caught between the Bahamas and the Florida coast, somewhere east of present-day Miami, Echeverz and Ubilla knew their ships were little more than fragile wooden floats trapped between unyielding land masses. Powerful winds blowing east or west could smash them against the shoals of either coast. The two options for a ship expecting a powerful storm were to either seek anchorage in a harbor sheltered from the waves by breakwaters or get as far away from the shore as possible. In this case, the latter was the only option.

Hurricane!

The voyage continued without incident for six days as the combined fleets sailed as rapidly as possible during the day and then more slowly at night to avoid collision. Their direction was northward along Florida's eastern coast. Although the skies had been blue when the ships set sail, by July 28 the conditions began to look entirely different.

On the morning of the July 29, sailors with arthritis complained that their joints were aching, calling it a sign that bad weather was coming. By that evening, Ubilla decided that bad weather was indeed on the way and ordered full sails unfurled for a high-speed nighttime run—despite the collision hazard such travel created.

Battling the Storm

The morning of July 30 dawned with an oppressive humidity that was followed by a darkening of the sky. Stern lanterns on the fleet's ships were lit to make the ships visible to one another. Powerful winds began to churn the seas as the hurricane moved toward them like a gigantic counterclockwise-spinning pinwheel covering hundreds of miles.

Sailors soon found the ships could no longer be steered, so they struck and secured their sails. This action reduced the speed at which the ships were being shoved by the wind. During the day, the five storm bands that were contained within the hurricane slammed at the ships, snapping their masts and flinging seamen to their deaths.

Echeverz's ship was badly damaged, and its bow was driving deeply into the sea. This sent tons of water over the ship's decks, and the stored goods and foodstuffs on board were flung about.

Destruction

By 2 A.M., Ubilla's ship, the *Nuestra Senora de la Regla,* was in the clutches of the hurricane's most powerful winds. The order was given for its heavy mast to be chopped down to reduce wind resistance and provide more buoyancy for the ship. This strategy would allow the ship to have a shallower draft, making it possible for the ship to float over reefs guarding the shore. Unfortunately, this commonsense tactic was not enough to save the ship. In the end, its bottom was clawed completely open as the ship grounded on a shoal.

People, cargo, and 120 tons of treasure spilled out of the ship as it wallowed in its death throes. Ubilla and 220 others drowned in the maelstrom as the hulk of the ship, lightened when it disgorged its contents into the sea, stayed afloat and moved closer to shore.

Miracles and Mayhem

The surf tore apart the small supply ship, *Nuestra Senora de las Nieves,* as it moved toward the shore, drowning two dozen aboard. Miraculously, the top part of the ship separated and floated raft-like to shore, carrying approximately 100 thankful survivors to safety.

The Hurricane's Toll

Of the 12 ships in the fleet, 11 were shattered or driven ashore by the relentless hurricane. The Frenchman Darié, who piloted the *Grifón,* had earlier angered Ubilla and Echeverz when he sailed farther away from shore than they instructed just before the storm struck. In the end, he proved to be the smarter—or luckier—mariner, as his was the only ship to escape the treacherous shoals.

Darié's brilliant seamanship had placed him so far ahead of the other ships that he had no idea a hurricane had struck them and even reported to Spanish officials upon his arrival that he thought they had been *becalmed* by a lack of wind.

Spanish officials estimated the toll of the 1715 Treasure Fleet's destruction at around 1,200 persons. In addition, a fortune in Spanish treasure— 14 million pesos—was lying submerged off Florida's coast, having been ripped from the bellies of the treasure galleons.

Know The Ropes

There are two things a sailor doesn't want: too much wind and not enough wind. However, a sailor facing a hurricane with 100-mph winds would always prefer no wind to too much! When mariners in sailing ships found themselves without enough wind to fill their sails, they were **becalmed,** meaning the ship was rendered motionless when winds were still.

Here is a summary of the losses:

➤ *Nuestra Senora de la Regla:* Ubilla's ship struck a shoal, tearing open its hold and spilling its treasure and passengers into the sea. Ubilla and 219 others died.

➤ *Nuestra Senora de las Nieves:* When this ship was torn apart by the massive waves near shore, two dozen people died, but 100 were saved when the upper part of the ship broke away from the hull and floated to the beach.

➤ *Santo Cristo de San Román:* The 450-ton Almiranta had its hull sheared off by the shoals. The death toll was 120 persons.

➤ *Nuestra Senora del Carmen:* The 713-ton Capitana carrying 72 guns managed to lighten its load enough that it floated close to shore with virtually no loss of life. This was Echeverz's ship, so Echeverz survived the calamity.

➤ *Nuestra Senora del Rosario:* The warship was completely destroyed, killing 124, including Echeverz's son, Don Manuelde de Echeverz, the ship's commander.

➤ *Urca de Lima:* The supply ship was the only ship of the fleet carried ashore that remained more or less intact and was anchored. When those aboard tried to reach the shore, 35 were drowned.

➤ Unnamed supply ship: The ship was smashed by waves, drowning 12.

➤ *La Holendesa:* A merchant ship that washed ashore with no loss of life.

➤ *La Francesca:* A small frigate lost with all hands.

➤ *La Galera:* A sloop of war lost with all hands.

➤ *Nuestra Senora de la Concepcion:* A supply ship lost with 135 on board.

Shiver Me Timbers

Except for the *Urca de Lima,* none of the wrecks has been positively identified, and one site has never been located. The wrecks are known by nicknames (from north to south along the coast): Pine Wreck, Cabin Wreck, Anchor Wreck, Green Cabin Wreck, Unnamed Wreck, Rio Mar Wreck, Sandy Point Wreck, Wedge Wreck, Colored Beach Wreck, and another Unnamed Wreck.

Looting

The wrecks were scattered offshore in a 30-mile line from Sebastian to Stuart, Florida, and the survivors were clumped in various groups awaiting death or rescue.

As hundreds of bodies washed upon the beach, many of the survivors began to carefully examine the dead, looking for jewelry and other treasures. Soon survivors were picking up silver coins and other forms of treasure washed ashore by the violent storms.

A number of the survivors decided to help themselves not only to the treasure spilled from the galleons but also to the belongings of the dead. Because looters outnumbered the officers demanding a halt to the looting, it continued until reinforcements arrived to restore order and strip looters of their ill-gotten gains.

Shiver Me Timbers

Officials were so concerned about widespread looting of the wrecks that residents of Saint Augustine (whose city was around 110 miles distant) were ordered to turn over to authorities all of their boats and canoes. The citizens were also ordered not to travel north or south of their town without special permission. Soldiers garrisoned the area around the town, searching people for treasure pilfered from the wrecks. The oldest city in the continental United States treated the survivors graciously, even though the residents' own homes and crops had been smashed by the same hurricane that sank the 1715 Treasure Fleet.

Salvaging Spain's Treasure

Not much had gone right for Spain on July 31, 1715. In a matter of hours, it had lost 14 million pesos, as well as 1,200 men, women, and children. Spain dispatched salvage teams and soldiers to the site to begin salvage operations. Officials were still so concerned about looting that a Catholic priest, Father Manuel de Quiñones, threatened to excommunicate anyone who attempted to keep any of the recovered treasure for themselves.

As you can well imagine, the last thing Spain needed at this point was bands of pirates on the prowl, grabbing tons of Spanish treasure. Unfortunately, that is exactly what the country got.

Word was already ricocheting around the Caribbean about the massive treasure loss from the 1715 Treasure Fleet, whose value had already been reported by spies to British officials in Jamaica prior to the fleet's departure.

One sea robber who jumped in with both of his felonious feet was British pirate William Jennings; his massively profitable raids upon the Spanish salvage efforts are discussed in Chapter 5.

Endless Looting

Hapless Spanish officials tried to recover their badly needed treasure for four years following the 1715 disaster but met with little success for two reasons: The scuba equipment that would have greatly helped them would not be invented for another 228 years, and pirates and freebooters were crawling all over the wrecks. Although Spanish officials claimed to have recovered 30 percent of the lost treasure, many today believe that figure is much too low.

Twentieth-Century Booty

Although the plunder of the 11 wrecks went on for years, it eventually settled down and most people forgot about the matter altogether. In 1821, America acquired Florida from Spain, and life went on.

After World War II, home builder Kip Wagner began to hear about people finding silver on Sebastian Inlet near Vero Beach, Florida, which was close to his residence, and he decided to try some beachcombing. Sure enough, Wagner found silver—and lots of it! In fact, Wagner eventually discovered the general location of many of the offshore wrecks.

Wagner's treasure-hunting acumen was so profitable—and famous—that he is credited with starting the fad—if not the outright business—of treasure hunting in America. Even the famous treasure hunter Mel Fisher was Wagner's partner in the early 1960s.

Millions in silver and gold have been recovered from the waters and beaches off Florida since Wagner's first amazing discovery in the 1960s.

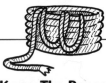

Know The Ropes

Anyone wishing to search for treasure in publicly owned waters off the Florida coast must enter into a "contract for salvage" with the state of Florida's Department of State, Division of History and Records Management. A $1,200 fee is required. Searchers are limited to one boat, and they must relinquish 25 percent of any recoveries to the state. The state also has the option of keeping all of the recovered treasure and reimbursing the finder for its market value.

Treasure Regulation

Mel Fisher's Universal Salvage group, working under contract with Wagner, located gold on one of the 1715 wreck sites in 1964. This created suspicion among state officials that Florida was getting cheated out of its 25 percent cut of recovered treasures, even though officials later determined no such thing had been happening.

By 1965, as Fisher and others found more gold and tourists began to pour into the area, Fort Pierce, Florida, was calling itself the "Treasure Coast." With the additional notoriety being garnered by Fisher's successes, state officials began to keep closer tabs on the treasure hunters.

Even beachcombers said they felt they were being watched during the 1960s when strangers struck up conversations with them.

Tourist Attraction

The area of the *Urca de Lima*'s wreck off Fort Pierce became the state's original Underwater Archaeological Preserve in September 1987. The *Urca* was the only ship that managed to be shoved ashore mostly intact during the 1715 storm.

Its cargo of privately owned silver was the first to be salvaged by Spanish crews, since the ship was so easy to reach. After the salvage operation, the ship was burned to conceal its remains from pirates and official British plunder expeditions.

Florida's Underwater Archaeological Preserve allows divers to visit the remains of the ship—just 200 yards offshore in about 20 feet of water. But it's a look-don't-touch visitation! Plunder of artifacts is not allowed, and officials ask visitors to take only pictures and leave only bubbles.

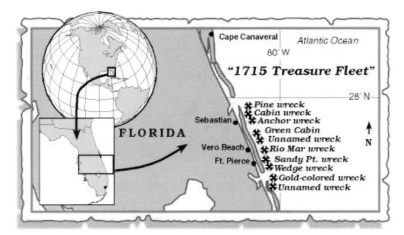

A map of the wreck sites of the 1715 Treasure Fleet.
(Drawn by Ken Ellis)

The Least You Need to Know

➤ Philip V, king of Spain, was a weak man who allowed everyone to boss him around—including his wives and his ministers!

➤ The French Ship *Grifón,* which defied the orders of Echeverz and sailed too far east, was the only one of 12 ships traveling in the 1715 Treasure Fleet to survive the hurricane that destroyed 11 other ships.

➤ Eighteenth-century sailing ships were dark and cramped, with the food becoming progressively more disgusting as the trip dragged on. Foodstuffs deteriorated, and worms began to infest the provisions.

➤ The extremely religious Catholics aboard the sinking ships the *Regla* and *Carmen* desperately wanted priests on board to hear their confessions and to pray with them just before the ships were smashed on Florida's south-central coast.

➤ The crews on Spanish treasure fleet ships lit lanterns at the rear of the vessels at night so the ships would be visible to one another.

➤ It's believed as many as 1,200 people died in the destruction of 11 of 12 ships of the Spanish treasure fleet by a hurricane.

A Rose Blossoms Again

Ever seen the old films from the late 1950s and early 1960s when America's fledgling space program was embarrassed by one missile explosion after another? Build a special one-of-a-kind device, pack it with new technology, and the probability of failure is uncomfortably high.

We have the same problems when we make modern improvements to existing works of technology. Sometimes things get improved so much that they no longer work at all. Teens do this to their cars. And, sometimes, kings make too many poorly thought-out improvements to their favorite warships—which leads us to the *Mary Rose.*

In sixteenth-century England, officials took this perfectly good warship and made it so incredibly powerful, well equipped, and innovative that it sank at the moment it was needed most. The fully loaded *Mary Rose,* which was maneuvering to do battle with the French on July 19, 1545, tipped over and drank a fatal dose of water through its open gun ports. It sank so swiftly that only 35 of the 700 men aboard escaped death.

Like the televised explosion of the space shuttle *Challenger* in 1986—another shocking technology failure—the *Mary Rose* disaster was witnessed by many, including King Henry VIII, who considered the ship a favorite.

What was fatal for the crew and soldiers aboard the *Mary Rose* and shocking to the nation of England, would become a boon for archaeologists and historical researchers 437 years later. This was when, after a 17-year effort, the *Mary Rose,* her artifacts, and the bones of those aboard were finally rescued from the ooze of Portsmouth Harbor.

The events leading up to the sinking are complicated, and the reasons are numerous. We're going to return to merry olde England for a look at the era, the military crisis that prompted the disaster, and the incredible remains of a ship that failed in battle but, in death, managed to capture the hearts of the world.

Words To Treasure

England long ago learned that, as an island, it would have to build one of the world's most powerful navies if it were to prevail against her enemies. This fleet was known for centuries as England's **"Wall of Oak."**

Mary Rose: England's Pride

The island nation of Britain has long known its survival depended on its ability to build and maintain a navy that could help it fight off invaders and make the seas safe for trade.

For centuries, ships like the *Mary Rose* have fulfilled the role of being England's *"Wall of Oak,"* serving as floating fortresses to preserve that nation's sovereignty. The ships and the men who served in them were England's salvation and heroes. While there were many ships in England's history, one stands out as very special, and it was the *Mary Rose.*

Henry VIII's Favorite Ship

Henry VIII—mostly famous for having six wives (and executing two of them)—also took serious steps to build up England's navy and make it one of the most powerful and modern in the sixteenth-century world.

Gus: Bronze = Tin and Copper Alloy

Construction on the *Mary Rose* began the year that Henry took the throne in 1509 at age 18. A year later, as part of his crash program to strengthen the navy, Henry VIII ordered so many bronze naval cannon that he caused a tin shortage. Nevertheless, he still demanded the forging of even more guns. It was crucial to Henry VIII that England be able to defend itself against invasion.

For many years the *Mary Rose* was known to be Henry VIII's favorite ship, and others thought highly of it as well. Admiral Sir Edward Howard proclaimed in a letter to the King, "The *Mary Rose,* Sir, she is the noblest ship of sail and a great ship at this hour that I trow [trust] to be in Christendom." Howard wasn't one to toss about empty flattery regarding ships, since he bitterly complained that other ships under his command were downright lousy.

Everyone loved the *Mary Rose,* except her enemies, of course.

Treacherous Political Waters

Trying to understand the politics of early sixteenth-century Europe is a tough chore, especially if you didn't have European history pounded in your head as a schoolchild. But things were at least as complicated then as they are today, though affairs between nations were punctuated by a lot of rather mean-spirited raids if not outright warfare.

So let's get some background on just one historical example of this era, of course, one that eventually includes the *Mary Rose* herself!

England, threatened by France and neighboring Scotland, occupied the French city of Calais for 111 years beginning in 1347 to guarantee a toehold in Europe. (England, after all, needed to protect its foreign trade across the English Channel.) France, in turn, conducted frequent raids across the channel, burning crops on England's east coast. Hence, there was generally a lot of friction between the two nations. I know it's confusing, but this is why Britain needed warships and why the *Mary Rose* was built.

The *Mary Rose,* constructed between 1509 and 1511, was part of England's military infrastructure for competing in a world where combat seemed to consume most of the time, treasury, and manhood of European nations.

Words To Treasure

It was obvious that Henry VIII was partial to the *Mary Rose,* since it was built the same year he was crowned King of England. He also chose to name the warship after his favorite sister, Mary Tudor. The Tudor family symbol was the rose, hence the name "Mary Rose." It's an awfully sweet name for a war machine!

Mary Rose's Wars

The *Mary Rose* had been in naval service nearly a year when England decided to align itself with Spain to fight none other than their old nemesis France across the rainy English Channel. The *Mary Rose* took part in a naval raid on the French port of Brest in August 1512.

Sailing through a harbor containing 222 French ships, the *Mary Rose* led an attack force of 25 English ships. The force captured and burned 32 French ships while taking 800 men prisoner. The *Mary Rose* was the flagship for Admiral Sir Edward Howard, indicating that she was considered one of the most impressive ships England had at the time.

During the battle, *Mary Rose* took on the ships of the French fleet, pounding it with cannon fire and killing or disabling as many as 300 French sailors and soldiers.

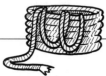

Know The Ropes

A **refit,** or **overhaul,** is a necessary part of a ship's life. Ships are victimized not only by everyday wear and tear, battle damage, rot, shipworms, and fires but also by becoming outdated. Warships are large financial investments even today. They remain expensive, since they must be modernized and kept shipshape, or they risk falling victim to either the enemy or their own lack of seaworthiness.

Words To Treasure

A ship's **displacement** tonnage is a unique nautical term. A ship's weight is measured by how much water it displaces while still remaining afloat; thus if it weighs 700 tons, it will displace 700 tons of water. (These are long tons weighing 2,240 pounds with each consisting of 35 cubic feet of water.) Ships have an empty weight and a loaded weight, meaning that the ship is designed to have enough hull area and freeboard (distance from the waterline to the main deck) to allow adequate flotation when it is fully loaded with people, weapons, and provisions.

Fatal Improvements

By 1536 the *Mary Rose* was ready for her second *refit*— or *overhaul*—to repair bad wood, make various improvements, and possibly to add gun ports with doors that opened and closed below the main deck. No one's sure whether the ship was built with these doors or whether they were added 26 years after its construction.

Unsafe Safety Measure

Another addition to the *Mary Rose* prior to its final battle was the weaving of strong netting to cover the main and upper decks. This rope netting was designed to keep enemy soldiers from jumping down onto the deck during a boarding action from another ship.

This brilliant innovation meant anyone on the deck could not climb over the gunwales to safety in case of a sinking. The "protective" netting would ensnare anyone trying to flee the ship. Those aboard the *Mary Rose* were essentially caged when the netting was erected. Though cannon were important long-distance weapons in naval warfare at the time of Henry VIII, infantry was still used when ships came close enough to board one another.

Putting on Weight

The *Mary Rose* had been improved while undergoing at least two major refits during its lifetime, but the ship also received more firepower in the form of heavy bronze cannon and smaller guns. By 1545 the original complement of 15 cannon was increased to a total of 71 guns, not counting 20 small antipersonnel weapons that fired hailshot, or cubes of iron, for ripping people apart.

Many of these new guns were added on the upper decks of the *Mary Rose,* meaning that its center of gravity was much higher than it was originally.

Strengthened and upgraded, the *Mary Rose* was approximately 120 feet long and 35 feet wide and was considered to have a 700-ton *displacement* at the time of its final overhaul in 1536.

A Nautical Balancing Act

Though landlubbers don't often think about this, ships have to be finely balanced to sail properly. They need a proper amount of ballast, or weight, in the bottom of their hold to counterbalance the weight of the ship's tall superstructure, the part of the ship above its waterline.

In the days of sailing ships, ballast usually consisted of stones, which were stacked in the hold along the keel. Ships also needed to be balanced, or trimmed, fore and aft (front and back, to you matey!). If you fail to provide a ship's proper balance, you have a dangerous situation. Lacking proper ballast, a ship could flip over sideways (capsize). Insufficient trim can send the bow (the front of the ship) or the stern (its rear) too deeply into the water.

Just remember this naval engineering stuff later when we talk about what sank the *Mary Rose* and killed almost 700 men.

The Final Battle

England is quite a nation. Its history is loaded with situations in which it faced unbelievable odds only to calmly survive as if there were nothing to snatching victory from the jaws of inevitable defeat.

In July 1545, Henry VIII and his realm found themselves facing a French fleet determined to enter the waterway behind England's Isle of Wight and to destroy the English navy once and for all.

Don't be fooled—this fight wasn't taking place over French outrage that no one called the English Channel the "French Channel." Things were a bit more serious than that. The French, like the English, wanted to control the waterway—regardless of its name—and besides, Henry VIII had been fighting with the Spanish against France. Unfortunately for Henry VIII, France and Spain agreed to a truce, leaving France free to invade irksome England.

Bad Odds

The French assembled 225 warships to deliver a massive blow against the English navy positioned in Spithead Strait on the northeast edge of the Isle of Wight. The stakes were high. Henry VIII's army had captured the French city of Boulogne, and the French wanted the Isle of Wight so they could make a trade. All Henry VIII could muster was around 100 ships to face a French naval force more than twice as large.

Henry VIII's smaller fleet was guarding Spithead's entrance in a defensive action and had wisely decided to not fight it out in the open waters of the English Channel. Between the Isle of Wight and the English mainland, Henry VIII's fleet was also covered by shore guns, making it tough to root them out.

Death of the Mary Rose

The French sailed up to the entrance of Spithead Strait to lure England's fleet out to fight in the open spaces of the English Channel, but the English did not take the bait, choosing instead to hold their defensive position in the narrow strait as the French approached.

As the *Mary Rose* sailed forward into battle, a breeze came up, and Henry VIII's favorite ship made what looked like a sudden turn. The *Mary Rose* leaned sharply, took on water through her gun ports, and sank in a matter of seconds. Perhaps as few as 35 or as many as 50 of the 700 aboard lived. The French sailors rejoiced, believing that their magnificent gunnery had done the trick.

Shiver Me Timbers

Henry VIII watched in horror from Southsea Castle, along with thousands of other spectators along the shore, as the *Mary Rose* suddenly heeled over and sank. The king could even hear the screams of the men on the sinking ship. As usual, with any maritime disaster, the confusion began to mount regarding what happened to the *Mary Rose*. By one account the *Mary Rose* turned too hard, and the cause of its loss was bad handling. Other accounts related that a mild wind filled her sails and knocked the precariously unbalanced ship over so her gun ports took on water. Just before the ship sank, the *Mary Rose*'s ranking officer, Sir George Carew, told another officer, "He had the sort of knaves whom he could not rule." Carew had complained that all the sailors were such superb mariners that they disdained the small tasks, causing the ship to be poorly handled.

Eventually, the French withdrew after burning up a few more crops and villages on the Isle of Wight. The invasion had been repelled, but the *Mary Rose* was sitting on the bottom of Spithead Strait with only its masts protruding from the water.

Weighing the Evidence

Although the loss of the *Mary Rose* was blamed on bad seamanship, the sudden sinking may have been caused by numerous errors, one stacked upon another, as is often the case in modern aviation mishaps. It seems the *Mary Rose*, pretty as it was, might have had a weight problem.

The *Mary Rose* had been nearly doubled in weight—to 700 tons—because of successive refits during its 35 years of service. The number (and weight) of its guns had been increased nearly fivefold, and the ship was carrying 285 more men than normal on the upper decks and in fighting positions in the masts. (Ordinarily, the crew was only around 415.)

Remember our discussion about balance, ballast, and freeboard? It seems a good circumstantial case can be made that the ship was a bit top-heavy. The extra men alone, with their armor, bows, and other weapons, would have contributed as much as 25 tons to the ship's weight, distributed not in the hold for stability, but on the main and upper decks and masts for fighting, making the ship less stable.

English explorer and sailing legend Sir Walter Raleigh commented decades after the sinking that the *Mary Rose* lacked enough freeboard between her gun ports and the water and that she was poorly balanced. A lot of evidence points to a good ship having too many people and guns placed on it to make it more powerful. In the case of the *Mary Rose,* less may have been more when it came to survival.

Casualties

Why did so many die? Speculation has it that the only survivors were the soldiers and archers (with their famously accurate and powerful longbows) posted in the mast-mounted fighting positions. (Though the *Mary Rose* bristled with cannon, the famous English archers were still capable of launching deadly arrows hundreds of yards at enemy ships.)

The other soldiers and sailors, it is believed, may have been trapped under the antiboarding net stretched taut over the main deck. As the ship sank, they could not escape the wreck. Also, many were in combat armor, making swimming or floating next to impossible.

Early Salvage Attempts

Although the 1982 raising of the *Mary Rose* was a worldwide media event, efforts to bring up the valuable warship and its guns started immediately after it was lost. An August 1, 1545, letter from Charles Brandon, Duke of Suffolk, predicted the *Mary Rose*'s salvage within days. He called for a detailed list of salvage equipment and personnel, including "Venetian maryners and one Venetian carpenter."

His prediction was only off by nearly 350 years.

Time Takes Its Toll

Within 150 years, the *Mary Rose*'s protruding masts and other parts above the mud had rotted away. However, the complaints of fishermen plying Spithead Strait about something snagging their nets led the inventors of the diving helmet, John and Charles Deane, to another attempt to salvage the wreck.

Know The Ropes

Innovative salvors of the period were quite accomplished and intended to use a proven method to raise the *Mary Rose.* Using a pair of ships displacing 700 tons each, cables would have been attached to the *Mary Rose*'s mainmast and then to the ships on either side. As the tide rose, so would *Mary Rose.* It would then be carried back to the docks. However, the mast appears to have been torn out in this effort, and free divers may not have been able to place cables beneath the heavy ship resting in the mud for another try.

In 1836 the Deanes rediscovered the wreck and were diving to it in hopes of recovering something of value. What they found were the ribs of an old ship protruding from the mud along with four cannon that they recovered. They later found 19 more guns, human skulls, and other artifacts.

Having a Blast

The Deanes then allegedly did something to make modern nautical archaeologists shudder in horror. They obtained explosives and began to blast away at the wreck site to expose more of the *Mary Rose*. This effort apparently provided little help to the Deanes who gave up their salvage attempts in 1840, but only after they commissioned a beautiful set of watercolor paintings of the artifacts they recovered.

Lost and Found Again

British journalist Alexander McKee had a lifelong interest in the undersea world and diving and has written many books on shipwrecks and undersea archaeology. McKee was an adventure journalist who often did something dangerous and exciting and told his readers about it.

By 1965 McKee decided he wanted to locate the *Mary Rose* and organized an effort known as Project Solent Ships. One of the early members of the team was terrestrial archaeologist Margaret Rule, who was then excavating Roman ruins in Britain.

Many dismissed the effort as a foolish waste of time, claiming that the *Mary Rose* had long since rotted to nothing. But McKee and Rule believed that the mud of the Solent Strait (which included Spithead Strait) had buried what remained of the *Mary Rose*, protecting it from decay.

Salvage on a Shoestring

With a rowboat budget for their battleship task, the searchers paid much of the early costs of the expedition out of their own pockets. Their early efforts included using a small boat and a magnetic compass in attempts to locate the wreck. The compass would serve as a crude magnetometer to alert them to iron cannon beneath the water.

McKee put on diving gear, and keeping an eye on the compass, he was towed around the suspected wreck site of the *Mary Rose*. Incredibly, his compass needle fluctuated, indicating that iron was below. However, he and his companions had to dodge the ships coming and going in the busy channel. The compass method was inexpensive but dangerous and inconclusive.

Seeing Through Mud

After two years, the group decided it needed some way to confirm whether it really knew where the *Mary Rose* was before embarking on an expensive attempt to recover the ship. In 1966 the group obtained an 1841 Royal Navy chart showing the location of the *Mary Rose* found by the Deanes.

This information promised to be a great help, but it was imperative to pin down the precise location of the wreck before further archaeological efforts could be financed. In 1967 the resourceful McKee talked a British representative of the American firm EG&G into using its side-scan sonar equipment to provide an image of the seafloor at the suspected site. The scan indicated something was there.

Harold "Doc" Edgerton, one of the founders of EG&G and an inventor of side-scan sonar, came in person in 1968 to use the latest equipment to investigate the possible *Mary Rose* wreck site. Again the side-scan sonar showed something under the water.

Shiver Me Timbers

Though his name doesn't often come up when people talk about the discovery of the *Titanic* and the *Bismarck* or the *Mary Rose*, Harold "Doc" Edgerton's side-scan sonar innovation is the tool of choice for those hunting shipwrecks. A friend of explorer Jacques-Yves Cousteau, Edgerton developed underwater photographic techniques and later decided to use sound waves to "profile" the seafloor and produce images beneath the mud. These systems are still in use, though many manufacturers now produce side-scan systems. Side-scan sonar not only can provide an image of the bottom but also can "see" through the mud to what is buried below.

Success! Finding the Mary Rose

After years of digging underwater trenches with hand tools, blowing clouds of silt with water jets, and generally being cold, tired, and unsuccessful, Alexander McKee and his volunteers finally achieved success.

On Saturday, May 1, 1971, divers began their yearly search for the *Mary Rose* in the Solent's murky, dark water. Soon after, diver Percy Ackland popped to the surface to report he had found the *Mary Rose*'s timbers protruding from the muddy bottom. Experts believe that the currents of the Solent had temporarily revealed the remains of the *Mary Rose,* allowing its discovery where hundreds of dives had occurred during previous search attempts.

Raising Money

The discovery of the *Mary Rose* actually created as many problems as it solved. Now, the "picnic-party archaeology," as it was described by archaeologist Margaret Rule, would have to become a serious and expensive expedition. The site needed to be completely mapped and surveyed, and eventually the wreck and its remains would need to be recovered.

Volunteer divers continued the difficult work in the dank conditions under the Solent, attempting to determine the size and condition of the wreck and the location of its artifacts. Raising money now became as much of a chore as the archaeology itself.

Know The Ropes

In July 1980, as mapping and survey work proceeded on the *Mary Rose's* wreck, diver and scientist Louise Mulford descended to begin a day of underwater work. The experienced diver failed to return to the surface, and her body was seen floating near the wreck site. It was later determined that she had vomited underwater and drowned. This involuntary reaction, known as a "glottal spasm," is nearly impossible for a diver to recover from because vomiting forces a diver to remove the air regulator from his or her mouth. Diving while suffering any sort of ailment, particularly a stomach bug, is not advised.

Royal Assistance

Help was on the way in the form of attention given the project by His Royal Highness Prince Charles, Prince of Wales. Charles, an avid scuba diver and a former student of archaeology, dove upon the wreck in 1975.

By 1979, Prince Charles agreed to become president of the Mary Rose Trust that had been formed on January 19 of that year. The money, which had trickled into the project, now poured in. In fact, the entire world became aware of the *Mary Rose* project.

Excavation

Using water jets to blow away silt, the *Mary Rose* volunteers had excavated the wreck from its muddy bed by 1981 and began dismantling various parts of the ship and its components.

Thousands of artifacts were brought up from the wreck site in preparation for the eventual raising of the ship's remnants that included roughly half the hull, which looked as if it had been sliced diagonally like a loaf of bread cut in two from front to rear.

By 1982 the ship's brick galley was dismantled, and the wreck was cleared of loose objects and artifacts. Airlifts, used by Florida treasure hunters since the 1960s, were employed to clear the silt from around the wreck.

Up, Up, and Away

By 1982 the *Mary Rose's* remaining timbers were mostly excavated from the mud, its artifacts and loose timbers were removed, and the ship was ready to be raised. However, the fragile nature of the hull would make the raising tricky and technologically complex. The five-stage process required the use of a specially designed lifting device and a cradle.

A four-legged platform known as the underwater lifting device (ULF) was lowered over the remnants of the *Mary Rose's* hull where pins and suspension wires were attached to its wooden timbers. The device was slowly raised as divers used airlifts to suck silt and mud from beneath the wreckage.

When the wreckage was free from the mud, a crane lifted the ULF that held the *Mary Rose*'s hull and lowered it upon a special steel cradle that had been submerged beside the wreck site. The ULF was then connected to the cradle and converted into a single unit.

The entire rig, now containing the remains of the *Mary Rose,* was then hoisted out of the water and taken by barge to a dock.

Archaeological Treasures

The *Mary Rose* was no treasure ship, since the only gold found at its wreck site was the pocket money carried by officers and crew hoping to buy a stiff drink following the naval battle.

However, nearly 400 years underwater had not robbed the *Mary Rose* of its historical treasures. Some 2,500 arrows in near-perfect condition were recovered, along with 139 longbows that the archers were to have used against the French. Nearly new wooden chests were recovered as were personal items, leather shoes, dinnerware, and numerous pocket sundials (the Rolex wrist watches of the time).

The most perfectly preserved artifact was a Tudor-period nail that was as shiny and bright as the day it was forged. More than three centuries before, a carpenter had accidentally dropped it into a vat of tar, thereby preserving it.

Seagoing Critters Found

Even the skeletons of rats were found, indicating that the sailors were sharing their food with unwelcome stowaways. The skull of a dog was also recovered, which proved once and for all that there really is such a thing as a sea dog. The four-legged mariner may have earned its keep chasing the rats.

The strangest animal remains aboard were those of a frog that learned the hard way it isn't easy being green. Careful study showed that the frog, like the pooch, may have been a productive member of the crew, although the ugliest of a tough lot. It was long believed by sailors that a frog, if dropped in water, would swim toward land. Frogs, it seems, were carried as backup compasses until the 1800s, although there's no indication that a frog has any better sense of direction than your ordinary lost tourist.

Conserving the Past

The *Mary Rose*'s wooden hull immediately presented serious issues related to its preservation, since the timbers would crack and warp if allowed to dry out. Therefore, the *Mary Rose* was kept wet with chilled water in the Mary Rose Museum at Her Majesty's Naval Base, Portsmouth.

However, preservationists determined that this method was not doing the job, so in 1994 conservators began drenching the ship's reconstructed hull with a wax mixture. Various concentrations of polyethylene glycol will be sprayed on the ship's timbers until around 2014.

The wax will replace the water inside the ship's timbers, allowing the wood to gain strength and to prevent further decay.

A map of the Mary Rose *wreck site.*
(Drawn by Ken Ellis)

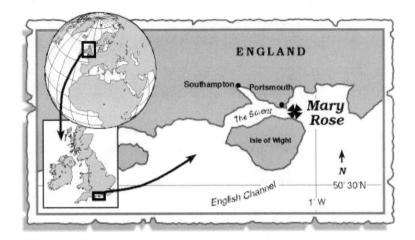

The Least You Need to Know

➤ Henry VIII witnessed the July 19, 1545, sinking of the *Mary Rose* from Southsea Castle and was so close to the scene that he could hear the screams of those aboard as they drowned.

➤ Volunteer diver Louise Mulford died in July 1980 while conducting underwater archaeological work on the *Mary Rose* wreck site when a vomiting episode caused her to drown.

➤ Sonar inventor Harold "Doc" Edgerton personally came to the site of the *Mary Rose's* sinking to use his device to help confirm the position of the sunk warship mostly buried beneath the mud off Spithead.

➤ Although some attempted to blame the crew of the *Mary Rose* for the disaster, it's generally believed the ship sank because it was poorly balanced and overloaded.

➤ The *Mary Rose,* completed in 1510, was the flagship of the English fleet when it led an attack on the French fleet at Brest in 1512, which was its first military action.

➤ The *Mary Rose* was long believed to be completely decomposed beneath the water but persistent archaeologists and enthusiasts pressing for its rediscovery found much of its hull and many of its artifacts were intact.

Chapter 15

A Bountiful Tale

In This Chapter

➤ The harsh era of the HMS *Bounty*

➤ The *Bounty's* silly breadfruit mission

➤ Cruel Captain Bligh and Mutinous Mr. Christian

➤ Mutiny!

➤ The tragic getaway of the mutineers

➤ Finding the *Bounty's* wreck

Most shipwrecks are famous mostly just for sinking. Some were floating behemoths with hundreds of victims like the *Titanic*, while others, like the *Edmund Fitzgerald*, were lost mysteriously and later popularized by a hit song.

But of all the lost ships that ever slumbered out of sight upon the seafloor, the HMS *Bounty* is one remembered most for what happened before it sank. It was an English vessel that earned a reputation as the most unhappy ship afloat in a navy famous for having a lot of very unhappy ships.

More than 120 years before the *Lusitania* and the *Titanic* made their names household words, the HMS *Bounty* had become notorious in maritime history. It was seized in a mutiny on April 28, 1789, by a group of men in a spur-of-the moment coup to rid them of their hated Lieutenant William Bligh.

The *Bounty,* like other lost ships with tragic stories, had an ironically positive name, but it really wasn't that much of a ship! It was a converted coal hauler pushed into Royal Navy service for the ridiculous job of fetching breadfruit trees from the South Pacific. The plants were to serve as a food source for African slaves working on British plantations in the West Indies. However, this floating fast-food restaurant's fate was not going to be as dull as its mission.

When it was lost, the *Bounty* and her mutineers were actually fleeing, and it was sunk on purpose in one of the most inaccessible spots in the world. Although the *Bounty's* intentional sinking was in a relatively shallow bay well-known to many just a few years after it was lost, the remains of its wreck were not located for 168 years.

But don't be fooled! The story of the *Bounty* is far more than that of a ship; it's the tale of an era and is perhaps the greatest story of the sea ever told. This true story has been well documented and has served as the foundation for numerous films and countless books. The incident gave us a paranoid villain and an unlikely hero in Lieutenant William Bligh and his former favorite officer, Fletcher Christian.

The story is no brief two-hour soap opera like that of the *Titanic* but an epic tale lasting years. This incredible historical episode also gave the world a second shipwreck in the form of the pursuing HMS *Pandora* upon which some of the captured mutineers would perish in a violent shipwreck. Not only were both ships and their crews plagued with tragedy, but both had equally malignant commanders.

The story of the *Bounty* and her crew begins not with the cruelty of Lieutenant William Bligh, but with the institutionalized cruelty that had become part of the way the Royal Navy operated at the time. The *Bounty* was a dysfunctional seagoing workplace that reflected the unhealthy system that spawned it. The strange, instantaneous transformation of Fletcher Christian from Bligh's favorite officer to mutiny leader is one twist that has never been fully explained.

If the mutineers thought deposing Bligh would mean happiness, they were sadly mistaken. They would find little happiness after seizing the ship, and many—including Christian—would die violent deaths on their island hideout of Pitcairn. And Bligh would continue to be a dishonest and paranoid tyrant for the remainder of his naval career.

Words To Treasure

A **collier** is a word used chiefly in England for a ship that carries coal among various ports, though it is also used as another name for a coal miner.

The Harsh Era of the HMS *Bounty*

The shipwreck of the HMS *Bounty* is unique in a hundred ways. While as famous a ship as the *Titanic,* the *Bounty* has been famous for far longer. The story of the smaller ship is not one involving the wealthy and the famous like that of the "unsinkable" liner. In fact, the *Bounty* was an unglamorous *collier* converted into a floating nursery for plants. Although members of the *Bounty's* crew did die, none perished because of the ship's sinking.

A replica of the HMS Bounty with its sails unfurled was built for the 1962 movie Mutiny on the Bounty.
(Courtesy of the Tall Ship Bounty Foundation)

Without cheating, can you name the captain of the *Titanic* or of the *Lusitania?* But you certainly know that Captain Bligh commanded the *Bounty,* and you've probably heard of his mutinous officer Fletcher Christian. Kind of amazing, isn't it, that even a small ship without any great treasure aboard could still become so famous!

The story behind the wreck of the *Bounty* began long before its mutineers stripped it, burned it, and then allowed it to sink in their island sanctuary's bay. The roots of what happened to the *Bounty* lay within the personalities of its men and officers, interwoven with the crushing weight of institutionalized cruelty in England's legendary Royal Navy.

The eighteenth century saw a level of criminal punishment in England that would make many of us shudder with horror. Until 1832 shoplifters could be executed, and until 1870 traitors were still disemboweled after they were hanged!

The Royal Navy of that era used equally harsh measures, since the entire navy was a virtual floating prison system. Filled with thousands of men that had been forced into naval service, the Royal Navy had almost as much trouble fighting its wars as it did trying to keep its sailors. The conditions aboard the English warships were made unbearable with frequent floggings and the occasional *keelhauling.*

Words To Treasure

Keelhauling was a punishment that could be ordered by a Royal Navy warship's captain. This barbarous punishment involved throwing a bound sailor into the sea and dragging him from one side of the ship to the other under the keel, and frequently resulted in death.

Pressed Into Service

England, with its far-flung colonies and almost-unending wars, was constantly in need of sailors for its navy. The law allowed the government to issue a hated "Special Warrant" in order to draft any number of men the navy required for as long as they were needed. Those who conducted this "recruiting" were members of "press gangs." They brooked no argument from their prospective sailors.

Because the men were forced into service, they often deserted at the first opportunity. For the navy, the answer to this problem was to make life worse for the sailors. For example, usually only officers were granted leave, or permission to go ashore, a circumstance that was despised almost as much as the floggings.

Some statistics tell a rather sobering tale about conditions in the Royal Navy during the late nineteenth century. Between 1774 and 1780, a whopping 42,069 men out of a total of 175,900 sailors deserted. Only 1,243 sailors were killed in combat during this period. Obviously, those in charge of the Royal Navy's gentle brand of recruiting were in a very difficult footrace trying to keep pace with desertions.

Shiver Me Timbers

Because there were more than a few wrinkles in the morale of Royal Navy, it was necessary for the British to "press" men into naval service. Desertion plagued the Royal Navy that ruled an empire held together by seapower. At first, the Special Warrant specified that only men who were mariners would be placed into involuntary service. That changed when the navy's need for personnel became so great in 1778 that any able-bodied man could be snatched up for duty. The Royal Navy decided it might as well conscript some former English subjects as well and began forcing seamen on American ships into naval service. This action was one of the causes of the War of 1812 between England and the United States.

For Flog and Country

This despicable situation in the Royal Navy was perhaps best highlighted by the issue of flogging, which is a punishment based upon an ancient Hebrew law that allows a man to be whipped one time less 40 lashes. Interestingly, this punishment was given to Jesus Christ prior to his crucifixion.

We're not talking about anything minor here. Flogging is a flesh-ripping, bone-exposing torture delivered by a cat-o-nine-tails—a whip made out of steer hide with nine lashes at its end, that are sometimes tipped with barbs. The navy actually issued these disciplinary instruments to English ships! It was a horrible punishment, one the entire crew was forced to watch. The infractions leading to a flogging could range from theft to insubordination.

English lawmakers—not to mention the public—were getting a bit sick of the harsh treatment of their sailors, and when an antiflogging bill was introduced into the House of Commons in 1871, it became pretty clear to the admirals that the days of floggings were numbered. Even though the 1871 bill was eventually withdrawn, the admirals saw the handwriting on the wall and essentially ended the practice that year. Nonetheless, the regulations allowing the infliction of corporal punishment was not removed officially from the Royal Navy until 1949.

But in 1789 as Lieutenant William Bligh prepared for his mission, the harsh rules of the Royal Navy still prevailed, and that suited Bligh just fine.

The *Bounty's* Silly Breadfruit Mission

What must go down as one of the most amazing pieces of bureaucratic foolishness is the recommendation that a Royal Navy ship be dispatched to Tahiti so it could be loaded with breadfruit trees. These fruit-bearing plants were to be taken to the West Indies and planted as a source of food for African slaves.

English explorer Captain James Cook determined that breadfruit was an excellent—and inexpensive—way of replacing bread as a staple. English plantation owners took this idea to heart and pressured the government to finance an expedition to retrieve these trees so they could feed their slaves more economically (as if getting the free labor wasn't enough!), and the government agreed to do so.

Shiver Me Timbers

Lieutenant William Bligh's background as a sailor was rather impressive, since he served as the sailing master on Captain James Cook's final voyage that began in 1778. Bligh's hot temper and ability to twist the truth may have cost Cook his life. When Cook went ashore in Hawaii on February 14, 1779, to confront the Polynesians about thefts, he ordered Bligh and another officer into different boats to prevent the escape of Polynesians aboard canoes. When one canoe attempted to leave, it was not merely halted, but fired upon by both boats, which resulted in the killing of a chief. This news provoked Cook's own death at the hands of the natives. Bligh beat the rap by falsely claiming that Cook was dead before the shooting incident.

Years later, after breadfruit trees were finally taken to the West Indies in the wake of the mutiny on the *Bounty* and other tragedies we discuss, plantation owners learned that the slaves despised the fruit. Despite the bitterness of the *Bounty*'s voyage, it turned out its cargo was completely tasteless.

The Silliest Ship

The *Bounty* began life as a coal-carrying ship named the *Bethia*. Its displacement tonnage was 215 tons—by comparison, the *Mary Rose* weighed in at 700 tons and the *Titanic* at 52,310 tons. The Royal Navy purchased the ship in 1787 for 1,950 English pounds and refitted it at a cost of 4,456 pounds.

The large cabin over its stern that was usually the captain's quarters was converted into a seagoing arboretum. The wooden planks of the floor were covered in lead to protect them from water, and racks containing lead drainpipes were erected inside the cabin. The runoff from watering was collected and used again.

A Bounty of Desertion

Even though it didn't start out as a navy ship, the *Bounty* didn't go untouched by the personnel problems of the Royal Navy. Among the 46 men aboard the ship, including a botanist to care for the trees, 32 deserted while the ship was in Portsmouth, England, awaiting departure on its botanical mission.

Despite the desertions, there's no indication that anyone aboard the *Bounty* had been pressed into service against his will. Regardless, this rate of desertion was not unusual for the period.

Cruel Capt. Bligh and Mutinous Mr. Christian

Though William Bligh and Fletcher Christian are often thought of as complete opposites, the truth is that their backgrounds were similar. In fact, Christian was so well-liked by Bligh that he became Bligh's favorite officer—for a while. Both were well educated, and both were officers. At the time of the voyage, Bligh was 33 and Christian was 24.

Christian had even served under Bligh on several occasions while both were in the civilian merchant service following the American Revolution. The art of navigation was a skill Christian had picked up from Bligh during these voyages.

Handpicked Mutineer

Bligh's affinity for Christian ran so deep that he personally selected Christian to be the master's mate of the *Bounty*. Christian, wrote Bligh, "had a bright, pleasing countenance and tall commanding figure well adapted to those feats of strength and agility which he so frequently exhibited on the passage to Otaheite [Tahiti]."

Later, when things had gone sour between the two men, Bligh would describe Christian in less glowing terms. He subsequently wrote that Christian was "… strong made and rather bowlegged; subject to violent perspirations and particularly in his hands so that he soils anything he handles." Well, as they say, familiarity breeds contempt, and Bligh and Christian got very sick of one another before Operation Breadfruit was over.

Christian's personality has been dissected time and again, but it's generally believed he was a bit on the sensitive side. He eventually allowed Bligh's vile treatment of him to push him too far.

The Bounty's Blight

Bligh's biggest problem was his inability to control his temper. This lack of bearing cost him the leadership of the crew. He didn't command as much as he raged. He picked favorites and then converted them into enemies with unfair treatment and bad decisions. One of his worst traits was his lack of truthfulness regarding his performance. His logs and correspondence are filled with self-serving statements and outright lies.

The man whose name is synonymous with bad leadership once repudiated allegations that his crew was unhappy under his command by saying, "His [Bligh's] treatment of them was such that songs were made on him extolling his kindness."

How did Bligh get the job? One of the wealthy West Indies planters pushing for the expedition was Duncan Campbell for whom Bligh had worked as a merchant ship officer. Campbell pushed for Bligh's selection as expedition commander. The Royal Navy, ignorant of Bligh's ineptitude as a leader, gave him command.

Although famous for ordering 10 members of the crew flogged at various times during the infamous voyage, Bligh was generally no more cruel than your average Royal Navy officer of the period. But his willingness to order floggings, coupled with wicked and hurtful tongue-lashings of his crew, were the causes of the mutiny.

Know The Ropes

A ship's master was an extremely old and traditional job generally given to a master mariner who knew how to handle a ship and its sailors, and the master's mate was just beneath that position. Hundreds of years earlier, English warships held two ranking officers with one being in command of the soldiers on board and one in charge of running the ship itself.

Mutiny

The *Bounty* left Spithead—the site of the *Mary Rose*'s sinking 242 years previously—on December 23, 1787, and was headed for Tahiti to purchase breadfruit. The *Bounty* made its way down Africa's western coast, around the turbulent seas of Cape Horn, and eastward toward Tahiti, a distance of 27,000 miles.

Bligh, a highly capable mariner, immediately got off on the wrong foot with his crewmen when they learned that he had removed cheese from the ship's provisions and taken it to his home before the journey. Though this action may have been legal, it didn't sit well with the enlisted men.

Morale Worsens

Food was crucial to sailing ships, since sailors often fell victim to many nutritional illnesses. Bligh, who understood the importance of keeping the crew safe from illnesses of all types, ordered that pumpkins be eaten aboard the ship, instead of bread, since the pumpkins were going bad.

This sensible order was resented when Bligh made it clear he would flog any sailor who lodged a complaint about the food.

By the time *Bounty* had reached Tahiti on October 26, 1787, the crew had already become tired of Bligh's rigid behavior and his long tirades.

Desertion and Punishment

The *Bounty*'s stay in Tahiti was to last nearly six months during which time the sailors became friendly with the natives—most particularly the native women. On January 5, 1788, while the *Bounty* was still anchored off Tahiti, the crew discovered that William Muspratt, John Millward, and Charles Churchill had deserted. Since Churchill had been the ship's corporal and in charge of discipline among the enlisted men, things were obviously not going well!

On January 22, all three men surrendered. The punishment was meted out swiftly. Muspratt and Millward would receive 48 lashes apiece, while Churchill would get 24. The lashes would be delivered in two installments. Mate Thomas Hayward, who was on watch at the time the men escaped, was placed in irons.

Christian's Disillusionment

After the ship left Tahiti on April 4, 1788, Bligh continued to be an equal-opportunity abuser. Not even his fair-haired boy Fletcher Christian was spared, and Christian didn't take the browbeatings well at all. Ship's master John Fryer noted Christian's protest of his treatment when Christian told Bligh, "Sir, your abuse is so bad that I cannot do my duty with any Pleasure. I have been in hell for weeks with you."

Bligh, spoiling for another food fight, then began to accuse people on April 27 of stealing coconuts that he had purchased during one of the stops. Even though the entire crew had purchased the coconuts that were scattered about the *Bounty*'s deck, his wrath fell upon Christian—whose defense was that he had consumed only a single coconut. Bligh went into a screaming accusatory rampage before the entire crew.

Christian's now-famous inquiry then followed: "Why do you treat me thus, Captain Bligh?" To end the affair, Bligh seized everyone's coconuts and had them taken below decks, thereby treating every member of the crew as a criminal.

Christian Mutineer

Christian was obviously at the end of his rope, and he started behaving strangely. Predicting nothing but more hell at the hands of Bligh, Christian gave away his personal possessions and began tearing up his letters from home. He also discussed using some planking as a float and swimming from the ship.

When sailor George Stewart awakened Christian for his 4 A.M. watch, Stewart implored Christian to not swim from the ship, but to instead consider leading a mutiny. This is just what Christian decided to do on the spur of the moment. By dawn of April 28, 1789, Fletcher's mutineers had arrested Bligh and seized the ship. Standing next to Christian throughout the mutiny would be Charles Churchill, who had been sentenced to 24 lashes by Bligh.

Bligh Is Set Adrift

Christian at first ordered Bligh and those loyal to him to board a small, leaky boat but later relented and allowed the ship's captain to take a larger boat in better condition. Into that boat went Bligh and 18 other men.

The 23-foot-long craft had a sail, but stuffed as it was with people and laden with supplies and water, the boat had just over a half-foot of *freeboard,* or distance between the deck of the boat and the water. It was a dangerous situation. Needless to say, the breadfruit trees went over the side soon after Bligh did.

Words To Treasure

The **freeboard** of a ship is the distance between the surface of the ship's deck and the water.

Lieutenant William Bligh and the members of the crew who did not mutiny are set adrift from the HMS Bounty *by mutineer Fletcher Christian. (Courtesy ARTTODAY.COM)*

High and Bligh: An Amazing Journey

The journey that followed was nothing short of a miraculous feat of seamanship and survival at sea, which actually made Bligh something of a hero upon his return to England.

Amazingly enough, the small, overloaded boat managed to sail 3,618 miles between April 28 and June 12 without losing a single person. Of course, during the voyage, Bligh barked orders at everyone and drove them mercilessly until they arrived at the island of Timor in the Dutch East Indies.

Court-Martial

Upon Bligh's return to England on March 14, 1790, he faced a court-martial over his loss of the *Bounty* but was exonerated of any wrongdoing. He was allowed to complete the mission and did so this time with two ships and a complement of highly disciplined Royal Marines as insurance against future mutinies.

The Tragic Getaway of the Mutineers

Soon after Bligh and his 18 companions were turned loose upon the sea, Christian returned to Tahiti where 16 of the mutineers asked to remain. Staying with Christian and the *Bounty* were eight mutineers, six Polynesian men, a dozen Tahitian women, and a small girl. They finally landed at a nearly unknown place named Pitcairn Island, roughly 1,200 miles southeast of what is now French Polynesia.

Shiver Me Timbers

Christian knew about Pitcairn Island from a book he read while aboard the *Bounty*. The book was written by Captain Philip Carteret of the Royal Navy, who discovered the island in 1767. It was named after Royal Marine Major John Pitcairn, who was the first to spot it from the deck of Carteret's ship. Eight years after the discovery, Pitcairn would command the British troops in the April 19, 1775, Battle of Lexington and Concord in Massachusetts, the first fatal confrontation between the Americans and the British. When the Boston merchant ship *Topaz* came to Pitcairn in 1808, its New England sailors were most interested to learn the name of the island.

The mutineers and their Polynesian friends removed everything of value from the ship while it lay anchored in what would later become known as Bounty Bay. When the ship was emptied of its goods and stripped of usable materials, Christian ordered the hull of the *Bounty* burned to prevent it from being spotted by a passing ship.

What was left slipped beneath the powerful waves of the bay where it would remain undiscovered until 1957.

Murder and Mayhem

Christian divided the uninhabited island among the white mutineers but provided no property to the Polynesian men. This action alienated and angered the Polynesians, and the result was a steady drumbeat of discord and small-scale warfare that lasted for years.

By the time the American merchant ship *Topaz* arrived at Pitcairn Island in February 1808, all but one of the English mutineers were dead, as were many of the Polynesian men who had come there 19 years before.

John Adams was the sole surviving mutineer on the island, and he told the *Topaz*'s captain, Mayhew Folger of Nantucket, that Christian had died of natural causes. Christian's death in 1793 was followed by the killings of the other Englishmen by the Polynesian men. The Tahitian wives of the mutineers then killed the Polynesian men in retribution. The crew of the *Topaz* also learned of the *Bounty*'s fate and reported this information to English naval authorities.

What Was Christian's Real Fate?

Adams's story changed considerably when a pair of English warships came to the island in 1814 while hunting for an American warship during the War of 1812. Adams said Christian had been murdered by a native while gardening and that the other murders had been organized by mutineers William McCoy, who died in a drunken fall, and Matthew Quintal, who was executed by Adams and fellow mutineer Edward Young.

Shiver Me Timbers

What exactly happened to Fletcher Christian? In 1808 (the same year the *Topaz* came to Pitcairn), Christian was allegedly seen in England by Peter Heywood, a former officer of the *Bounty*. Oddly, the Royal Navy did nothing when Captain Folger reported that Pitcairn was the island refuge of Christian and his mutineers. Christian's boyhood friend, poet William Wordsworth, dropped from view for several periods during which Christian was "sighted" in England. Both were from the same town of Cockermouth. It appears that Elvis was not the first celebrity to be spotted frequently after his death!

Opening Pandora's Box

Eager for justice, the Royal Navy dispatched the HMS *Pandora* with its 24 guns and 160 sailors to search the South Pacific for Fletcher Christian and his mutineers. At the time it left, Bligh predicted that the *Pandora* would not return, since its captain, Edward Edwards, was unfamiliar with the Endeavour Straits that lie off of Australia's northern coast and had to be navigated to get to Tahiti.

On October 22, 1790, the *Pandora* sailed off on its South Pacific manhunt. Although Edwards was known to be as tyrannical as Bligh, he wasn't nearly as good a mariner. But even though he glided right past Pitcairn Island during his hunt for the *Bounty*'s crew, he still managed to arrest 14 of the surviving mutineers who had remained in Tahiti. The *Pandora* left Tahiti on May 8, 1791. A pair of mutineers who didn't survive their stay on Tahiti to be arrested were Matthew Thompson and Charles Churchill. In the end Thompson murdered Churchill and was in turn executed by avenging islanders sometime in 1790.

Although several of the captured survivors truthfully stated they had been kept on the *Bounty* with the mutineers against their wishes, Edwards considered anyone left behind guilty of mutiny and imprisoned them all aboard his ship.

Pandora's Sweatbox

Edward's wrath against the alleged mutineers knew no bounds. He had the ship's carpenter build a covered box that measured only 11 feet by 18 feet on the deck of the ship in which he placed the prisoners. They were kept there 24 hours a day with their arms and legs bound with iron chains. The crude enclosure was locked, and the men were forced to lie in pools of sweat swimming with maggots—Princess Cruise Lines this was not!

Wreck of the Prison Ship

Not knowing his way around Australia's Endeavour Straits, Edwards blundered into the Great Barrier Reef in the middle of a storm on August 28, 1791. This storm shoved the *Pandora* over a reef, ripping open its hull. When the prisoners realized that the *Pandora* was doomed to sink, they broke their chains so as to not go down with the ship. The ever-cruel Edwards ordered them secured again.

Men pumped seawater from the leaking ship for hours until it finally began to sink. Most of the mutineers made it out of the box as the ship slipped beneath the Pacific; however, four mutineers and 31 members of the crew perished. Edwards was among the 99 who survived and made their way 1,000 miles to the island of Timor in the Dutch East Indies—the same location Bligh reached after the mutiny.

Shiver Me Timbers

Edwards was a pretty mean guy. Soon after the wreck, the lifeboats from the ship carried the crew and the mutineers to a tiny desert island, where Edwards refused to let the mutineers find shade under a canvas sail. They had to bury themselves in the sand to escape the broiling sun. Without clothing or hats, their heads, faces, and necks became horribly sunburned and were soon covered with painful sunburn blisters. Edwards, who was the policeman in the mutiny, was acting as judge and jury and had already begun dispensing justice.

Justice?

The 10 accused mutineers who survived the *Pandora*'s wreck finally went to trial on September 12, 1792, more than three years after the mutiny. Of these, six were convicted; James Morrison was given a suspended sentence and Peter Heywood was heavily criticized but absolved of blame. A legal technicality made William Muspratt a free man.

Tom Ellison, Thomas Burkett, and John Millward received the ultimate penalty and were hanged from the *yardarm* of a warship in Portsmouth Harbor. They died without complaint of slow strangulation in front of an audience of sailors and officers.

Bligh would eventually be named governor of New South Wales in 1806. Not to break with tradition, his vile temper led him to verbally abuse a sheep farmer whose land Bligh threatened to confiscate. This sort of talk went over like an iron ballast bar and led to an armed revolt of local soldiers. The revolt put Bligh on a ship to be returned to England.

Words To Treasure

A **yardarm** is the end of a **spar,** or horizontal support pole that is part of a vertical mast. Its actual purpose, when not used as an execution platform, is to hold the square sails of a ship.

Back in England, a government report blasted Bligh's "longing to gratify his insatiably tyrannical disposition." Bligh's military career was finally at an end. Nearly 15 years after avoiding any responsibility for the mutiny that cost him his ship, Bligh's luck had nonetheless run out because of his inability to control his foul temper and self-serving behavior.

Finding the *Bounty's* Wreck

Although many knew where the *Bounty* sank after the 1808 visit to Pitcairn Island by the American ship *Topaz,* no one actually went looking for the ship until intrepid *National Geographic* writer and photographer Louis Marden dove in Pitcairn Bay in 1957.

Marden, a legend among adventure writers, traveled the globe for his prestigious magazine. He went to the island with his scuba equipment specifically to locate the wreckage of the ship. When he found the ship's heavy iron ballast bars on the floor of the bay, Marden had essentially determined the precise location of the Bounty's sinking. With the bars as a reference point he then calculated the probable position of ship's other remains and was successful in finding additional artifacts.

Touching the Past

Diving in the rough waves of the dangerously turbulent bay, Marden located a lead pipe that had apparently been part of the plumbing system for the breadfruit trees. Shipworms that proliferated in the warm, tropical waters had devoured all the wood, leaving only bits of copper, hull sheathing, and other metal parts.

Words To Treasure

A **pintle** is a type of pin that attaches a rudder to the rear of a ship and is ordinarily made out of a corrosion-resistant metal such as bronze. The **rudder,** mounted at the stern of the ship and used for steering, is usually wooden and sheathed with copper.

In 1933, Parkin Christian, the great-great-grandson of Fletcher Christian, used a grappling hook to recover the *rudder* and *pintle*—used for attaching the rudder to the hull—of the *Bounty.* Parkin Christian was 73 when he met Marden on Pitcairn Island in 1957.

Believe it or not, anyone who might be interested in getting a good look at a full-size version of the *Bounty* can do so. A replica of the ship—based upon its original plans—was constructed for the 1962 Metro-Goldwyn-Meyer film *Mutiny on the Bounty.* The ship is now owned by the nonprofit Tall Ship Bounty Foundation that teaches sailing skills. Another replica of the ship was built for the 1935 film version starring Clark Gable and Charles Laughton.

Discovering Pandora

Filmmaker Ben Cropp and naturalist Steve Domm believed they knew where they could find the HMS *Pandora* but needed a little help from above—in the form of a Royal Australian Air Force plane known as a Neptune. Since this plane was designed to hunt for submarines by using an airborne *magnetic anomaly detector* (*MAD*) device, it was perfect for the *Pandora* search.

The Neptune employed to search for the *Pandora* carrying a MAD in the tail and buzzed an area marked by Domm and Cropp. Eventually, the device registered a location where a significant amount of iron was interfering with the earth's magnetic field. Cropp and Domm's research had accurately predicted the approximate location of the *Pandora*. The divers were electrified to discover the ship during a dive to the site found by the magnetic anomaly detector.

With the discovery of the HMS *Pandora*'s wreckage off Australia's Great Barrier Reef, both ships made famous by the *Mutiny on the Bounty* had been accounted for. By 1983, Australian underwater archaeologists were mapping the site and recovering an incredible number of artifacts. The wreck was lying beneath 110 feet of water off the northern tip of Australia's Cape York Peninsula.

Pandora's "Treasures"

A tremendous amount of the *Pandora*'s wreckage remains, but some of the greatest finds are actually medical instruments. One of these is a urinary syringe used in the treatment of venereal disease. The syringe would send mercury into the urethra of indiscreet sailors as a pre-antibiotic treatment for sexually transmitted bacterial infections.

The pocket watch of the *Pandora*'s surgeon, Dr. George Hamilton, was found remarkably intact and may mark the time of the ship's sinking at around 11:12 P.M. on August 28, 1791. A marble mortar, used for the mixing of pharmaceuticals of the day, was located amidst a clump of colorful coral.

Continuing Recovery

Underwater archaeologists are still visiting the *Pandora*'s wreck site. The expeditions carefully map the area to be worked on by installing a grid of plastic pipe. They then meticulously remove silt to expose objects whose position is carefully noted before recovery. The objects that are recovered are then turned over to preservation experts who restore the artifacts to prevent future damage.

The recovered items are being restored and prepared for exhibition at the Museum of Tropical Queensland in Townsville, Australia.

A map of the wreck site of the HMS Bounty. *(Drawn by Ken Ellis)*

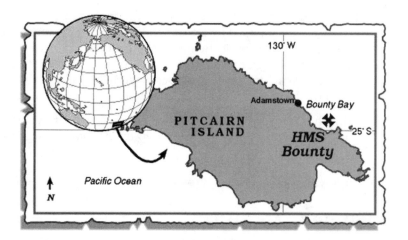

The Least You Need to Know

➤ Although none of the sailors aboard the HMS *Bounty* were "pressed" into service by the Royal Navy, many thousands of sailors were forced into open-ended service to meet England's military needs.

➤ Flogging has been practiced for thousands of years in other cultures and was not an English invention.

➤ The HMS *Bounty* wasn't originally a warship, but a coal delivery ship that was purchased and refitted for its mission of sailing to the Pacific and retrieving breadfruit trees.

➤ Fletcher Christian was a junior officer aboard the HMS *Bounty* and was something of a favorite of Bligh's for a brief period. It was during this time that Christian was named master's mate on the ship.

➤ Although Bligh ordered 10 men to receive lashes for various infractions of regulations, he was not considered any more eager to use the whip on his sailors than the average English naval officer of the period.

➤ Although Fletcher Christian is believed to have been murdered on Pitcairn in 1793, some witnesses claimed to have seen the mutineer in England in 1808. According to one rumor, Christian may have secretly visited his boyhood friend, poet William Wordsworth.

Chapter 16

Wreck of the Royal Charter

In This Chapter

➤ Outback gold rush

➤ Famous and fast

➤ Final voyage home

➤ Storm of the century

➤ It takes a village to raise a fortune

➤ Laying the blame

The wreck of the *Royal Charter* is a fatal example of being in the wrong place at the wrong time. Although the ship had sailed more than 20,000 miles during a two-month trip from Australia to England, it had few problems until it was just hours away from its home port.

It was the same old story in a lot of ways. It was an advanced ship with an innovative design that had proven itself time and again on the high seas; nevertheless, with its homecoming a seemingly sure thing, the beautiful ship was grabbed by fate and destroyed. The *Royal Charter* was considered one of the most capable ships of its time and was only four years old at the time of her loss.

This steam- and sail-powered clipper had the incredibly bad misfortune of having its arrival coincide with one of the worst storms to strike the British Isles in 100 years. Nearly 500 people died when the ship was beaten to pieces by the storm.

It seems that every time we start to think that we've outsmarted Mother Nature with some new technology, the old girl swats down our best efforts just to keep us humble. The *Royal Charter* stands as yet another example of human vulnerability stumbling headfirst into the power of nature.

And so—with a superb captain at the helm and a capable crew aboard—the *Royal Charter* sailed into a hurricane. By the time the winds quit blowing, at least 447 people (including all the women and children on board) were dead, most killed before the eyes of Welsh villagers working to save them.

The ship had been built to swiftly ferry people to and from Australia's gold rush, which was booming during the mid-1800s. Aboard the ship were prospectors of the lucky and unlucky variety, along with an assortment of other passengers including women and children.

Despite its bad finale, the *Royal Charter's* final voyage was initially a speedy and enjoyable one for its passengers. Although there's little mystery in this shipwreck, people did attempt to point the finger of blame, but it was ultimately recognized that in this situation a reliable ship lost a valiant struggle with the forces of nature.

The wreck of the Royal Charter *as it smashes upon the rocks of the Welsh island of Anglesey. (Courtesy of the National Maritime Museum, Greenwich, England)*

Unlike the *Titanic* disaster with a mighty ship sinking slowly into frigid, glass-smooth water as a doomed band played music, the sinking of the *Royal Charter* was not picturesque. In fact, the death of the *Royal Charter* was a horrifyingly ugly display of nature's power along the bleak northern coast of Anglesey, a Welsh island protruding into the Irish Sea.

The *Royal Charter's* death occurred in a cove barely large enough for its 320-foot hull, but a deathtrap perfectly designed by nature for chewing the ship to pieces with the aid of a storm.

Put your bow into the wind, turn your smoking pipe over to keep the rain out, and steady yourself for the terrible ordeal you're about to experience.

Outback Gold Rush

After the American colonies so rudely booted out England's soldiers and taxmen during the American Revolution, the English decided that Australia was the next land of opportunity. It would prove for many immigrants to be just as wild, beautiful, and profitable as America.

After the 1851 discovery of gold in Australia, gold fever swept through England, and thousands of would-be prospectors wanted to get to the "land down under" immediately! They didn't have time to waste on a three-month voyage.

Shiver Me Timbers

Although Australia's gold made it a land of opportunity following the ore's discovery in 1851, the continent had rather inauspicious beginnings as the site of English penal colonies. The convicts actually played a major role in developing the country prior to the arrival of un-shackled settlers that began streaming in during the last half of the nineteenth century.

People began to flood to Australia, which had been claimed by Captain James Cook during his 1770 expedition of discovery to the region. The continent, first used as a penal colony, was later viewed as a fairly promising place to colonize. Instead of traveling in shackles like the convicts taken to Australia previously, the regular folks heading for Australia dined with the ship's captain.

In the five years following 1852, when the settlers really began pouring in, more than 226,000 people flooded into Australia. While many came to prospect for gold, others arrived to earn a living in other businesses. Of this number, only 3,000 were Americans and another 1,500 were French. Many others were English (100,000), Irish (60,000), and Scottish (8,000). And they were all in a hurry.

The Need for Speed

The distance to Australia from England was about 20,000 miles, and on a slow ship the voyage might take six months. Sailing ships could literally move like the wind—when the wind blew—but when it didn't, the ships lolled about on the sea like giant fishing corks. Some way had to be found to make ships move without depending on the capriciousness of the weather.

The solution came in the form of the steam engine, which was put into use on sailing ships by 1850. Speedier hull designs accompanied this innovation. Although the steam engines of the day weren't very powerful—and were prone to blowing up and breaking down—they still provided a way to keep a ship moving despite being caught in the *doldrums.*

Don't Go Overboard!

After reading this book and deciding you're not worried about being in a shipwreck, you'll probably want to purchase a schooner or another type of extremely expensive sailing ship. But beware the **doldrums**—a region known for slack or nonexistent winds that runs along the equator. Crossing this belt is tough in a sailing ship, since you might find yourself **becalmed** (left motionless due to a lack of wind). Just be patient and in a few days—or weeks—you'll be on your way. Take a good book!

A Time of Seafaring Innovation

Traditionally, it's been hard to let go of one technology as another one comes along, and the *Royal Charter* was ultimately a victim of this tendency. In the 15 years preceding 1850, American shipbuilders had been refining a sleek, fast, strong sailing ship that was known as a clipper. It was no longer a fat, round ship but more like a really big racing yacht.

The clipper revolutionized shipbuilding for a while, since it made sailing ships faster. But then steam power came along, and shipbuilders found themselves unable to resist this promising new technology. Rather than jump into building what later became known as steam-ships, shipbuilders first combined the sleekness of the clipper hull and its sails with steam power.

At the same time, shipbuilders began to use iron for ship hulls. These new ships were strong and no longer susceptible to shipworms.

For a brief period during the mid-1800s, ships would carry both sails and steam engines. Though wind against the sails would provide most of the propulsion, the steam engine could provide power when the wind didn't cooperate.

For the first time in history, a captain could snort at a lack of wind and order the steam engine started. You can imagine that getting the steam engine chugging didn't mean you were suddenly in a speedboat, but it did mean you could at least keep moving.

Record Breaker: The *Royal Charter*

Built at the Sandycroft ironworks in Flintshire in 1855, the *Royal Charter*'s birthplace in the British Isles was not to be far from where its death would occur four years later. As if to provide an omen of things to come, the *Royal Charter*'s birth did not come easily.

The shipbuilder originally constructing the iron-hulled *Royal Charter* went bankrupt, and the task of completing the ship fell to its owners, the Eagle Line, a firm that specialized in making shipping runs to Australia. The ship was lengthened during final construction so it was seven times as long as it was wide, a critical element of clipper design.

The *Royal Charter* had a displacement tonnage of 2,179 and a keel length of 320 feet (although its actual length with bow and stern overhang was around 336 feet). A trio of masts shot toward the sky for the massive sails that would be used for most of the trip as propulsion. In addition, the ship could carry 700 tons of anthracite coal to fuel the 200-horsepower steam engine when the winds died down.

Difficult Beginnings

The *Royal Charter* was designed to be fast, strong, reliable, and safe, but no one could build luck into it, and that shortcoming plagued its early days.

Attempts to launch the ship in 1855 proved abortive, since the water was too shallow for it to float. Getting it off the ways—the wooden platform upon which ships are built and launched—would involve a digging operation before it could be launched. Shortly after the launching debacle, the *Royal Charter* ran aground on a sandbar, causing substantial damage to its hull.

Disaster nearly struck early when a naval engineer who helped design the *Royal Charter* prompted the crew to place 400 tons of unnecessary ballast in the hold to compensate for the weight of the towering mast. This unneeded weight robbed the *Royal Charter* of two feet of freeboard. Water was only six feet from the deck, instead of the required eight feet. When it began its maiden voyage for Australia from Liverpool on January 18, 1956, rough seas sent water crashing over the *Royal Charter*'s deck, soaking the belongings of passengers below. The overly heavy ship wallowed in the choppy seas.

As its sails pulled the *Royal Charter* forward faster than the steam engine could move it, the propeller was raised to keep it from causing drag. But the ship was so low, the propeller still plowed through the water, creating resistance.

The *Royal Charter* was in such bad shape that the captain decided to risk embarrassment and return to port to correct the situation. The 400 tons of useless ballast were dumped, and the lightened ship sped on its way, handling like a graceful clipper instead of a partially submerged log.

Don't Go Overboard!

Ballast is weight placed at the bottom of a ship along its keel to provide balance so its hull stays solidly in the water and doesn't bob like a cork. However, too much or too little ballast can be trouble for an otherwise capable ship. Too much ballast can cause a ship to ride dangerously low in the water, making it easier for waves to crash over its decks. Too little ballast can make a ship dangerously uncontrollable, or at least so unstable that everyone gets seasick.

Words To Treasure

A **propeller** is a device whose blades are designed to push water backward or forward depending on the direction of its rotation. So effective were propellers that they replaced paddlewheels on early steamships.

Famous and Fast

The *Royal Charter* then roared down Africa's west coast and streaked eastward across the treacherous waters of Cape of Good Hope and through the Indian Ocean. Its maiden voyage was nothing short of a complete success.

First-class passengers—as they still do—enjoyed delicious food and the company of the captain. A pair of seagoing dairy cows even provided fresh milk. With the wind usually in its favor and the chugging steam engine to move the ship when fair winds failed to blow, the *Royal Charter* made the trip to Melbourne in just shy of 60 days.

Although a good airliner can take us the same distance in about 20 hours of flight time, getting around the world in less than two months made a big splash in the nineteenth century. You'd think the ship had broken the sound barrier the way people went on. It was a terrific feat, and one the Eagle Line proudly displayed in its advertising. Its slogan was "The magnificent steam clipper *Royal Charter*—Australia in under 60 days."

Final Voyage Home

The gold rush was still booming in Australia as miners continued to pour into the country along with farmers, sheep ranchers, businesspeople, grocers, and families looking for a fresh start in a new land. And the *Royal Charter* was carrying people as quickly as it could to this mysterious continent.

On August 26, 1859, the tried-and-true *Royal Charter* was preparing to depart for Liverpool with 390 passengers and a crew of 112. It was also carrying two tons of gold brought on board in wooden crates. The value of the gold was then worth about four British pounds an ounce.

With the pound equaling roughly five American dollars at the time, this treasure of 256,000 ounces of gold was valued at about $1.28 million dollars. On today's market the gold would be worth approximately $60 million.

In a rare occurrence, a few wooden boxes turned an ordinary ship into a "treasure ship."

Capable Captain

Signing for the gold was the *Royal Charter*'s captain, Thomas Taylor, who was considered a tough, no-nonsense seafarer with a rock-solid reputation. He had sailed to Australia as a passenger aboard the *Royal Charter* on its maiden voyage to Melbourne nearly four years earlier.

Physician William Gilmour, who sailed as surgeon aboard the *Royal Charter* on four of its Liverpool-Melbourne voyages, later described Taylor as a strict disciplinarian and as a man who had climbed to the top of his profession through skill and hard work instead of connections. Said Gilmour of Taylor: "A better commander and seaman never had charge of a ship."

Pocket Money

Although tons of gold were stowed in the *Royal Charter*'s strong room, dozens of passengers—particularly returning gold miners—were carrying their profits with them as gold coins tied around their waists in money belts.

The farsighted James Dean put his accumulated wealth in the form of a check carried in a watertight pouch. Dean's foresight would later save both his life and the three years of wages he was bringing home to his wife.

Like the sinking of the SS *Central America* that had occurred two years before the loss of the *Royal Charter,* many passengers were carrying gold on their persons. This extra weight would pull many travelers to their deaths when the *Royal Charter* ended up on the rocks two months later.

An Uneventful Trip—Almost

Being in the Southern Hemisphere as it departed Melbourne, the *Royal Charter* had to pick its way through icebergs breaking off from the glaciers of the South Pole region. Unlike the RMS *Titanic* 53 years later, the *Royal Charter* avoided a collision with any floating chunks of ice.

The voyage back to Liverpool was relatively calm with the only real excitement provided by the Australian parakeets brought aboard by the passengers. These valuable birds often escaped from their cages in mid-ocean, and—finding nowhere to go—winged up to the masts and their horizontal spars where the birds perched until they were recaptured or flew away.

The *Royal Charter* made its way toward Liverpool with its collection of wild and woolly miners, correct clergymen, mothers, children, and entrepreneurs. Among those on board was the Anglican Reverend Charles Vere Hodge, whose unhappy wife had moved to New Zealand, leaving him with their 10 children. He had followed her at first, but after two years was forced to return to his duties as a minister.

At least two on board were traveling under false names, including a William Gardiner (passing as "Garden") and a mysterious man named S. Perry whose real name was never determined. It is known that Gardiner had stolen nearly 4,000 pounds. On October 25, 1859 (the 58th day of the voyage), the scoundrel Gardiner departed at Queenstown on Ireland's coast with 12 other passengers. A day later Gardiner's wife and 447 people would be dead.

Storm of the Century

On October 24, Captain Taylor received a flattering letter of thanks from the passengers to whom he had promised an arrival in Liverpool within 24 hours. However, as they sighted Holyhead Island just off the coast of North Wales around 1:30 P.M., many on board began to take note of a strange haze in the air and a correspondingly odd-looking sky.

Regardless of the appearance of the skies, the pressure on the *Royal Charter's* three barometers held steady—indicating no storms were imminent. Because all systems seemed to be on the mark, Taylor never had reason to seek shelter in the nearest harbor, particularly since he was less than 100 miles from his destination.

Shiver Me Timbers

Although a severe change in barometric pressure usually precedes and accompanies a cyclonic storm, no such warning was available prior to the terrible hurricane that slammed the *Royal Charter* into the north coast of Anglesey Island. A scientist at the Liverpool Observatory would later testify that barometric readings there had hardly changed even when the massive storm was overhead. The only warning that bad weather was on its way was a thin black cloud formation that choked the light from the sky. As the *Royal Charter* moved ever closer to its rendezvous with fate, the storm that was heading northward had already slammed English cities to the southwest of Anglesey.

Fighting the Storm

By 8 P.M., the *Royal Charter* found itself in the worst possible spot. As powerful winds—approaching a force of 80 mph—created huge waves, the clipper found itself being pushed into the shore that was no more than five miles away.

Taylor attempted to use his steam engine to propel him through the winds toward the open waters of the adjacent Irish Sea, but the ship could make no headway against the great winds. He then contemplated chopping down the masts to reduce the ship's wind resistance but hesitated to do so, since the felled masts could cause nearly as much damage to the ship as the storm.

Taylor began firing a cannon and launching rockets to signal that he needed a pilot on board to help him navigate the dangerously close rocky coast, but no pilots could reach the ship. It was now 7 P.M., and the sea was growing wilder by the hour. To make matters worse, the high seas and heavy rain prevented any potential rescuers from seeing the *Royal Charter's* struggle.

Out of Control

With four crewmen straining on the ship's wheel in a mighty effort to turn the *Royal Charter*, Taylor ordered that the ship be steered directly into the wind. The men strained on the wheel until the rudder was finally moved, only to find that the ship was no longer "answering," or responding, to the rudder's movements. With its

200-horsepower engine unable to push the *Royal Charter* into the Irish Sea, Taylor knew the ship was little more than a giant piece of driftwood following nature's command.

Final Efforts

As winds rose to 100 mph, buffeting the ship, Taylor ordered men into the rigging to unfurl a small sail to help turn the ship in an effort to regain control. The crew struggled valiantly, but storm damage to the masts and powerful winds made the attempt impossible. Taylor gave up on regaining control in the wild winds and waves and ordered the ship's two anchors dropped, believing—and hoping—this action would halt the *Royal Charter*'s drift to shore.

The two anchors sank to the seafloor, and hundreds of extra feet of heavy iron chain were *paid out* to hold the ship steady. However, even this step did not help, and the ship was slowly pushed backward toward the rocky shore of a small village named Moelfre, which lies on the north coast of Anglesey. All the while, the propeller of the ship was pushing the bow toward the wind.

One of the seamen struggling with the sails was sailor Isaac Lewis, who was born and reared in Moelfre on Anglesey. Within hours the *Royal Charter* would be smashed upon Moelfre's shore, and seaman Lewis would endure the most horrifying and tragic homecoming imaginable.

Fatal Indecision?

As the hurricane howled and the *Royal Charter* was slowly pushed toward the grim, rocky shore of Anglesey Island, Taylor hesitated to chop down the ship's three masts, hoping the puny engine would push the clipper away from shore. Eventually, however, Taylor did order the masts chopped down. (You'll recall that the Spanish treasure fleet captains used this technique to both slow and lighten their storm-driven ships.)

The masts had provided a sail-effect during crucial hours when the *Royal Charter*'s crew fought to keep the ship from drifting. But at 1:30 A.M., October 26, Taylor finally decided to fell the three masts with axes to slow the ship's progress toward shore and the dangerous breakers. The snapping of one of the ship's two anchor chains prompted Taylor's decision.

Words To Treasure

To **pay out** is not to give away money but to release slack on a line or anchor chain.

So Near and So Far

With the masts cut down, the crew and passengers held on to anything they could in the bucking, rolling ship as 60-foot waves crashed into the *Royal Charter*. At 6 A.M. those aboard peered into the gray dawn light to see they were a mere 75 feet from land. This predicament was both heaven and hell.

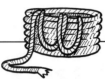

Know The Ropes

Captain Taylor was dealing with a lot of complicated circumstances. His ship would not respond to steering commands and was being blown toward shore by 100–mph winds. He had no way of precisely knowing how quickly he was moving toward a shoreline he couldn't see. Cutting the masts earlier would have slowed the rate at which the *Royal Charter* was being blown to the coast, but the hundreds of feet of rope running through the masts might have fouled the pathetically small propeller trying to push the ship to safety. He also had to be worried about the masts crashing through the decks and causing injuries.

Words To Treasure

A **bosun's chair** is a chair rigged with a pulley at its top that is used for transferring people and items between ships at sea, or between a ship and the shore. It can usually carry only one person at a time and is relatively slow, since it is pulled by hand.

The huge masts cut down hours earlier danced madly in the waves crashing against the rocky shore. The waves were incessant and massive, with some as high as 60 feet. The 320-foot *Royal Charter* lay parallel to the shore as waves continuously hammered its iron hull. The 25 yards of water between the ship and the shore was a deathtrap, and lifeboats were useless in the violent seas.

A fleet of rescue helicopters would have been the only option for sea rescue, but those were still 90 years away from being invented. Virtually all aboard had only two hours to live.

Desperate Measures

Seaman Joseph Rodgers leaped into the wild surf with a rope tied about his torso hoping to reach shore. If he survived, the smaller rope about him could haul a heavier line ashore so a *bosun's chair* could carry the passengers to safety. Rodgers was grabbed by the waves and heaved upon the rocks where he was fortuitously saved by locals from the village of Moelfre, just behind the shore.

Once the bosun's chair was erected, it hung so low that huge waves swamped it while it was pulled between the *Royal Charter* and the shore. As you can well imagine, many passengers were afraid to get into the chair.

A group of 11 riggers that had hitched a ride aboard the *Royal Charter* from another boat on October 25, however, were not so shy about using the chair. They rushed the contrivance only to be ordered back by a clipper crewman. The sailor demanded that passengers be evacuated first with preference given to women and children.

However, many women declined outright to climb aboard the flouncing conveyance, fearful not only of using the chair that was slammed by the seas but also of leaving their husbands behind. Members of the crew then tried, and several were washed off to their deaths. Eventually, perhaps only as few as three men were saved by the bosun's chair.

The End of the Royal Charter

A foot of water sloshed over the deck of the ship as huge waves shoved and battered the giant hulk. The *Royal Charter*'s iron hull made horrible grinding noises on the rocks at the bottom of the small bay until, at last, one huge wave ripped the once-beautiful clipper in two. The two ends of the ship broke open like a snapped pencil, exposing passengers in the decks below.

Passengers spilled out of the ship's innards and were swept up on the howling sea and flung against floating debris or the unyielding rocks ashore. Many, particularly the women, were heavily dressed, while others were weighted with their heavy gold in money belts.

Apprentice Seaman Walter Hughes was thrown into the churning water as the ship broke apart but not before glimpsing a scene that haunted him for the rest of his life: that of "three small children, standing on the deck, holding each other's hands, screaming."

Stripped for Survival

James Dean watched as people struggled in the crashing waves and realized that most who struggled were heavily clothed. He removed most of his clothing and, still keeping the check representing his savings, leaped into the water. A nonswimmer, Dean grabbed onto a floating box only to end up struggling for possession of it with a drowning man.

Dean surrendered the box, found another, and was then thrown onto the rocks by a huge wave. Before he could get his footing, he was grabbed by another wave and hauled back into the watery maelstrom. On the fourth time he was thrown to the rocks, Dean managed to grab a rope tossed by a Moelfre villager, and both he and his money were pulled to safety.

Sudden Death

It was not even 8 A.M., and hundreds of bodies were already floating in the water.

Many of those killed had not drowned, but had been beaten to death or knocked unconscious by heavy debris from the wreck. People with terrible wounds were everywhere, including a man whose skull was smashed open. It was obvious to those who saw him that his brain had been washed free from its cavity.

In addition, those wearing clothing and heavy boots were often too weak to pull themselves up to the shore even if they managed to be thrown onto the rocks alive.

Before it was over, there would be at least 447 dead and only 41 survivors, of which all were men. Of these, 18 were crewmembers. Captain Taylor and all of his officers perished in the breakup of the *Royal Charter*.

One of the dead was Isaac Lewis, whose father had come down to the wreck only to recognize his son on the doomed ship. Lewis' body was later found along the shore.

Shiver Me Timbers

Seaman Isaac Lewis was standing on the bow of the *Royal Charter,* now torn into two pieces at its center by the waves, when he and his father spotted one another. The elder Lewis had come to the horrific scene to help out and soon realized that his son was aboard. Much legend has developed around this event, with some accounts claiming the son called to his father as he was swept to sea. What is certain is that Isaac Lewis's body was discovered less than a mile from his boyhood home in the coastal village of Moelfre.

It Takes a Village to Raise a Fortune

As villagers formed human chains in the raging surf to pull the injured from the water, one survivor, Seaman George Suaicar, held on to the end of one chain and grabbed nine people who still had signs of life.

As he did so, showers of gold coins began to wash about the bay, broken free from the strong room where the gold had been stored. The waves had cracked open the room like an egg. Wrapped about many of the bodies being flung on shore were money belts packed with gold coins, nuggets, and dust, making them perhaps the wealthiest corpses in history.

Inevitably, Moelfre villagers would be accused of both stealing the ship's spilled treasure and stripping the bodies of the dead for their gold. Though how much gold local villagers took was never determined, they knew better than anyone where such items would wash up on the shore.

Reports of looting and pilfering of the dead prompted authorities to call in soldiers and marines to patrol the site of the wreck. Only 1,200 British pounds' worth of gold was returned as recovered from the dead.

Salvage

Salvage efforts followed within a month as helmet divers and salvage barges appeared at the sight of the fearsome and fatal wreck. By early November, divers were pushing their way past decomposing bodies in the submerged tangle of the wreck, looking for the gold cargo valued at 322,400 English pounds. By the end of December 1859, salvors had recovered at least 275,000 British pounds' worth of gold.

> **Shiver Me Timbers**
>
> As divers went down to the wreck to search for the gold, more bodies had begun to float to shore. Family members who had flocked to Moelfre to identify the dead thought the efforts of the divers were dislodging the bodies. However, bodies that sink will usually rise again owing to the effects of gases generated by decomposition. By this time, drowning victims are horribly bloated and seldom recognizable. Families were eventually encouraged to stay away from Moelfre, as identification of the bodies was becoming nearly impossible.

Golden Legacy

Over the years, a number of salvage attempts have been made on the wreck of the *Royal Charter* with one of the most recent taking place in 1986. This well-financed expedition did a large amount of work clearing sand and rock from around the wreck in search of the remaining gold.

Ironically, all this hard work was ruined when hurricane Charlie roared through the region and smashed the efforts of salvors Jack Smart and Peter Day. The pair had attempted a previous salvage in 1972 but found little.

Laying the Blame

Although some distraught survivors wildly accused Captain Taylor of being drunk in the final hours of the *Royal Charter*'s life, they subsequently withdrew their accusations.

A Board of Trade hearing was held and testimony heard. In a report issued to the board on November 28, 1859, the ship's design was considered strong and capable, and it was believed her captain and crew had done their jobs well.

However, the hearing report pointed out that Taylor should have removed his masts sooner than he did while adding, "… the officers and the crew to the last were indifferent to the preservation of their own lives and solely intent on their duty."

*A map of the wreck site of
the* Royal Charter.
(Drawn by Ken Ellis)

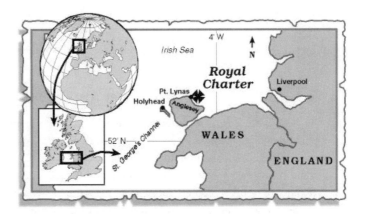

The Least You Need to Know

➤ The *Royal Charter* was built on the fast clipper hull design but with an iron hull and an auxiliary steam engine that helped it move even when there wasn't enough wind to fill its sails.

➤ Some angry survivors of the *Royal Charter* disaster accused Captain Thomas Taylor of being drunk, though these charges were later determined to be false.

➤ The *Royal Charter* broke a record for traveling to Australia by completing its maiden voyage there within 60 days, a very fast time for the mid-1800s.

➤ On its final voyage, the *Royal Charter* had to pick its way through a section of the Pacific Ocean dotted with icebergs from the Antarctica region, though the ship managed to do so without incident.

➤ The 447 who died aboard the *Royal Charter* included all the women and children on board, although 41 men, among them 18 crewmen, managed to survive.

➤ Some Moelfre villagers may have helped themselves to gold that washed ashore with many of the victims of the wreck.

Slow Death of the SS *Central America*

Ships are big things, and they can take a long time to sink—especially if those aboard pitch in and fight the sea. If collision or a storm damages a ship, its agony can go on for days. This is just the sort of slow death that happened to the SS *Central America,* which sailed into a powerful hurricane 200 miles off Cape Hatteras, North Carolina, on September 11, 1857.

What resulted was a 36-hour struggle between the damaged ship and the stormy waters of the Graveyard of the Atlantic. The ship and the 578 aboard eventually lost their unequal struggle with the sea. Although 154 were rescued from the ship, another 426 men perished. The storm, for its part, simply howled on without taking notice.

But the *Central America* was more than just a passenger ship. It was virtually an American version of a Spanish treasure galleon, carrying an estimated $1 billion in gold in today's value from California's gold rush to the East Coast.

It may seem bizarre to you and me that anyone would choose to go from California to New York by sailing to Central America's Pacific coast, cross the Isthmus of Panama, and then board another ship for a voyage through the Caribbean and northward to New York. Well, just remember, it was 1857, and the Transcontinental Railroad was 12 years in the future.

The loss of the *Central America* represented not only the greatest loss of life and treasure in the history of American peacetime shipping but also an event marked by the heroic leadership of a captain who became a U.S. Navy hero.

The *Central America* plummeted 8,000 feet beneath the Atlantic with its estimated 21 tons of gold and its victims. It decomposed in darkness until one of the most carefully planned expeditions in the history of treasure hunting lighted the wreck site with remotely operated vehicles and retrieved much of its gold.

Words To Treasure

The abbreviation **SS** placed before the name of an American ship is sometimes thought to mean "state ship" but instead stands for "steamship."

After a nail-biting search, encroachment by aggressive would-be salvors, and all the problems of deep-ocean recovery, as much as $1 billion in gold was plucked from the wreck site by a consortium spawned in landlocked Columbus, Ohio.

"All aboard" for the last voyage of the SS *Central America*. After more than 130 years, its amazing cargo has finally made it home.

Thar's Gold in Them Thar Depths

Sometimes the worst tragedies start with the most joyous events, and no one has ever claimed the discovery of gold near Sacramento, California, in 1848 was anything less than wonderful.

The California gold rush coincided with the end of the Mexican-American War that resulted in Mexico ceding California to the United States as part of a peace treaty. It also happened at the time when Americans were already bored with the so-called West that extended only to the Great Plains. All eyes were on California, and the prospect of finding gold just lying about fueled the American concept of *Manifest Destiny*.

Though gold had previously been found in areas of California, it was the discovery of a lump of the yellow ore gold by carpenter John Marshall on January 24, 1848, that led to the realization that California contained massive gold deposits. He had been building a sawmill for John Sutter at the time of the discovery. The word shot around the world, and those who could traveled by land or sea to arrive in California in time to be dubbed "forty-niners," for the year in which they arrived.

However, the gold rush wasn't open-ended. By 1883, the California gold fields were already depleted. This unfortunate circumstance forced subsequent generations of Californians to abandon their gold mines and become Hollywood producers and scriptwriters. As much as $15 billion in gold in today's prices may have been panned, sluiced, dug, and scratched out of California between 1849 and 1868—the height of the gold rush.

American Treasure Ships

To those forty-niners, getting on a horse and heading east to return home with fortunes in gold didn't seem like the prudent thing to do in the 1840s and 1850s. The Indians were still a bit upset about their treatment at the hands of the white man, and the geographical obstacles were daunting. Let's also not forget the wild animals and the lack of convenience stores along the way. All these factors combined to make a dangerous trip at sea a veritable joy.

To make this trip, some ships departed from California or New York to round Cape Horn on the Southern tip of South America. This voyage was extremely long and not for the fainthearted. Others made a relatively short voyage to Panama where passengers and cargo were unloaded for a quick overland trip to the Pacific or Atlantic coasts where another ship waited to continue the voyage.

U.S. officials were convinced that providing reliable sea transportation to California was essential to speed up the colonization of California. This prompted the federal government to subsidize construction of a fleet of steamships that would carry people and goods to and from California under the command of U.S. Navy officers. One of these ships was the *George Law*, which later was renamed the SS *Central America*.

Words To Treasure

A general feeling among the American populace that became national policy was **Manifest Destiny**. This policy said that Americans were entitled to control all the territory between Mexico and Canada and from the Atlantic to the Pacific Oceans.

A Famous Captain

The steamships that carried thousands to California during the mid-1800s were commanded not by civilian ship's masters but by U.S. Navy officers supervising civilian crews. As it turned out, one of America's most famous Naval officers was commanding the *Central America* in 1857, and his name was Captain William Lewis Herndon.

This 43-year-old had explored the Amazon River on orders from the U.S. Navy when he was 36. His published account of the adventure, *Exploration of the Valley of the Amazon*, was widely read. Herndon's exploration and writings represented the deep interest the American people had in exploration and Manifest Destiny, or the conquest of the territory they perceived as their own.

A Fight for Life

Before those in California could board the SS *Central America* for the final leg of their journey from Panama to New York, the travelers would first have to board the SS *Sonora* in San Francisco for a 14-day trip to Panama. Once in the tropical nation, people and possessions would be loaded on a train for a 50-mile trip across the isthmus to the Caribbean coast to board the *Central America*.

Words To Treasure

Learning your way around a ship means learning a whole new set of terms. **Starboard** means anything to the right side of a ship, and **port** means the left side. A **list** is a constant leaning of a ship due to improper balancing brought about by a leak or bad loading. A **hatch** is a door you **secure** instead of close, and a **passageway** is a hallway. A **space** is a room, and a **cabin** is a living space. The **deck** is the floor, and a **bulkhead** is a wall. Have you heard enough of this **bilge**? (Bilge, of course, is the dirty water inside the lowest portion of a ship's hull.)

The side-wheel steamer *Central America* took her passengers aboard and sailed for Havana, Cuba, for a stopover before proceeding up America's East Coast on September 8, 1957.

Rising Water

Two days sailing out of Cuba, the *Central America* encountered heavy winds and high seas but all went well until Friday, September 11, 1857, when Chief Engineer George Ashby determined that the ship was taking on water faster than it could be pumped out.

Ashby could not locate any leaks other than water spurting through the shaft of one of the side wheels where it entered the hull. Though this was plugged, the force of the sea slamming the boat spat out the packing and the water continued to rise. It collected on one side of the boat giving it a *starboard list*.

The severe list created another problem as crewmen found it impossible to push coal to the steam engine furnaces in wheelbarrows. Notified of the situation, Captain Herndon ordered waiters into the hold to form a line moving the coal with baskets to keep the ship's two steam engines running.

Leaks Abound

The *Central America* had been taking a beating from the waves, and Ashby discovered that water was hip high in some of the starboard staterooms. Seawater, he found, was being pushed through the ship's closed porthole covers by the pounding wave action.

Water Race

By noon of September 11, the water continued to rise inside the ship, prompting the order to be given to begin bailing the ship by hand since the steam-driven pumps were not equal to the task. Holes were cut in the staterooms to allow the water trapped there to flow into the hold to be pumped out.

So much water was entering the ship that Ashby believed the hull's oakum, or caulk filling, had been beaten out between its hull planks. The male passengers, many hardened by years as California prospectors, were asked to lend a hand bailing water from the ship using buckets. The men immediately complied and helped the crew move thousands of buckets full of water from the *Central America's* bleeding hull.

Despite the crew's efforts, the water had risen so high that it extinguished the starboard boiler furnace and made it impossible to get coal to the port furnace. The remaining furnace was then fueled with wood torn out of the ship until that furnace flickered out, too. Without a furnace, the ship's steam-driven bilge pumps no longer worked, and all subsequent bailing had to be done by hand.

Hopeless Situation

Captain Herndon listened to all the reports about water entering the hull, the loss of the steam engines, and the attempts to use buckets to remove the water. Evening began to fall as hurricane-force winds of at least 75 mph battered the sinking ship. Herndon recognized that it was only a matter of hours before the ship would sink. He determined he would stay aboard as long as one other person remained. He put on his dress uniform and positioned himself in the wheelhouse of the ship.

Know The Ropes

The *Central America's* problems stemmed from the central issue of keeping the ship buoyant. Once the ship lost enough buoyancy to allow water above its deck, the ship would be swamped. Wooden ships always take on water, since few are perfectly watertight, but bilge pumps compensate for this problem. When the leakage gets excessive, it can outpace the capacities of the pumps. Mariners can calculate the rate of the leak with the rate of water removal and arrive at a fair idea of when the ship will no longer be buoyant enough to remain afloat.

Because the ship was carrying lifeboats for only a fraction of those aboard, Herndon ordered the crew to rip out the wood from the ship's superstructure and cabins and to use it to make rafts. Many knew the end was very near. One man aboard took out a heavy bag of gold dust and poured it out. Another threw down a bag of gold coins before a group of passengers and told people to take what they wanted. His offer had no takers aboard the dying ship.

Partial Rescue

Because the *Central America* was traveling in a heavily used shipping lane, roughly 160 miles off North Carolina's coast, Captain Herndon hoped a passing ship might come to his aid. Salvation did come in the form of the *Marine,* a ship that had sailed from Cuba on August 29.

Although not nearly as large as the 278-foot-long *Central America,* the 120-foot *Marine* was willing to fight the rough seas despite the difficulty of maneuvering due to the loss of its sails. Though badly damaged, the *Marine* was still seaworthy.

Words To Treasure

A **brig** is a ship equipped with two masts supporting square sails, although the word also refers to a compartment used for the temporary confinement of prisoners on a warship.

Fighting Marine

The *brig Marine*, with its captain, Hiram Burt, commanding five seamen, had fought for its own life against the smashing winds and waves of the hurricane but quickly came to the aid of the *Central America*. Even so, the rescue almost didn't happen, since the sound of the signal guns fired by the *Central America* was blotted out by the roaring storm. However, the darkness of the cloudy afternoon allowed Burt to see the bright muzzle flashes of the guns around 2 P.M. on that fateful Saturday.

Lacking an engine, Burt had to fight to keep the *Marine* close to the *Central America* and was at the mercy of the winds and currents because of the loss of his sails.

Women and Children First

As Burt began to maneuver his damaged ship toward Herndon's, the *Central America*'s captain ordered his ship's five lifeboats to be made ready to transfer passengers to the approaching ship. Herndon sternly ordered that women and children would leave the sinking ship first and even organized passengers as guards to ensure that the rescue operation would occur without interference.

The first step was to lower the lifeboats with their six oarsmen and a helmsman. The women and children were then lowered by ropes into the lifeboats rising and falling on the wild seas. Many people were injured when they fell into the boats or the water during this transfer that was as slow as it was precarious. One woman, a passenger named Lucy Dawson, died when she was smashed between a lifeboat and the hull of the *Marine*. Otherwise, all women and children were evacuated from the *Central America*.

During the evacuation, the storm forced the *Marine* several miles from the *Central America,* and a pair of lifeboats rowed by exhausted crewmen took two hours to return to the sinking ship. Although some men were allowed to leave with the women—and at least one man leaped into a boat without permission—the evacuation was orderly. Remaining aboard the *Central America* were 426 men.

The *Marine* had taken aboard precisely 100 evacuees from the *Central America*. There were 30 women, 26 children, and 44 men, most of whom had crewed the lifeboats.

The Last Helpful Try

Another ship, named the *El Dorado,* appeared and approached the *Central America* as the sun began to set. The *El Dorado* was under the command of Captain Samuel Stone and came alongside the *Central America* but could not remain close by because of the winds. Herndon decided against sending any men over the side for evacuation in the darkness, since it was now nearly 7 P.M.

WRECK OF THE STEAMSHIP CENTRAL AMERICA.

APPALLING DISASTER.

On Saturday, September 12th, 1857, Capt. Herndon, bound to New York, from California, with the Pacific Mails, Passengers and Crew, to the number of 592 persons, and treasure to the amount of over $2,000,000, foundered in a hurricane, off Cape Hatteras.

Whole number on board, 592.   Number saved, 166.   Number on board whose names are known, 134.   Names unknown, 292.

The SS Central America *finally lost its fight with the sea. The ship sank beneath the storm-tossed waters of the Atlantic while hundreds of its passengers flounder in the waves.*
(Courtesy Peabody Essex Museum)

Death at Sea

Around 8 P.M. on the night of September 12, 1857, the *Central America* lost its battle with the storm. The steamer slipped beneath the sea, creating a huge suction that drew dozens of those who still remained aboard to their deaths—including the stalwart Captain Herndon who had chosen to stay on board as long as anyone else remained there.

As in the case of the *Royal Charter* (see Chapter 16, "Wreck of the *Royal Charter*," for a reminder), floating debris became as great a danger as drowning soon after the *Central America* sank. Buoyant objects such as massive wooden pieces of the ship began rocketing up from the depths to leap out of the water. Much of this debris injured or killed many on the water's surface.

Captain Herndon went down with the *Central America,* holding true to his word to remain with the ship and to allow women and children to evacuate first. The passengers, as a rule, had also remained orderly, with many married men encouraging the women to leave quickly, promising to join them soon.

Only 54 men were rescued as they drifted at sea. The Norwegian ship *Ellen* picked up 50 men the day after the wreck, while a British vessel named *Mary* found four men adrift on wreckage. They were discovered four days after the wreck, 476 miles from the wreck site.

Shiver Me Timbers

U.S. Navy Captain William Lewis Herndon's professionalism during the sinking of the *Central America* earned him hero status in the United States. Herndon's reputation for courage and discipline prompted the construction of a monument for him in 1860 at the U.S. Naval Academy. Both the obelisk and his fame have become part of a rather odd ritual. At the end of each school year, the monument is smeared with lard. First-year midshipmen must then climb the 21-foot obelisk to retrieve the hat worn by one member of their class. If they succeed, they replace it with an upperclassman's hat. The ceremony is known as the "Herndon" or the "Plebe Recognition Ceremony," since a "plebe" is a first-year U.S. Naval Academy student.

The Stranded Rescuer

The *Marine,* carrying the survivors of the *Central America,* had been becalmed following the sinking of the other ship and was unable to sail on. As the small rescue ship ran out of provisions to feed the large number of people aboard, Captain Burt hailed the *Euphrasia* as it neared on September 16. The master of that ship provided the *Marine* with barrels of water, potatoes, hams, chickens, and other provisions while refusing payment. He then offered to take any passengers who wanted to go on to his destination of New Orleans.

Don't Go Overboard!

For those thinking they might like to find a sunken ship or invest in such an effort, success is far from assured and, the effort is astronomically expensive. Ships are tough to find and, if located, hard to identify as the one being sought. Often, shipwreck searches end up without the desired results. Money and patience may be required in equal amounts in order to achieve success.

Cash-and-Carry Help

Not all who would near the stranded ship would be as generous as the captain of the *Euphrasia,* however. Still without wind to propel his damaged ship, a tug boat arrived and offered to pull the *Marine* to port for $500, but Burt said he and those aboard were without adequate cash to pay for such a tow. The tug captain refused to take them into tow unless paid. Eventually, the widows and the handful of men aboard were able to scrape up $300 to satisfy the captain, and they arrived at last in Norfolk, Virginia.

Quest for Gold

If you want to find a lost treasure ship, you need only do a few things: First, raise $12 million. Second, rent, invent, and lease the best technology you can (which includes side-scan sonar and remotely piloted vehicles).

The only other thing you need is single-minded dedication to the task of locating a sunken treasure considered lost forever. This element is crucial because—as we've pointed out—finding sunken ships is extremely difficult under the best circumstances. Columbus, Ohio, engineer Tommy Thompson managed to do all of the above.

Eccentric Searcher

Tommy Thompson proved he was an eccentric scientist at the age of eight when he invented a "telephone" that allowed him to eavesdrop on his mother's calls. But Ma Bell's equipment detected the presence of two phones in a house that was only paying for one. A telephone technician came and went away amazed.

Thompson obtained an engineering degree from Ohio State University and along the way established a rock-solid reputation as one strange dude, although a brilliant one. He sought a specialized field of training in ocean sciences and took to driving a small amphibious car with a propeller in the back. As is the fate of any brilliant individual, some people hated him, some loved him, and everyone thought he was extremely intense.

The Making of a Treasure Hunter

After college, Thompson ambled to the Florida Keys in 1976 where he eventually ended up working for a year as a diver for treasure hunter Mel Fisher. Thompson never found any treasure, but he studied Fisher's search methods and began taking note of what he thought was being done wrong.

To Thompson, Fisher's team suffered feast-and-famine funding, failed to use the latest technology, and did not incorporate a strict search methodology to prevent the same area from being searched several times. Eventually, Thompson would apply the lessons he learned in his search for the *Central America*.

When he went to work at Battelle Institute in Cleveland, Ohio, Thompson was assigned to study deep-ocean mining and salvage issues on behalf of federal government clients. By 1983 the prospect of using an improved form of side-scan sonar to locate deep-ocean objects turned his mind back to treasure hunting.

Know The Ropes

The redoubtable Mel Fisher may be the last of the old-style treasure hunters to literally spend years searching for a sunken ship. Since deep-water wrecks are the ones remaining untouched, they are prohibitively expensive to locate and recover using robotics. Searchers must now refine their search area using historical research and mathematics before zeroing in on a shipwreck with deep-ocean expedition. Fisher's family operation is giving way to well-organized corporate efforts.

Picking the Central America

Thompson began to think seriously about finding the *Central America* and recovering its gold based upon a list of requirements. Since the ship was beneath 8,000 feet of water, it was undoubtedly untouched; and since it contained tons of gold, the project could be profitable. Though the *Titanic* was also in deep water, Thompson thought it essentially worthless as a treasure ship because it had no stockpiles of gems or precious metals and scratched it off his list.

He had long since determined that other famous and more recent shipwrecks were red herrings when it came to rumors about their being good salvage prospects for treasure. The *Andréa Doria* was probably not carrying the fabulous treasure that many whispered about and would be too difficult to get into because of its steel hull.

After conducting preliminary research, Thompson surmised that the *Central America* sank between 100 and 200 miles off North Carolina's coast. The ship was in international waters, which met another important criterion for Thompson in that no government could claim the ship.

Shiver Me Timbers

Everyone who knew a treasure ship from the "Good Ship Lollypop" knew that the *Central America* was filled with around three tons of registered gold and still more gold that had been carried by passengers. However, U.S. Army documents purported on April 2, 1971, that the ship was also carrying a secret shipment of another 15 tons of the precious ore mined from California's gold strike. This claim, if true, could make the wreck even more valuable and resulted in more than a few researchers spending years tracking down the whereabouts of the ship.

The Long Search

Before raising the treasure, Thompson had to raise money, and he started doing so in 1985 by convincing well-heeled investors in Columbus, Ohio, to back his project. Eventually he would raise more than $12 million to fund the search and recovery effort.

One of his primary concerns was complete security, since anyone could rent a boat, head for the suspected scene of the wreck, and claim it before Thompson's group (which eventually became known as the Columbus-America Discovery Group) did. Thompson was honest and precise about his plans, warning everyone the *Central America* might never be found.

By June 1986, Thompson and his crew embarked on their first search for the *Central America*. They decided to search in a location provided by the captain of a merchant ship known as the *Ellen*. Other coordinates they considered were those Herndon told to survivors of the wreck before his ship sank. The *Marine*'s captain also checked the position, but this location was not considered as reliable as it was determined with dead reckoning.

Searching with Sound

Using side-scan sonar in a submerged, towed sled known as the SeaMARC, Thompson and his team began the 40-day job of going back and forth over the waters off the coast of North Carolina, imaging the seabed hunting for the shape of the *Central America*'s wreck. Equipment problems with the SeaMARC plagued the effort. When the U.S. Navy showed up to conduct naval maneuvers, its sonar equipment blotted out the images Thompson's group was trying to obtain.

One of the images the team obtained using the sonar appeared to be a side-wheel steamer, but the "target" was too short to be the ship. However, the searchers reasoned that the *Central America* had been damaged upon impact and that much of its super-structure had been chopped away to make rafts prior to sinking.

Shiver Me Timbers

The time may soon come when the scene of scuba divers patiently excavating sunken treasure will become a thing of the past. Remotely operated vehicles that contain high-resolution video cameras for eyes and robotic arms, are now being sent down to deep wrecks to identify them and excavate their artifacts. This allows wrecks thousands of feet deep to be explored and reduces the possibility of human injury.

Thompson and his technicians worked to construct a remotely operated vehicle, which would help them retrieve artifacts from the seafloor when they returned to the wreck site the following year.

Wrong Wreck

By June 21, 1987, the team had its second look at the promising wreck using their camera sled. The sled revealed a decomposed shipwreck but one devoid of the tons of coal that should have marked the grave site of the coal-burning steamship *Central America*. The sonar image had led them on, but such images are often hazy and prone to interpretation, but the camera sled visually showed the team members that they were barking up the wrong tree.

This crushing realization forced the Columbus-America explorers to look at another sonar target they had acquired the year before. The image looked like a ghostly skull. They returned to the site, took a sonar image of it, and realized that it was dimpled with the piles of coal.

They knew it was crucial to obtain an artifact from the ship so they could arrest it legally in a federal court, thereby providing them the legal right to recover the wreck's treasure without interference. Thompson's team had "sued" the original wreck site to obtain the right to work the wreck, but it was now the wrong location.

Claim Jumpers

By the time Thompson's group began looking for the alternative wreck site, a ship named the *Liberty Star* out of Cape Canaveral came close by, towing what appeared to be a remotely operated vehicle and searching for something on the seafloor.

The presence of other treasure hunters prompted Thompson to move quickly, and the remotely operated vehicle under his control was sent down again to pluck an artifact from the wreck so that he could arrest it.

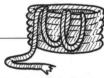

Know The Ropes

Side-scan sonar is an extremely useful tool that has become more capable during the intervening years since its development thanks to a raft of advancements including computer enhancements of the images returned from the seafloor. However, it has yet to reach the point where side-scan sonar images are as clear as photographs and some interpretation is required.

At first, the effort appeared to have failed, since the scoop and carrying basket on the vehicle were empty, until someone spotted a lump of coal jammed into the frame of the device. Thompson had anticipated this type of event and called for a seaplane that was standing by. The airplane, trailing a grappling hook, snatched the lump of coal suspended on a line held between the search ship and a rubber boat in which Thompson stood. The coal was then taken to federal court, and the wreck site claimed by Thompson was changed in the court records.

Legal Protection

Concerned about the mysterious *Liberty Star* still trolling its sonar sled, attorneys for Thompson's group obtained a temporary restraining order, ordering the interloping ship and anyone else to stay clear of the area designated by Thompson's search group.

Wrong Ship Again!

After examining the second wreck site carefully, Thompson realized that the second ship his group had found was still not the *Central America*! While it had coal and artifacts such as dishes dated around the time of the treasure ship's loss, no massive side wheels were to be found.

Images gathered during the previous sonar profiling runs were examined and reexamined, and it became apparent that a large mass on the seafloor that was thought to be geological formation of some kind was probably the long-sought *Central America*.

Another Try

Despite the group's mounting money woes in 1988, an improved remotely operated vehicle was developed, and a Columbus-America Discovery Group investor purchased a search ship named the *Arctic Explorer* and leased it to the expedition. The ship was refurbished and was to be equipped with thrusters to allow the use of "dynamic positioning." This technology involved a series of propellers that allowed the ship to remain in the same spot despite winds or currents.

Waiting for Thrust

A delay in getting the specially built thrusters delivered from Houston allowed Thompson and his crew the time they needed to refine the new remotely operated vehicle they had developed and to raise more money (always a good thing!). One investor came through with $3.5 million, but the investors were getting anxious and needed something to show for their money.

A Day to Remember

On September 11, 1988—exactly 131 years to the day after the *Central America* ran into the fatal hurricane—Thompson's team was stunned. Sitting in a darkened and chilly control center watching video screens, team members suddenly saw the image of a rusted side wheel being transmitted by the remotely operated vehicle's camera!

The ghostly images of the wreck site on the team's monitor left no doubt that the group had finally found the *Central America*. By October, still cameras recorded the location of tons of gold scattered about the wreck site.

High-Technology Recovery

The amazed team discovered stacks of federally minted $20 gold coins standing upright on the seafloor 8,000 feet beneath the surface. Gold, unlike silver or virtually any other metal, neither tarnishes nor attracts marine growth. Finding gold beneath the sea means that you find *gold!*

The group used a remotely operated vehicle, dubbed the *Nemo,* and a fascinating combination of technology to carefully lift the coins from their watery repository. Because thousands of the freshly minted coins were completely unused, their value as collector's items was immense. Understandably, dinging these items during recovery would devalue

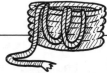

Know The Ropes

Simply recovering artifacts and treasure isn't good enough for today's treasure hunter using remotely operated vehicles. Since the items recovered often have increased value due to their condition, gentle methods must be employed. Use of a "grab" or claw-like device to lift treasure from the British liner *Egypt* during the 1930s was an effective but crude way to recover treasure and would give an archaeologist or one of today's treasure hunters nightmares. A nick or a dent in an otherwise pristine gold coin or a crack in a piece of recovered china would drastically reduce the value of the find.

the golden artifacts. The need for recovery with care presented a serious technical challenge to Thompson's group as it tried to haul up coins by giving commands to a robot through 8,000 feet of fiber-optic cable.

Sticky and Innovative Fingers

The *Nemo* was fitted with a system that allowed it to inject a silicone rubber gel over a pile of coins or other artifacts that would then solidify under water. Encased in the gel that would harden into a soft rubber, the sealed coins would then be lifted to the surface.

After the gold was brought to the surface, the pliable silicone compound could be peeled away without marring the finish of the coins. Because of the large amount of gold dust aboard the wreck, an underwater vacuum cleaner was used to suck the valuable litter from the ocean floor.

A Historical Lift

While recovering hundreds of millions of dollars in gold, the Columbus-America group also retrieved suitcases and clothing belonging to the passengers. Even after 131 years underwater, many of the items were still usable, and books found amid the wreckage could still be read. These items were later transferred to Ohio State University for preservation and study.

Legal Double Eagles

After finding and recovering millions worth of gold, including hundreds of gold *"double eagle"* coins, 39 insurance companies emerged to lay claim to the treasure in U.S. district court in Norfolk, Virginia. What followed was nearly a decade of legal wrangling.

Shiver Me Timbers

The $20 "double eagle" coin—officially known as a Liberty Double Eagle—was itself a product of the California gold rush since its production was prompted by the discovery of gold at Sutter's Mill. Previously only $2.50, $5, and $10 gold coins were minted in the United States. The coin was first minted in 1850 by the United States with the last such coins minted in 1907. Lady Liberty graces one side of the coin and the American eagle the opposite.

U.S. District Judge Richard B. Kellam dismissed the claims of 21 insurers and found that the remaining 18 had abandoned the cargo of gold, leaving it free for the taking by any salvor who made the effort to locate and recover the wreck. The decision was appealed, and in 1992 the Fourth Circuit Court of Appeals, saying that the "abandonment" had to be an overt act, sent the case back to Judge Kellam in Norfolk. Kellam heard more evidence and in 1993 granted Thompson's group 90 percent of the recovered treasure.

Eventually, Kellam granted Columbus-America 92.22 percent of the recovered gold carried as official cargo, 100 percent of the personal gold carried by passengers, and 100 percent of the U.S. Army gold shipment.

In another suit, Columbia University and treasure hunters Harry John and Jack Grimm claimed the *Central America* wreck was found using sonar images collected by the group during a 1984 expedition they conducted. Kellam dismissed the lawsuit filed by John and Grimm. On June 14, 1995, Kellam's decision to dismiss the John-Grimm suit was affirmed by the federal appeals court.

Shiver Me Timbers

U.S. District Judge Richard B. Kellam's decisions regarding the *Central America* salvage made legal history. They also paved the way for the 1994 ruling by fellow federal judge J. Calvitt Clarke Jr. that allowed the RMS Titanic, Inc., to arrest the wreck of the *Titanic*. Like the Columbus–America Discovery Group, RMS Titanic, Inc., had gone to the wreck site of a ship and, in this case, recovered a wine decanter to prove the discovery of the *Titanic's* wreck. The legal precedents in both cases were unique, since both saw a U.S. federal court extend American salvage law into international waters.

Following the resolution of these legal dilemmas, the final obstacles to the possession of the gold were overcome at last.

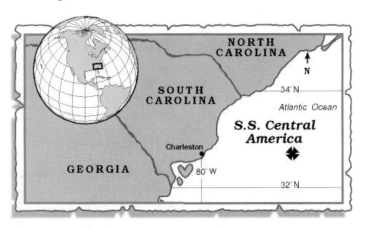

Map of the wreck site of the SS Central America. *(Drawn by Ken Ellis)*

The Least You Need to Know

➤ The Transcontinental Railroad wasn't built until 1869, forcing many East Coast forty-niners to travel by sea to and from California's gold rush.

➤ Captain William Lewis Herndon stalwartly remained at the bridge of the *Central America* and ensured the orderly evacuation of women and children, leaving 426 men to perish at sea.

➤ The *Central America* was originally christened the *George Law* after being built by William H. Webb and Company on New York's East River.

➤ Unable to move coal through the sinking *Central America,* the crew and passengers burned wood that they ripped from the ship to keep the boilers operating.

➤ The storm-damaged brig *Marine* battled rough seas to come alongside the *Central America* where it took aboard 30 women, 26 children, and 44 men.

➤ The captain of a tugboat that found the becalmed *Marine* with the survivors of the *Central America* refused to pull the ship into Norfolk, Virginia, unless he was paid $500. He finally settled for $300.

➤ Tommy Thompson, who masterminded the successful search and recovery operation for the *Central America*'s gold, once worked for treasure hunter Mel Fisher.

Part 4

The Bigger They Are, the Harder They Fall

Part 4 recounts the loss of the largest and most spectacular ships in events that shocked the world. The Titanic, Lusitania, Andréa Doria, *and* Edmund Fitzgerald *were ships that no one could have imagined would ever be lost, but they were. Although the loss of life on some was immense, as in the case of the* Titanic *and* Lusitania, *relatively few died on the* Andréa Doria *and the* Edmund Fitzgerald, *but these losses hypnotized the world nonetheless.*

Part 4 discusses the mistakes, the arrogance, and the avoidable errors that could have precluded these tragedies.

Never Say Never: The *Titanic*

It wasn't the biggest ship ever built, and it was far from the first ship to sink, but next to Noah's Ark, the Royal Mail Ship *Titanic* has become the most famous ship in history.

Touted as the ultimate luxury liner, the *Titanic* stunned the world by striking an iceberg on its maiden voyage. Its loss with 1,517 people aboard made it a transportation tragedy without historical rivals. The disaster reeked of scandal as the subsequent investigation revealed that unnecessarily excessive speed combined with antiquated safety rules led to the most costly peacetime shipping accident on record.

Some of America's wealthiest citizens were aboard the ship, as were the poorest prospective Americans—hundreds of emigrants who perished in steerage class. The tragedy of a massive new ship being punctured by an iceberg has developed into an epic tale of victims rich and poor, noble and ignoble, and villains real and imagined.

When the *Titanic* sank on April 15, 1912, it slammed into the ooze on the seafloor 13,000 feet below and hid with impunity for more than seven decades. The biggest piece of evidence of the great event—the *Titanic* itself—was gone, as if it had never existed.

Deep-ocean geologist Robert Ballard, who had dreamed of finding the *Titanic* for much of his life, organized an expedition in 1985 that discovered the liner. His successful search of the *Titanic* triggered an international sensation over the decomposing wreck lying in two large sections three miles beneath the surface.

Entrepreneurs would arrive nine years later to claim the wreck under American salvage law. When RMS Titanic, Inc., began retrieving objects from the seafloor, the activity created more turbulence than the propeller of a giant ocean liner. Some, like Ballard, wanted the ship left alone as a gravesite. Of course, others were more than willing to pay to stand in line for a chance to see the jewelry, the ship's china, and other artifacts retrieved from the depths.

Well, the water is cold, the night is clear, and the ship is going down, so let's hurry and find out what we can about the most famous shipwreck to ever make it to the top by hitting bottom.

A poster depicting the steamship Titanic *for the White Star Line presents a majestic view of the liner that would perish during its first voyage. (Courtesy of the Mariners Museum)*

Shiver Me Timbers

When the *Titanic* fell nearly 13,000 feet to the bottom of the North Atlantic, it was as if the 852.5-foot liner had fallen 15 times its own length or 9.5 times the length of New York's World Trade Center (which measures 1,350 feet in height). For avid readers of highway mileage signs, that's about 2.75 miles straight down to Davy Jones's locker. By now you've probably gotten a pretty good picture of how far the *Titanic* fell before it reached the seafloor.

Hype, Hope, and Bad Luck

Bigger, better, faster. It isn't a new thing for people to be clamoring for more. Long before we got involved with the space race, turbocharged sports cars, and supersonic intercontinental flights, everyone wanted the best, and much of this was driven by plain old hype.

Even the earliest plans behind the RMS *Titanic*'s design revolved around not only making the ship one of the fastest, safest, and most beautiful, but also making it look faster with the addition of an unnecessary fourth smokestack. The original decision to build the *Titanic* and two huge sister ships came out of a 1907 conversation between J. Bruce Ismay, director of the White Star Line, and Lord James Pirrie, an executive with the Harland and Wolff shipbuilding firm.

The White Star Line steamship company operated passenger liners and was in hot competition with Cunard, another shipping company famous during the early 1900s for having some of the fastest passenger ships of the day. The three new ships would follow White Star Line's tradition of building innovative and comfortable ships to combine speed with luxury. Harland and Wolff's ships were considered the best built in the world, though not as fast as those constructed for the Cunard Line like the *Lusitania* by John Brown and Co. Limited at Clydebank, Scotland.

Building the Titanic

Harland and Wolff would build a trio of ships upon orders placed by the White Star Line. The first would be the *Olympic,* followed by the *Titanic,* and then by the *Gigantic* (whose tentative name was later changed to *Brittanic* after the *Titanic*'s loss). These ships would be the standard bearers for the White Star Line that provided service to various European ports and to New York.

The *Titanic*'s keel was laid down on March 31, 1909, in the Harland and Wolff, Ltd., shipyard in Belfast, Ireland. On May 31, 1911, the *Titanic*'s *hull* was launched, and the outfitting of the ship was completed by March 31, 1912.

249

Titanic Means Big!

Everything about the trio of ships planned by White Star Line had been big. The slips ordinarily used to hold three ocean liners under construction in Harland and Wolff's Belfast shipyard were redesigned to make room for only two—the *Olympic* and *Titanic*.

The bases of the slips were reinforced with concrete 54 inches thick, which also contained reinforcing steel. Even the docks of the destination city of New York weren't large enough to accommodate the new leviathans. Lobbying took place early to successfully get city officials to enlarge the docks at public expense.

This lobbying effort may have been helped along through the influence of J. Pierpont Morgan, whose holding company, International Mercantile Marine, had purchased White Star Line in 1902. He had earlier clenched the deal for the shipping line by promising to leave J. Bruce Ismay, son of its founder, in charge and agreeing to let the British use the ships in time of war.

Words To Treasure

The outfitting of a ship is a major part of the shipbuilding effort. Although the **hull** is completed enough for the ship to be launched, much of the machinery must be installed, and a large amount of skilled work was needed to make the *Titanic* a floating luxury hotel.

Bigger Than Its Sister

The *Titanic* received numerous improvements based upon lessons learned during the construction of the *Olympic*. The *Titanic*'s interior was altered to provide space for 163 more passengers, with most of those being added to the sumptuous first-class accommodations.

Shiver Me Timbers

The relationship between Harland and Wolff and White Star Line was old and strong. White Star Line was founded in 1845 and eventually focused on providing transportation to Australia following the 1851 gold rush there. Thomas Henry Ismay purchased the line when it went into bankruptcy in 1868. The shipbuilding firm Harland and Wolff, under the direction of marine engineer Sir Edward Harland, was started and received its first order from White Star Line in 1869. By agreement, all of White Star's ships would be built by Harland and Wolff, and the shipbuilders would build for no other company.

In addition, the *Titanic*'s furnishings and decoration were more elegant than those on the *Olympic;* for example, on the *Titanic* hardwood furniture replaced wicker items. As a result of these changes, the *Titanic* outweighed the *Olympic* by 1,000 tons, something most sisters wouldn't brag about.

Alexander Carlisle, the ship's chief designer, considered the *Titanic* Harland and Wolff's finest shipbuilding accomplishment despite the subsequent disaster. Newspapers at the time were effusive in their praise of the *Titanic*, even pitching in the phrase "the unsinkable ship." Among the Wall Street crowd, the *Titanic* was known as "the millionaire's special" because of the wealthy passengers it was designed to attract.

Titanic Dimensions

The specifications of the *Titanic* delivered to the British Board of Trade during the investigation into its loss showed the *Titanic* was 852.5 feet long, 92.5 feet wide, and 92.5 feet high from its keel to its main deck. When the ship was loaded so its hull was submerged to a depth of 34 feet, 7 inches, the *Titanic* displaced 52,310 tons of water.

Stiff Competition

The White Star Line was functioning in a very competitive environment, competing with the legendarily fast ships of the British Cunard Line as well as with German companies that had recently introduced fast and beautiful liners. Speed was an extremely important factor for passengers as was comfort. Those clamoring most loudly for these features were the increasingly affluent American tourists.

At the same time, a fierce ticket price war occurred at the turn of the century, coinciding with a serious drop in emigrant travel to America. These factors put a double pinch on the steamship lines. Although poor emigrants weren't clamoring for a faster, more luxurious voyage, the rich Americans were, and their dollars had to be pursued for a steamship line to survive. Speed was of the essence.

Ready, Willing, and Ably Crewed?

The massive *Titanic* conducted sea trials for half a day on April 2, 1912, although the amazingly brief trials simply determined that the ship could accelerate and then stop. Fully loaded, it displaced nearly 54,000 tons of seawater and boasted 159 furnaces to heat the steam-producing boilers powering the three engines. By the day the *Titanic* sailed, everything was working relatively well.

Although it would seem the beautiful and new *Titanic* would be filled with a magnificently trained crew, many of its hands had just arrived from other White Star liners prior to sailing. Some came from the *Olympic*, which had been damaged in a collision with a British cruiser, and some came from the smaller *Oceanic,* whose trip to North America had been canceled because of a British coal-mining strike. The new crewmen had to quickly learn their way around the massive *Titanic*. Along with the crewmen came the spare coal from both the ships not making the crossing due to the strike.

Lifeboat Concerns

Although ready for the April 10, 1912, sailing date with 20 lifeboats aboard, complaints about the small number of lifeboats equipping the White Star ship had already

Know The Ropes

The *Titanic's* 14 full-size lifeboats were extremely well built, containing copper flotation canisters to keep them afloat even if the boats filled with water. They were also extremely rugged boats, capable of being maneuvered on the open seas. They were equipped with sails, a compass, and provisions. Each could carry 65 persons. A pair of similarly equipped cutter boats could carry 40 persons apiece. Four collapsible Engelhardt boats were available, and their wood-reinforced, canvas hulls could be folded up until needed. There were no sails for these canvas boats, which could carry 47 persons each.

originated in the United States. Maritime expert E. K. Roden warned months before in the publication *The Navy* that "common sense" was being ignored by White Star Line, which persisted in equipping its ships with too few lifeboats.

Even *Titanic* designer Alexander Carlisle had argued that 50 lifeboats should be placed aboard the *Titanic,* but his plea was shunted aside. The *Titanic* carried 14 regular wooden lifeboats, two smaller wooden boats, and four folding, canvas and wood lifeboats.

British Board of Trade rules specified that any ship exceeding 15,000 tons should be equipped with a minimum of 16 lifeboats. The *Titanic* was four above this figure, though simple arithmetic would show the boats could carry only 1,178 people aboard a ship carrying 2,201 passengers and crew. The rules were badly outdated.

American regulations would have required a ship with the capacity of the *Titanic* to carry 42 lifeboats, providing room for 2,367 persons, wrote Union Iron Works naval contractor Hugo P. Frear shortly after the *Titanic* disaster. Americans perceived British safety regulations as lax and old-fashioned.

Abandon Ship!

On April 11, the *Titanic* steers for New York across a North Atlantic that had been plagued with a hazardous number of icebergs. It had been a strange year for iceberg activity, since warm weather had caused a larger-than-normal amount of ice to calve (or split) from glaciers on Greenland's coast. These gargantuan chunks of ice then drifted north on the Labrador Current to enter the shipping lanes.

By 9 A.M. on April 14, the *Titanic* received an ice warning from the *Caronia,* and at 1:42 P.M. another ice warning from the SS *Baltic.* The coordinates of the warnings indicated the *Titanic* would encounter ice that night. The *Titanic's* captain, Edward J. Smith, read the *Baltic's* message and then handed it to J. Bruce Ismay, the chief executive of White Star Line. For some reason, Ismay pocketed the note. It was not posted in the ship's chart room as a bulletin until 7:15 P.M. when Smith asked Ismay to return it.

A drawing depicts the Titanic *colliding with a huge iceberg. The rendering properly shows that much of an iceberg's bulk is submerged. (ARTTODAY.COM)*

Mixed Signals

The *Titanic*'s radio operators would receive at least three more iceberg warnings that day, including one from the German liner *Amerika*, which reported ice south of the *Titanic*'s track—or route—around 1:45 P.M. A fourth ice warning was received at 7:30 P.M. from the SS *Californian*. And an ice warning from the steamer *Mesaba* was received by the *Titanic* at 9:40 P.M.

The *Mesaba*'s ice warning showed plainly that ice was in the vicinity of the *Titanic,* but like several of the warnings, it had not been delivered to Captain Smith because the radio operators on board were busily transmitting paid messages on behalf of passengers.

In an odd arrangement, the wireless operators tapping out messages in Morse code were employed by the Marconi Wireless Company, which had a virtual monopoly on wireless communications. Part of the backlog of message traffic handled by the two operators on duty was caused by an equipment breakdown that had to be repaired.

Haste Makes Waste

The *Titanic* made virtually its entire trip across the Atlantic at "high speed," according to the British Board of Trade investigation and did not slow down until the iceberg was spotted dead ahead at 11:40 P.M. When the *Titanic*'s lookouts spotted the iceberg and clanged a warning bell three times, the ship was traveling at 22.5 knots, or nearly 25 mph.

The huge ship reversed its propellers and tried to turn away from the iceberg. Despite these efforts, the iceberg's submerged bulk still struck the starboard side of the *Titanic*. This type of glancing collision turned out to be the worst possible event. It's now believed that the *Titanic*'s hull steel may have been overly brittle and that the collision cracked and tore a 300-foot gash in the ship 10 feet above the *keel,* or the lowest portion of the ship's hull.

Words To Treasure

The **keel** of a ship is the structural backbone of a vessel running from its bow to its stern and forms a center line down the bottom of the hull.

This event opened up six of the ship's compartments to the sea. The *Titanic* filled with water, and the "unsinkable" ship would slip beneath the North Atlantic at 2:20 A.M., only 160 minutes after the collision.

Smith's apparent lack of concern about the iceberg warnings baffled many who thought the captain should have reduced the speed of the ship. Many believe that Smith felt pressured to keep the ship's speed high to provide good publicity for the ship's maiden voyage. If you'll recall, speediness was a very important boast made by the owners of the liner *Royal Charter,* which also rushed to disaster with a massive loss of life in Chapter 16, "Wreck of the *Royal Charter.*"

Confusion and Cold Water

The *Titanic* began to sink at the bow as tons of water rushed into its wounds. Lifeboats were ordered lowered, and in the confusion, many were lowered half-empty by their davits. Although women and children were to have been rescued first, at least 43 male passengers found safety in the boats. Many of the 107 crewmembers that survived the sinking had been ordered into the boats to man them.

Don't Go Overboard!

Hypothermia, or the reduction of body temperature due to exposure to cold, can kill a person within 30 minutes. The sea's temperature was around 28 degrees at the time of the collision. A person can survive a maximum of three hours in 50-degree water. Passengers afloat around the *Titanic* may have had as little as an hour to live in the water.

Part of the real tragedy is that virtually all of the boats left the ship with room to spare. One boat left with only 12 aboard, while many left half full! Only 711 were aboard the boats when the SS *Carpathia* arrived at the scene the following morning to take aboard survivors. Perhaps a thousand more could have been saved had the lifeboat loading been better organized.

Life Preservers

Although drastically short of lifeboats, the *Titanic*'s crew and passengers had life preservers running out of their ears. The ship carried 3,560 such "lifebelts," as the British called them. Unfortunately, all mariners know that the chill waters of the North Atlantic in the winter and spring mean quick death even if you can keep from drowning.

A Horrible Sight

Those who managed to row to safety from the sinking *Titanic* knew all too well that their boats could be tipped over by the masses of desperate people struggling to climb aboard. As a result, many lifeboat occupants either did nothing to help those in the water or actively beat them away even though many of the boats still had room for survivors.

Passenger Archibald Gracie recalled that an oar struck the head of crewman Harry Senior as he tried to climb aboard Gracie's lifeboat. Gracie had to turn away from the sight of people slowly dying of hypothermia as they begged for help.

Decades of Speculation

Perhaps the less said about the "mystery" of the *Titanic*'s sinking the better, since everyone knows the ship hit an iceberg. But as is usually the case, a raft of conspiracy theories floated to the surface after the ship's loss. Some claimed that the *Olympic* had actually been substituted for the *Titanic* and was sunk intentionally as part of an insurance scam, while others refused to accept the sinking of the "unsinkable" *Titanic*.

Distraught families were briefly convinced that their loved ones were trapped alive inside the ship at the bottom of the ocean and begged officials to raise the ship immediately.

However, speculation about the mystery of the *Titanic*'s loss seems silly, since everyone knows the ship struck an iceberg and that a 300-foot line of damage compromised its watertight compartments.

Some even claimed that Captain Smith shot himself with a pistol as the ship began to sink. However, it's now accepted that iceberg collision damage sank the ship and that Smith simply went down with the *Titanic* in the tradition of many captains before him.

Discovery

Robert D. Ballard at first seems like an unlikely sunken-ship hunter. An accomplished and highly respected deep-ocean geologist and oceanographer, Ballard may have spent more time on the deep-ocean seafloor than any other person.

He had long harbored a strong desire to find and visit the site of the *Titanic*, but the task would prove difficult. None of the ships involved with the rescue of the *Titanic*'s survivors or even those among the liner's crew had a good idea where it was lost.

Strange Seabed Fellows

It's hard at first to imagine what the May 22, 1968, loss of an American nuclear submarine named the USS *Scorpion* would have to do with the discovery of the *Titanic*, but the resourceful Ballard managed to make the connection. As a scientist with the

Words To Treasure

Argo was the name of the ship in Greek mythology that was sailed by Jason and his argonauts in search of the equally mythic Golden Fleece. *Thresher* and *Scorpion* are the names of fish. The U.S. Navy formerly used fish names for submarines.

Woods Hole Oceanographic Institute, Ballard worked with the U.S. Navy to develop technology that would allow the investigation of the deepest parts of the ocean.

Among the items developed under Ballard's supervision was the *Argo,* a remotely operated vehicle that would allow precise mapping of wreck sites and other items of interest to the Navy. One purpose of the technology was to keep an eye on the wreckage of a pair of sunken American nuclear submarines.

As we discussed in Chapter 2, "Underwater Sleuths," Ballard convinced the Navy to let him use this technology to hunt for the *Titanic* after conducting a survey of the wreck sites of the nuclear submarines *Thresher* (which was unarmed) and the *Scorpion* (which was carrying a pair of nuclear-tipped torpedoes).

Practice Makes Perfect

In the summer of 1984, Ballard and his Navy-funded team used the new *Argo* technology to examine the USS *Thresher*'s wreck site, and a year later they mapped and studied the *Scorpion* wreck site. Upon completing the *Scorpion* mapping expedition, Ballard was allowed to take the *Argo* to the suspected site of the *Titanic*'s sinking in August 1985.

The French Touch

Ballard was able to enlist the assistance of the French Institute of Research and Exploitation of the Sea (IFREMER) that had been established in 1984. Using its side-scan sonar system, a French team had already searched one segment of the suspected wreck site but found nothing. However, the work served the crucial purpose of revealing where the *Titanic* was not.

An American Try

The American team, funded in part by *National Geographic* magazine, which had secured photographic rights to the expedition, then took over with the *Argo* remotely operated vehicle. Conducting a video search, the group spotted the *Titanic*'s debris field around 1 A.M. on September 1, 1985.

Using *Silicon Intensified Target,* or *SIT,* technology to make it possible for video cameras to see in total darkness, Ballard was able to gather images of the *Titanic*'s remains in the blackness of the deep ocean. The media went wild, Ballard became famous, and the *Titanic*'s hiding was over, though Ballard kept the location quiet to discourage plunder of the wreck.

Sitting upright in the muck was the bow of the once-proud *Titanic*. Spread out behind and around the bow was a mile-long debris field containing massive piles of coal and the stern of the ship. Also scattered about were thousands of objects, including the shoes and boots of the dead. These items had lain in the same position for 73 years. The remains of the dead had long ago been consumed by marine organisms and bacteria.

Money Matters

To recoup their expenses, IFREMER and Ballard had agreed to sell images collected during the 1985 expedition, but an agreement to conduct a simultaneous release of images and films of the *Titanic* fell apart. When the images were released unexpectedly in the United States by the Woods Hole Oceanographic Institute, IFREMER filed a lawsuit. This rift between Ballard and Woods Hole Oceanographic Institute on one side and IFREMER on the other meant that cooperation between the two groups regarding the *Titanic* was over.

Returning to the Titanic

Returning without the French in 1986, Ballard's team collected clearer images of the *Titanic,* making the images of the wreck familiar to millions. Ballard dove to the wreck in the deep-submergence vehicle *Alvin.*

At nearly 13,000 feet, Ballard and the *Alvin*'s two-man crew saw the massive hull of the *Titanic* rising out of the muck.

As soon as they trained their powerful lights on the hull, though, they began losing power as water pressure approaching 6,000 pounds per square inch shorted out the *Alvin*'s oil-filled batteries. They surfaced for repairs and used the Argo for additional photography during the wait.

In subsequent dives, Ballard used another Navy-sponsored remotely operated vehicle known as *Jason Jr.* The small craft swam out of a "garage" in the bow of the *Alvin* to venture inside the wreck to deliver stunning images of the ship's once-magnificent staircase.

Mysteries Solved

Although accounts varied about the *Titanic*'s behavior when the massive ship stood on its bow for its final slide into the water, the location of the wreck resolved these differing recollections. Some said the ship went down as a single piece, while others said it snapped in two.

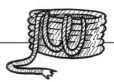

Know The Ropes

Water blocks light, and the deeper one goes into the ocean the more completely dark it becomes. Those wanting to take photographs or films underwater must come equipped with plenty of electricity and powerful lights. **Silicon Intensified Target** technology eliminates these hassles, since it boosts available light 10,000 times. A relatively small and energy-efficient light source can be used instead. The technology consists of a "camera tube" that allows video cameras to essentially see in near-total darkness.

The *Titanic*'s remains were found in a mile-long debris field with the bow and stern nearly a quarter mile apart. Apparently, the ship snapped in two during its sinking. The hulls of large ships are supported by water and aren't strong enough to support their own mass when not cradled by the wet stuff. It's also been learned that extremely large ships tend to be torn to pieces during sinking in the same way aircraft can be ripped apart when they go out of control.

Marketing History

The pleas of Ballard and others to leave the *Titanic* site alone fell on deaf ears when a group headed by George Tulloch, a Connecticut auto dealer and entrepreneur, mounted a 1993 expedition to locate and recover objects from the wreck.

Tulloch followed in the footsteps of Texas oilman Jack Grimm who, during the early 1980s, conducted numerous search expeditions for lost ships including the *Titanic* and the SS *Central America*. Grimm's searches had been unsuccessful, but Tulloch hired the expertise and equipment of IFREMER to assist in the search and recovery of artifacts. Since IFREMER scientists had already been to the wreck site, the organization knew how to locate the *Titanic*.

Claiming the Titanic

Tulloch's group managed to recover a crystal wine decanter from the *Titanic*'s wreck site in 1994. This fragile artifact was carried to U.S. District Court Judge J. Calvitt Clarke Jr. in the same Norfolk, Virginia, courthouse where the ownership of the *Central America* was granted to the Columbus-America Discovery Group. Clarke allowed the arrest of the *Titanic* wreck by Tulloch's group.

A Titanic Display

Since then, hundreds of *Titanic* artifacts, both large and small, have been recovered. A bearing journal ring for one of the *Titanic*'s engines has been raised along with a 20 by 26-foot section of the hull. Also recovered are delicate pieces of jewelry and documents.

One incredible discovery is the other half of a claim ticket presented to passenger Lawrence Beesley who deposited valuables with the *Titanic*'s *purser*. Beesley mentioned the ticket and its number, 208, during testimony about the disaster. The soggy half of that ticket has been recovered and restored and is part of the traveling exhibit that continues to tour the United States.

Though criticized for recovering objects from the *Titanic*'s site, Tulloch's organization has pledged not to split up the collection of artifacts for sale to individuals.

Words To Treasure

A **purser** is not someone who presses his or her lips together tightly or who designs women's handbags; he or she is the officer aboard a ship that handles all financial matters including the storage of passenger valuables.

No Pictures, Please!

RMS Titanic, Inc., even obtained a ruling from a federal judge in 1998 barring anyone from visiting or photographing the site without the consent of the firm, which now "owns" the *Titanic*. The ruling was sought after entrepreneurs organized tourist trips to the wreck aboard deep-diving submersibles. The ruling has been ignored by some who question an American court's jurisdiction over a British wreck in international waters. However, this ruling was reversed in 1999.

Disintegration of a Legend

One reason that proponents of artifact recovery give for venturing to the *Titanic* and removing objects is that the wreck of the *Titanic* is decomposing at an alarming rate. Though experts disagree on how long it will take for the wreck to collapse upon itself, much deterioration has already occurred.

While rust is a problem, bacteria are also eating the iron of the ship's hull, weakening it drastically. This process will continue for as long as the steel remains underwater to be devoured. Bacteria and worms have eaten virtually all of the wood fixtures aboard the ship, though glass, ceramic, and bronze objects remain in superb condition.

The great weight of the ship's remaining superstructure will do much to hasten ship's collapse once its steel has been sufficiently weakened by corrosion and bacteria.

Shiver Me Timbers

In 1996, George Tulloch's group organized a monumental media event when it invited 1,600 paying customers aboard two cruise ships to watch as crews attempted to lift a massive piece of the *Titanic*'s hull from the water. That attempt failed, but another two years later was successful. Tulloch's penchant for showmanship has brought him much criticism including accusations from *Titanic* Historical Society's Edward Kamuda that Tulloch is disturbing a "gravesite."

*Map of the wreck site of
the* Titanic.
(Drawn by Ken Ellis)

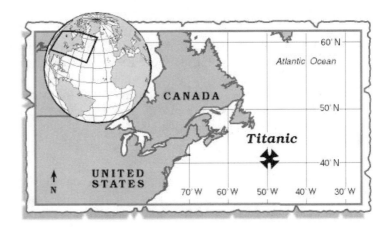

The Least You Need to Know

➤ The slips in which the *Titanic* and the *Olympic* were built had formerly been used to house three liners under construction but were enlarged and their floors were reinforced with concrete 54 inches thick.

➤ American maritime safety regulations would have required the *Titanic* to install more than twice the number of lifeboats it was carrying, boosting the number from the 20 aboard the White Star liner to 42.

➤ Although the 16 wooden lifeboats aboard the *Titanic* were equipped with collapsible sails, the four collapsible wood and canvas boats on board were not.

➤ Ships have been known to survive head-on collisions with North Atlantic icebergs, and speculation holds that the *Titanic* may have survived if it had done the same instead of striking a glancing blow.

➤ Numerous rumors abound regarding the *Titanic,* but one that is considered untrue is that Captain Edward J. Smith shot himself as the liner began to slide into the water.

➤ Before discovering the *Titanic,* oceanographer Robert Ballard had conducted a secret mission during which he located and photographed the wreckage of an American nuclear submarine named the USS *Scorpion.*

Chapter 19

Amazing Rescue: The Andréa Doria

In This Chapter

➤ The pride of Italy

➤ Knifed by the *Stockholm*

➤ The rescue

➤ Courtroom drama

➤ Diving's fatal Mecca

Some ships are downright beautiful, but one of the prettiest was the *Andréa Doria,* an Italian liner that represented not only style and elegance but also perhaps the final days of the era of transatlantic travel.

The *Andréa Doria* was not as big as the *Titanic,* but the disaster that caused the ship to be swallowed by the sea was equally mesmerizing and held the potential for being just as deadly. Only those aboard the *Titanic* saw that liner's demise, but millions saw the death of the *Andréa Doria.* Newsreel camera operators, still photographers, and reporters flew overhead, capturing and describing the scene.

By the time of *Andréa Doria*'s loss on July 26, 1956, it was already the twilight for transatlantic passenger service. Although the travel time had shrunk to as little as five days aboard the sleek liners, jet airliners had also emerged in 1952—making the trip a one-day experience. Steamships carried 27 million passengers between Europe and America from 1919 to 1956, but ocean travel would soon be supplanted by air travel.

Beginning in 1952, Britain's *de Havilland Comet,* the world's first jetliner, was winging people over the Atlantic 30,000 feet above turbulent weather at a speed of nearly 500 miles per hour. Though the lure of luxury accommodations gave the transatlantic liners a few more years, their use as a means of point-to-point transportation was at an end.

Like so many of the other shipwrecks we've seen, the *Andréa Doria* was a victim of the misplaced confidence the crew had in its design. Construction rules and technology had changed since the *Titanic* era, and the *Andréa Doria* was officially not supposed to sink. Not only that, but the 700-foot-long liner carried radar, a proven technology that could keep even the most inept fishing-boat skipper from running into things.

Despite its beauty and its radar, the *Andréa Doria* managed to collide with the liner *Stockholm* anyway, proving to a shocked world once again that technology cannot remove every danger in "modern" life. Then, because of hidden flaws in its design, another "unsinkable" ship sank, even though the damage shouldn't have been fatal.

The loss of the *Andréa Doria* is not a pretty sea tale when looked at up close. While there was heroism, there was also some poor behavior by the Italian liner's crew. When the story of how the collision occurred is peeled back, it's easy to see how giant ships can run into each other in the crowded Atlantic sea lanes.

The *Andréa Doria* took nearly four times as long as the *Titanic* to sink, allowing virtually all the passengers to be saved not only by the ship that struck it but also by other ships that rushed to the scene. The story of the *Andréa Doria* is mostly the story of a successful rescue at sea that remains unparalleled.

Step aboard one of the most ornate and beautiful ships ever built. Sure, it has some fatal problems, but try not to think about those as you enjoy a final evening at sea before disaster strikes.

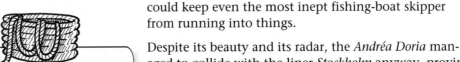

Know The Ropes

Ship construction had changed in the 40 years between the building of the *Andréa Doria* and the *Titanic.* The Italian liner was fueled by oil instead of the coal that propelled the *Titanic.* Welding had long since replaced riveting on ships, and the hull of the *Andréa Doria* was welded. While a welded seam can be as strong or stronger than a hull plate itself, some believe the *Titanic's* rivets popped loose upon collision with the iceberg. The *Andréa Doria* was also equipped with radar that could reveal the presence of other ships—and icebergs. Despite these improvements, the *Andréa Doria* ended up on the bottom of the Atlantic like the *Titanic.*

The Pride of Italy

After its ruinous experience in World War II as one of the least enthusiastic members of the Axis powers, Italy wanted to regain its traditional status in the world of maritime affairs. Half of Italy's commercial ships were sunk during the war, and the nation knew it needed to rebuild its fleet of merchant ships and liners.

Among its most ambitious projects was the construction of the *Andréa Doria,* a luxurious liner that intended to recapture Italy's glory as a maritime nation—and some badly needed money as well. The ship took nearly a year to build, while the outfitting of the completed hull took another 18 months.

A gracefully beautiful ship, the *Andréa Doria* was 697 feet long, 11 decks high, and could attain a maximum speed of 23 knots. On its final voyage, the ship would carry 1,134 passengers and a crew of 572.

The Andréa Doria *as it appeared during its heyday as one of the world's most beautiful transatlantic luxury liners.* (Courtesy of Italia de Navagazione *and the* Houston Chronicle Library)

Shiver Me Timbers

To those who speak the king's English, the name "Andréa Doria" is certainly a beautiful woman's name, but it's actually a man's name. To the Italians, Admiral Andréa Doria was the most courageous sea dog who ever lived. Doria's name graced the sides of many ships throughout Italy's history. It was the name of the first American ship ever saluted by a foreign navy following the American Revolution. He remained an Italian patriot until his death at the age of 94.

Floating Art Gallery

So much care had gone into outfitting the *Andréa Doria* that the liner was virtually a seagoing museum of artwork, sculpture, and interior design. A 1,600-square-foot mural representing paintings and sculpture by Italian artists enclosed the ship's lounge. In the middle of this same room, a life-size statue of Admiral Andréa Doria greeted passengers.

Throughout the ship were 31 communal rooms where artwork, sculpture, and paintings were displayed. Panels carved of exotic woods decorated walls, while mosaics and mirrors turned other walls into beautiful visual experiences. Some of Italy's best artists were employed to turn the ship into a work of art.

Built in 1953, the ship was the first to boast three swimming pools, one for each of its classes. It was fully air-conditioned and was considered one of the premiere ships of the day. The principal owner was the Italian government, though the ship sailed under the flag of the Italia Line.

Modern Design

While boasting beautiful artwork, the *Andréa Doria* also laid claim to modern engineering dictated by the 1948 International Conference for Safety of Life at Sea that established shipbuilding safety standards. The *Andréa Doria* was designed to survive flooding in two of its compartments. This rule and others, which affected all ships built after that year, were thought to render most ships invulnerable to sinking.

Know The Ropes

Although ships are designed to remain afloat even if a compartment fills with water, they are also designed to remain balanced because of their ballast, or weight along the bottom of the ship. However, a ship unable to equalize the weight of water entering the hull through a nonfatal leak can lean so far to one side that it will **capsize,** or turn over. Capsizing means death for a ship, even though it wasn't in danger of losing buoyancy because of the addition of water.

While many ships could remain afloat with one compartment flooded, it was reasoned that a collision might penetrate the boundary between two compartments. Unless there was a military attack or a fluke iceberg collision like the one that sank the *Titanic,* it seemed the two-compartment rule would hold water.

The Capsizing Hazard

A ship designed to remain afloat with two flooded compartments might ride low in the water, but it would nonetheless remain afloat. Since a leak or collision can cause any ship to take on water, the compartments must be able to redistribute the water so the ship doesn't become unbalanced. A ship weighted too much on one side can flip over and *capsize.*

Stockholm: *The Pride of Sweden*

The *Stockholm* was also a beautiful ship, though not nearly as luxurious as the *Andréa Doria.* The *Stockholm* was owned by the Swedish-American Line and was designed to be an efficiently run and comfortable ship. Though often thought of as nothing more than a freighter, the *Stockholm* was a transatlantic liner and carried 534 passengers; the Italian ship carried 1,134. The *Stockholm*'s crew numbered 213.

The 575-foot-long ship was built in 1948 and weighed 12,000 tons, or less than half the 28,000 tons of the *Andréa Doria.* The *Stockholm* was, however, the largest ship built in Sweden up to that time.

Bowing In

The *Stockholm,* being a ship that operated in cold Scandinavian waters, had a reinforced bow. Though legend often has it that the bow was designed so the *Stockholm* could serve as an icebreaker, the strengthened bow was designed to push aside ice while it followed an actual icebreaker through iced-over harbors and waterways.

Knifed by the *Stockholm*

Under the command of Piero Calamai, the *Andréa Doria* was 50 miles south of Nantucket Island approaching New York after an eight-day, 4,000-mile voyage. It was around 11 P.M., July 25, 1956, and fog had enveloped the ship.

Calamai was not just an extremely cautious captain but also a very dignified and kind man. However, he was under extreme pressure to arrive on time, since delays cost thousands of dollars an hour. Calamai knew the "Rules of the Road," which were regulations established by the maritime industry for the safe operation of ships, and the fog meant his ship should have probably come to a dead stop, though no ship ever did.

According to the rules, a ship is supposed to travel at a speed that would enable it to stop at half the length of visibility. It's no different from a car, really. If you were driving in low-visibility conditions, you would naturally slow down, right?

Since neither the captain nor his men could see anything, Calamai reduced his speed from 23 knots to 21.8 knots—that would be from 24 to 23 mph for turnpike drivers. After all, Calamai had radar and could electronically "see" all the ships surrounding the *Andréa Doria*. The 59-year-old captain came to the bridge of the ship at the first word of fog and remained there until the collision.

The Cautious Stockholm

Meanwhile, aboard the *Stockholm*, Captain Harry Gunnar Nordenson gave his orders for the night. The ship had departed from New York for Sweden seven hours earlier. Left in charge on the *bridge* of the *Stockholm* was officer Johan-Ernst Bogslaus August Carstens-Johannsen, known simply as Carstens. The *Stockholm* was traveling at its maximum speed of roughly 18 knots.

Carstens-Johannsen's ship did not enter the fog bank that worried Calamai, but the ship's officer had other problems—sea currents were pulling the *Stockholm* strongly to the north. The currents forced Carstens-Johannsen to make several course corrections to bring the ship back to the south. Eventually, both he and Calamai spotted one another's ships on their respective radar screens. The *Stockholm* was traveling east, and the *Andréa Doria* was heading west. No problem, right? Read on!

As the distance between the two ships closed to roughly two miles, Carstens-Johannsen saw the

Words To Treasure

The **bridge** of a ship isn't a gangplank for walking across but a command center for a ship where the ranking officer on duty directs the ship's operations from a high vantage point.

Andréa Doria's lights and determined they would pass port to port, or with the left sides of the ships facing one another.

A Turn for the Worse

As Carstens-Johannsen watched in disbelief, the *Andréa Doria* turned sharply to the left, heading south and placing itself directly in the path of the *Stockholm*'s sharp, strong bow. The Swedish officer ordered a hard right turn.

The westward-traveling *Stockholm*, moving at 18 knots, knifed into the Italian ship, crushing its own bow compartments while doing the same to compartments inside the *Andréa Doria*. Unfortunately, the collision occurred at 11:10 P.M. when many aboard both ships were asleep in cabins affected by the collision. The *Andréa Doria* continued moving, and the Stockholm pulled free from the Italian liner, leaving a 30-foot-deep hole in the left side of its hull shaped like an upside-down pyramid.

The smashed bow of the *Stockholm* then dragged along the side of the *Andréa Doria* in an amazing shower of sparks witnessed by passenger Dr. Horace Pettit. Hearing the collision, Pettit poked his head out of a porthole to see the *Stockholm* scraping along the *Andréa Doria*'s moving hull in a brilliant fireworks display of grinding steel.

Don't Go Overboard!

Failing to obey the maritime "Rules of the Road" can be as deadly as driving the wrong way on a highway. Internationally recognized "Rules of the Road," known officially as the Collision Regulations, clearly state that ships must travel at speeds safe for the weather and traffic conditions they encounter. Ships coming at one another head–on are both required to make sharp turns to starboard, or to the right.

Sudden Death

A total of 51 people died in the collision. Aboard the Italian ship, 43 were killed immediately, and another three would die later of injuries. Aboard the *Stockholm,* five crewmen would die of injuries they received while inside their smashed bow compartments.

"Miracle Girl"

When a seasick sailor from the *Stockholm* ventured out to get some fresh air soon after the collision, he heard a girl's voice calling for her mother in Spanish near the *Stockholm*'s shredded bow. In a bizarre twist of fate, Bernabe Polanco Garcia of Spain was perhaps the only Spanish-speaking crewman aboard the *Stockholm* and could understand the girl's cries.

Garcia found 14-year-old American Linda Morgan in yellow pajamas where she had been deposited by the collision on the *Stockholm*'s deck from her own cabin on the *Andréa Doria*. Though an American, Morgan spoke Spanish because she had been raised in Spain where her stepfather was a correspondent for the *New York Times*.

Her stepfather Camille Cianfarra and her half-sister Joan died in the collision. Dubbed the "Miracle Girl" by the media, Morgan would later marry and become a librarian at the San Antonio (Texas) Museum of Art.

The Rescue

Although Linda Morgan was saved by providence, others would have to struggle to make their way out of the ship that quickly listed 20 degrees to starboard. This tilting of the ship shocked Captain Calamai and his officers, since the *Andréa Doria* was supposed to list no more than seven degrees. A SOS signal was immediately sent out.

Shiver Me Timbers

Since the *Titanic* disaster, when some ships heard the distress signal and some had not, a new system was in place that allowed ships to automatically generate an alarm signal aboard other vessels even when their radios weren't being monitored. This alarm would awaken sleeping operators who could then take down the message. The message sent contained the *Andréa Doria's* code letters ICEH, the time of the message, and the crippled ship's location of latitude 40.30 north 69.53 west. It also contained the plea: "Need Immediate Assistance."

As on the *Titanic* and ships today, the *Andréa Doria's* lifeboats were arrayed along the port and starboard sides of the ship—which makes sense as long as the ship is sinking straight down. The severe starboard list or tilt of the sinking liner lifted the port or left-hand lifeboats far from the water and angled them toward the ship, making them unusable. As a result, only half the boats ship's 16 lifeboats were releasable. A ship—that moments before the collision had more than enough lifeboats—now had room in its lifeboats for only 1,004 of the ship's 1,706 passengers and crew.

The *Stockholm,* while "down at the bow" to a depth of three feet, seven inches, was intact. The only water rushing into the ship was from its own water lines that were soon shut off. Captain Nordenson rushed to the wheelhouse to take charge. Carstens-Johannsen was still stunned by what had happened.

When Nordenson was confident that the watertight compartment behind the smashed bow wasn't leaking, he dispatched Carstens-Johannsen to the *Andréa Doria* in one of four *Stockholm* lifeboats sent to retrieve passengers.

Swedish Hospitality

By 12:30 A.M., survivors began to arrive at the *Stockholm,* which would eventually take on 542 crew and passengers from the *Andréa Doria.* Among those taken aboard the *Stockholm* were 234 of the ship's 572 crew members, indicating that women, children, and male passengers were not the first to leave the sinking ship.

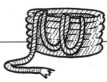

Know The Ropes

When it comes to working aboard a ship, there are true sailors and then there are folks doing a job at sea that they might do on land. In the minds of a ship's crew, a division is made between able-bodied seamen and waiters and other service workers on luxury ships. Despite having a crew of nearly 600, Calamai found himself short of real seafarers able to use signal lights and handle rescue chores.

Tough Decision

Although it's romantic to believe that any ship's captain will immediately respond with a courageous crew to save another ship imperiled on the sea, reality is a bit less clear-cut. Ship captains have the safety of their own ships and passengers to worry about without mentioning the massive cost of delaying their voyage to rescue others.

Worried Hero

One such hesitant hero was Baron Raoul de Beaudéan who was serving as replacement captain on the French liner *Ile de France.* After receiving the SOS from the *Andréa Doria,* he began to wonder whether his ship would arrive in time to do any good. He also was concerned about endangering his own passengers who were expecting to arrive in Europe on time.

After figuring that a 36-hour "rescue" delay would cost his company nearly $50,000, de Beaudéan nonetheless turned his ship around to answer the *Andréa Doria's* pleas.

Fleet Helpers

Although the U.S. Coast Guard dispatched 11 ships to the scene of the sinking, the ones reaching the site first included the aging luxury liner *Ile de France,* merchant ships, and two U.S. military ships. This odd collection of rescue ships would prove to be extremely effective.

Along with the magnificent liner *Ile de France,* a U.S. Navy transport named the *Private William H. Thomas* would respond to the sinking quickly. Other ships that arrived were the United Fruit Company freighter *Cape Ann* and the destroyer USS *Edward H. Allen.* The tanker *Robert H. Hopkins* would arrive in time to rescue the last passenger taken off the ship at 4:30 A.M.

Frantic Passengers

With the then 44-year-old *Titanic* disaster still fresh in their minds, many passengers quickly assumed the *Andréa Doria* had struck an iceberg. Many believed the ship would sink immediately, though such fears soon subsided as the crew proclaimed the ship was in no danger.

Many of the Italian emigrants on board became frantic not only because of the collision but also because they feared having to return to Italy after enduring the long bureaucratic process required before they were allowed to come to America. This anxiety was only heightened by the fact that they were now faced with clambering down ropes and cargo nets on the tilted deck to reach the remaining lifeboats below.

When lifeboats from other ships finally did arrive, some passengers panicked and began leaping into the water, forcing their rescuers to fish them out. One frantic man on deck dropped his daughter into a boat below causing her to suffer a serious head injury. Eventually, lifeboat crews began catching children in blankets, like firefighters do.

A Quick Save

Though minutes seemed like hours to passengers of the *Andréa Doria,* the hastily organized rescue worked well. Virtually all aboard the *Andréa Doria* were rescued by 4:30 A.M., or four hours after the accident. The *Ile de France* took aboard 576 passengers and 177 crewmen, while the *Private William H. Thomas* took on 146 passengers and 12 crewmen. The destroyer USS *Edward H. Allen* took 77 members of the crew.

Don't Go Overboard!

The next time you ram a reef or find your ship sinking because someone unplugged the bilge pump, you better provide full details when you radio for help. The 1929 Conference for Safety of Life at Sea determined that anyone getting a radio call must rush to provide help, but the 1948 conference watered down this ruling by stating that captains could go at their discretion if they knew other vessels were responding. If you call for help, be specific or your would-be rescuers might assume you don't need them.

Captain Calamai and 11 of his officers remained aboard, but everyone had forgotten about Robert Hudson. The merchant sailor had transferred aboard the *Andréa Doria* near Gibraltar for transportation back to America for an injured back and hand. If you can believe this, he was sleeping in the ship's hospital and had not been awakened by the collision!

Shiver Me Timbers

Anthony Grillo was a three-year-old toddler traveling with his mother aboard the *Andréa Doria* when the accident occurred. Like other children, he was dropped to safety into a tautly stretched blanket held by rescuers. Grillo, who now lives in New York, has created a Web site on the disaster and has been gathering information about the event. Nearly 20 years after the accident, Grillo discovered that a coworker, Mario DeGiralomo, was also a survivor of the sinking.

When the tanker *Robert E. Hopkins* arrived at 4:30 A.M. to provide what help it could, it found a panicked Hudson clambering down a rope to the water's edge. He was then taken aboard to be the tanker's only rescue.

A Hopeless Struggle

The impact of the collision began a small drama when it trapped and seriously injured Martha Peterson in the first-class stateroom she shared with her husband, Thule. Her uninjured husband, wearing nothing but a curtain wrapped around his waist, worked for hours with the help of steward Giovanni Rovelli to free his wife.

They struggled valiantly to save the badly injured Mrs. Peterson. When they finally obtained a jack and began lifting the wreckage pinning her legs, Mrs. Peterson gasped her last and died. Though many of the crew fled the ship far ahead of the passengers, Rovelli was touted as a hero for his selfless rescue efforts.

Stockholm's Troubles

The *Stockholm*, though not in danger of sinking, fought two separate battles. Its anchor chain had fallen to the seafloor and pinned the ship so that movement was impossible. Meanwhile, a team of rescuers began to cut its way through the crumpled cabins in the bow of the ship to rescue trapped sailors.

One of the most popular sailors on the *Stockholm* crew, Alf Johansson, was discovered with most of his bones broken and his skull fractured in the smashed remains of his cabin. Johansson was one of five people plucked from the scene of the disaster and flown by helicopter to shore for treatment. Unfortunately, Johansson died soon after.

The body of a woman pinned in the remnants of the Swedish ship's bow was lost when the *Stockholm* finally wrenched its anchor chain loose to fall into the sea. A search for the body was conducted, but all that was seen were sharks that proliferate in the area.

Salvaging Hope

The *Andréa Doria*'s officers left the ship at 5:30 A.M. only after an argument between Captain Calamai, who wanted to remain, and his subordinates, who wanted him to leave. Calamai agreed to leave only after his officers threatened to remain aboard with him. (The Italian Merchant Marine minister radioed an order for Calamai to abandon ship, but it arrived after he had done so.)

Calamai knew a U.S. Coast Guard boat that was equipped for towing was on its way to the site. He hoped it would arrive in time to drag the *Andréa Doria* onto a sandbar nearly 25 miles away. This action would have allowed the grounded ship to be re-floated relatively easily after minor repairs. However, Calamai knew that abandoning the ship would make it available as a salvage prize to any passing ship able to take it into tow.

When the U.S. Coast Guard ship *Hornbeam* arrived, Calamai and 44 crewmembers went aboard around 9 A.M. The *Hornbeam* was ordered not to tow the ship, since the Italian Line had already contracted for seagoing tugs to tow the *Andréa Doria*.

The Andréa Doria *nears its final moments as it leans heavily on to its starboard side on the morning of July 26, 1956. (Courtesy of the Mariner's Museum)*

Lost at Sea

Calamai's hopes of salvage were to be dashed. Towing was not practical, since the liner was now listing 50 degrees on its damaged right side with its *promenade deck* touching the water. It would sink at 10:09 A.M. on July 26, 1956, and settle intact on its starboard side in 225 feet of water.

Courtroom Drama

Perry Mason couldn't have provided a better show than the legal proceedings following the disaster. The buildup to the legal wrangling was immense, since the accident had been photographed, televised, broadcast on radio, and splashed across newspapers worldwide.

Nothing's more emotional than an accident in which hundreds of lives are put in peril. Follow this with the grueling give-and-take of in-depth courtroom interrogation, and you have a venue in which to relive the tragedy.

A pair of beautiful ships carrying hundreds of people had collided despite the use of radar, nighttime running lights, and common sense. Fifty-one people were dead, and the public hungered for more information.

Words To Treasure

A **promenade deck** is an upper deck of a ship, with much of it open to the sun and breeze, where passengers can take walks while the ship is underway. Promenade is a fancy word for a sociable walk with another or it can even be a dance.

High Seas, High Speed

In preliminary federal court hearings, a clear picture of what caused the collision between the two liners began to emerge. Although lawsuits had been filed, the real battle was between the lawyers who were representing the ships' owners.

Carstens-Johannsen, in charge of the *Stockholm* at the time of the collision, pointed out that his ship's speed was not excessive. He knew the *Stockholm* could stop within half the distance he could see, as stipulated in the "Rules of the Road." The *Stockholm,* he maintained, was not in fog at the time of the collision.

The Swedish officer also pointed out he had been turning away from the *Andréa Doria* when that ship turned left in front of him.

Too Fast

Under the normal pressures to arrive in New York on time in order to keep down expenses and to prevent longshoremen from being paid while waiting for the ship, Piero Calamai admitted he reduced his speed only slightly despite being in a thick fog bank. (However, few captains in Calamai's shoes slowed to a crawl, so his decision to maintain a high speed was not unusual.)

Shiver Me Timbers

Ships, like airplanes, carry a variety of lights so other ships in the dark can determine the direction and orientation of a ship at long distances. A green light is carried on the right side of a ship, and a red light marks the left side of a ship. Carstens-Johannsen was dumbfounded when he saw the right-side light of the *Andréa Doria* where the left-hand, or port, light had been moments before. It meant the Italian ship had turned in front of him in the darkness.

Eventually, it became clear that confusion in the wheelhouse of the *Andréa Doria* lead to Calamai's thinking that the *Stockholm* was farther away than it really was. When the ships appeared headed for collision, Calamai ordered a hard left turn, thinking his ship would pass safely in front of the *Stockholm*.

At the same moment, Carstens ordered a turn to the right to avoid the looming ship in accordance with the "Rules of the Road." The result was the deadly collision.

Tired Captains

The stress of the event was so hard on Captain Piero Calamai and Captain Harry Gunnar Nordenson that both were hospitalized soon after the event. Calamai was hospitalized for nine days after the accident, and Nordenson spent two weeks in the hospital after feeling faint during his testimony at the preliminary hearing in federal court.

While Calamai had endured the strain of losing a ship, Nordenson was working night and day to supervise $1 million in repairs to the *Stockholm*'s bow while also taking part in the legal proceedings.

Case Closed

Eventually, both the Italian Line and the Swedish-American Line decided to settle the suits filed against one another out of court, and each absorbed the cost of its own losses. The *Andréa Doria* was a $30-million ship, and the *Stockholm* needed a new, $1-million bow.

A lawsuit settlement fund of $5.8 million was established with the Italian Line contributing $1.8 million and the Swedish-American Line contributing $4 million. All death and property claims were paid from this amount.

Shiver Me Timbers

One of the most interesting cargo items aboard the *Andréa Doria* was a $100,000 concept car designed by Chrysler and called the Norsemen. The car was returning from Italy's auto design house of Ghia that designed and constructed its sleek body. The car was the first fastback design and sits somewhere inside the cargo hold of the liner. Diver John Moyer, who holds salvage rights to the *Andréa Doria,* intends to locate the car and bring it to the surface.

Fatal Flaw

When the *Stockholm* knifed into the *Andréa Doria,* the empty fuel tanks on right side of the ship were punctured, causing them to fill with seawater. Another group of fuel tanks on the left side of the ship were empty, thereby causing the ship to list heavily to the right. This proved to be a problem more serious than the collision itself.

The empty fuel tanks had never been ballasted, or filled with water, testified officers of the Italian liner. When full, the tanks held the ship lower in the water and provided additional ballast. If equally empty on the left and right sides of the ship, the liner would be balanced.

The rapid and unexpected leaning, or listing, of the ship immediately after the collision may have happened because the *Andréa Doria* suddenly found itself hopelessly unbalanced.

Diving's Fatal Mecca

The *Andréa Doria* still lies in darkness in a shark-infested part of the North Atlantic. French undersea explorer Jacques-Yves Cousteau dove upon the wreck with his team and declared it too dangerous due to strong currents and an unusually large number of sharks.

It's believed that at least 12 divers have died descending to the *Andréa Doria* wreck since its loss in 1956. In 1998 one diver died each month in June, July, and August while diving on the wreck.

The wreck is precisely what divers look for. A big, beautiful ship that is almost completely intact and accessible is a great temptation to divers who want an exceptional challenge. Because the ship is 225 feet below the surface, it is far below the 130-foot limit of ordinary recreational diving.

Divers who want to visit the wreck have used special mixes of gases in their breathing tanks. The gases help them reduce the possibility of suffering injury or death due to decompression sickness or nitrogen narcosis that can dangerously impair judgment. Nitrogen collects in the tissues in deep water and can expand upon surfacing with terrible effects.

Don't Go Overboard!

Only the most experienced and proficient divers should attempt diving below the ordinary 130-foot level. Many experts have called diving on the *Andréa Doria* dangerous. Some of those include Jacques-Yves Cousteau and department store heir Peter Gimble, who made the first dive on the ship shortly after it sank and returned to it many times over the years. One diver who died while exploring the wreck in July 1998 was found floating inside the first-class lounge of the *Andréa Doria*.

A map of the wreck site of the Andréa Doria. *(Drawn by Ken Ellis)*

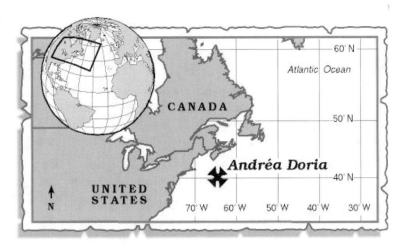

The Least You Need to Know

➤ The *Andréa Doria* was one of the most beautiful ships ever designed and was made exquisite with the artwork of many Italian artisans.

➤ Though his name has a lyrical and feminine sound to non-Italians, Admiral Andréa Doria was an extremely tough and brilliant naval commander.

➤ The Swedish-American Line ship *Stockholm* was the largest ship ever built in Sweden at the time of its construction in 1948.

➤ The *Stockholm*'s reinforced bow was not strong enough to allow the liner to serve as its own icebreaker but had been strengthened to allow it to push through ice while following an icebreaker.

➤ In the 43 years since the loss of the *Andréa Doria* on July 26, 1956, at least a dozen divers have perished while descending to the dangerous 225-foot depths where the ship lies on the seafloor.

➤ "Miracle Girl" Linda Morgan was the 14-year-old deposited on the deck of the *Stockholm* from her *Andréa Doria* cabin during the collision.

Chapter 20

The Torpedo That Launched a Thousand Ships

In This Chapter

➤ Fast and fabulous

➤ Fog of war

➤ Death blow

➤ Sinking into mystery

➤ Owning the *Lusitania*

It's really quite amazing how shipwrecks and maritime disasters can rivet our attention through the decades. One example of this phenomenon is how so many of us know of the World War I loss of the Cunard Steamship Company liner RMS *Lusitania*. A German torpedo sank the *Lusitania* on May 7, 1915, killing 1,198 men, women, and children in sight of the Irish coast.

The event is known by many, even though other, more ghastly events related to the Great War can't be recalled. Have you heard of the Battle of the Somme in France? On the first day of this battle, July 1, 1916, Britain alone suffered 57,470 killed and wounded.

Of all the things that happened during that four-year war in which 47 million people died, the one event still grabbing headlines is the sinking of the *Lusitania*.

The disaster's circumstances made the event both a human tragedy and an international incident that still lives in infamy. Carrying more than 1,859, the *Lusitania* was sunk by a German Imperial Navy U-boat when submarine warfare was considered a cowardly form of piracy. This treacherous form of killing, fanned by Allied wartime propaganda, made the sinking of the *Lusitania* synonymous with murder.

Although the pointless, wholesale slaughter that marked World War I was obvious to those paying attention to the course of the war, the sinking of the *Lusitania* officially announced the end of gentlemanly warfare with the finality of a dropping anchor. An age of unrestricted warfare that would target both civilians and combatants had arrived. The result was the rag doll-like bodies of children washing up on Ireland's bleak southern coast. The disaster still lives in the collective psyche of many.

The Germans saw the *Lusitania* as a legitimate military target that happened to be carrying civilians. The Germans knew that the liner was part of a wartime maze of high-level intrigue in which the British government circumvented American neutrality to ship war goods home.

Because British policy had severely blurred the line between civilian passenger liners and warships (the *Lusitania* was designed to carry guns in the event of war), the Germans were put in the unhappy position of having to kill civilians to halt war supplies.

Germany, whose own ports were blockaded by the British, decided to stymie Britain's floating supply line with the establishment of a zone around the British Isles. Allied ships entering these zones would be sunk by Imperial German Navy U-boats. Germany even published a warning to the United States about this policy prior to the May 1, 1915, departure of the *Lusitania* from New York.

Shiver Me Timbers

Britain's subsidization of the shipbuilding industry came with a price, and that was a require-ment for ocean liners to be capable of minimal military duty. Liners like the *Lusitania* were equipped with fittings to allow the emplacement of a dozen six-inch naval guns. Although merchant ships and liners carried self-defense armament in both World Wars, commercial ships are not purpose-built for war and are ineffective as actual offensive combatants.

Despite the published warning, the *Lusitania* was carrying 159 Americans when it left. Of those, 124 died when the *Lusitania* was torpedoed six days later. Though the event didn't immediately propel America into the conflict against the Germans, the attack hardened American opinion and was a great propaganda resource for Britain. After sinking more American ships and asking Mexico to go to war against the United States, Germany did find itself at war with America 23 months later.

So this event raises some big questions. Was the *Lusitania* an armed warship? Was it carrying dangerous explosives that detonated when a U-boat torpedo struck it? Did the British government engineer the disaster to drag America into the war?

The *Lusitania* was and is a ship of mystery, and there are still more questions than answers about its loss. The once-magnificent ship now lies in total darkness 315 feet beneath the Celtic Sea. Since it doesn't mind a few new visitors, let's drop down and feel our way through the green water made even darker with speculation and conspiracy theories.

Fast and Fabulous

What an odd history the Royal Mail Ship *Lusitania* had. It was built to be both a partial warship and high-speed luxury liner, and its competitor in both war and peace was Imperial Germany. Fast new German liners were gaining ground in the transatlantic shipping business in the early 1900s at the same time Britain feared Germany was gearing up for war.

When the British government loaned 2,600,000 British pounds to Cunard to build the ships the *Lusitania* and the *Mauretania,* the government wanted them to be capable of traveling at high speeds and capable of carrying six-inch guns. In time of war, British liners such as the *Lusitania* would be available for any purpose the government demanded. The liners would recapture transatlantic passenger business and also be ready for war.

Built by John Brown and Co. Limited at Clydebank, Scotland, the *Lusitania* and its sister ship the *Mauretania* were to be marvels of their time. Construction began on the *Lusitania* in May 1905. It was launched 13 months later on June 7, 1906. The liner was 785 feet long and weighed 32,000 tons fully loaded.

The Lusitania *proudly sails with smaller ships as escorts to show the comparative sizes of the liner and the other vessels. (Courtesy ARTTODAY.COM)*

Speed Matters

To be a commercial as well as a military ship, the *Lusitania* had to be the fastest ship around. A great deal of research went into its design and power plants. The decision was made to use turbines instead of reciprocating engines to provide the amount of power needed to propel the ship at 26 knots.

On the first of its 201 successful voyages across the Atlantic, the *Lusitania* broke a speed record by traveling from Liverpool, England, to New York City in four days, 19 hours, and 52 minutes. That's right ... if you blinked, you missed the whole trip! It was capable of achieving 25.88 knots.

Shiver Me Timbers

The *Lusitania* was unique in that it used some of the most advanced propulsion concepts of its day. Instead of being pushed through the water by a steam-powered reciprocating engine with pistons and a crankshaft, the *Lusitania* was equipped with four gas turbines powered by steam. These engines harnessed pressurized steam to generate 70,000 horse-power for turning the ship's screws, or propellers. Instead of one or two propellers, the *Lusitania* had four.

Iffy Innovations?

The *Lusitania* was designed with little thought given to where to put the tons of coal it would need to feed its furnaces, so engineers had to scramble to make room for the black stuff. It was decided to cram the 6,600 tons of coal needed by the *Lusitania* for an Atlantic crossing into the ship's longitudinal bulkheads. These watertight compartments ran the length of the ship on both sides to provide buoyancy.

Filled with coal and positioned between the sides of the hull and the ship's engines, it was believed these compartments could absorb the force of a collision or the explosion of an enemy shell or torpedo. But there were problems with this idea. Chunks of coal can act as hard sponges absorbing water, which meant that the ship could retain unnecessary weight even after leakage had been pumped out.

It's also obvious that scattered chunks of coal would make it hard for coal stokers to completely seal the watertight doors built into the compartments for access to the coal. Should damage allow water into the longitudinal compartments (which were split into five sections each), it might rush into the hull through poorly closed hatches.

Floating City

The *Lusitania* was built to be a luxurious home at sea to thousands of people and contained every convenience that could be jammed into a ship in the first decade of the 1900s. Electricity played a big role on the ship, powering everything from telephones and elevators to safety devices such as automatic waterproof doors. The massive ship also contained beautiful woodwork, fireplaces, a hospital, and a nursery with a special kitchen for preparing meals for infants.

Fog of War

Every sea captain knows the danger of fog. The conscientious masters of ships often have a standing rule to be called whenever fog is in the area. Captain Piero Calamai of the *Andréa Doria* did. Being blinded by fog can mean sudden death for a ship. Unfortunately, there are many types of fog and the *Lusitania* found herself lost in the *fog of war*.

World War I was complicated by the fact that the world was a very interconnected place in the 1900s. More people were traveling between continents than ever before, and the complex web of industrial trade between nations was an essential part of world commerce. In some cases, a nation unable to receive necessities such as food and raw materials by sea faced starvation or economic ruin.

Words To Treasure

The **fog of war** describes the confusion and misunderstanding that permeates not only combat but also the political circumstances surrounding war. The fog of war is often blamed for troops shooting at their own side and other mishaps that make the horror of war just a little worse.

Consequently, combat at sea became a form of economic warfare as the Allied powers of Britain and France kept supplies from sailing to Germany through a successful blockade. The Germans similarly intended to starve the British, using a small number of U-boats to sink merchant ships bound for Great Britain. Unfortunately, many civilians sailed on these ships, making the fog of war even thicker.

Ship or Warship?

Complicating matters even more was the British policy of subsidizing ship construction (as in the case of the *Lusitania*) so the government could require the ships to do everything from serving as floating military hospitals to actually carrying guns and engaging in combat.

Although mountings were put on the *Lusitania*'s deck to allow the ship to be equipped with 12 six-inch guns, there's no indication such weapons were in place at the time it was sunk. However, the Germans knew of these plans and tended to regard most British ships as potential men-of-war. When the Germans launched a submarine campaign against British shipping, the attackers decided to shoot first and ask questions later when uncertain of a ship's combat potential.

Another measure taken early in World War I to militarize the *Lusitania* was the addition of extra steel to its upper decks for protection from enemy shells. This extra weight may have made the *Lusitania* slightly top-heavy.

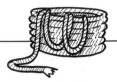

Know The Ropes

We won't pick up a calculator and start working complex formulas. Let's realize that naval engineers and architects know a ship's weight must be distributed properly for it to remain stable. The addition of heavy, naval gun mounts to the *Lusitania's* upper deck made the ship top-heavy. If the weight was great enough, it might have required additional ballast, or weight, to be added along the *Lusitania's* keel. If too much weight is added high in the ship without adding ballast, the ship may have a tendency to careen or list too easily. (Remember what happened to the *Mary Rose* in 1545 when it leaned too far over and took on water?)

Total War

Germany declared a "war zone" around the British Isles in February 1915, meaning that the Germans would consider any Allied ship coming into the coastal waters of Britain fair game to German submarines.

The British blockade of the North Sea was doing a fairly good job of reducing food supplies in Germany. Germany was going hungry, and its navy was going to do the same to England. Britain's first lord of the admiralty, Winston Churchill, had ordered German U-boat crewmen shot upon capture and advised British ships to fly neutral America's flag to avoid attack.

Germany's discovery of these orders (which were probably more hyperbole than policy) could only have stiffened the attitude of the highly motivated U-boat crews.

Everyone Fights

The British government decided that captains of merchant ships who failed to fight or ram German U-boats would be prosecuted. Everyone was a combatant according to this type of thinking. This attitude indicates how desperate the British were to mitigate the sneaky and dastardly U-boat menace that the nation was unprepared to fight.

What's in the Hold?

Through complex relationships with famous American industrialists like J. P. Morgan and ranking government officials, the British were successfully buying and shipping war materials from American suppliers despite America's neutrality policy. The policy precluded trade with belligerents (who are otherwise known as "warring nations").

Obviously, one of the ships used in this trade was the *Lusitania,* though it was never designed as a true cargo ship. For years, speculation swirled around whether the *Lusitania* carried tons of high explosives on its last voyage. If it had, wondered many then and now, did its own cargo explode to finish off the *Lusitania*?

We know that the *Lusitania* was carrying six million rounds of rifle ammunition for British forces. However, such a cargo is unlikely to explode with anything approximating the force of a widely used explosive of the time, called "gun cotton."

Shiver Me Timbers

A week before the *Lusitania* sailed on its last voyage on May 1, 1915, British agents, working through J. Pierpont Morgan's offices, purchased 600 tons of a gun cotton called **pyroxyline.** This form of gun cotton can detonate upon contact with seawater. No one knows whether the pyroxyline was loaded on the *Lusitania,* but 323 bails of "furs" came from locations in Maryland near Du Pont plants that made the explosive. Some other curious cargo that was loaded on the *Lusitania* included 60 tons of so-called cheese destined for the British navy's "Experimental Establishment." New York's docks were home not only to very large wharf rats but also to a lot of intrigue at the time.

Forewarned Is Forearmed

World War I was blazing, the Germans and the British navies were knuckling down to a no-holds-barred naval war, and people were boarding the *Lusitania* in New York for a luxury ocean voyage into a war zone. Meanwhile, the British and the Germans were trying to schmooze with rich and powerful—but neutral—America. British and German spies swarmed over New York's waterfront as the *Lusitania* prepared to set sail for Liverpool on May 1, 1915.

A German-American group was concerned that a large number of Americans killed in a German torpedo attack would stink up the political situation worse than a bowl of overripe sauerkraut at a dessert table. The group drafted a warning to Americans against sailing on British or Allied ships, saying they will be "liable to destruction."

The Imperial German Embassy signed the letter that was published adjacent to Cunard newspaper ads. These ran throughout the United States the week before the *Lusitania* sailed. However, the warning had little effect other than to raise suspicions later that the Germans knew, all along, they were going to sink the *Lusitania.*

An Aging Ship

Captain William Thomas Turner had been at sea since the age of 13, and in March 1915 at the age of 59, he had been given command of the *Lusitania.* Turner was an unlikely skipper for Cunard, since the company expected its captains to charm the passengers. The highly regarded Turner despised socializing with the passengers, calling them a "a lot of bloody monkeys." Another officer was hired to take care of the dinner table chitchat while Turner ran the ship.

Turner had concerns more worthy than repeating the latest joke over dinner. Upon taking command of the *Lusitania,* he found numerous problems with lifeboats and safety equipment. The caliber of the crew also disturbed Turner. There was a war on, he was told, and all the best chaps were either in the Royal Navy or enduring barrages on the Western Front. Although he couldn't do anything about his crew, he did fix many of the safety shortcomings, and the *Lusitania* sailed from Liverpool on April 17, 1915.

Shiver Me Timbers

One problem not fixed was the *Lusitania's* turbine engine used for generating "astern," or reverse, propulsion when backing away from the dock. If thrown into use too quickly with too much steam, the pressure could cause the system to explode. This problem was considered minor at the time, since it seemed that the *Lusitania* would have little need of reverse thrust. However, the faulty engine proved to be a shortcoming when the ship was unable to slow adequately to allow lifeboat evacuation after it was torpedoed.

Death Blow

Traveling at high speed, the *Lusitania* arrived in New York on April 24 and was readied for its return trip to Liverpool. It also took on cargo that may or may not have contained potentially dangerous explosives. Passengers were abuzz over German Embassy warnings about traveling on the *Lusitania,* but everyone boarded nonetheless.

On May 1 the ship edged away from its berth at New York's Pier 54 as a male chorus on the ship sang the "Star Spangled Banner." In less than a week, the *Lusitania* would have a deadly rendezvous with a German submarine.

Perhaps the richest passenger aboard was New York millionaire Alfred G. Vanderbilt, 38, who was traveling alone to England. The best-known passenger was American theatrical producer Carl Frohman, 41. Both would turn out to be extraordinary men in the horrible events that would ensue.

Survivors row from the Lusitania *as it sinks off Old Head of Kinsale after being torpedoed by the German submarine U-20. (Courtesy ARTTODAY.COM)*

Almost Home

After seven days of sailing, the *Lusitania* was only hours from docking in Liverpool. However, the final few hours of the *Lusitania's* voyage were the most dangerous because submarines prefer to do their hunting in *choke points,* or narrow waterways. These exist in areas where harbors and ports attract an ample supply of seagoing victims.

Captain Turner brought the *Lusitania* in from the relatively safe vastness of the Atlantic to the smaller, U-boat killing zone of the Celtic Sea and traveled north along Ireland's west coast. Here, German navy Kapitän-Leutnant Walter Schwieger waited in his surfaced U-boat for another victim. As he did so, he ran his air-breathing diesel engines to charge the batteries that powered his submarine when submerged.

Unknown to Captain Turner, German submarines had sunk 23 merchant vessels in the area since his departure from Liverpool two weeks previously. Schwieger's submarine, known as the *U-20,* had sunk three of those and was targeting the *Lusitania* for his fourth kill.

Straight into Trouble

Captain Turner had decided he needed to take an extremely accurate navigational fix before completing the voyage to Liverpool. To do so, he would have to travel in a perfectly straight line at a steady speed for 40 minutes. U-boat commander Schwieger couldn't have asked for a better target.

Words To Treasure

Choke points are narrow straits that are heavily traveled entry and exit points for shipping, and are considered prime hunting areas for submarines.

Bonus Blast

Schwieger kept the *Lusitania* in his sights until the massive liner was 700 yards away. At 2:10 P.M., he launched a single type G torpedo but held out little hope of sinking the ship, which he initially thought was the *Mauretania*. Schwieger's lack of enthusiasm was well-founded: His torpedoes were notoriously unreliable and sometimes exploded weakly if at all.

Aboard the *Lusitania,* 18-year-old seaman Leslie Morton spotted the torpedo's wake coming toward his ship like a straight white line drawn against a blue-green canvas of water. This particular type G torpedo detonated with a vengeance on the right side of the ship just behind the bridge.

Then Schwieger saw something unexpected through his periscope that the *Lusitania's* passengers also experienced—a second explosion.

Shiver Me Timbers

Torpedoes carry sizeable warheads and are extremely effective against the hulls of even warships that were often equipped with "torpedo blisters," or thick belts of additional armor just below a ship's waterline. Merchant ships, while strong, are not made to resist torpedoes or naval gunfire. The *Lusitania,* for all its attributes, had no protective armor plate and its hull was easily penetrated by the shockwave of the torpedo's high-explosive warhead.

The Unexplained Explosion

The second blast occurred almost immediately after the first, and its cause remains hotly debated nearly 85 years later. It was heard and felt by many aboard the *Lusitania*. Some claim it was the detonation of contraband munitions, while others say it was an accumulation of coal dust in the longitudinal bulkheads. Some witnesses say there was no second explosion.

Sinking Fast

The *Andréa Doria* took nearly 11 hours to sink, and the *Titanic* took two hours and 40 minutes to go down. The *Lusitania's* death dance to the bottom of the Celtic Sea, 11 miles off Old Head of Kinsale, took just 18 fear-packed minutes.

The ship was quickly thrown into a starboard list that rendered most of its 22 wooden lifeboats impossible to launch. The boats on the port side were leaning back onto the deck, while those on the other side swung too far out.

The ship, which was traveling at nearly 18 knots, still surged forward as Captain Turner heard his ship begin to die. To slow this movement and allow the lifeboats to be lowered, "full astern" was ordered. This action only caused the malfunctioning low-pressure turbine to burst. Turner then steered the ship for land.

Eventually, the bow of the *Lusitania* began to sink. The prow of the 785-foot ship struck the granite bottom of the Celtic Sea 315 feet below while the stern was still pitched high in the air.

Bad Behavior

In a display of supreme ignorance, an American passenger named Isaac Lehmann grabbed his handgun and made his way to the leaning deck. There he began ordering crewmen—whom he didn't think were working courageously or quickly enough—to lower boats. At gunpoint he forced crewmen to prematurely release a boat that swung backward, smashing passengers as it careened down the sloping deck.

A sobbing Lehmann later admitted to his bad behavior, as he was one of the 761 survivors.

Heroes

Alfred G. Vanderbilt and Carl Frohman found themselves in the liner's nursery where dozens of infants were lying in baskets. Both men began to tie life preservers to the baskets in the hope that the children might be able to float free of the wreck and be recovered.

As these two men were going about their chore with an air of calmness, Third Officer Alfred Bestic warned them the ship was on the verge of sinking. In response, Vanderbilt only shrugged his shoulders.

As the water swallowed the *Lusitania,* Frohman was widely reported as quoting a line from *Peter Pan:* "Why fear death? It is the most beautiful adventure in life." Frohman was a friend of J. M. Barrie, the author of the children's story.

Shiver Me Timbers

Third Officer Alfred Bestic was swept through the nursery by a rush of water and was struggling for survival. All around he could hear the cries of infants as their baskets foundered in the water. This scene caused him such distress that he wanted to commit suicide but was too exhausted to take off his own lifejacket. The cries slowly faded as the infants drowned one by one. In fact, 94 of the 129 children aboard the *Lusitania* died. Of the 1,198 victims of the wreck, 785 were passengers and the remaining 413 were crew members.

Frohman's body was recovered and returned to New York for burial. Despite the offer of 1,000 British pounds for the body of Vanderbilt, it was never found. A single British pound was offered for the body of a British subject and two British pounds for the recovery of an American. The bodies of victims washed ashore for days following the disaster.

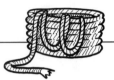

Know The Ropes

An explosion outside the hull of a ship will generally produce a shock-wave that will either dent or fully penetrate the steel inward. An explosion occurring inside a ship, if powerful enough, will deform the hull outward or even peel the steel away in an outward fashion. Although this seems simple enough, hull damage studies have fueled decades of debate over what caused the loss of the battleship USS *Maine* and that of the nuclear submarine USS *Scorpion* (which is discussed in Chapter 24, "The Cold War's Deepest Mystery: The USS *Scorpion*").

Sinking Into Mystery

If you want to see a bunch of historians and authors get into a fight, just shout, "*Lusitania.*" It will set them off like a ringside bell at Madison Square Gardens. Everyone has a theory about what "really" sank the *Lusitania.*

A longstanding theory that a second fatal explosion shortly after the torpedo blast actually led to the sinking of the *Lusitania* had some cold water dashed on it by none other than ocean explorer Robert Ballard. A 1993 expedition using the remotely operated vehicle *Jason* from Woods Hole Oceanographic Institute found no internal explosion damage to the hull.

Although this discovery is unlikely to halt the specula-tion, it does add fuel to the belief that the *Lusitania*'s dusty—and nearly empty—coal bunkers may have provided the ideal environment for a second explosion triggered by Schwieger's torpedo. However, the physical evidence tends to indicate the second blast was not enough to compromise the integrity of the hull.

Laying the Blame

The causes of the *Lusitania*'s loss are probably numerous. Blaming Turner because he was torpedoed seems a bit ridiculous. The Royal Navy's inability to sweep its coastal waters clear of enemy submarines combined with design flaws in the *Lusitania* may have doomed the ship.

If Schwieger's torpedo had penetrated both the outer hull and the starboard longitudi-nal bulkhead, the ill-fitting doors leading into the engine compartments may have allowed water to pour uncontrollably into the hull. Perhaps it was merely bad luck that sank the *Lusitania:* The *U-20* and the *Lusitania* could just as easily have missed one another.

The British Board of Trade was to conduct an inquiry into the loss of the *Lusitania* under the direction of Lord Mersey (who was being heavily pressured by ranking Royal Naval officials including Churchill to blame Captain Turner). However, Mersey found that the seafarer conducted himself properly. The blame, said Mersey, who had investigated the *Titanic* disaster three years previously, must rest on the U-boat crew and those who commanded them to sink the ship.

In short, Mersey decided the technological ruthlessness of modern war was the culprit.

Descending Into War

Woodrow Wilson had long sought to convince the European powers to find a peaceful way out of the war and its slaughter, but desperate German naval policy that encouraged the sinking of American merchant ships in British waters brought America closer to war.

The 1915 sinking of the *Lusitania,* which made Americans violently angry, was widely denounced as a crime, though public reaction did not goad President Woodrow Wilson into making war on Germany that year. Nonetheless, Germany's stupidity solved that problem in relatively short order.

A telegram sent by the German Ambassador to Mexico, Arthur Zimmerman, seeking to create an alliance with Mexico and Japan against the United States was intercepted by the British and delivered to President Woodrow Wilson in February 1917.

Around the same time, Germany began practicing unrestricted submarine warfare and sank three American ships. An angry Wilson then sought and obtained a declaration of war against Germany on April 6, 1917.

Owning the *Lusitania*

Over the years, the *Lusitania* was rumored to have been carrying tons of gold from New York to Britain. Other untrue stories about fabulous treasures being aboard the ship were also circulated.

To date, not much of real value has been pulled from the wreckage that, at 315 feet, lies 185 feet deeper than ordinary divers can go. The currents are strong and treacherous, and the water darker than the inside of a closet at midnight.

During the intervening decades, various companies and individuals have obtained salvage rights to the wreck. At present the ship's salvage rights mostly belong to Gregg Bemis of Sante Fe, New Mexico, who has salvaged items from the wreck. Bemis had asked to be declared the sole owner of the wreck and its contents, but the Supreme Court of the United States denied his request. Irish courts have declared Bemis owner of the wreck but not of its contents or the personal effects of its passengers. Bemis first laid claim to the wreck in the 1970s.

The Irish government, in whose waters the *Lusitania* lies, forbids unauthorized diving on the wreck and strictly enforces this ban.

Words To Treasure

Lusitania was the word used by ancient Romans for the region that included western Spain and all of Portugal. The Lusitani were the courageous and warlike people who inhabited the region.

A map of the wreck site of the Lusitania.
(Drawn by Ken Ellis)

The Least You Need to Know

➤ The *Lusitania* broke a world transatlantic liner speed record during its maiden voyage to America by making the trip three hours and eight minutes short of five days.

➤ The *Lusitania,* in competition with other luxury ships of the period, was richly decorated and contained virtually every amenity that could be found ashore, including a nursery for children and a hospital.

➤ Germany suffered heavily under the British blockade of its ports in the North Sea, causing the Germans to retaliate with unrestricted submarine warfare that allowed them to sink any Allied ship in the coastal waters of the British Isles.

➤ The *Lusitania*'s captain, William Thomas Turner, was considered a superb ship's master but a lousy dinner companion, since he despised the passengers he was carrying across the Atlantic.

➤ Type G torpedoes, like the one that destroyed the *Lusitania,* often failed to explode and were considered unreliable by U-boat commanders who launched them.

➤ Ocean explorer Robert Ballard used a remotely operated vehicle to view the *Lusitania* off Ireland's west coast in 1993 and reported there was no damage in the hull of the sunken ship to indicate that a second explosion had played a role in its loss.

Chapter 21

Wreck of the *Edmund Fitzgerald*

Maybe someday at least someone'll write a song about this...

In This Chapter

➤ *Edmund Fitzgerald:* "Pride of the American Side"

➤ Fighting the storm

➤ The "Big Fitz" disappears

➤ Investigating the wreck

➤ Visiting the "Fitz"

Okay, so it wasn't a high-speed luxury liner, and its cargo was rusty iron ore instead of a shinier treasure, but the bulk carrier *Edmund Fitzgerald* attained near-mythical status after its mysterious loss with 29 hands on November 10, 1975. As a fierce storm agitated Lake Superior, sending huge waves crashing down on the *Fitzgerald,* the massive ship disappeared!

The *Fitzgerald* had been famous for years around the Great Lakes region following its 1958 launching. In shipping—where size does matter!—the *Edmund Fitzgerald* was the largest ship to navigate the Great Lakes and remained so until 1971—four years before its loss. Whenever the ore carrier broke a new hauling record, the owners publicized the fact.

This was a working man's ship in many ways. Those aboard were regular blue-collar guys mostly from the Midwest and the Great Lakes region. The *Edmund Fitzgerald's* purpose was utilitarian: pick up iron ore on one end of Lake Superior and deliver it to the blast furnaces on the other to sate the auto industry's infinite hunger for steel. The *Edmund Fitzgerald* was not only part of the area's maritime realm but also a crucial thread in the region's economic tapestry.

No Vanderbilts or Astors would sink with the *Edmund Fitzgerald,* just working stiffs enduring a dangerous environment to provide America with fenders and bumpers. Although *"blue water" sailors* have always disparaged mariners who plied lakes and rivers instead of the open sea, anyone who's worked offshore knows a sailor can drown in 16 feet of water as easily as in 16,000.

When the *Edmund Fitzgerald* departed on its last trip from Superior, Wisconsin, the 729-foot ore carrier had yet to meet a storm it couldn't endure, but November 10, 1975, would be different. The "Fitz," as lake sailors knew it, was headed for trouble from which it would never return. Those who have sailed Lake Superior believe they've seen storms the equal of any Pacific typhoon or Atlantic hurricane.

Made famous by Gordon Lightfoot's 1976 hit song "Wreck of the *Edmund Fitzgerald*," the ungainly looking ore carrier would become the focus of sadness for a ship and crew who dared and lost.

Meanwhile, the regular folk who lived along the shores of what the American Indians called *Gitche Gu' Mee,* or "The Big Sea Water," still talk of the November 10 storm. Authors and experts are still arguing over what caused the *Fitzgerald* to sink, and television documentaries are still being made about the tragedy.

Torn in two and lying in 530 feet of water 17 miles north of Michigan's Whitefish Point, the *Fitzgerald* is far from lonely—it's one of at least 3,700 shipwrecks littering the waters of the Great Lakes.

Gulp down some steaming java that's as black as the night outside, pull on your foul-weather gear, and fight your way across the pitching deck because the "gales of November" are still blowing!

Words To Treasure

A **"blue water" sailor** is one that sails far out at sea where the water is often an extremely deep blue color as opposed to near-shore and fresh-water sailors who sail in shallower depths that are often just muddy.

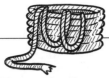

Know The Ropes

Lake Superior is the largest lake in the Western Hemisphere and acquired its name from French explorers who called it *Lac Superieur* meaning "upper lake." Superior is 350 miles wide from east to west, 160 miles wide from north to south, and reaches a depth of 1,300 feet in places.

Edmund Fitzgerald: **Pride of the American Side**

Every great shipwreck begins with a great ship, and the *Edmund Fitzgerald* was one of the greatest. In 1958, America stood astride the world like an industrial colossus, building the best of everything in massive quantities. Iron ore by the millions of tons was needed to keep the steel plants operating, and much of that ore sailed across the Great Lakes by ore carriers.

When Northwestern Mutual Life decided it wanted to invest, it avoided the allure of the stock market and real estate to instead build the largest bulk iron ore carrier ever launched on the Great Lakes. Originally known as "hull 301," the work on the ship began on August 9, 1957, and a 729-foot ship slowly began to grow at Detroit's Rouge River Shipyard. It was launched on June 7, 1958, before a crowd of 15,000.

The ship, whose length was equal to the height of a 60-story skyscraper, slid down its *ways* into the Detroit River. As it was coming into the world, the ship leaned far over to its port side—making some believe it was going to sink then and there! The ship seemed unsure about whether to capsize or come back straight but righted itself and headed for 14 weeks of outfitting work to prepare for its September 22, 1958, maiden voyage. Written immediately after its loss, Canadian Gordon Lightfoot's song about the *Edmund Fitzgerald* described it as the "pride of the American side," which the "Fitz" really was for much of its life.

Words To Treasure

The *Edmund Fitzgerald* was named after a man who, coincidentally, was named Edmund Fitzgerald and who was the former president of North-west Mutual Life, the insurance company that owned the ship. **Ways** are the timbers upon which a ship rests while undergoing construction.

The iron ore carrier Edmund Fitzgerald *as it looked in May 1975, a mere six months before it was lost with all 29 aboard in a vicious storm on November 10, 1975. (Photograph Courtesy of Robert Campbell)*

The "Big Fitz"

Shipping is a business and a demanding one. Profit margins can be thin, while the cost of operating even a modest ship is enormous. An elementary rule of shipping econom-ics is to carry as much as possible at the lowest possible cost. Hence the increase in the size of ships with a parallel reduction in the size of the crew during the past 3,000 or so years of sailing.

The *Fitzgerald* was made so big because it had to be profitable—and technology now allowed gigantic ships to be built, powered, and maneuvered. The *Fitzgerald* was immediately leased to the Columbia Transportation Division of the Oglebay Norton Company of Cleveland, Ohio, that would provide the crew and operate the giant ship. By comparison, the cargo ship *Arthur M. Anderson*—built for Great Lakes duty in 1952—originally measured 647 feet and had a capacity of 20,150 tons. At the time, the *Anderson* was considered one of the larger ships on the Great Lakes.

A 7,500-horsepower, coal-fired steam turbine engine originally powered the *Fitzgerald*, although the engine was converted to burn oil in 1972. The ship could accommodate a crew of 35—including VIPs as well as guests. A tunnel ran the length of the ship to allow the crew to walk from one end to the other without being exposed to dangerous weather conditions on deck.

At the bow of the ship was a pilothouse where the captain and the officers spent their working day. At the stern were the dining area and living quarters of the crew. Lying in between were 21 gigantic cargo holds covered with flat, seven-ton steel covers. Each cover was an inch thick and was secured to the hold opening with 68 *Kestner clamps* tightened with a special wrench.

Shiver Me Timbers

The *Fitzgerald* broke a number of records for hauling iron ore and eventually carried its record load of 27,402 tons in 1969. This load is comparable to those carried by many carriers plying the Great Lakes today, though newer ships like the 1,000-foot *Columbia Star* launched in 1981 can carry nearly 79,000 tons. The *Edmund Fitzgerald's* increase in capacity was due to the relaxation of Coast Guard regulations establishing the ship's **freeboard requirement**—the distance between the deck and the water. Originally set at 12 feet in the summer and 14 feet, 3 inches in the winter, these distances were eased to 11 feet, 2 inches and 11 feet, 6 inches, respectively. After the *Fitzgerald's* loss, some critics wondered whether the rules had become too lax.

Dents and Scratches

One reason ships are so expensive to operate is that they always require repair, and the *Fitzgerald* was no exception. Like most gigantic ships, the *Fitzgerald* was rather ungainly. This can lead to collisions and groundings, and the ship suffered a few of both.

On September 6, 1969, the *Fitzgerald* grounded near Sault St. Marie, Minnesota, bending some of her hull plates and the internal stiffeners supporting them. She collided with another ship on April 30, 1970, and four months later banged into the wall of a lock. Another lock wall was struck in May 1973.

In September 1974, the crew inadvertently attempted to lift one of the ship's giant hatch covers with a crane without removing all the Kestner clamps and managed to bend the *coaming* and the cover. All these problems were corrected during the icy winter months when the ship was taken out of service for repairs.

Cracking Down

One of the most serious problems found on the *Fitzgerald* was not the result of a collision, but of natural stresses on the ship. A 1969 inspection of the ore carrier revealed serious cracking along its *keelson,* the reinforcing steel that runs along the top of the ship's *keel,* or backbone.

A naval architect was consulted and additional stiffening was added to the keelson to keep it from flexing. Later inspections showed some minor keelson cracking but nothing that required other than minor welding repairs.

Words To Treasure

A **Kestner clamp** is a massive fastener tightened with a heavy bolt. It fits over the hatch cover and a lip of the coaming upon which the hatch rests to provide a hopefully watertight fit.

Fitzgerald's Captain

By November 1975, Ernest R. McSorley had been captain of the Fitzgerald for nearly four years. The 62-year-old ship's officer had served on ships for 44 years, becoming the youngest ship's master on the Great Lakes at 37. Decent and fair to his men, he also maintained a strict code of discipline.

Considered a leader more than merely a barker of orders, McSorley fully understood the common crew member's job and how to command without humiliation (obviously someone had learned Bligh's lesson!). He also understood the necessity of distance between the man in command and those commanded, so McSorley retained an appropriate reserve.

Words To Treasure

A **coaming** is an opening on a deck with raised sides to prevent water from sloshing in. A **keel,** of course, forms the spine of a ship, but a **keelson** is the application of additional steel plates or beams on top of the keel for extra strength.

Fighting the Storm

By dawn of November 9, 1975, McSorley's crew was opening the *Fitzgerald*'s 21 hatches to receive 26,116 long tons of taconite iron ore as it sat alongside the Burlington Northern Railroad Dock in Superior, Wisconsin. As the crew worked, death in the form of a powerful and capricious storm front was making its way north from Texas. The storm would roar out of northern New Mexico and western Texas on November 8, 1975, with its northern tip aiming straight for Lake Superior.

Thousands of tons of iron ore thundered into the open holds from dockside bins as chief mate Jack McCarthy kept an eye on a lighted indicator indicating the trim, or the balance, of the ship. As the ship filled with iron ore, McCarthy pumped water out of the Fitzgerald's eight ballast tanks to keep the ship from riding unevenly in the water. The loading took nearly six hours. And, through it all, the storm was traveling north.

Weather Warning

The National Weather Service knew the front was on its way and issued a gale warning for the Lake Superior region. A gale warning was broadcast on November 9, 1975, at 7 P.M.—when the *Fitzgerald* was nearly five hours into its trip across Lake Superior to Detroit to unload the iron ore.

The forecast was nothing too frightening, just another of the gales of November. The 7 P.M. report warned of winds reaching 34 to 40 knots. By 2 A.M., Monday, November 10, the gale warning had become a storm warning with winds of 35 to 50 knots. Waves as high as 15 feet were expected during the day Monday.

Traveling a dozen miles behind the *Fitzgerald* was the *Arthur M. Anderson,* an ore carrier commanded by Bernie Cooper. The *Anderson* was actually larger than the *Fitzgerald* and one of several vessels that had dethroned the Big Fitz from its position as the biggest on the lake—but only by 38 feet in length. When built in 1952, the *Anderson* was shorter than the Fitzgerald but was lengthened by 120 feet in 1975.

Shiver Me Timbers

A **gale** is a weather disturbance with winds of 34 to 40 knots, while a storm carries winds of 48 to 55 knots. November storms have claimed many ships on the Great Lakes. On November 11, 1913, for example, 18 ships were lost with 254 killed. From November 11 to 13, 1940, another 57 were killed aboard three ships. On November 29, 1966, the freighter *Daniel J. Morrell* went down in Lake Huron, taking 28 crewmen with it.

Taking note of each other's position, McSorley and Cooper communicated by radio and at 2 A.M. decided their best course was to get on the protected, or lee, side of the Canadian coast. The two ships pulled out of the ordinary shipping lanes and moved farther north. The captains wanted to hug the Canadian shore as protection from the heavy waves and winds that were now 52 knots strong.

Rough Water

The waves slamming the *Fitzgerald* and the *Anderson* were not rounded rolling swells, but sharp, fast staccato attacks of water blown by a 52-knot wind from the northeast. By 2 A.M. the waves were 10 feet high and snapping over their decks and bow.

By dawn on November 10, the storm had tightened into a smaller, more intense system, swirling in a counterclockwise direction. The rotating winds then slammed across Lake Superior from the northwest. Weather Service officials predicted waves of 16 feet by that afternoon with northwest winds gusting up to 60 knots.

The waves were so large that they crashed down upon the decks of the ships, submerging them momentarily until the water washed over the *railing* and through the *scuppers*. At 2 P.M. both ships entered a blinding snowstorm. An hour later, Cooper noted the *Fitzgerald* was sailing close to an underwater rise known as the Six Fathom Shoal, an obstacle that extended a mile farther out than charts of the time revealed.

Words To Treasure

A **rail** is either steel cable or metal piping that serves as a safety fence around the decks of a ship. **Vents** allow air to enter and escape ballast tanks as they're filled and emptied with water. **Vent covers** keep water from splashing into the vents. A **scupper** is a drain on the deck of a ship below the railing that allows accumulated water to run off.

Damaged Ship

At 3:35 P.M. McSorley called Cooper to report that the *Fitzgerald*'s railing was down and that a pair of ballast tank *vents* were missing. Worst of all, McSorley told Cooper that the *Fitzgerald* had a list—that is, the ship was leaning because it was filling with water.

Cooper asked whether McSorley was using pumps to get the water out, and McSorley replied, "Yes, both of them." By 4:10 P.M. there was more bad news when McSorley told Cooper that his (McSorley's) radar had stopped working.

Walls of Water

By 6 P.M. the *Anderson* was fighting its way through 25-foot-tall waves that rose up and then crashed down upon the deck. Cooper noticed on his radar that the *Fitzgerald* was ahead of him by 15 miles and a mile to the right but seemed to be drifting to the left.

Disappearance of the "Big Fitz"

After learning that McSorley's radar was knocked out, Cooper provided directions to the electronically blinded *Fitzgerald*. When the *Anderson*'s radar spotted a ship heading their way, an *Anderson* mate called the *Fitzgerald* at 7:10 P.M. to warn McSorley. As an afterthought, the mate asked about the *Fitzgerald*'s problems. A taciturn McSorley gave a reply that has now become famous: "We are holding our own."

Soon after, Cooper realized the *Fitzgerald* may have disappeared from the *Anderson*'s radar screen and began unsuccessful attempts to radio McSorley. Visibility improved suddenly, but the *Fitzgerald*'s lights still weren't visible. For nearly an hour, Cooper tried to reach the U.S. Coast Guard in Sault Ste. Marie. When he did, he told them he believed the *Edmund Fitzgerald* was lost in an area roughly 20 miles north of Whitefish Point, Michigan.

The Search

The Coast Guard took Cooper's call at 8:25 P.M., unsuccessfully tried to radio the *Fitzgerald,* and finally had a local radio station broadcast a message to the ship that also failed to elicit a reply.

Aircraft were sent aloft with powerful searchlights and flares. While airborne searches seem promising to the uninitiated, small lifeboats and tiny people are notoriously hard to spot from a fast-moving aircraft covering hundreds of square miles of turbulent water. A 647-foot ore carrier, named the *William Clay Ford,* and the *Anderson* also embarked on a search for the *Fitzgerald* and its survivors but without success.

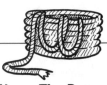

Know The Ropes

When the *Fitzgerald* lost its radar, the ship was fortunate to have the *Anderson* nearby, since the *Anderson* could plot the movement of both ships. Navigating near land is extremely tricky business and radar provides an instant map of what's above the water. The *Anderson's* radar essentially acted as the remote eyes for the *Fitzgerald's* Captain McSorley.

Sickly Rescuers

The Coast Guard's plucky little fleet of rescue vessels was not in good shape. A cutter named the *Naugatuck* was receiving maintenance when Cooper's call came in. The ship was headed out to the scene of the loss when it broke down. Adding to its ineffectiveness were instructions that precluded the *Naugatuck* from operating in winds above 60 knots. It didn't reach the area of the *Fitzgerald's* disappearance until 16 hours after it was dispatched.

Many of the Coast Guard's other ships were either undergoing maintenance or were unequal to the challenge of pounding seas and high winds. However, it became obvious that the crew had not had time to escape and had gone down with the ship.

Shiver Me Timbers

Upon hearing of the loss of the *Fitzgerald* with all hands, Father Richard Ingalls made his way to the Old Mariners' Church in Detroit, Michigan, where he was rector. He rang the church's 3,000-pound Brotherhood Bell once for each person aboard the *Fitzgerald.* Gordon Lightfoot mentioned Ingalls's action in the ballad "Wreck of the *Edmund Fitzgerald.*" The church was built in 1842 for use by Great Lake sailors.

Three other ships in the area—the *Benfi, Nanfri,* and *Avafors*—refused to help in the search, saying the weather was far too dangerous for such an undertaking. The Big Fitz and its crew of 29 were swallowed whole by Lake Superior, and the lake was tenaciously guarding her latest catch.

Giving Up

By November 11, 1975, a massive three-day search had been geared up with aircraft and boats searching for survivors or wreckage. However, everyone knew that even those who managed to climb into a lifeboat would have long since died of *hypothermia*—the fatal reduction of body temperature due to exposure to cold.

Finding the Wreck

Although finding sunken ships is hard, the superb directions provided by Cooper allowed a rapid location of the wreck site. Knowing generally where to look, a U.S. Navy P-3 Orion submarine-hunting plane was borrowed for the task of finding the *Fitzgerald*'s wreck. Equipped with a magnetic anomaly detector for locating steel-induced disturbances of the earth's magnetic field, the aircraft managed to find the sunken ship's precise location on November 14.

Debris

Very little was left adrift to mark the spot where the *Fitzgerald* was lost. The *Anderson* discovered a chunk of one lifeboat roughly nine miles east of the wreck site. A larger segment of a smashed lifeboat was later found, as well as the twisted remains of a third.

Searchers would eventually recover a sounding board used for recording the water levels in the ballast tanks, life preservers, spare tanks of propane, and flotation rings. Even a searchlight from the *Fitzgerald* was found bobbing on the surface.

Unlike older ships that were mostly built of wood, the wrecked *Fitzgerald* didn't leave masses of wood planks bobbing on the surface. The steel ship was made of very little that could break free and float.

Investigating the Wreck

If you think finding a sunken ship is hard, trying to figure out what causes one to sink when there are no surviving witnesses can be incredibly tough. Even when there are witnesses and everyone basically knows what happened, competing theories spring up anyway, arguments break out, and books are written. The rest of us are left to guess among ourselves.

Don't Go Overboard!

If you've been watching a lot of Hollywood movies about shipwrecks and you've seen people survive by floating around on debris, don't count on that if you sink on a modern ship. Steel and other metals are now used in ship construction. Because metal is denser than water, metal sinks, so forget having giant chunks of wood for makeshift rafts. You might consider sleeping in your life preserver if things don't look very safe.

When the *Fitzgerald* went down, the event had all the necessary elements to confound and shock the public. It had been the biggest ship sailing the Great Lakes for 13 years after its 1958 launching, and its captain was among the best in the business.

As is customary in the loss of a merchant ship, the U.S. Coast Guard rapidly convened an inquiry, known as a Marine Board of Investigation. Meeting in Cleveland, a Coast Guard admiral and two captains heard sworn testimony from 45 witnesses during a dozen days of proceedings. The transcript of the inquiry would create a 3,000-page document.

The Usual Suspects

There was the usual list of suspects to be considered in the wreck, and a few things were known. Whatever sank the *Fitzgerald* happened so quickly that McSorley couldn't make a distress call. He also reported the ore carrier had been taking on water, which caused the ship to list, and had radioed that the ship had suffered damage on her deck. The ship's radar had also been knocked out as it fought the storm.

Clearly, the storm churning Lake Superior's surface into waves as high as 25 feet had created a vile and dangerous environment for the *Fitzgerald* and the other ships navigating Superior that night.

The usual suspected causes of the wreck included gouging open the hull on rocks, a stress fracture of the hull caused by the high seas, or leaking hatch covers that allowed the ship to take on water from the crashing waves.

Conclusions

The Coast Guard considered the evidence but needed more information following the inquiry, so it borrowed the U.S. Navy's remotely operated vehicle known as CURV. The vehicle, whose name means "cable controlled underwater research vehicle," was sent down to the wreck to gather photographs of the scene 530 feet below. This investigation began May 20, 1976, and 12 dives were conducted in seven days.

CURV contained video cameras, side-scan sonar, and manipulator arms that could actually pick up objects from the lake bed. However, the images shot by CURV's cameras did nothing to resolve what happened to the *Fitzgerald*. The hull was split in two with the bow sitting upright in the mud and the stern resting upside-down some distance away. Thousands of tons of iron ore pellets littered the scene.

The U.S. Coast Guard's final report, issued 18 months after the inquiry, concluded that there was no evidence that McSorley and his crew were to blame for the loss of their ship.

Safety Problems

However, the report did note some glaring safety issues regarding the construction of ore carriers like the *Fitzgerald*. Incredibly, the ship's cavernous central hull was not subdivided by watertight transverse bulkheads (like those of the *Titanic*). Consequently, a leak in one part of the hold could not be locally contained.

Another amazing shortcoming was that the *Fitzgerald* lacked a *fathometer,* which uses sound waves to measure water depth under a ship. This omission startled many observers, since even bass fishermen can purchase these devices for a few hundred dollars to help them avoid grounding.

The inquiry also learned that McSorley had no way of knowing where water was inside his hull, since the ship did not have a simple electronic monitoring system. McSorley would only know his ship was leaking when it began to ride lower in the water or developed a list, which it did.

Words To Treasure

A **fathometer** operates on the same principle as sonar. It generates a noise and records its echo to determine the depth beneath a vessel.

Official Guess

One mysterious aspect of the *Fitzgerald*'s damage is the loss of two mushroom-shaped vent covers that prevent water from entering the vents of the ballast tanks. As water is allowed into the tanks, the displaced air escapes through the vents. That something knocked two of these heavy steel objects off the deck and smashed railing around the deck was mystifying.

The Coast Guard report speculated that a floating object could have struck the ship or that the *Fitzgerald* could have ground severely enough to cause the damage by bending the ship. However, the Coast Guard concluded that the entry of water through the missing vents would not have been enough to sink the ship.

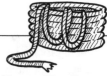

Know The Ropes

Navy and Coast Guard inquiries into ship losses are essentially legal proceedings. They are held to discover the facts behind the loss of a ship so future accidents can be avoided. The language used to report the findings of these hearings is a combination of legal and nautical jargon with the intent of making it a very scientific proceeding. Because the loss of a ship can be a complex thing, the word "probable" is widely used in inquiry findings.

Maybe, Could Be

Although the Coast Guard could not be completely sure of what happened, it stated that "the most probably cause" was flooding through the openings of the massive, seven-ton hatch covers. These flat covers had been subjected to tons of water crashing on the decks during the storm.

Lax Regulations

The Coast Guard's report also criticized the relaxation of its own regulations that allowed ships to operate with less of their hulls out of the water and mentioned the ruling as a possible contributing factor. This reduction in freeboard increased the amount of water crashing down on the *Fitzgerald*. Even the largest ships need an adequate amount of freeboard to provide stability.

Controversy

The Lake Carriers Association, an industry group that represented 15 shipping companies operating 135 ships on the Great Lakes, fired off a blistering letter at the time stating it "completely rejects the Coast Guard's theoretical cause of the *Fitzgerald* sinking."

The association was upset because it believed the Coast Guard should have given more credence to a grounding mishap as the cause. The organization pointed out that changes to hatch covers and reverting to stricter freeboard regulations could cost the shipping industry millions.

Despite the protests, the Coast Guard did not change its ruling, and its findings were later backed by the National Transportation Safety Board, which determined the 25-foot waves crashing on the *Fitzgerald*'s deck could have even crushed the hatch covers.

Shiver Me Timbers

An October 1977 inspection of the *Fitzgerald*'s sister ship, the *Arthur B. Horner*, revealed serious problems with the hatch covers that fit on the deck coamings, or square walls surrounding the hold openings upon which the hatches are secured. When inside the *Horner*, inspectors could see sunlight shining through the "closed" hatches, indicating they didn't fit and would have allowed water to enter the hull if waves were crashing on the deck.

Visiting the Fitz

After the October 1976 Coast Guard search of the *Fitzgerald* wreck, using the CURV remotely operated vehicle, a number of other expeditions explored the wreck, which lies just inside Canadian waters.

Jacques-Yves Cousteau's team of explorers dove upon the wreck in a two-man submersible on September 24, 1980. With Cousteau's son Jean-Michel supervising the expedition, the explorers spent only half an hour looking at the wreckage. The Cousteau team concluded the ship broke apart on the surface, floated in two sections, and sank, speculation rejected by the official findings.

A Clearer Look

A group of deep-sea technology firms, *National Geographic Magazine,* the Michigan Sea Grant organization, and numerous other historical groups took part in an August 22 to August 25, 1989, expedition at the *Fitzgerald* wreck to test a remotely operated vehicle (ROV) designed by Deep Diving Systems in Massachusetts.

The ROV glided along the wreckage, taking images many times better than those collected by the CURV vehicle 13 years previously. During the expedition it became apparent that the fame of the *Fitzgerald* tragedy remained a worldwide phenomenon with news agencies descending on the scene to interview participants and researchers.

Body of Evidence

In 1994 two expeditions visited the *Fitzgerald,* gathered even more images, and created more discussion about the loss of the ship. The first, which took place from July 3 to July 5, was headed by Canadian physician Dr. Joe MacInnis and used a 22-foot research submarine named the *Celia.* This craft allowed the first real inspection of the ship by people since the brief Cousteau expedition 14 years before.

High-quality photographs and video images revealed even more information about damage to the *Fitzgerald.*

A second expedition, from July 25 to July 27, was privately funded by Michigan businessman Frederick J. Shannon. Diving to the site in a 16-foot research submarine named the *Delta,* Shannon's team photographed a body wearing a life jacket near the bow of the wreck.

This information stunned many, since it proved that at least one member of the crew knew the ship was sinking. This inadvertent discovery upset some family members of the *Fitzgerald*'s crew. However, the body might not be that of a *Fitzgerald* crewman, since the clothing and life preserver it's wearing appears far older.

The Bell

On July 4, 1995, another expedition descended upon the wreck of the *Fitzgerald.* The lead diver, Bruce Fuoco, was wearing an armored diving suit known as a *Newt Suit.* Fuoco was part of an expedition sponsored by *National Geographic Magazine* and assisted by the Canadian navy ship *Cormorant.*

Once at the wreck, Fuoco used an underwater cutting torch to melt through the three steel stanchions holding the 200-pound bell. When it was hauled up through 500 feet of water, among those awaiting its arrival were family members of the *Fitzgerald*'s lost crew.

Know The Ropes

A **Newt Suit** is a major improvement over the relatively crude armored diving suits developed in the 1920s. Made out of exotic materials and propelled by thrusters attached to the suit, the robotic-looking enclosure allows a diver to use manipulator devices for work underwater while avoiding the problems associated with sea pressure.

The restored bell now sits in the Great Lakes Shipwreck Museum at Whitefish Point, Michigan.

A map of the wreck site of the Edmund Fitzgerald. *(Drawn by Ken Ellis)*

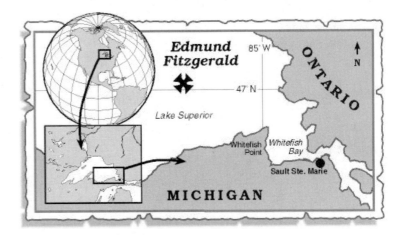

The Least You Need to Know

➤ The 729-foot *Edmund Fitzgerald* was the largest ship of its type operating on the Great Lakes at the time it was completed in 1958.

➤ The storm that slashed across the Midwest and eventually collided with the *Fitzgerald* originated in western Texas.

➤ The U.S. Coast Guard and the National Transportation Safety Board both believed water may have entered the *Edmund Fitzgerald* through its cargo hatch covers.

➤ The U.S. Coast Guard's pathetic attempts to rescue survivors of the *Fitzgerald* were hampered because many of its boats were down for repair at the time of the storm.

➤ Very little debris was recovered from the *Fitzgerald;* most of the items found were life rings and life jackets, along with the remnants of three lifeboats that broke loose during the sinking.

➤ Explorers under the direction of Jean-Michel Cousteau used a two-man submersible to perform a 30-minute inspection of the *Edmund Fitzgerald*. The team concluded that the freighter had broken apart of the surface, a finding that disagreed with the official U.S. Coast Guard report.

Part 5
Sleeping Warriors

War has long contributed a large share of shipwrecks to Davy Jones's locker, and three lost warships are included in Part 5. Of these, two were also treasure ships: the Japanese Imperial Navy submarine I-52 and the British cruiser HMS Edinburgh that were lost during World War II in different parts of the world.

One of the most confounding mysteries of the Cold War—the loss of the nuclear submarine USS Scorpion—is also discussed in this part. Shrouded in secrecy, the submarine failed to return to its home base and was later found 12,000 feet beneath the Atlantic, where it still perplexes those trying to unravel the reasons behind its loss and the deaths of 99 men.

Chapter 22

The Strange Story of the Japanese Submarine *I-52*

> ### In This Chapter
>
> ➤ An unusual mission
>
> ➤ Atlantic ambush
>
> ➤ The deepest treasure
>
> ➤ Uplifting proposal
>
> ➤ Honoring the dead

Most sunken ships, including those with treasure, usually have rather simple stories explaining how they ended up on the seafloor. Some are slammed by storms, others just spring a leak. While plenty of ships are sunk during wartime, a military treasure ship is a strange fish indeed.

Since the end of the Spanish treasure fleets in the nineteenth century, real treasure shipwrecks have been few and far between. Only a handful of ships have hit the bottom fat with gold or silver in the past century. A very small number of these date back from World War II when military ships carrying treasure were lost during dangerous wartime situations.

One of these rare wartime treasure ships is a craft that sank many times—and came back to the surface—the Japanese submarine *I-52*. The story of its 4,000-pound cargo of gold and its demise is entwined with a highly secret military operation that has only recently become well-known.

Although Japan fought its portion of World War II in the Pacific Ocean, 15,000 miles from the Atlantic, the Japanese submarine *I-52*'s odd fate was to make it the largest submarine sunk by the Allies in the Atlantic! The complexity of the story makes the *I-52* all the more interesting and, in the world of sunken treasure, such notoriety may inflate its golden cargo far beyond its mere price on the world gold market.

The *I-52* died in the middle of a South Atlantic storm, thousands of miles from its sister submarines. Those aboard the *I-52* had no way of knowing its death was preordained weeks before by the U.S. Navy. Nothing was in the *I-52*'s favor. The Allied cracking of the Japanese and German communication codes and the use of a top-secret torpedo sealed its fate.

Shiver Me Timbers

During World War II, the American, British, and Polish intelligence agents worked together to steal and then unravel the secrets behind a code machine developed by Nazi Germany and adopted by the Imperial Japanese Navy. The machine used a series of cipher keys to encrypt messages in a different way each time it was used. Intercepting coded German and Japanese messages during the war led to some major allied victories as well as lesser-known successes—including the interception and sinking of the *I-52* submarine.

Its 4,000 pounds of gold have remained on the seafloor since 1944, but a group that has located the wreck is raising money and plotting its recovery. The entrepreneur who pioneered the search for the *I-52* is seeking to raise not only the gold but also the entire submarine.

However, the Japanese Imperial Navy submarine was still awaiting recovery as of 1999. It could prove to be the richest and most interesting modern treasure ship awaiting the tender touch of a remotely operated vehicle. No human hand will sweep away seafloor sediment to look at the golden treasure of the *I-52*. The unique treasure ship is submerged in crushing pressure 4,500 feet deeper than the *Titanic*.

So, open the pressure hatch, come up on the bobbing deck, and suck in a chest-ful of night air. Your submarine's diesel engines are throbbing as you make your final dash past the U.S. Navy's antisubmarine patrols. You're heading for an Atlantic ambush, but at least the tons of gold inside your submarine are giving you a steadier ride in the choppy water.

Unusual Mission

A lot of folks weren't around during World War II (1939–1945), so a little history lesson is necessary to understand why Japan and Germany decided they had to risk the lives of submarine crews to send supplies and gold around the globe.

Germany was locked in the center of Europe and conquered every European country it could lay its hands on. It had few friends left, and the British and Americans sank any ship coming in and out of occupied Europe. Japan, which went to war to conquer the natural resources of its Pacific neighbors, instead became completely isolated by American submarines that eventually sank 90 percent of its merchant fleet.

Japan and Germany were about each other's only friend (except for Axis partner Italy, which surrendered in 1943). Isolated but desperate to share technology and crucial raw materials, they realized exchanging war materials and technology would have to be done by the sneakiest ships available: submarines.

Long Commute

The Japanese Imperial Navy sent its first submarine to Europe in 1942. This was the *I-30* that had been on a normal war patrol in the Indian Ocean and could carry a scout plane inside a large waterproof cylinder on its deck. The plane would come out, fly around, land in the water, and then end up back in the can! The *I-52* was also designed with a submersible airplane hangar.

After completing a routine war patrol, the *I-30* was sent to Lorient in German-occupied France to determine whether it was possible for Japanese submarines to make it to France. The *I-30* did make it to France after a long and harrowing journey. Though the British essentially controlled the Atlantic, the German U-boat menace was extremely strong in 1942 and the unprepared Allies were on the defensive. This may explain why the *I-30* made it to France at all.

The *I-30* then headed south along the west coast of Africa so it could then head for the Indian Ocean and back to Japan. On the way, the *I-30* tried to stop at Penang Island in Malaysia but struck a British mine, killing 13 of the 100 men aboard.

Know The Ropes

World War II–era submarines were powered by air-breathing diesel engines on the surface and by electric batteries when submerged. These submarines were almost always on the surface using their diesel engines and dove only to attack or avoid being attacked. Their hulls were shaped like traditional ships, which helped them move better on the surface, where they spent most of their time.

Successful Trip

Despite the last-minute loss of the *I-30*, the idea of sending Japanese submarines around the world still seemed realistic to the Japanese high command. The leaders decided that the *I-8* would be the next submarine to head for the German naval bases in France by heading west through the Indian Ocean. The submarine departed Penang, Malaysia, accompanied by another submarine that would return after refueling the *I-8*.

The *I-8* sailed far south of Africa's Cape of Good Hope to avoid detection by British patrols. This forced her crew to fight a desperate battle with the wild seas below Africa's southern tip. Arriving near the Azore Islands in the North Atlantic, German technicians equipped the submarine with what amounted to a naval "Fuzzbuster," so it could detect the radar signals of antisubmarine aircraft.

Shiver Me Timbers

World War II not only provided a proving ground for treasure-hunting technology, like metal detectors and magnetic anomaly detectors, but also the invention of the radar detector so the rest of us can drive irresponsibly fast down the highways and byways. However, radar detectors on ships warned of a pending aviation attack, since the Allies had perfected ways of spotting surfaced submarines using radar. When the submarines got a signal, they sank themselves voluntarily before being sunk involuntarily.

Carrying weapons and critically important equipment back to Japan, the *I-8* made the mad dash across the Bay of Biscay off France's coast where it was attacked unsuccessfully by Allied aircraft. The submarine completed its 30,000-mile round trip in 125 days.

Rough Sailing

In November 1943, a pair of Japanese submarines started the trip to Germany to exchange war supplies and technology, but both voyages ended in disaster. The *I-29* left Penang for France first, followed shortly afterward by the *I-34*.

The *I-34* was torpedoed by the British submarine *Taurus* on November 13, 1943, before leaving Asia. The *I-29* almost survived its 30,000 round-trip cruise to Europe. The submarine made it to the coastal waters of Formosa (now Taiwan) where it was sunk on July 26, 1944, by the U.S. submarine *Sawfish*.

The Last Try: The I-52's Turn

By now, the Japanese sailors knew that jumping into the old submarine for a four-month trip to the other side of the world and back was incredibly dangerous. Only one of the four previous boats made it, and Allied navies guarding every inch of the route were getting stronger by the month. Nevertheless, the *I-52* began its voyage from Japan on April 23, 1944.

The Germans had a lot of technology the Japanese needed, and, in turn, the Japanese had raw materials the Germans were desperate for. The Japanese owed the Germans for the technology they were buying, so the *I-52* brought along two tons of gold with which to pay the tab.

Words To Treasure

Molybdenum is a metal that can be used for numerous industrial applications but is often used as an alloy material to make extremely hard steel or for making heating elements used in superhot furnaces. It was almost as hard for the Germans to obtain as it is for us to say. **Tungsten** is a metal whose hardness and heat resistance make it perfect for rocket motor nozzles and armor-piercing shells.

Also inside the giant submarine were 228 tons of tin, *molybdenum,* and *tungsten;* a whopping 268 tons of liquid opium; three tons of quinine; and 54 tons of raw rubber. The opium was for painkillers such as morphine, and the quinine was the basis for other medicines. Of course, the rubber was for any number of militarily important products from tires to gaskets.

The Boat

The *I-52* was big for a World War II submarine, weighing 2,564 tons and measuring a whopping 356 feet long and 30 feet across. It could travel 27,000 nautical miles on the surface, using its two diesel engines at 12 knots. It could only travel under water for 105 nautical miles using battery power. (Remember that a nautical mile is equal to about 1.1 regular, or statute, miles.)

The *I-52* was built in the Kure Navy Yard in Japan in 1943 and was commanded by Commander Kameo Uno. It had a large waterproof cylinder on its deck for storing a small airplane. It could dive down to 330 feet to enable it to hide from attack or to sneak up on victims for torpedo attacks. It normally carried a crew of 94.

Atlantic Ambush

Things didn't quite work out for the *I-52*'s mission for a lot of reasons. One of the biggest problems is that the British and Americans figured out how to understand German and Japanese radio messages sent using a code machine they called Enigma. The German invention was adopted by the Japanese and had only one drawback— British scientists had already decoded the machine's complex signals.

Because of this, the British and Americans knew about the secret mission. After Berlin requested and received an update on the *I-52*'s cargo and passenger list, the U.S. Navy had it decoded seven days before American aircraft destroyed the Japanese submarine on June 24, 1944.

Not only did the Americans know what was on the submarine, they also knew the names of 14 Japanese technical experts on board for eventual arrival in Germany.

Shiver Me Timbers

The U.S. Navy document containing the decoded list of the submarine's occupants and its cargo still exists! It was located in the National Archives and copied by Paul Tidwell, who is spearheading the effort to salvage the submarine from 18,000 feet beneath the Atlantic.

To make things worse, the Allies invaded France on June 6, 1944, making it impossible for the *I-52* to go to Brest, France, its intended destination. Ignorant of how naked its intentions were to the Americans, the *I-52* plowed past Africa's southern coast and north through the center of the Atlantic.

Hunt for the I-52

Though few remember it, the U.S. Navy controlled the South Atlantic and flew massive antisubmarine patrols from South America's east coast to the shores of western Africa. America was determined to crush the Nazi U-boat menace that had sunk thousands of ships and killed tens of thousands of military and civilian sailors. Now, a Japanese submarine was swimming into this huge web.

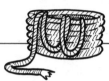

Know The Ropes

Fido was a torpedo with electronic ears that could hear submarines and hunt them down. If it found a submarine within its 15-minute life span, its 92-pound warhead was designed to explode against a submarine's hull. If sonobuoys dropped by an Avenger torpedo bomber transmitted submarine noises, a Fido would be dropped into the water to fetch a submarine for Davy Jones's locker. Of the four Japanese submarines destroyed by Fidos in World War II, one was the *I-52*.

On June 15, the American aircraft carrier USS *Bogue* was ordered to ambush the *I-52* and a German submarine coming to meet it about 1,000 miles west of the Atlantic's Cape Verde Islands.

The *Bogue* carried Avenger torpedo bombers designed to destroy ships and submarines. Just prior to this, the Navy had introduced a secret new torpedo whose code name was *Fido*. It was an acoustic homing torpedo designed to work in association with sonobuoys (listening devices) dropped from aircraft. Fido would be the weapon that would execute the *I-52* and the 100 men huddled inside.

From decoded communications between Japan and Germany, the U.S. Navy knew where the *I-52* was going to meet the German submarine, the *U-530*. During the mid-Atlantic rendezvous the Japanese submarine would receive a German-built radar detector to notify it of a pending American attack. It would also take aboard a German navigator as well as a German sailor to operate the detector. The radar would be installed during the remainder of the trip to Europe.

Springing the Trap

On the rainy night of June 23, 1944, Lieutenant Commander Jesse Taylor and his crew took off in their fat, ungainly torpedo bomber from the *Bogue* to hunt for the two submarines. As he lifted off the deck, the Japanese and German submarines found one another. The submarines came together and the German personnel leaped aboard the wallowing deck of the rain-slicked *I-52*. The radar detector was also passed aboard the *I-52*. The two boats then went their separate ways.

High above, Taylor discovered half of his radar display was conked out, meaning he was able to observe only 50 percent of the normal area. However, his half-blind radarscope managed to pick out the *I-52* churning on the surface of the rough seas toward Europe.

The *I-52* didn't know it was being observed electronically, since there had been no time to set up the detector that was packed uselessly away. Taylor dove on the submarine, dropping illumination flares and a pair of 500-pound depth charges. Commander Kameo Uno took his submarine beneath the black water believing he would never be found.

Death from Above

Taylor's crew then dropped *sonobuoys* into the water that began transmitting the sounds of the *I-52*'s propellers to the torpedo bomber. Once he had an idea of where the submarine was, Taylor dropped the Fido into the water, where the torpedo began its circular search. An explosion was heard followed by what Taylor believed was the sound of a submarine imploding and breaking apart as it sank.

An hour later another torpedo bomber crew from the *Bogue* also heard submarine noises in the same vicinity prompting them to launch another Fido. About 15 minutes later there was a very long explosion followed by noises of a submarine breaking up. The sound of the propellers faded as they slowed to a stop.

The apparent destruction of what seemed to be two subs remains a mystery to this day and led to confusion over who sank the *I-52*. Either way, the *I-52* was destroyed that night.

Words To Treasure

Dropped into the water by an aircraft, a **sonobuoy** has the ability to gather and transmit underwater sounds back to the aircraft so torpedoes can be dropped on the submarine's approximate location.

Marking the Position

The flares dropped by Lieutenant Commander Taylor caught the attention of the *U-530*'s Kapitän-Leutnant Kurt Lange who looked back to see the antisubmarine attack on the *I-52*. He charted what he believed to be the location of the attack and made his way back to Europe. The *U-530* and its records of the attack on the *I-52* would survive the war.

Two Heroes

Since no one at the time could unravel the mystery of the second set of submarine noises or who really destroyed the *I-52*, the Navy decided to commend both Taylor and Gordon for the sinking of the submarine. The secrets behind the sinking remain classified as "SECRET" by the Navy for more than 35 years after it happened.

Debris floated up from the wreck, including blocks of natural rubber, but there were no survivors among the crew or the passengers of the *I-52*. It sank in 17,000 feet of water, beyond the reach of 1940s technology.

The Deepest Treasure

Paul Tidwell was a veteran of infantry combat in Vietnam who made his living researching the locations of shipwrecks. In 1990 he came upon information about a wreck so rich and so astonishing that he decided he had to try and recover it himself. He was about to join a very small group of risk takers known as deep-ocean treasure hunters.

The wreck that electrified Tidwell was that of the *I-52* lying undisturbed more than three miles beneath the Atlantic. So deep is the wreck site, it would take a person walking very briskly more than 45 minutes to cover the distance equaling the 17,000-foot depth of the *I-52*.

However, no one could unravel the location of the attack. The locations gathered from the *Bogue* and reports filed by Taylor and Gordon didn't agree. Tidwell believed he could find the boat with the tools of the deep wreck treasure hunter: plenty of money, a lot of technology, and maniacal dedication. The hunt was on.

Although others were hot on the trail of the *I-52*, Tidwell had located the *U-530*'s logbooks, convincing him Taylor was the aviator who sank the Japanese submarine, and making Tidwell confident he could find the *I-52*'s hiding place.

Shiver Me Timbers

Incredibly, thanks to technology, the sounds of the destruction of the *I-52* were recorded from the sonobuoy transmissions. You can hear the swish–swish of the *I-52*'s propellers, the explosion of the torpedo, and the implosion of the submarine as it descended into the depths. The recordings are held near Washington, D.C., at the National Archives and Records Administration. Also, several Web sites enable people to listen to these sounds using their computer.

Long Hard (and Deep) Look

Tidwell knew enough about wreck recovery to understand that finding the *I-52* beneath the great depths would be complicated by the fog of war. By April 1995, Tidwell had put together an organization known as Cape Verde Expeditions and mounted an expedition to find the submarine.

Tidwell also hired the services of Meridian Sciences, Inc., of Maryland to use its computers and expertise to locate the wreck. Meridian combined all the available data and computed it with the ocean conditions at the time to ascertain the approximate location of the *I-52*'s wreck site.

Tom Dettweiler, with Meridian Sciences, would be part of the expedition to the wreck site. Dettweiler previously worked to locate the wreck of the *Titanic* and was well versed in the difficulties of finding a deep-ocean wreck.

Vodka and Water

Tidwell hired the Russian oceanographic research ship *Yuzhmorgeologiya* and its high-tech camera and sonar sled to help locate the *I-52*. Departing Barbados, the ship took on a load of bad fuel that fouled its engines. The resourceful Russian crew went to work solving the problem in mid-ocean, modifying the engine to accept the contaminated diesel.

Borscht was served daily and the work of "mowing the lawn" by the systematic towing of the sensor-equipped sled over the suspected wreck site dragged on for two weeks. With their search time slashed by a week due to fuel problems, the tension began to mount. The ROV sent a constant stream of side-scan sonar images back to the ship, but none contained the *I-52*.

Dettweiler and Meridian Sciences worked out a new search area based on revised calculations, and the side-scan sonar soon located the *I-52* nearly 17,000 feet beneath the Atlantic. It was 10 miles from where the Navy believed it went down, and its discovery proved that Lieutenant Commander Taylor had sunk the submarine. Out came the vodka aboard the unpronounceable Russian ship, and the party commenced.

Know The Ropes

Deep-ocean treasure hunters looking for an edge frequently hire research firms that conduct highly technical computations to locate shipwrecks. Another such firm is Wagner and Associates, which helped locate the lost USS *Scorpion* submarine in 1968 using mathematics.

Uplifting Proposal

As of 1999, great secrecy still surrounded the *I-52* treasure-recovery project, but Tidwell still wants to recover the gold and intends to do so in the most efficient and complete way possible. The Cape Verde team may first drill a small hole in the *I-52*'s hull and insert a fiber-optic cable to confirm the presence and location of the gold bullion.

Getting the gold will be a technical challenge. If it remains inside the submarine, Tidwell's team will have only two choices: cutting into the boat using deep-diving submersibles with manipulator arms or raising the nearly 360-foot submarine to the surface. The sea pressure at 17,000 feet is immense and creates nearly 7,500 pounds of pressure per square inch.

Cold War Bonus

Tidwell has said he's conducted talks with the Smit International, a leading salvage firm that developed secret technology in the early 1990s to raise the wreck of a Soviet submarine named the *Komsomolets*. On April 7, 1989, the virtually new Soviet submarine caught fire and sank in roughly 6,000 feet of water, 300 miles off Norway's northern coast.

Though the Soviet salvage project was never attempted, Smit retained the technology and represents the only firm that could possibly raise the *I-52*. The technology being considered for use in possibly raising the *I-52* remains highly secret, and Tidwell won't discuss it.

Raising the I-52: Easier Said Than Done

Tidwell's dream of raising the entire submarine would prove to be a daunting task. Damage to the *I-52* from the torpedo attack could have weakened its hull, making it hard to lift in one piece. In addition, implosion damage to the submarine's compartments also could have weakened the structure of the submarine. Though only one fifth the weight of the 13,000 ton *Edmund Fitzgerald,* lifting the 2,560-ton submarine will be no easy task.

Submarines have been raised successfully in the past, but only from shallow water. The U.S. Navy has raised several submarines using salvage divers. In a monumental and dangerous job, divers spent nearly six months raising the *S-51* submarine that sank off Rhode Island's Block Island on September 26, 1925. The task nearly killed several divers, although this submarine lay in only 132 feet of water.

Smit's effort to recover the *Komsomolets* never materialized, since the submarine was leaking radiation. International environmental protests against disturbing the wreck prompted the Soviets to scrap the salvage plan. Instead, deep-diving Russian *Mir* submersibles descended upon the wreck to seal the boat's open torpedo tubes to prevent further radiation leakage.

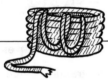

Know The Ropes

Any salvage work on the *I-52* will be done either by robots or by deep-diving submersibles equipped with manipulator arms. Some theories discussed for raising the *Titanic* included filling the ship with table tennis balls, but this idea is ludicrous, since the sea pressure would crush such objects immediately. However, some believe a special foam could be injected into the *I-52* to give it buoyancy and allow it to be towed back to port.

Money Boat

The *I-52*'s gold may be worth from $16 million to $25 million, depending on world gold prices, but Tidwell and others in the sunken-treasure business know you don't melt down gold and sell it by the ounce at world gold prices. The gold bars aboard the *I-52* have even more value as collector's items.

If the story of the *I-52*'s loss and notoriety continues to grow, the gold bars found aboard the ship can increase in value, as they become sought-after collector's items. The gold recovered from the *Central America* in 1989 has also achieved a far higher value than its mere worth as gold.

Honoring the Dead

Cape Verde Expeditions faced two very delicate emotional and legal issues as it planned the incredibly complex operation of recovering the *I-52*'s gold. The submarine is believed to still contain the remains of most of the 100 aboard. Knowing the reverence the Japanese place on their deceased, especially their war dead, a major part of Tidwell's effort has involved meeting with Japanese relatives of the dead and representatives of the Japanese government.

Tidwell intends to treat whatever human remains are found with dignity, according to the wishes of the families. However, the Japanese government passed legislation erasing all of its claims to such wartime treasure.

Perhaps an even more complicated legal issue involves the 268 tons of liquid opium that is still intact aboard the *I-52*. At least one container has been recovered and disposed of properly by Tidwell's team. Cape Verde Expeditions is now working with the U.S. Drug Enforcement agency on the best way to deal with and dispose of the valuable substance, since the opium could be used to make heroin.

Shiver Me Timbers

Even more than a half century after the end of World War II, Japan and the United States still pay close attention to proper treatment of the remains of their respective war dead. Although military graveyards dot the Pacific, the chance location of human remains belonging to military personnel usually results in respectful reburial. American officials are still looking in the jungles of Vietnam for Americans killed there more than 30 years ago.

A map of the wreck site of the I-52.
(Drawn by Ken Ellis)

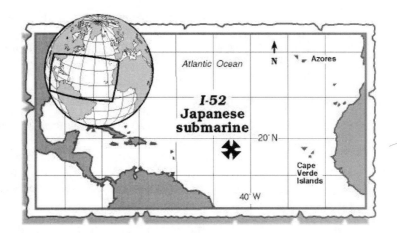

The Least You Need to Know

➤ By 1944, Germany and Japan had essentially created a situation in which they were unable to freely trade goods on the open seas, since their cargo ships were frequently sunk by American and British warships.

➤ The *I-52* was built with a large, waterproof cylinder on its deck that was originally made to house an airplane for reconnaissance and bombing missions.

➤ Only one submarine, the *I-8,* successfully made the unbelievably dangerous 30,000-mile trip from Asia to France and back in a voyage that took 125 days.

➤ The two tons of gold aboard the *I-52* was being carried to France for transfer to Germany to pay for technology being purchased by the Japanese military.

➤ Although two pilots dropped once-secret acoustic homing torpedoes in the vicinity of the *I-52* and both heard submarine noises, it took the search efforts of Cape Verde Expeditions to determine that Lieutenant Jesse Taylor was the pilot who sank the submarine.

➤ A British search effort named Project Orca also tried to locate the *I-52* submarine the year before Paul Tidwell's group successfully located and photographed the wreck 17,000 feet below the Atlantic.

Cold, Cold Cache

Some shipwreck stories are so full of incredible plot twists, intrigue, and drama they seem too amazing to be true. The agonizing World War II destruction and subsequent discovery of the British Royal Navy cruiser HMS *Edinburgh* is one of those tales.

The *Edinburgh* was a powerful and sleek cruiser—a miniature version of a battleship—that was converted by the capriciousness of war into one of history's richest treasure ships. It was May 1942, and the Allies in Europe were fighting not just to win but to survive against Nazi Germany.

The Soviet Union's war-machine, beset by shortages and defeats, required massive shipments of food, aircraft, and other supplies to remain in the fight against the Germans. The way to the stomach of the Red Army was through the mouth of its port at Murmansk in what is now Northwest Russia. In return, the Soviet Union's leader, Joseph Stalin, was to pay for his war supplies in gold shipped out of Murmansk.

North of the Arctic Circle, Murmansk is located on the Kola Gulf, which is an inlet wider than the Mississippi River running south from the Barents Sea like a steep-walled fjord. It was the Soviet Union's best place for resupply, since the waters around Murmansk were kept free of ice year-round by the warmth of the North Atlantic current.

Shiver Me Timbers

The route to Murmansk was so dangerous, American and British sailors dubbed it the "Suicide Run" and the "Murmansk Run." Cluttered with icebergs, Nazi warships, and mines, the "Run" claimed one in eight ships. Although American merchant seamen suffered one of the highest casualty rates during the war, they have been denied official status as veterans of World War II.

During World War II, hundreds of sailors and merchant seamen died in the icy waters that led across the northern roof of Europe while shepherding supplies to the Soviets. If you were a sailor aboard one of those wartime ships, a torpedo from the swarms of Nazi U-boats skulking in the waters could instantly seal your fate. If the explosion didn't kill you, the cold water would finish you in half an hour.

By April 25, 1942, the cruiser *Edinburgh* had just navigated this route known as the "Suicide Run," escorting a supply convoy to Murmansk. It sat dockside in the grim port city awaiting orders. Someone, somewhere decided the cruiser would carry five tons of Soviet gold back to England. Luck would not be on the ship's side. Within a week from being filled with treasure, the *Edinburgh* would lie at the bottom of the Barents Sea with nearly $50 million in frigid gold sleeping inside its armored ammunition hold. The ship also held the remains of 57 crewmen who would never again see England.

By the late 1970s, the gold started looking good to the governments of Britain and the Soviet Union, who each owned a part of it. An unlikely hero—the son of a poor, single mother in Northern England—would show them the way to the treasure.

Keith Jessop, the working-class salvor who eventually located the gold and masterminded the expedition to recover it, was nearly financially and legally ruined despite his success and his good intentions.

Let's step onto the ice-slickened deck of the HMS *Edinburgh* as it races across the Barents Sea. It's 11 degrees Farenheit, and you're on watch. To protect Stalin's gold, you're on deck with binoculars to hunt for submarines cloaked by the frozen fog. Nothing will save your ship, but you already know that, don't you?

Rescuing Stalin's Gold

When a Nazi submarine torpedoed the HMS *Edinburgh,* it contained at least 5.5 tons of gold being paid by Soviet Joseph Stalin to Britain for war material. Oddly, the malevolent dictator had no one to blame but himself. Afraid of Adolf Hitler, Stalin signed a

1939 peace treaty with Germany instead of standing up to his fellow dictator and possibly scaring Hitler enough to halt Adolf's conquests.

Hitler signed the treaty only so he could invade France without worrying about the Soviet Red Army. On June 22, 1941, after the conquest of France, Hitler attacked Stalin's unprepared forces. This action shocked a disbelieving Stalin, who like most thugs and murderers, considered fleeing for his own safety. He eventually calmed down, but faced more than 100 German combat divisions and a four-year struggle to retake his country.

Though the Soviet citizens fought like tigers and literally died by the millions (often due to bad military decisions), they needed the food, trucks, and aircraft that only the Americans and British could provide. While much aid was simply given to Stalin's regime, he agreed to pay a billion dollars for the assistance. Soviet paper money wasn't very attractive, so Stalin had to pay his bills in gold, and it had to go by sea. The decision was made in April 1942 to put 93 wooden crates of gold on the British warship HMS *Edinburgh* for the dangerous trip to England.

Shiver Me Timbers

A portion of the 5.5 tons of gold placed aboard the *Edinburgh* for shipment to England may have had something in common with the silver and gold treasure plundered from the New World by Spain. One of the richest gold deposits in the world is in the Kolyma region of Siberia where an unknown number of political prisoners were worked to death mining gold for Stalin's regime. Beginning in the late 1920s, as Stalin secured his power with the imprisonment of millions, Kolyma's gold mines enjoyed an abundance of laborers.

An Odd Cargo

It was a gray Arctic day on April 25, 1942, when crew members of the *Edinburgh* noticed some unusual activity around their snow-covered warship moored at Murmansk. A pair of barges, guarded by soldiers, pulled up next to the ship. Royal Marine commandos aboard the *Edinburgh* were also on guard during the loading of what appeared to be ordinary ammunition boxes. The mystery ended when one of the wooden boxes broke to reveal five bars of pure gold.

The gold bullion was placed back into its sawdust-filled box and carried deep into the strongest part of the ship—its ammunition magazine. This compartment was located near the bottom of the *Edinburgh*'s hull. Its roof was two inches of steel armor, and its side walls a hefty six inches of steel. The "ammunition boxes" were stacked around the real munitions including the six-inch shells used by the *Edinburgh*'s 12 naval guns.

In addition to the gold, the *Edinburgh* took aboard 200 passengers. Most were survivors of ships sunk while making the insanely dangerous cargo run to Murmansk. Some of these men were suffering from frostbite after being immersed in the frigid water. Others were so badly injured that the ship's aircraft hangar was turned into an emergency hospital where the ship's surgeon began amputating gangrenous limbs. Now all they had to do was travel 1,000 miles across waters swarming with German submarines.

Unlikely Treasure Ship

The *Edinburgh* was perhaps one of the most modern and capable ships in the Royal Navy. It was virtually new, having been completed on July 6, 1939, by the Swan Hunter shipyard. It was 613 feet long and could travel at an incredible 32.5 knots or nearly 36 mph. It carried a dozen six-inch guns, torpedo launchers, and on its last mission, a crew of 550. A four-inch belt of armor around the waterline served as protection against torpedoes.

However, all this strength wasn't enough to make the *Edinburgh* impervious to torpedo attack. The *Edinburgh* needed what naval officers called a "screen" of destroyers that could swarm after a sonar contact and either drive away or destroy a lurking U-boat. Large ships were luscious targets, and the *Edinburgh* was a real prize.

The powerful and graceful ship was designed for the task of slugging it out in long-range gunnery battles with other surface ships. Alone, in a sea filled with Nazi submarines, it was little more than a big target. Ignoring this military reality would send a lot of treasure to the bottom of the Barents Sea.

The British cruiser HMS Edinburgh *as it appeared shortly after being launched in 1939. It was destroyed in World War II while carrying a fortune in Soviet gold.*
(Photograph courtesy of the Imperial War Museum)

Slow Death

Making it through the Barents Sea meant overcoming numerous obstacles including the mines, aircraft, submarines, and surface warships of the Nazis. Other than that, travel north of the Arctic Circle was no problem. Returning to England with the *Edinburgh* was a convoy of 13 merchant ships, six destroyers, four corvettes, four minesweepers, and an armed trawler. A pair of Russian destroyers also came along. This convoy departed on April 28, 1942.

Although the *Edinburgh* was under the command of Captain Hugh Faulkner, the cruiser was actually under the authority of Rear Admiral Sir Stuart Bonham-Carter, a higher-ranking officer aboard the ship for the return voyage. The ships traveled straight north out of the Kola Gulf. The ships would go as far north as possible until ice fields forced them to turn west for the dash across the Barents Sea.

At 8 A.M. on April 29, a German reconnaissance plane spotted the convoy and carefully took note of its position and composition. The report excited German naval commanders who mobilized a force of three destroyers to hunt down the convoy. In addition, prowling U-boats were directed toward the slow-moving convoy. Known as *wolfpacks,* the teams of U-boats then lined up in the path of the convoy to await a chance to sink a ship.

By April 30, the convoy had traveled 200 miles north of Murmansk, but the icy waters were hot with U-boat activity. The escorting destroyers began launching attacks on lurking German submarines while the *Edinburgh* crept along with the rest of the convoy at a measly six knots. Knowing the ship was a slow, easy target for the U-boats, Bonham-Carter committed a fatal mistake by ordering the *Edinburgh* to go ahead of the convoy and patrol without an escort of destroyers.

Torpedoes Away

The submerged *U-456* was rolling with the calm seas as its commander, Kapitän-Leutnant Max-Martin Teichert, raised his *periscope* for a look around. It was 4 P.M. April 30. Teichert, whose

Words To Treasure

Owing to the effective Nazi U-boat tactic of flocking together to attack merchant ship convoys, German submarine crews soon began to refer to themselves as **wolfpacks** since wolves also attack their prey in packs.

Words To Treasure

Torpedo is a Latin word for an electric ray, but in the naval context it stands for a self-propelled bomb launched from a surface ship or submarine that swims to its target just below the surface. A submarine **periscope** is an optical device that allows submerged personnel to see above the water and is used for aiming torpedo attacks. **Amidships** is the middle portion of a ship, while the **stern,** of course, is the rear. The **rudder** is a steering surface that turns the ship left or right.

submarine had only two torpedoes left, was on the verge of turning back to restock his supply of the deadly weapons when he spotted the *Edinburgh*.

At that same moment, nearly 20 miles ahead of the convoy, Bonham-Carter was about to make another expensive mistake. When the *Edinburgh*'s sonar operator warned of a nearby submarine in the cruiser's path, Bonham-Carter dismissed the report as incorrect.

Teichert took aim through his periscope and ordered his final two torpedoes launched. Unlike the scene on the *Lusitania*, sunk 27 years before by another U-boat, no one on the *Edinburgh* even saw the white wakes of the two torpedoes launched against it. At 4:13 P.M. the torpedoes detonated, with one ripping a massive hole *amidships,* while the other literally blew the *stern* of the ship off along with its *rudder* and two of its four propellers.

Hopeless Situation

The ship began filling with water but did not sink because enough of the *Edinburgh*'s watertight bulkheads remained intact to give the ship buoyancy. However, the ship was impossible to steer and only one of its two remaining propellers could be powered, making its progress extremely slow. To tow the cruiser back to Murmansk, four destroyers left the convoy, but made little headway even after towing the cruiser throughout the night.

Of the four destroyers helping the *Edinburgh*, the two Russian destroyers were low on fuel and had to return to Murmansk. The two remaining British destroyers could not tow the *Edinburgh,* since they needed to be free to maneuver in case of attack. The once-fast *Edinburgh*'s speed was now only eight knots, and it circled lazily without a rudder. On May 2, a group of four minesweepers arrived from Murmansk to take the *Edinburgh* into tow, but the trio of German destroyers including the *Hermann Schoemann* began to shell the ragtag fleet and the crippled *Edinburgh*.

In a wild fight, one of the two remaining British destroyers was crippled. But, in a miraculous retaliatory shot, a six-inch shell from the badly damaged *Edinburgh* ripped into the German destroyer *Hermann Schoemann,* destroying its engine room. German torpedoes launched at the two British destroyers missed, but one struck the *Edinburgh* opposite the side of the original damage with another massive explosion. Still, the *Edinburgh* did not sink.

Abandon Ship

Nearly blasted in two, the bent and mangled *Edinburgh* had to be abandoned, leaving the five tons of gold inside its flooded magazine. The minesweepers came alongside and took on the nearly 700 survivors from the cruiser. Incredibly, despite a trio of torpedo hits, only 57 men died aboard the *Edinburgh* with most trapped inside flooded compartments.

Scuttled

After the evacuation, Admiral Bonham-Carter ordered the cruiser scuttled. One of the minesweepers went to the task by pumping 20 shells from its small four-inch gun into the armored hull of the *Edinburgh*. The cruiser could not be left floating as a derelict to be retrieved by the Germans, if for no other reason than to keep the gold out of Nazi hands. Unfortunately, the puny shells that were used to scuttle the ship had no effect!

Shiver Me Timbers

Like the Japanese submarine *I–52* and its commander, Teichert and his *U–456* fell victim to a Fido acoustic homing torpedo on May 12, 1943. The *U–456* attempted to evade the British aircraft that launched the torpedo by diving but suffered an unknown accident and was lost with all 49 aboard.

Bonham-Carter finally ordered the destroyer *Foresight* to launch its remaining torpedo into the dead ship, creating another huge explosion. Finally, the *Edinburgh* had taken all the damage it could bear. It sank at 8:55 A.M. on May 2, 1942 after its ruptured hulk filled with water and slammed into the sediment 800 feet beneath the Barents Sea.

When Kapitän-Leutnant Teichert heard the *Edinburgh* sink, he peered through his periscope to see nothing but an oil slick and floating debris on an empty sea.

Finder of the *Edinburgh*

Enter Keith Jessop, a rough and tumble lad from the landlocked British town of Keighley. Born to an unwed mother who had spent her life as an impoverished fabric-mill worker, Jessop finished his formal schooling at 15 and went straight into the depressing mills to work for three years. Despite being poor and illegitimate, Jessop found his refuge in risk-taking. He eventually became a competitive bicyclist and a rock climber. Taking physical risks was inexpensive for the poor teen but the payoff in heightened self-esteem from such accomplishments was immense. Jessop metamorphosed into an adventurer willing to take any type of risk to escape the dullness of the mills.

His interest in rock climbing spurred the 18-year-old to join the Royal Marines in 1951 after he learned through a newsreel that all British marines participate in rock climbing as part of their commando training. While posted on the island of Gibraltar in 1952, he began skin diving for recreation, using a mask and flippers in the clear waters near shore. He soon fell in love with the ocean, just as Frenchman Jacques-Yves Cousteau had done during his own military service in the 1930s.

Shiver Me Timbers

Looking downward into the clear waters around Gibraltar, Jessop also experienced a common but brief sense of panic among divers looking into the transparent water with a face mask for the first time. Jessop was momentarily seized with the fear that he was going to fall to the bottom!

A civilian once again, Jessop eventually became a self-taught explosives expert and began salvaging valuable components from sunken ships around England. At the end of the day, he and his friends would haul massive propellers and copper pipe to scrap dealers. The plainspoken Jessop was a genuine entrepreneur. He would eventually go to work as a diver on offshore oil rigs around the world. In his spare time he continued his research into lost ships, particularly the HMS *Edinburgh,* whose fate and treasure were well known among those in salvage work.

Know The Ropes

Decompression sickness, or **DCS,** is caused when a diver fails to allow nitrogen shoved into his or her tissue by sea pressure to be safely released by gradual ascending, or decompressing. **Saturation diving** simply means the divers are subjected to the pressure they will work at underwater and then kept at that pressure when brought back to the surface. Instead of spending four hours decompressing each day after an 11-minute dive at 450 feet, saturation divers need to decompress only once—saving hundreds of hours.

Saturated with Possibilities

While working on the offshore rigs, Jessop became an expert in *saturation diving.* This technique kept divers pressurized for days or weeks so they could forgo daily and time-consuming decompression periods. Developed in the United States in the 1950s, saturation diving allowed divers to descend to the seafloor in a pressurized diving bell and then return to a chamber to live for weeks if necessary.

Like scientist Robert Ballard, who knew that a new titanium hull on the *Alvin* submersible could allow him to someday visit the *Titanic,* Jessop knew saturation diving would allow divers to recover the gold from his dream wreck, the HMS *Edinburgh.*

Although ordinary scuba divers seldom go below 130 feet, and only highly trained divers should descend deeper using exotic mixes of breathing gases, saturation diving provided a system by which divers could go down to nearly 1,000 feet. Minutes under water at such depths translated into hours of decompression time and it was incredibly inefficient. Long periods required for decompression could now be spent working under water since decompression was done only once, when divers left their pressurized saturation chamber following a shift that could last for days or weeks.

Unlucky Search

Having lined up a group of partners, Jessop obtained permission from the British Salvage Association in 1979 to conduct an October search for the *Edinburgh's* wreck site. A friend who was a commercial fisherman once snagged a net on what he believed was the *Edinburgh* in the Barents Sea and gave Jessop a general idea of its location.

Armed with this information and with Admiral Bonham-Carter's records detailing the location of the wreck, Jessop's team went to the site using side-scan sonar but still could not locate the *Edinburgh*. After the team returned to Norway to rethink its strategy, Jessop met some trawler fishermen who claimed that their seafloor-scraping nets had set off explosions. They also reported a large wreck near the explosions had also snagged their nets. (The lowly fishermen and their simple nets had beaten technology once again!)

Jessop went to sea again, this time shadowed by a Soviet trawler conducting surveillance on their efforts. At one point Jessop became so angry at the trawler's interference that he attempted to chase it away—this of course only earned him a scolding from the commander of a Norwegian destroyer. As luck would have it, when the team's side-scan sonar images finally began showing bits of debris, Jessop's time was up. By the end of October 1979, Arctic storms had begun to make the waters of the Barents Sea too rough for locating the *Edinburgh*.

Competing for the Gold

Soon three consortiums were ready to seek British and Soviet government permission to recover the still-undiscovered treasure. All of these consortiums were to be heard by British officials.

Jessop bought a new suit and laid out a plan that the British officials accepted. As salvor, he and his partners would take 45 percent of the recovered gold. Although Jessop became something of a folk hero in Britain for beating the "old boy" system, he hadn't yet found the gold. The job would be done on a *no cure, no pay* basis.

Very Grave Concerns

Jessop's group was able to sell itself as the salvor because most of its members were British, and they

Words To Treasure

The **no cure, no pay** term is a classic bit of legalese that has been around for at least 100 years. Under these conditions salvors agree to recover a wreck or its goods with the knowledge that they'll receive payment only if they're successful. In addition, expenses in the operation belong to the salvor, not the wreck owner's.

also promised not to use explosives on the wreck. This promise was especially important, as the government had classified the *Edinburgh* as an official war grave. The remains of sailors were still aboard the ship. Understandably, the recovery of the ship's gold had created a media flap as family members of the *Edinburgh's* dead protested the salvage effort out of deference to the remains of their loved ones.

Golden Rumor

Jessop's research originally led him to believe that the *Edinburgh* was carrying 10 tons of Soviet gold at the time it sank. A Soviet manifest showed the *Edinburgh* received 10 tons of gold, but the ship's records showed that it took aboard only 5.5 tons.

This discovery was made just as Jessop was getting permission to salvage the gold, and he was floored. His research indicated the other 4.5 tons might be elsewhere on the ship and may have been intended for the private use of Stalin and his high-ranking henchmen. Jessop knew his divers could never search the whole interior of the wrecked cruiser in the pitch-dark waters of the Barents Sea, and he was now faced with the harsh reality that he and his partners would have to settle for a paltry 5.5 tons of gold. The remainder of the "treasure" turned out to be the product of the rumor mill, not Stalin's gulag of slave mines.

Da or Nyet? Soviet Approval

The Soviet Union was very much alive in 1979, and the Cold War couldn't have been colder between Britain and the USSR. After much nervous waiting by Jessop and his partners, the Soviets finally agreed to allow the recovery as long as their representatives were present to ensure that all the gold was accounted for. Everyone's glasses were filled and vodka was knocked back all around. The search was on—as soon as the hangover wore off.

A Grave Undertaking

Jessop's research and a lot of theories boarded the search ship for the location phase of the expedition, but Jessop himself stayed behind. On May 12, 1981, the salvage ship *Dammitor* began imaging the seafloor with a towed side-scan sonar device. After only two hours of searching, the wreckage of the *Edinburgh* appeared on the sonar printout.

A remotely operated vehicle with television cameras was lowered into the Barents Sea, and the eerie image of the smashed *Edinburgh* came into view. Keep in mind that by the time Jessup's crew had found it, the ship had been undisturbed for 39 years. The team then began studying the plans of the HMS *Belfast*, a sister ship of the *Edinburgh*, to learn the best way to use underwater cutting torches to gain entry into the fully loaded ammunition magazine.

Because some of the relatives of those killed aboard the *Edinburgh* were upset about plans to recover its gold, Jessop's plan promised that cutting torches instead of explosives would be used. Ironically, the torches would be potentially far more destructive to the divers and the bones of the dead if the flame detonated the tons of shells inside the filled magazine. The public's recoil at using explosives on a sunken war grave sounded terrible and cutting torches "seemed" like a less destructive means of entry. Jessop wanted the contract so he offered to do the job with the torches.

Shiver Me Timbers

The HMS *Belfast* survived World War II and was donated as an exhibit to the Imperial War Museum. The *Belfast* now sits on the south side of the Thames River, across from the Tower of London beyond the river's north bank. Except for some modernization during the postwar years, it is a carbon copy of the *Edinburgh*. The *Belfast* was completed on August 3, 1939, in the shipyards of Harland and Wolff in Belfast, Ireland, the same shipyard that built the *Titanic* and the *Olympic*.

High-Pressure Work

The 12-diver recovery crew arrived on the site of the wreck of the *Edinburgh* three months after its discovery. On September 2, the first team of divers was pressurized in a chamber as if the group were at 750 feet of water. (At 750 feet the sea pressure is 330 pounds per square inch.) Once *blown down,* in diving parlance, the divers were lowered to the wreck site in a diving bell. Disaster almost struck the crew before it had even gotten started when a malfunction in the bell allowed too much potentially lethal carbon dioxide to build up inside. Thankfully, the divers were brought up safely, and a second team was prepared for the dive after the problem was fixed.

For the next five weeks, the 12 divers would rotate working on the wreck. Pressurized inside a chamber to their working depth, they could descend to the wreck and return in a pressurized diving bell that was then locked to a larger chamber. They would live there in air pressure of 352 pounds per square inch until their next dive. After making a number of dives, they could "decompress" and reenter the normal world of a single atmosphere of pressure.

The near-freezing temperature of the water was counteracted by the use of diving suits warmed by circulating hot water pumped from the surface. Adding to the diver's burden of working 800 feet beneath the ocean, the circulating hot water systems malfunctioned, and some of the divers were terribly scalded. Highly contagious ear infections encouraged by the high pressure also plagued the divers who worked daily to clear wreckage and cut through the steel of the magazine.

Unfortunately, this was all in a day's work for the divers whose workplace was complicated by freezing-cold water, temperamental equipment, and massive water pressure.

Bones and Treasure

To reach the magazine where the gold was stored, the divers had to clear debris from a cavernous bulkhead that had once contained fuel oil. By dive 25, a nine-foot-by-seven-foot hole had been cut through the thick armor to allow entry into the room. During the work, some human remains were inadvertently sent to the surface as the divers placed unexploded munitions in bags for disposal. These human remains were then reburied at sea.

Words To Treasure

Being **blown down** isn't a line from the sea shanty "Blow the Man Down" but describes the pressurization of a chamber in which saturation divers become physiologically acclimated to the sea pressure they will work in.

Eventually divers began to send up bags filled with gold covered with a thick scum of congealed fuel oil. Jessop himself stepped in and took on the job of scrubbing the gold with diesel fuel and a wire brush. The gold was then stacked on the floor of a locked compartment for counting—and recounting—by the Soviet officials on board. The Soviets even searched the inside of the decompression chamber where the divers lived to ensure that each bar was accounted for.

By early October 1981 the weather had gotten so bad that Jessop and the others knew it was time to halt the search before any divers were seriously hurt. Following dive 67, a total of 431 gold bars were hauled up for a meeting with Jessop's scrub brush. Only 34 of the bars were left behind, but even those few are worth an estimated $6 million.

Treasure Trouble

After the recovery and the attendant publicity, Jessop found himself being accused of all sorts of wrongdoing—from allowing divers to intentionally desecrate a war grave to bribing a British salvage official to gain permission to do the recovery. Jessop was cleared of any wrongdoing in the desecration charge following a Ministry of Defense investigation. A British court simply dismissed the bribery charge as groundless.

In the highly charged atmosphere surrounding the recovery, Jessop was even tried on charges of defrauding two salvage firms in the recovery effort but was acquitted by a jury that deliberated for only a handful of minutes. The legal haggling consumed two years of Jessop's life and took some of the tarnish off his successful golden quest.

Like Columbus-America Discovery Group that located and recovered the gold of the *Central America,* Jessop learned that finding sunken treasure also meant finding yourself in court.

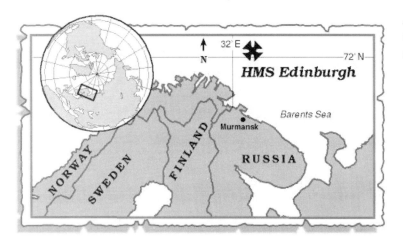

A map of the wreck site of the HMS Edinburgh. *(Drawn by Ken Ellis)*

The Least You Need to Know

➤ Although much of the equipment and food sent to the Soviet Union during World War II was given to the Soviet war effort against the Germans, Stalin agreed to pay $1 billion in gold for the assistance.

➤ Although Soviet records indicate that 10 tons of gold were placed aboard the HMS *Edinburgh*, British records show only 5.5 tons aboard the warship when it was lost.

➤ Despite being struck by three German torpedoes, the HMS *Edinburgh* refused to sink until a British warship fired a fourth torpedo in an effort to prevent its capture by the enemy.

➤ Divers descending to the gold 800 feet beneath the Barents Sea suffered terrible scalding burns when the water-heating system malfunctioned inside their diving suits.

➤ British diver and salvage expert Keith Jessop who organized the search for the HMS *Edinburgh* was later accused of bribery, fraud, and war-grave desecration, though he was finally cleared of all charges.

➤ There's a good possibility that slave labor from Soviet prisons in Siberia (themselves testimony to Joseph Stalin's iron grip on power) mined some of the gold recovered from the HMS *Edinburgh*.

Chapter 24

The Cold War's Deepest Mystery: The USS *Scorpion*

In This Chapter

➤ Sleek and deadly

➤ Cold War pressures

➤ Final mission

➤ The mystery begins

➤ Myths and evidence

The mysterious 1968 loss of the nuclear-powered submarine USS *Scorpion* killed 99 highly trained men and spawned decades of speculation that may never be put to rest. While coffee shop discussions still simmer over the "real" reasons behind the losses of famous sunken ships, the *Scorpion* disaster left us with a genuine enigma that technology and investigation can't seem to answer.

The event itself seemed hidden by the social cacophony of 1968 America. Riots, assassinations, and the Vietnam War left little room for the *Scorpion* disaster to purchase a place in the American psyche. Much of the resulting Navy investigation into the incident would be conducted behind closed doors because of the secrecy surrounding nuclear submarine operations.

Upbeat publicity surrounding America's still-young fleet of nuclear submarines made the *Scorpion*'s loss all the more unbelievable, even though a more modern nuclear submarine was lost with all hands five years previously. The May 22, 1968, death of the *Scorpion* was yet another reminder that challenging the seas is never a sure thing.

The speculation about the submarine's loss started early, with some wondering whether the *Scorpion* had been destroyed by the Soviet Union's own aggressive submarine fleet. The Bermuda Triangle, a mythical zone in the Atlantic that supposedly devours ships, was blamed as another culprit. Did the sub blow itself up with its own torpedo? Was a bomb planted aboard by a terrorist? Take your pick.

Perhaps the biggest miracle regarding the *Scorpion*'s loss was that the Navy managed to find the submarine on a flat plain curving up to a submerged mountain range. Lost 400 miles southwest of the Azores, more than 11,000 feet beneath the Atlantic, the sounds of the *Scorpion*'s death were actually recorded by underwater listening systems that later allowed its discovery.

Despite two sessions of a Navy court of inquiry, photographs of the wreckage, and studies conducted by dozens of experts, officials were unable to explain what happened to the USS *Scorpion*. Knowing wouldn't have brought the men back, but not knowing made the loss even harder for the families.

"Who else but a submariner would go out and sink a perfectly good ship?" ask the undersea sailors poking fun at their own risk-taking. The gallows humor of the United States nuclear submarine fleet is born out of the daily risk of sailing 500 or 1,000 feet beneath the oceans. Enclosed in a submarine, all the normal hazards are magnified. Should a fire or mechanical malfunction occur, the crew only has minutes or seconds to resolve the problem.

Shiver Me Timbers

After the end of World War II, the U.S. Navy wanted to keep track of submarines all over the world by installing a secret system of **hydrophones,** or underwater microphones, that could locate and identify submarines through their sounds. When the USS *Scorpion* was lost, this system and two other unrelated listening systems helped scientists to determine the *Scorpion*'s location within 200 feet.

This daily drama occurs within a few feet of a controlled nuclear reaction inside the belly of the submarine's reactor. Sealed inside a submarine's steel tube, its sailors serve as smaller symbiotic organisms necessary for the survival of a larger creature.

Welcome to the coldest part of the Cold War. As they say in the U.S. Navy's submarine fleet: "May the number of your dives equal the number of times you come to the surface." For reasons that continue to confound everyone, this would not be the *Scorpion*'s destiny.

Sleek and Deadly

Early submarines were called "pig boats" by those who served in them. Small and unstable in rough seas, the boats spent most of their time bobbing on the surface of the ocean, since they were unable to operate submerged for more than an hour. When nuclear energy went from theory to reality with World War II's atomic bomb project, the U.S. Navy sat up and took notice.

Navy designers knew nuclear energy would provide a way of powering submarines without forcing them to come to the surface. Submarines could now be designed in a modern, bullet-shaped form, discarding the old-fashioned ship hull necessary for surface sailing. After the sleek shape was refined and nuclear power was placed in prototype submarines, the Skipjack-class submarines began construction, of which the *Scorpion* was one.

The USS *Scorpion*, known within the Navy as *SSN589*, was commissioned at Electric Boat Co. in Groton, Connecticut, on July 26, 1960, following two years of construction. It was the second boat of the six built within the Skipjack class, named after the USS *Skipjack*, which was the lead boat of the series.

Words To Treasure

The **USS** prefix ahead of an American warship's name means "United States Ship" while the **SSN589** suffix behind the submarine's name identifies the type. **SSN** means "submarine service, nuclear (powered)" and the number is the hull number of the *Scorpion*. It was the 589th American submarine.

The USS Scorpion *is put through acceptance trials after being launched December 19, 1959. Standing at left on its sail plane is the father of the nuclear navy, Admiral Hyman Rickover. (Courtesy U.S. Navy)*

The Newest Technology

Submarines have to be three things: fast, silent, and deadly. The *Scorpion* was definitely all three. It could dive to approximately 700 feet (though some estimates claim it could go deeper), and its sleek shape meant it would encounter less resistance in the water than older submarines with angular ship-type hulls.

The *Scorpion* was equipped with an S5W nuclear reactor that produced 15,000 horsepower and could propel the submarine at least as fast as 28 knots or 31 mph. A lot of these numbers are still classified, but we know enough to understand the *Scorpion* and its sisters could cross the Atlantic submerged about five knots faster than the *Lusitania* or the *Titanic*—and do so underwater no less! The nuclear reactor near the middle of the hull produced steam that powered a turbine that turned the submarine's single propeller shaft.

The *skin* of the *Scorpion* was two-inch-thick steel known as HY-80 or "high yield" steel. Although designed to provide greater strength to the submarine, the steel also had its problems. It was prone to cracking and needed occasional repairs. When built, the *Scorpion* carried the latest radar, sonar, and radio equipment available. The *Scorpion* was 252-feet long and weighed 3,575 tons when submerged. Despite being crammed with equipment, the 31-foot wide submarine still provided living space for up to 100 sailors.

The Scorpion's Sting

The *Scorpion* carried its torpedoes in the forward part of the submarine, including 14 Mark 37 torpedoes and two others known as ASTORs. These ASTORs were nuclear-tipped torpedoes possessing an 11-*kiloton* yield. The rest of its torpedoes contained conventional high-explosive warheads. The Mark 37 acoustic homing torpedo was the modern descendant of the weapon that destroyed the Japanese submarine *I-52* in 1944.

Know The Ropes

When referring to the yield of a nuclear weapon, a **kiloton** is an amount equal to 1,000 metric tons of the explosive TNT.

Underwater Sports Car

With its virtually unlimited power, the *Scorpion* could maneuver like a dolphin rather than a plodding boat that's temporarily submerged. The submarine was so fast and its handling characteristics so tricky that helmsmen had to be sure they didn't perform any unauthorized maneuvers. Although submariners are sailors and proud of it, they tend to refer to the sailing of submarines as "flying," since modern submarines are so maneuverable.

Deadly Work

The *Scorpion* was a member of the Atlantic Submarine Fleet based at the U.S. Navy base in Norfolk, Virginia. The *Scorpion*'s original assignment was to patrol the Atlantic looking for Soviet submarines, particularly any with ballistic missiles that could be aimed at the United States. This duty marked the early days of cat-and-mouse games between American and Soviet submarine commanders. The *Scorpion* was also employed in a number of other missions whose purposes remain classified.

During the 1961 Cuban missile crisis, the *Scorpion* also conducted a patrolling operation around Fidel Castro's island paradise and managed to break a record for remaining submerged longer than any other submarine up to that time.

To help it patrol the Atlantic for submarines, the *Scorpion* received intelligence information about where Soviet submarines were located off the East Coast. Then it would try to avoid detection while searching out its Soviet counterparts. It was serious business, since American submarine commanders might have to sink a Soviet submarine near the American coast if the sub made noises indicating it was preparing to launch a missile.

Cold War Pressures

As you already know, keeping ships operating safely means maintaining them properly. Although the public perceived the American nuclear submarine fleet as a world of precision and excellence, cracks were beginning to show in the system. On April 10, 1963, the nuclear attack submarine USS *Thresher* was lost with 112 sailors and 17 civilian employees. Incredibly, it sank during its first test dive off the coast of New England following a lengthy overhaul.

Shiver Me Timbers

Using a telephone that transmitted and received voice sounds through the water, the submarine rescue ship USS *Skylark* waiting above the *Thresher* heard the final words spoken to the outside world by the *Thresher's* crew. Soon after, all that was heard were the terrible sounds of the seapressure collapsing the steel compartments of the submarine. It was lost in 8,000 feet of water but was subsequently located after a lengthy search.

Although the U.S. Navy had seen other submarines sunk during peacetime accidents, this was the first time a nuclear-powered submarine was lost. This fact, combined with the large loss of life in the sinking of the *Thresher,* created a national scandal. It was determined that piping designed to carry water through the submarine to cool equipment had broken at a faulty weld and shorted out the nuclear reactor's control panel.

A court of inquiry determined that the damage prevented the submarine from "driving" to the surface, in submariner's language. The crew's last hope of survival—expelling air from its ballast tanks—was dashed when a defective design made it

337

impossible to expel water from the ballast tanks against the terrific seapressure. Heavier than the surrounding water and without power, the submarine sank to its death.

Better Safe Than Sorry

The loss of the *Thresher* nixed a suggestion floating about that the *Scorpion* would be able to skip its first overhaul in 1963 because it was in such good condition. Instead, the submarine was completely reworked with special attention paid to its cooling water piping welds. Many welds were found to be faulty and were fixed. During this extensive overhaul, the *Scorpion* spent 10 months in the Charleston Naval Shipyard and was returned to service on April 28, 1964.

Maintenance Nightmares

After the *Thresher* was lost, the Navy decided to correct safety flaws in its submarines. This program, known as the Submarine Safety Program, or SUBSAFE, was necessary to make the submarines safe and prevent another catastrophe. One of the systems the Navy wanted to improve on the *Scorpion* was the ballast tank *blow system* that had failed on the *Thresher*.

Because the *Thresher*'s ability to push water from its ballast tanks had failed, attempts were made to place an improved system on the *Scorpion*, but that new system failed when a vacuum caused ice to clog the system and could not be repaired. The emergency blowing system would remain unfixed until the *Scorpion*'s death five years later.

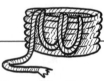

Know The Ropes

Known by submariners as the **blow system,** the emergency main ballast tank system is the means of introducing high-pressure air into the submarine's ballast tanks to force out the water. This system can make a submarine lighter, heavier, or just as buoyant as the surrounding water. In case of an emergency, submariners prefer the faster method of "driving" to the surface by using their propeller instead of slowly floating upward. The system allows any submariner to grab a control to lighten the submarine in an emergency.

Cold War operating pressures, the Vietnam War, and the massive program of retrofitting submarine safety improvements had overwhelmed the Navy's maintenance system. Unable to provide the *Scorpion* the time-consuming safety work, the submarine was ordered to not exceed certain depths and speeds as an interim safety move.

Overhaul Woes

The Navy's maintenance system was creaking and groaning under the $500-million program to refit its submarines with the required safety systems. New problems were also beginning to appear as more nuclear-powered submarines were coming in for overhaul work.

Nuclear submarines going in for overhauls during the 1960s disappeared into a black hole. Civilian shipyard personnel were not used to the systems on the newer boats, and virtually all other work on the submarines had to stop during the complex refueling of the nuclear reactor. The USS *Skate*'s overhaul in 1966 became something of a maintenance scandal when its scheduled 13-month overhaul took nearly 29 months.

Memos began flying, and it was decided the *Scorpion* would receive only a fraction of its scheduled maintenance work plus the refueling of its nuclear reactor, whose radioactive fuel was seriously depleted. This task meant cutting out a *patch* or section of the hull to reach the reactor, another reason that nuclear submarines were more difficult to maintain.

While the other nuclear submarines were receiving two-year-long maintenance periods, the *Scorpion's* was to last only eight months.

A memo written from the headquarters of Submarine Squadron Six, under which the *Scorpion* served, warned that the difficulty in maintaining the submarines "… stands as a source of acute political embarrassment." The memo was written as plans were being made to reduce the *Scorpion's* maintenance.

> **Words To Treasure**
>
> A **patch** to a nuclear submarine sailor is a section of his boat's pressure hull that's cut out with a cutting torch so equipment can be removed or repaired.

A New Commander

By October 1967, the *Scorpion* had completed its abbreviated maintenance and received a new skipper, Lieutenant Commander Francis A. Slattery, a 1954 graduate of the U.S. Naval Academy. Born in Minot, Maine, Slattery was a conscientious officer who took over command of the ship from Commander James R. Lewis, under whose command the *Scorpion* had received numerous honors for its performance. The crew remained extremely busy preparing the submarine for duty after its compressed maintenance period.

While conducting familiarization training, the *Scorpion* made a high-speed underwater run to the Caribbean in November 1967 and began to corkscrew out of control. Crew members, who had worked long hours on the submarine, were beginning to distrust their ship. One was frustrated Electrician's Mate Dan Rogers, who was willing to disqualify himself from submarine duty to escape the *Scorpion*.

Rogers's wish was granted in January 1968, but he was nonetheless allowed to remain in the submarine service and transferred to another submarine, the USS *Lapon*. Whether the *Scorpion* was as bad as he said it was or not, Rogers nonetheless saved his life by his action.

Final Mission

The USS *Scorpion,* which had never before been sent to the strategically important Mediterranean Sea, received orders to depart for the area in 1968. Although now eight years old, the *Scorpion* was still a sleek example of a nuclear submarine and a powerful symbol to friends and foes alike. Submarines like these were called *showboats* by their crews, since their port calls were reassuring to America's allies.

On February 15, 1968, Dan Rogers helped cast off one of the mooring lines to the *Scorpion* as it eased away from the Norfolk Navy base's pier. Rogers and his former crew exchanged shouts as the boat moved out into the gray waters of Chesapeake Bay.

Laura Stone looks admiringly at her brother, USS Scorpion *Machinist's Mate David Stone, while the sailor was home on leave before he was lost with 98 others on the submarine. (Courtesy Vernon and Sybil Stone)*

Only two days after leaving Norfolk, the *Scorpion* developed a severe hydraulic fluid leak within its sail, or the upright structure on submarines frequently called a "conning tower" in Hollywood movies. The leak forced the submarine to surface in mid-ocean to repair the problem. The *Scorpion* then made its way to Rota, Spain, by March 15 before it swam past Gibraltar. The submarine made port calls in Italy at Taranto, Augusta Bay, Sicily, and Naples.

Photographed by Robert Ballard's team in 1986, the detached sail of the USS Scorpion *lies in nearly 12,000 feet of water southwest of the Azores Islands. (Courtesy U.S. Navy)*

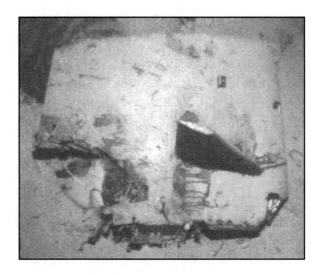

Although crew members got to see some of Italy's most beautiful sights, they also found themselves deep under water participating in U.S. Mediterranean Fleet exercises. After more than three months, the *Scorpion* was ordered home.

A Good and Bad Trip

The cruise to the Mediterranean had been both fun and hard work for the crew. Slattery had proven himself a capable submarine commander and treated his men in a gentlemanly way. Upon encountering a group of the *Scorpion*'s enlisted men ashore in Italy, he insisted they have a drink on him. As a nuclear submarine officer, his technical background reflected a lack of familiarity with submarine warfare tactics, but reports indicated he was getting the knack of the undersea cat-and-mouse game.

However, the submarine's mechanical condition was commented upon by hard-working crewmen like Machinist Mate David Burton Stone, who accompanied his letters home with beautiful ink drawings of the ports he visited. A letter dated April 12, 1968, to his parents in Iowa stated, "We have repaired, replaced and jury-rigged every piece of equipment … at one time or another and the boat hasn't been overhauled in four years." Stone was pointing out that his submarine's last complete overhaul occurred in 1963 and its most recent maintenance period was far from a complete overhaul. Submarines of the period received full overhauls at least every three years.

Only three days after Stone penned a letter to his parents complaining about the submarine's condition, Slattery himself transmitted a message to his headquarters, Submarine Squadron Six, warning that the *Scorpion* needed work. Said Slattery, "Delay of this work an additional year could seriously jeopardize *Scorpion*'s *material* readiness."

Words To Treasure

When Naval officers talk about their ships, they have personnel and material matters, with the **material** matters pertaining to a ship's physical or mechanical condition. A **showboat** is a sleek nuclear submarine sent to domestic and foreign ports to impress the public.

The Mystery Begins

During the night of May 16, 1968, while on its way back to the United States, illness and a family emergency forced the *Scorpion* to surface near Rota, Spain, and allow two crewmen to depart. Crewman Bill Elrod, who needed to fly home for family matters, and crewman Joseph W. Underwood, who had a lung infection, were unknowingly sidestepping death. The *Scorpion* then slipped into the night and was soon underway.

On May 20, the *Scorpion* was ordered to eavesdrop on a Soviet flotilla near the Canary Islands off Africa's northwest coast. That mission was completed by 7:54 P.M. on May 21 when the *Scorpion* radioed it was located 250 miles southwest of the Azores. It announced it would arrive in Norfolk on May 27 around 1 P.M.

Sounds of Destruction

In the old days when a ship was lost in the deep ocean, a survivor might live to tell the tale, but advances in technology meant the *Scorpion*'s death would be recorded by a trio of underwater listening systems. Roughly 24 hours after the *Scorpion*'s May 21 message announcing its impending arrival in Norfolk, the terrible sounds of a submarine breaking up underwater were recorded. Of the three systems that heard it, one belonged to the U.S. Air Force and another belonged to a university under government contract. The third was the Navy's underwater surveillance system called SOSUS, for "sound surveillance system."

Although the recordings were often made by remote control and were unintelligible to all but expert operators, they would be invaluable later when the Navy decided to review them.

Shiver Me Timbers

If you were around during 1968 and don't remember the *Scorpion* disaster, it's probably not your fault. Although the *Scorpion*'s loss made headlines at the time, the event was buried not only beneath water but also by a host of terrible events. Civil rights leader Martin Luther King Jr. was assassinated April 4, 1968, and presidential candidate Robert F. Kennedy was assassinated June 5. Domestic issues such as race riots and war protests were also dominating the news.

Waiting in the Rain

On May 27, 1968, at 1 P.M., families of the *Scorpion* crew went to the *Scorpion*'s pier at the Norfolk Navy Base to greet their husbands and fathers. Many of the wives bought their children new clothes for the big day that ominously began with a thunderous rainstorm. Rain fell with such intensity that trees lost their grip in the soggy soil and fell over. The minutes turned into hours, and disappointed families slowly left the pier and straggled home as Navy officials scrambled to find out what had happened.

Though the families didn't know it, Vice Admiral Arnold Schade, commander of the Atlantic Submarine Fleet, had already grown concerned over the *Scorpion*'s fate and ordered a search of the *Scorpion*'s route of return on May 24. This was ordered after the *Scorpion* failed to respond to radio messages, and the concerned Schade wanted to determine whether anything was wrong.

However, by 3:15 P.M. on May 27, Schade issued a "submarine missing" or "SubMiss" bulletin. The news initiated a massive air and sea search for the *Scorpion* and its 99 men. However, a subsequent review of the underwater recordings revealed a series of noises in the central North Atlantic—eerily similar to those made by the *Thresher*'s death five years previously—close to where the *Scorpion* would have been at the time.

Myths and Evidence

As in the case of the *Edmund Fitzgerald,* an inquiry was rapidly assembled. Within days of the *Scorpion*'s failure to return, its crew was declared dead. This was not a heartless act, but a way of expediting benefits to the survivors of those aboard. It was obvious that the men aboard the *Scorpion* were lost.

For days, airplanes, submarines, and aircraft had zigzagged across the Atlantic in a fruitless search for signs of debris from the wreck. Aboard the USS *Lapon* taking part in the search was a devastated Dan Rogers, whose concern about the sub's condition had convinced him to leave the *Scorpion*.

The Official Inquiry

Retired Admiral Bernard Austin chaired the Navy's inquiry into the *Scorpion*'s loss. Austin had presided over the inquiry into the loss of the *Thresher* in 1963. The legal proceeding was gaveled into session in June 1968 and heard testimony from 76 witnesses including *Scorpion* crewmen Elrod and Underwood. The "material condition" of the *Scorpion* was said to be good by Schade and other officers.

The inquiry ruled out sabotage, enemy attack, or an irrational act by a crew member. Before the wreckage of the *Scorpion* was located, scientists began studying 190 seconds of sounds of the *Scorpion* imploding and sinking to the bottom. Some believed the submarine had been blown apart by a Mark 37 torpedo that experienced a *hot run*, meaning it had been activated accidentally and then exploded.

As a massive scientific effort was underway to locate the *Scorpion* using underwater recordings and camera sleds taking thousands of pictures, the court placed the accidental torpedo explosion at the top of the list of possibilities. This Finding of Facts was classified SECRET, and the inquiry was adjourned.

Words To Treasure

A **hot run** is a situation in which a torpedo with a detonating mechanism in its warhead has been somehow switched on while still stored inside the submarine.

Miraculous Discovery

Besides providing clues as to what happened to the Scorpion, underwater recordings from three different locations allowed scientists to *triangulate* the *Scorpion*'s position. These computations led the Navy to the general area where the *Scorpion* sank.

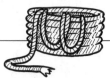

Know The Ropes

Triangulation of a position is the drawing of a line from three or more fixed points toward another location. The intersection of these lines will show an extremely accurate position of the location in question. Triangulation is often done using radio signals but in the case of the *Scorpion*, audio signals were plotted to their point of origin.

Using the triangulation data, the Navy research ship USS *Mizar* had been patiently towing a camera sled across the bottom of the Atlantic. The sled was what scientists call a "dope on a rope," since it blindly took still pictures as it moved across the seafloor. Each photograph carried the time so the searchers would know where they were when the picture was snapped.

On October 30, 1968—six months after the *Scorpion*'s disappearance—photographs from the sled revealed wreckage belonging to the *Scorpion* in 12,000 feet of water. The sled went back down for thousands of additional pictures, and the court of inquiry was reconvened to analyze the new evidence. To the court's surprise, there was no evidence of a torpedo explosion inside or outside the hull. Instead, the submarine is lying in three main pieces on the seafloor. Its sail, bow, and stern had separated during the sinking.

A Second Look

The Navy reopened its inquiry and ordered a deep-submergence investigation of the *Scorpion*'s wreck site, using the *Trieste II* deep-diving vehicle. This secret investigation was done in the summer of 1969.

While conducting dives on the seafloor, the *Trieste II* personnel made a pair of haunting discoveries. On one dive, the body of a *Scorpion* crewman was discovered lying near the wreck wearing a lifejacket, indicating the crew had forewarning that the submarine was in trouble. The second revelation was the recovery of a piece of battery casing belonging to the *Scorpion*'s massive batteries. Analysis of the recovered fragment indicated the submarine's massive bank of batteries had exploded.

Shiver Me Timbers

Woods Hole Oceanographic Institute scientist Robert Ballard was dispatched to study the *Scorpion*'s wreck site in 1985, while testing new remotely operated vehicles and camera equipment on behalf of the U.S. Navy. After determining that the *Scorpion*'s nuclear reactor and two nuclear weapons were not emitting radiation, Ballard used the same equipment to conduct the successful search for the *Titanic*. Despite the fame of the *Titanic*'s discovery, the *Scorpion* mission remained a secret for years.

However, the second investigation still failed to locate any torpedo debris or other physical evidence of an internal or external torpedo explosion. Scientists again pored over the evidence that had been collected. Although various groups of investigators had their own theories, Navy officials determined it was impossible to say what caused the *Scorpion*'s loss.

Endless Speculation

Although rumors of the *Scorpion*'s demise at the hands of an angry Soviet Union have hovered over the *Scorpion*'s Atlantic grave for more than 30 years, all the hard evidence available indicates this did not happen. The acoustical recordings that revealed the sound of the *Scorpion*'s death throes also showed there were no Soviet ships within 1,000 miles of the *Scorpion* at the time of its disappearance.

Some still claim a malfunctioning torpedo detonated inside the submarine. This theory seemed disproved when the *Scorpion*'s bow section—where the torpedoes are stored— was located intact. When it became known that a torpedo similar to the ones carried by the *Scorpion* could catch fire, others speculated this could have caused a detonation. Navy officers and scientific investigators who were part of the official investigation into the *Scorpion*'s loss insist there is no evidence of a torpedo explosion.

Still Grieving

On May 22, 1998, several hundred relatives and friends of the *Scorpion*'s crew gathered for the thirtieth anniversary of the submarine's loss. The families are still living in the crossfire of media theories about the *Scorpion* disaster, which was featured in a PBS *Nova* documentary and a Discovery Channel program in 1999. Navy officials have expressed surprise at the interest in having a memorial service so many years after the *Scorpion*'s loss but were gracious hosts. Just as it had on the day the *Scorpion* failed to return, rainy weather lashed the pier during the event.

The *Scorpion*'s loss may always be a mystery. This was made clear from the 1968 inquiry testimony of submariner and former *Scorpion* crewman Torpedoman James M. Peercy. When questioned during the inquiry about his theories as to the loss of the *Scorpion*, Peercy said, "I don't know sir. There are a lot of things that can sink a submarine."

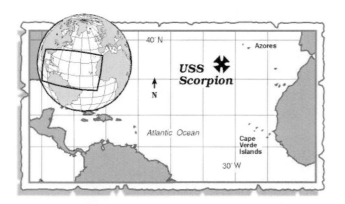

A map of the wreck site of the USS Scorpion. *(Drawn by Ken Ellis)*

The Least You Need to Know

➤ Early submarines were known as "pig boats" because they wallowed so much in the water when they traveled on the surface, and the tight confines led to serious problems when it came to cramming a larger crew into a small space for long periods.

➤ The *Scorpion* was a member of the Skipjack class of submarines that first combined the innovations of the bullet-shaped, streamlined hull and a nuclear reactor.

➤ The USS *Scorpion* was prone to cracking in its hull due to the use of a new steel known as High-Yield 80, but these cracks were discovered and repaired.

➤ The *Scorpion*'s nuclear fuel was nearly depleted at the time it went to Norfolk Navy Shipyard for refueling and a greatly abbreviated maintenance period.

➤ No debris from the wreck of the *Scorpion* was ever recovered on the surface despite weeks of searching by dozens of aircraft and ships.

Part 6

Pirates and Other Treasure Hunters

What sort of folks hunt for sunken treasure? Everyone! Treasure hunter extraordinaire Mel Fisher was a businessman who became both showman and shaman for treasure hunting. In Part 6, we follow him as he makes some of the richest finds ever, including those of the legendary Spanish treasure ships Atocha *and* Margarita. *His landmark legal battles spotlight the ongoing three-way war between archaeologists, the government, and treasure hunters.*

Part 6 also covers the history of piracy and explains that governments actually encouraged piracy against their enemies during times of war. This bad behavior was a genie not easily put back into the bottle and resulted in the "golden age" of piracy during the 1700s and early 1800s. Part 6 concludes by looking at the lives and exploits of notable pirates such as Blackbeard, Henry Morgan, and Jean Lafitte.

Chapter 25

"Today's the Day!": Mel Fisher, King of Treasure Hunters

In This Chapter

➤ Hatching a scuba pioneer

➤ Treasure fever

➤ King Fisher of controversy

➤ Victory and tragedy

➤ Endless treasure

Mel Fisher wasn't the first dreamer to search for sunken treasure, and he won't be the last. But during his 30 years of treasure hunting, this tall, smiling showman became the symbol of the American finder of sunken treasure ships. Although he was not a scientist like Robert Ballard, Fisher was among the first to use advanced technology to find shipwrecks. And while he may not have been an environmental crusader like scuba pioneer Jacques-Yves Cousteau, Fisher was one of the first scuba shop owners and dive instructors in the United States. Fisher, like the French undersea pioneer, was also a pioneering underwater filmmaker.

A World War II veteran who started selling scuba equipment from a shed at his parents' California chicken farm, Fisher would later build one of the largest scuba businesses in America and train thousands of divers. The restless Fisher would also begin diving on shipwrecks off California's coast. When he realized all the real sunken treasure ships were in Florida's waters, he packed up his wife and children and headed east.

During his decades of fabulous successes and crushing heartbreak, the one-time chicken farmer found the fabled Spanish treasure ships *Atocha* and *Margarita*. Along the way, he was triumphant in numerous legal battles with Florida and the

U.S. government to maintain possession of the treasures he found. Along with other famous personalities such as Ernest Hemingway and songwriter Jimmy Buffet, Fisher became an icon in the *Florida Keys* where he eventually came to live and make his greatest finds.

While the father of five seemed an unlikely treasure hunter, Fisher actually fit the definition like a glove. In many ways, he was the quintessential twentieth-century adventurer. He was a regular guy who initially ran a shoestring treasure-hunting operation and often lived on recovered Spanish pieces of eight when regular cash wasn't available.

Words To Treasure

The **Florida Keys** are a string of islands curving down from the southern tip of Florida's peninsula and extending about 150 miles to the west with the southernmost island city being Key West.

At the dawn of the 1960s, the religious and fair-minded Fisher gathered a multiracial team that included an electronics wizard, a Panamanian diesel mechanic, and some raw-boned scuba divers. By happenstance, Fisher later added to his team a historian who would decipher Spanish archival material that eventually led to the discovery of the *Atocha,* one of the richest treasure ships ever found. After plucking treasure from the previously discovered wrecks of the 1715 Spanish Treasure Fleet, Fisher plunged into other treasure hunts until becoming obsessed with the *Atocha* and *Margarita*—treasure galleons lost in 1622.

Despised by archaeologists angry that his discoveries would strip historically sensitive wrecks and hounded by Florida state officials eager to pour the treasure into state coffers, Fisher even found himself accused of wrongdoing by jealous treasure hunters. True to form, Fisher usually emerged smiling and victorious. The federal government would challenge his claim to the *Atocha* in a case that eventually made its way to the United States Supreme Court. His hero status among treasure hunters rose further when the Supreme Court ruled Fisher was entitled to the treasure and chastised the government for attempting to deprive Fisher of the treasure he fought so hard to locate.

Controversy would follow Fisher to the end. Just months before his death on December 19, 1998, Fisher was accused of selling replica treasure as the real thing, a charge hotly disputed by Fisher's representatives and disbelieved by everyone who knew him. After nearly four decades of treasure hunting, Mel Fisher's battle cry of "Today's the day!" was heard for the last time when he succumbed to a long battle with cancer.

Hatching a Scuba Pioneer

Mel Fisher didn't hail from a long line of mariners or explorers. In fact, Fisher came from Hobart, Indiana, a state whose "coastline" is 45 miles of waterfront facing Lake Michigan. Though sunken treasure was as rare as hen's teeth in Indiana, Fisher's interest in sunken treasure and things maritime was fueled by his childhood reading of *Treasure Island.*

Born on August 21, 1922, to a carpenter and a housewife, Fisher reached his junior year at Purdue University when the U.S. Army called him up for World War II service. He moved across Europe with American forces, building and rebuilding anything necessary as a member of a combat engineer unit. At war's end, he was the divorced father of a boy. His parents moved to California, and Fisher decided to wander the country.

In Tampa, Florida, Fisher talked a man skin diving with a swim mask and flippers into showing him how it was done. Like Cousteau (see Chapter 2, "Underwater Sleuths") and British diver and treasure hunter Keith Jessop (see Chapter 23, "Cold, Cold Cache"), Fisher was mesmerized by the ability to swim submerged while viewing the sea life clearly through a swim mask. At the dawn of the 1950s, he saw an ad in a California paper for Cousteau's Aqualung and bought one from sporting goods store operator Rene Bussoz. Fisher wanted to sell the air tanks and breathing regulators, but scuba diving was so new that Fisher couldn't even find a place to recharge his own scuba tank with air.

Shiver Me Timbers

Mel Fisher was so interested in the new scuba equipment that he didn't buy his through the mail but drove 2,300 miles to Los Angeles to purchase it personally from Rene Bussoz, who began selling the Aqualungs in 1949. Bussoz eventually named his company U.S. Divers. In 1957 the company that had the rights to the "Aqualung" bought the firm and installed Aqualung inventor Cousteau as its president. Cousteau remained in that position until his death in 1997. Fisher was one of the first people in the United States to purchase the underwater breathing rig.

Laying the Foundation

Six months later, Fisher moved to California where he worked with his parents who had started a chicken farm near Torrance. Fisher helped his parents oversee a spread of 10,000 egg-laying employees who worked for chicken feed. The farm was a success, but Fisher still dreamed of the sea and what was beneath it. He soon appropriated a 20-foot-by-20-foot shed on the chicken farm and was selling scuba equipment and recharging air tanks with an air compressor.

Living only a handful of miles from the Pacific, Fisher honed his skills as a member of a spear-fishing club and assembled a machine shop so he could design and build spear guns that he also sold. Like other diving entrepreneurs, Fisher would eventually design and sell *neoprene* wet suits before they were available from manufacturers. Divers from all over southern California showed up at his chicken farm dive shop for supplies or air tank refills. The sideline soon became more profitable than the farm.

Diving for Dollars

When the Fishers negotiated to sell the chicken farm, Fisher discovered that the family purchasing it had a fetching daughter named Deo. The 30-year-old Fisher took her diving, and marriage soon followed. Their 1953 honeymoon was a trip to Florida where the newlyweds dove in Florida's clear waters. During the drive back to California, Mel and Deo decided to open a dive shop.

Words To Treasure

Neoprene is a synthetic, rubberlike material manufactured to contain bubbles that create millions of tiny, insulating dead air spaces in the material. When used to make diving suits, the material—used in World War II to insulate air-conditioning ducts on warships—protects divers from the heat-robbing effects of being under water for extended periods.

Money was limited for the venture so Fisher purchased a pair of lots at a bargain rate. He then sold one of the lots to cover the cost of his own location. The couple dove for lobsters off California's southern coast and then sold the catch to upscale restaurants, using the money to purchase construction materials. Without $5,000 to spend on plans, the building was almost put on hold, but luck rewarded Fisher with a gift of architectural plans from the owner of a building whose layout Fisher admired.

The couple endured the cold Pacific water, with Mel moving across the bottom dragging the crustaceans from their holes while Deo dove into the water to relay the lobsters to the surface. The dive shop was built and—by the mid-1950s—was thriving.

School for Scuba

Even before building his dive shop, Fisher was giving scuba diving lessons and eventually employed instructors to help teach a tidal wave of enthusiasts. His local diving show sent flocks of students to Fisher who estimated that he and his instructors provided instruction to as many as 65,000 students during nearly a decade of instruction.

Fisher began one of America's first scuba diving courses in 1954. The instruction lasted five days and cost the students $35. A graduating diver obtained a certificate from Fisher indicating he or she completed the course. Many students learned their craft in the pool of the Hermosa Biltmore Hotel, which Fisher used instead of the chilly Pacific.

Soaked Celebrity

With content-hungry television in its infancy, Fisher soon took a page out of Cousteau's diving logbook and began shooting still pictures and photographs underwater. In time he had his own local undersea television show filming increasingly dangerous segments involving sharks, barracudas, and various hazardous inhabitants of the deep.

Sponsored by swimsuit manufacturers like Jantzen and corporations like Pan Am, Fisher began traveling to Mexico's Pacific coast and to the Caribbean to film the underwater adventures he wrote about in a column for *Watersports* magazine.

Deo Fisher claimed a bit of fame for herself when she spent 55 hours and 37 minutes underwater in an observation tank at the Hermosa Ocean Aquarium in 1958. Holding a sign plugging "Mel's Aqua Shop," Deo Fisher ate and drank while underwater to claim the world's record for a submerged diver.

Treasure Fever

A tireless and charming promoter, Fisher decided to tout the excitement of gold prospecting to his California customers. Once Fisher had his audience stricken with gold fever, he sold more scuba equipment and gasoline-powered dredges for sifting for gold in California's mountain rivers. However, Fisher himself would eventually become the most famous treasure hunter to ever suffer treasure fever.

Fisher's appetite for shipwrecks and their artifacts was whetted while diving off California's Pacific Coast. During the mid-1950s, Fisher heard a rumor about a pile of sunken cannon and set off to find it with television news crews close behind. Fisher was filmed raising the growth-encrusted guns, but a closer inspection revealed the "guns" were nothing other than 60-year-old sewer pipes!

Don't Go Overboard!

Mel Fisher decided during one of his movie-making trips off the Virgin Islands to spear a huge leopard ray. The fish immediately dragged Fisher out to sea for a wild ride. When Fisher climbed on the back of the angry ray to mug for the movie camera, the fish then slammed two of its eight-inch long tail barbs deep into one of his biceps. Fisher survived his wounds, though he required surgery. Not all sea creatures are as friendly as Flipper and should be approached with caution if at all.

Caribbean Cruise

While he continued to dive on shipwrecks off California and collect anchors and other artifacts, Fisher knew that the real treasure ships lay in the Caribbean and beneath the emerald waters off Florida. After purchasing a boat in 1960 and naming it the *Golden Doubloon*, Fisher mounted a treasure-hunting expedition that would take the boat through the Panama Canal to the Caribbean.

Sinking Treasure Hunters

Soon after the ship left Panama, a storm slammed the *Golden Doubloon*, causing it to slowly sink at the *stern*. A distress call was sent while Fisher's fellow treasure hunters used buckets to bail the boat. As water lapped over the nearly submerged stern, Fisher and Molinar grabbed sheets of plywood and nailed extensions on the stern's *gunwale* to keep out the encroaching water. The move saved the boat that was able to limp back to Panama for repairs.

First Find

As the *Golden Doubloon* made its way, Fisher and his group located three wrecks smashed upon Caribbean reefs and discovered a small cannon that was hauled to the surface as a souvenir. Despite their good fortune at stumbling upon what might have been Spanish treasure ships, Fisher and his companions had neither the knowledge nor the equipment with which to conduct a proper salvage operation.

Words To Treasure

The **stern** of a boat is the rear of a ship's hull and is usually more rounded than the sharp **bow,** which is designed to slice through the water. The **gunwale** is the short wall extending above the deck to prevent waves from sloshing aboard and to keep crew members from going overboard too easily.

Don't Go Overboard!

Few ships are perfectly watertight, and all face the prospect of damage that could fill the ship with water. This is why all ships carry pumps for removing water. Those ships and boats whose pumping capacity is less than the rate of water flowing into a boat will eventually sink, so before you buy a boat for yourself, you better make sure that its pumping capacity is up to snuff!

After returning, Fisher tallied up the cost of the trip that indicated the expensive nature of treasure hunting. Fisher invested $25,000 at the beginning of the trip and found himself $25,000 in debt before it was over. This didn't faze Fisher, whose dive shop and scuba instruction paid off the debt in a year.

Treasure Team

Not long after Fisher put Mo Molinar on the payroll to maintain his diving shop's boat, Fisher began adding other members to his treasure-hunting team.

When electronics expert Fay Feild called Mel's Aqua Shop in the early 1960s, Feild told Fisher how he'd invented an improved version of the magnetometer used to locate sunken ships. Feild, an electronics engineer and a pioneering cave diver, called Fisher to rent his boat. Soon Feild was towing his magnetometer behind Fisher's *Golden Doubloon* hunting for shipwrecks along the California coast. Their relationship would span more than 30 years.

Diver and adventurer Rupert Gates along with coin collector and construction foreman Walt Holzworth soon joined with Fisher and Feild for treasure hunts that would eventually take them from California to Florida.

Serious Salvors

With his initial band of treasure hunters ready for action by 1962, Fisher was provided the use of a 78-foot boat and financing by the boat's owner John Leeper, who went along on Fisher's first serious treasure expedition. Their target was the 1641 wreck of the Spanish treasure ship *Concepción* off Hispaniola that was partially salvaged in 1687 by adventurer William Phips, an episode recounted in Chapter 5, "Treasure Hunting's Soggy History."

The group used Feild's magnetometer to locate iron objects and dove repeatedly for the *Concepción* but without success. As luck would have it, a hurricane swirled across the Caribbean nearly swamping Leeper's boat, the *San Pedro*. A large wave smashed a window in the *San Pedro,* and Deo Fisher held a piece of plywood against it with her feet to keep waves from crashing into the boat. The treasure hunters operated a manual bilge pump and saved the boat, but the trip produced no treasure.

A third Caribbean treasure expedition mounted by Fisher also failed to produce riches in 1962, but the attempt to once again find the *Concepción* and her treasure built experience among his team members.

Florida or Bust!

Just prior to Fisher's 1962 treasure expedition, Lou Ullian, a member of the Real Eight treasure-hunting group in Florida (which is discussed in Chapter 11, "Rich Disaster: Wreck of the 1622 Treasure Fleet"), stopped by Fisher's dive shop to inspect one of the gold dredges sold by Fisher. Over dinner, Ullian told Mel and Deo Fisher of the Real Eight group's license to salvage the riches of the 1715 wreck.

After nearly a month of unsuccessful searching for the remnants of the *Concepción*'s silver during the 1962 trip, Mel and Deo Fisher met with Kip Wagner, who organized Real Eight. Wagner and Fisher made an arrangement that would plunge Fisher, his family, and his merry band of treasure hunters into the waters off Florida's "Treasure Coast." Fisher and his "experienced" team would operate under Wagner's license to search the 1715 wrecks. Fisher's group would pay its own expenses and split any finds with Real Eight on a 50-50 basis after Florida took its 25-percent share.

After selling his inventory and leasing his store, Fisher convinced Feild, Holzworth, Gates, Molinar, and merchant marine radio operator Dick Williams to sell everything and head for Florida in 1963. In a convoy of overheating cars, the group began its exodus. They struggled to cross the vastness of the Southwest and spent days driving from one end of Texas to the other. The travelers finally arrived in Florida and went straight to Kip Wagner's home.

Lyon Tells the Truth

After settling in Florida, Fisher met a fellow churchgoer named Eugene Lyon and was surprised to learn Lyon was a scholar trained in the form of Spanish used to record the history of the Spanish treasure fleets.

By 1970, Lyon was assisting Fisher's search for the *Atocha* and made a discovery as to the real location of the treasure ship that led to recovery of its magnificent treasure. Lyon's contribution to the discovery of the *Atocha* is recounted in Chapter 11. He was a key addition to Fisher's treasure-hunting team.

The King Fisher of Controversy

Kip Wagner was a bit surprised to actually see Mel Fisher and his group on his doorstep, but Wagner was unsure the group could be successful where others had failed, and assigned Fisher's team a 1715 wreck site that had been picked over by dozens of divers. The innovative thinking of Fisher and his team would soon make them wildly successful and would inadvertently ignite decades of suspicions and hostility from Florida officials.

Before their first dazzling success, the group endured nearly a year of unspectacular treasure finds, fighting harsh weather and poor seafloor visibility due to silt stirred up by bottom currents. Feild and Fisher discussed the problem and came up with the idea of using the propellers of their search boat to blow clear water to the seafloor. The development of what would be dubbed "mailboxes" was described in detail in Chapter 8, "Inches from Millions." To Fisher's surprise, the device not only cleared away the underwater "dust" but also excavated sand from the wrecks.

Words To Treasure

The word **cob** is derived from the Spanish term *cabo de barra*, which means "end of the bar." Early New World coins were minted by crudely stamping them from discs cut from the end of a thin bar of gold or silver.

On May 24, 1964, Fisher and his team used the mailboxes to blow away the sediment near a wreck off Florida's Douglass Beach (once a segregated strip of sand known as "Colored Beach") and were amazed to find the seafloor littered with thousands of gold coins. They salvaged 1,003 on the first day and 900 the next. Eventually, 2,500 *cob* type coins were plucked from the seafloor. Fisher estimated his portion of the treasure at $1.6 million. When word of the find eventually got out, Fisher was famous.

Suspicious Officials

To ensure security, the 1964 find had to be kept a secret until the recovery was completed. Unfortunately, secrecy came into conflict with Florida regulations requiring salvors operating under state license to report their finds as soon as possible. Before the treasure find was reported and the state received its share, suspicions prompted a comical investigation of Fisher and Treasure Salvors. It was the beginning of decades of official scrutiny aimed at Fisher's treasure-hunting efforts.

Know The Ropes

Some Florida officials, being neophytes at treasure-hunting operations, were under the misguided impression that gold and silver were just waiting to be hauled up by the ton. Officials didn't realize that sunken treasure is hard to find! The foolish expenditure of millions in tax dollars in dubious searches that often produced nothing would have been a political nightmare for officials trying to justify official treasure hunting.

While recovering gold from the wreck off Douglass Beach, Fisher and his crew noticed a man leaning out of a light plane peering at them through binoculars but thought little of it. Unknown to Fisher and his group, state officials had heard rumors of the treasure find and mounted an investigation. Agents hid in bushes to watch the salvage operation 600 feet from the beach. One investigator donned a fake beard and, posing as a fisherman, visited the Treasure Salvors's recovery boat.

Although state officials were satisfied that no treasure had been hidden from the state, the *Miami Herald* published a story that suggested a million dollars in treasure had been pilfered from state waters. This prompted years of debate over whether Florida should salvage the Spanish treasure ships so the funds could go straight into public coffers.

Bad Press

Newspaper reports depicted Fisher and his group as being little more than a gang of thieves, whose plunder of wrecks off Florida was taking money out of the public's pocket while damaging historical sites. Despite the publicity, Fisher had an unexpected supporter in the governor of Florida, Farris Bryant, who backed the free enterprise element in treasure hunting and decried state participation in treasure expeditions. Bryant's successor, Haydon Burns, was elected in 1966 and was also in favor of leaving treasure hunting to the private sector.

A Lawsuit Surfaces

Eric Schiff, a California investor in one of Fisher's earlier treasure-hunting efforts, filed a lawsuit claiming part of the Douglass Beach treasure when he heard news of Fisher's discoveries. Schiff's case was initially dismissed, but he filed it again and kept it alive for nearly four years until it simply faded away. It was to be the first of much legal wrangling Fisher would face.

By 1968, Fisher had moved his family—which by now included three sons and a daughter by wife Deo—to the Florida Keys to hunt for wrecks in deeper water. Fisher would find not only treasure but also an abundance of controversy and a lawsuit that would eventually be settled in the United States Supreme Court.

Victory and Tragedy

In June 1973 when Fisher began locating significant artifacts and treasure of the 1622 Spanish treasure ship *Atocha,* jealous competitors began claiming to the press and Florida officials that Fisher had not found the wreck as he claimed. The incredible story of the *Atocha* find is recounted in Chapter 11.

Soon after competing treasure hunters began carping about Fisher's honesty and reliability, state officials brusquely arrived for a scheduled pickup of 2,000 silver coins and a collection of exquisite and valuable artifacts collected from the *Atocha*. The officials then announced Fisher's permit to work the *Atocha* site would be revoked, since he had failed to file the appropriate paperwork. Deo Fisher halted that move by presenting the documentation to Robert Williams, then in charge of Florida's Division of History, Archives and Records Management.

When a U.S. Supreme Court decision placed control of the *Atocha* wreck site under the federal government in 1975, Fisher's maritime lawyer, David Paul Horan, filed a lawsuit in federal court to arrest the wreck under salvage law. U.S. District Court Judge William O. Mehrtens ruled in Fisher's favor, but federal officials appealed, forcing the case to the U.S. Supreme Court. In 1982 the Court ruled the *Atocha* and its cargo belonged to Fisher's treasure-hunting organization.

Shiver Me Timbers

The decision in favor of Mel Fisher was viewed as a victory for free enterprise and the American way of life. U.S. District Judge William O. Mehrtens's original ruling blasted the federal government, saying, "It would amaze and surprise most citizens of this country, when their dream, at the greatest of costs, was realized that agents of respective governments would, on the most flimsy grounds, lay claim to the treasure."

Casualties: Treasure-Hunting Nightmares

Despite the seemingly light-hearted nature of treasure hunting, the work is conducted above and below the potentially hazardous element of water. Fisher paid a terrible personal price on July 19, 1975, when his son, Dirk Fisher, and Dirk's wife, Angel, drowned aboard their work boat that capsized at night during the search for the *Atocha*'s main treasure. Diver Rick Gage also perished.

Only two years before, another death occurred when 12-year-old Nicki Littlehales was sucked into the mailbox blowers of one of the work boats during the *Atocha* recovery operation. He was the son of *National Geographic* photographer Bates Littlehales. Both tragic episodes are recounted in Chapter 11.

Mother of All Treasures

By April 1980, a team hired by Fisher located the *Margarita*, the *Atocha*'s sister ship, and recovered nearly 200 pounds of gold ingots, coins, and chains in the process. But bad news followed when Fisher learned in 1982 that he had cancer. He would undergo treatment off and on for the next 17 years.

After spending more than 16 years hunting for the *Atocha*'s main treasure, Mel Fisher's team located a small cannon on July 19, 1985. They dove upon the site to discover the bulk of the *Atocha*'s treasure. The *Atocha*'s estimated $400-million treasure had been found for the first time in 360 years, and Fisher was again in the news.

Shiver Me Timbers

When the mother lode of the *Atocha*'s treasure was eventually found, the six-foot, three-inch Mel Fisher himself couldn't be located. A Key West radio station began to broadcast announcements for Fisher to call his office as family and friends looked for him. Fisher was running errands and couldn't be reached by telephone or radio. He learned the news from a passerby while coming out of a diving shop, carrying his purchase of a diving mask and fins.

Silver Jubilee

When the *Atocha*'s main treasure was found, people raced to the location and piled aboard Fisher's salvage boats for a huge floating party. Singer and Key West denizen Jimmy Buffet arrived to play for the celebration while seated on a pile of silver ingots. The boat became so overloaded Fisher had to transfer revelers to another to avoid capsizing.

Immediate cultural heroes of the 1980s, Mel and Deo Fisher became the subjects of a 1986 television movie starring Cliff Robertson and Loretta Swit titled *Dreams of Gold: The Mel Fisher Story.*

King Conch

During the 1980s, Fisher found himself fighting an attempt by the federal government to establish the Florida Keys National Marine Sanctuary that would restrict activities in the environmentally sensitive area. In 1997, Fisher's treasure-hunting operations, which flushed thousands of holes into the sediment using boat-mounted mailboxes, was fined almost $590,000 for damaging sea grass in the first sanctuary damage case to go to trial.

The rowdy and free-spirited Florida Keys, long known as the "Conch Republic," was split over the issue of restricting activities affecting the underwater environment. Fisher, who proclaimed himself king of the Conch Republic, held that blowing away silt was good for the environment. Nonetheless, the sanctuary was established in 1990 to provide protection for the distressed coral reefs and sea life around the Florida Keys.

Final Controversy

Fisher established the Mel Fisher Maritime Heritage Society museum in 1982 in Key West, and it is still in operation. However, for tax reasons Treasure Salvors, Inc., was dissolved in 1986. Fisher opened Mel's Treasure Hunting Gift Shop in Key West, where the *Atocha* treasure is still being sold to those who can afford to buy one of its rare coins or artifacts.

In a stunning turn of events, Fisher was accused of selling counterfeit gold coins. Because of this, his gift shop was raided in May 1998. Since that raid, Fisher's staff claims to have determined that the coins are encrusted with microscopic organisms, proving they spent centuries under water. State and county police officials were still conducting their investigation in 1999, holding fast to their claim that the coins are counterfeit. However, a previous claim of selling counterfeit coins had been disproved years ago by Fisher.

While this controversy brewed, the 76-year-old king of the Conch Republic succumbed to cancer on December 19, 1998. He successfully battled the sea, the federal government, and personal tragedy to recover one of the richest treasures ever located beneath the sea.

Know The Ropes

The 220-mile Florida Keys National Marine Sanctuary is administered by the National Oceanographic and Atmospheric Administration and is designed to protect the fragile reef system around the Keys, along with the wildlife, from human activity. NOAA is attempting to assess humans' impact on the environment while preventing or reducing further damage to the reefs caused by such events as ship groundings.

Endless Treasure

Since Fisher owned the wrecks of the *Atocha* and *Margarita* under salvage law, he was able to allow other treasure hunters to contract with him for the recovery of artifacts and treasure at these wreck sites. Treasure is still coming to the surface despite the passage of years and the amount of recovery already conducted.

In November 1998, divers recovered 125 emeralds, along with three pieces of jade and other artifacts, near the widely dispersed *Atocha* wreck site. Prior to that discovery a trio of silver spoons were recovered. The search continues.

The Least You Need to Know

➤ Mel Fisher was born miles from the sea in Indiana, a state whose only significant coastline is a 45-mile stretch that faces the southern edge of Lake Michigan.

➤ While he would eventually return to Florida to live nearly 15 years later, Mel Fisher was living in Florida just after World War II, which is where he learned how to dive using a dive mask and swim flippers.

➤ Although he worked a number of jobs and had once been a student at Purdue University, Mel Fisher spent several years helping to manage his parents' chicken farm in Torrance, California, where he started his first scuba equipment store.

➤ To create interest in his dive shop and scuba diving lessons, Mel Fisher starred in his own local television show near Los Angeles, where he showcased his adventures and the underwater films he made showing sharks and other dangerous sea creatures.

➤ Mel Fisher's first treasure trip organized to the Caribbean was far from profitable. The entire trip cost $50,000 and put Fisher in debt for a year until his diving business paid off the entire amount.

➤ A Florida investigator, wearing a fake beard, came aboard Mel Fisher's boat during his 1964 recovery of treasure from one of the 1715 Spanish Treasure Fleet wrecks to determine whether Fisher was hiding any of the treasure from the state, which owned 25 percent of the recovered items.

Chapter 26

The Rudest Treasure Hunters

In This Chapter

➤ Piracy: The eternal scourge

➤ Caribbean sea robbers

➤ The pirate life

➤ Horror, hokum, and punishment

Most of what we know about pirates comes from works of fiction—you know, books like *Treasure Island*—and the images have often been less than accurate. Errol Flynn movies such as *The Sea Hawk* and *Captain Blood* transformed the pirate into a misunderstood hero with noble intentions. Other fictional pirates, such as Captain Hook in *Peter Pan,* have been portrayed as silly. In the opera *The Pirates of Penzance* the pirates were portrayed as musically inclined and not all that scary.

The elevation of the pirate to the level of cult hero seems like an odd turn of events, since true pirates, who were nothing more than sea robbers, were a rather horrible lot. Even during the eighteenth century's golden age of piracy, when an estimated 2,000 pirates plundered and butchered in the Caribbean and the Atlantic, these criminals were the subjects of best-selling books written by authors such as Daniel Defoe. The public couldn't get enough of their disgusting behavior.

Pirates were the original terrorists. They kidnapped, stole, raped, and murdered their way across the seas. Their primary weapon was the terror inspired by their reputation for brutality that allowed them to capture ships without a shot. They conquered cities, took hostages, tortured anyone who irked them, and committed murder on an industrial scale. Can you imagine someone elevating a modern terrorist to the status of cult hero in a book or film? How about a Broadway musical with a modern homicidal terrorist singing his way through his horrific acts against innocent people?

Although piracy is as old as sea travel itself, some of the most brutal, flamboyant, and famous piratical activities occurred in the Caribbean and along America's East Coast. A look at the history of piracy in this area from the 1600s through the 1800s reveals a complex historical and cultural puzzle in which governments and social conditions shared the blame for the flourishing of piracy in the New World.

Europe's wars saw thousands of sailors placed into service and then returned to hopeless unemployment upon the arrival of peace. With their only skill being seamanship, a life of crime at sea seemed like a natural choice. Hunger, disease, and harsh laws at home made a criminal life at sea seem like a viable alternative to returning to the wretched poverty of England in the 1700s.

Words To Treasure

The word **pirate** means to rob and plunder at sea but has been subsequently applied to those who illegally reproduce and sell music recordings or who operate radio stations without the proper licensing by "pirating" the public airwaves.

Ironically, sovereign nations that would later declare piracy a scourge and sweep it from the seas, ushered in widespread piracy through the centuries-old practice of hiring *privateers* to attack enemy shipping. Privateer sailors who developed a taste for wartime plunder often stayed with the vocation after the peace treaties were signed. It was not unusual for pirates to drift between crime and officially sanctioned piracy.

Being murderers and criminals, any pirate could ascend to the command of a pirate ship through mutiny or murder. As a result, a strange form of democracy prevailed on pirate ships that could not be found on the navy ships of the time. To prevent anarchy, pirates were frequently required to sign *articles* that bound them to a certain code of conduct. Everyone on the ship was frequently given a percentage of the booty as well as a voice in the pirate operations. Break a rule, however, and you could end up marooned on a desert island to die.

Words To Treasure

A **privateer** is a sailor or ship given governmental permission to attack and seize enemy vessels and cargo during war.

If you've got your flintlock pistols in your belt and you've slid your thumb along the edge of your cutlass, tell your foul-mouthed parrot to hang on because we're headed for an overview history of piracy!

Piracy: The Eternal Scourge

Before we start talking about how old piracy is, you ought to know that piracy is still with us. As you read this, modern pirates in Asia are scanning the horizon for their next prize ship in Indonesian waters. Instead of sharpening their sabers and tamping stone cannon balls into bronze cannon, Philippine pirates are readying assault rifles and rocket-propelled grenades for their next raid. Off Brazil's Atlantic coast, late-twentieth-century pirates are sneaking out to ships and yachts at anchor to commit robbery.

Although most of today's piracy occurs in the waters of Indonesia, Malaysia, and the Philippines, pirates off the Greek Island of Corfu seized a luxury yacht on September 27, 1996. Alerted by shotgun blasts fired at the pirates by yacht owner Keith Hedley, Greek police arrived to have a gun battle with the pirates who had overpowered Hedley. During the shoot-out, Hedley was killed. The pirates escaped in a speedboat.

First Treasure, Then Pirates

The history of piracy stretches back thousands of years to the time when hard-working folks put goods on boats and paddled them across a river or harbor to conduct trade. Some local thug probably figured out that robbing on the water was as good as doing it on dry land, and piracy was born.

As the technology of shipbuilding and navigation allowed ships to travel far out to sea, pirates moved their operations accordingly. Whenever merchant ships transported things worth stealing, pirates got down to the business of stealing it. Robbing at sea is great from the criminal's point of view: The seas are massive, and law enforcement agencies are far, far away. And because you're already on a ship, the getaway is a snap.

Ancient Pirates

In 4,000-year-old texts, historians recorded that the Sumerian civilization was plagued by a race of barbaric raiders who arrived by boat to plunder the city of Sumer and also to seize their boats at sea. As bad as the Sumerians thought these pirates were, the Sumerians apparently learned a thing or two about the profits of piratical activities.

By 3000 B.C.E., the Sumerians were also conducting sea raids upon coastal communities from the Persian Gulf up through the Tigris and Euphrates rivers. Piracy was so highly thought of by this time that a Sumerian holy man is said to have led one of these piratical expeditions. Unfortunately, this priest was a complete foul-up who ended up being killed and thrown into the Euphrates River by his crew who had had enough of his stupidity.

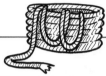

Know The Ropes

Piracy is so ancient that a saying has evolved claiming it is the third oldest profession behind prostitution and medicine. Coincidentally, prostitution and medicine figure heavily into a pirate's life. Since they frequently engaged in warfare at sea, pirate ships often employed their own busy physicians. The proclivity of most pirates to spend much of their booty in debauchery with prostitutes meant the physicians would be equally busy tending to venereal disease after a visit to port.

Know The Ropes

Sumer was an ancient but advanced civilization in what is now known as southern Iraq. Its origins have been traced back nearly 7,000 years, when Sumer dominated the region militarily and economically.

Early Pirate Laws

By 1905 B.C.E., King Hammurabi of Babylonian, had issued a legal code whose inscription can still be seen in the Louvre museum in Paris. It contained a law that demanded restitution equal to 30 times the value of a ship seized from the government and a tenfold restitution for a private ship captured by pirates. Pirates who couldn't pay the fine got to pay a one-time visit to the executioner. Like most other laws, those by Hammurabi were probably derived from even older regulations.

Et, Tu Blackbeard?

It would seem that in the old days no one was free from piratical predators. Years before Julius Caesar fell under the charms of Cleopatra, or the knives of his assassins, Caesar fell victim to piracy. He was captured and ransomed by pirates in the Aegean roughly 75 years before the birth of Christ. Relatives paid 20 talents of gold for the release of Caesar, who got along with his captors rather well.

A cocky Caesar taunted his piratical captors to ask for more money because he was insulted by the low price they placed on his head. It is said the pirates rather liked the devil-may-care attitude of the future Roman hero. They were less pleased when the tough-as-nails Caesar returned with soldiers and warships to capture and crucify his kidnappers.

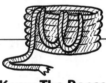

Know The Ropes

Letters of marque is a term derived from the Latin word *marcare,* which had a more specific business meaning. A *letter of marque* allowed the seizure of a ship or cargo as security against a debt. Such seizures usually occurred in ports where the ship was unable to pay for its supplies or repairs. Constant warfare prompted the issuance of letters of marque allowing the seizure of ships at sea to aid military efforts. This tradition gave many ordinary merchant sailors a taste of legal "piracy" as privateers.

War, Piracy, and Business

With the rise in merchant shipping in Europe by 1200, piracy began to take place with official approval, since pirates often augmented national fleets. England's first famous pirate was Eustace the Monk, who left life as a clergyman after dueling with and killing a man. Eustace was a good pirate commander and successfully raided French ships and coastal communities on behalf of England's King John. Eustace, who was Flemish, later changed sides and raided England for King Philip II of France. Eustace's reputation was one of cruelty and violence. He was eventually captured and executed.

Piracy augmented an official naval force through the issuance of *letters of marque*. Originally, such letters gave merchant sailors permission to settle debts by seizing the ships and cargo of those who owed them money. However, letters of marque eventually became official government permission forms to attack and seize enemy ships. Such civilian raiders were known as privateers and functioned as temporary members of official navies.

The issuance of letters of marque and official backing of pirates opened the door to an age of piracy that plagued the Atlantic from the Americas to Europe from the 1500s to the early 1800s. This era, chronicled by authors such as Daniel Defoe, Robert Louis Stevenson, and Charles Ellms, and later by filmmakers, was the well-known swashbuckling period of piracy.

Caribbean Sea Robbers

If you know anything about pirates, you may have heard of pirate names like Blackbeard and Henry Morgan. These pirate captains and thousands of their compatriots were cruel, cunning, and avaricious—traits of a good pirate. They accurately represented the pirates of the Americas and were the products of complex and historic events.

Constant wars between Spain, England, and France meant numerous letters of marque were issued to privateers to plunder enemy ships across the world, but the Spanish treasure fleets sailing through the Caribbean to Spain gave the boldest privateers the most obvious region to patrol. Spanish ships and settlements in the New World were targeted by privateers who later returned as pirates without official permission to plunder.

Perhaps the most famous official pirate to cut a swath of plunder through the Caribbean was Sir Francis Drake. The English privateer conducted raids on Panama's Atlantic coast in 1570, capturing large amounts of gold. You'll find a closer look at his exploits in Chapter 29, "Notable Pirates."

Booty: Piracy's Purpose

Although piracy flourished around the world for thousands of years, the greatest hunting ground in the history of piracy would result from the 1492 discovery of the New World by Christopher Columbus. The Spanish plunder of silver, gold, and gems from Mexico and Central and South America produced the greatest piles of treasure ever shipped across the seas up to that time. Chapter 9, "Fish Scales of Justice: Modern Salvage Law," provides the background of this extraordinary period that turned the Caribbean into a highway of silver and gold.

When asked why he robbed banks, American bank robber Willy Sutton replied, "Because that's where the money is." Perhaps Sutton's simple answer also explains why so many pirates flocked to the Caribbean and America's East Coast between the 1500s and 1800s. The pirates of the Caribbean would have undoubtedly said the same thing.

The Spanish ships plying the Caribbean loaded with precious metals and gems even became known as the "treasure fleet" and provided the most tempting targets a pirate could have dreamed about. Crowded with both treasure ships and pirates, the Caribbean was to become piracy's hot spot for the next three centuries.

Easy Come, Easy Go

Another important ingredient to the blossoming of piracy in the Caribbean and the Americas was the fact that this region was sparsely populated and governments were hard pressed to police the area. As larger Spanish fleets hauled tons of silver and gold to Europe while carrying manufactured goods to colonists, the pirates could plunder anything they wanted and make their escape with ease.

Pirate Ports

Although romantic notions of piracy might envision the pirates as constantly sailing the seas in search of their next victim, these robbers of the sea needed a base of operations. Sailing ships are notoriously labor intensive and require constant repairs. Ships needed to be *careened,* or leaned over on a protected beach, so the hull could be scraped clean of speed-robbing marine growth and caulked. The sailors themselves needed time ashore to escape the dangers of life at sea, so various ports provided haven to the pirates as well as their money.

Words To Treasure

The word **careen** refers to several things including the sharp turning of a ship under sail, but it was often used to describe the beaching of a sailing ship and leaning it over so its hull could be scraped free of marine growth and repaired.

Lafitte's Lair

Pirates sometimes lived along the coast of America; for example, Gulf Coast pirate Jean Lafitte inhabited a swamp known as Barataria south of New Orleans. When the authorities drove him out, he moved his operations to Galveston, Texas, where he continued an uneasy alliance with the respectable inhabitants until disappearing from that location in May 1821 under pressure from the U.S. Navy. (We'll read more about Lafitte in Chapter 29.) Civilization and a growing number of naval patrols eventually spelled the end for piracy's golden age by the mid-1800s.

A Royal Hideout

The most notorious pirate hangout in the Americas was Jamaica's Port Royal. After England captured Jamaica from the Spanish in 1655, Port Royal began to grow into a city and was the hub of trading activity in the region. Because Spanish warships prowled the area in great numbers, the English governors of Port Royal encouraged the presence of pirates, since it was believed (and correctly so) that they would discourage a Spanish attack.

In turn, the pirates were able to sail from Port Royal to conduct raids on Spanish shipping and then return with

Words To Treasure

The **Pirate Round** was named after the route taken by pirates that traveled from the Caribbean bases to the Indian Ocean and the Red Sea to plunder shipping before returning to sell goods to colonists in North America.

money or goods to trade or sell. After committing their robberies, pirates were little more than glorified smugglers carrying stolen goods to a location where they could be converted into cash or traded for needed items. Pirates actually became relatively important in some coastal areas of America and the Caribbean by becoming a link in the chain of commerce known as the Pirate Round that operated from 1690 until 1720.

Although England eventually ordered a halt to Port Royal's embrace of the pirates, the city met a catastrophic end on June 7, 1692, when an earthquake caused a major portion of the city to sink beneath the sea, killing as many as 2,000. Surviving pirates quickly found boats and began to loot the remnants of the city, as well as the bloated corpses of those who were drowned. The remnants of Port Royal recovered, but the town had seen its heyday. The submerged remains of the city are still being explored by archaeologists.

By the early 1700s, Port Royal had become a symbol for the coming end of piracy as English colonial authorities began to crack down on buccaneers. Pirate Charles Vane was hanged there on May 22, 1720, for torturing the crews of two captured sloops two years previously. In November of the same year, pirate captain John Rackam (also known as Calico Jack) was also hanged. Two years after Rackam's execution, 41 pirates were hanged en masse at Gallows Point near Port Royal. A hundred years later in 1823 pirates were still being hanged, with 20 Spanish pirates marched to the gallows near Port Royal for their misdeeds.

Know The Ropes

Not all pirate booty was in the form of gold and silver. Pirates would often end up robbing a ship of anything from grain to fine fabrics or other manufactured goods. It was not uncommon for "respectable" businessmen from Boston to Barbados to purchase such goods from pirates for sale on the shelves of legitimate stores. Public officials and so-called legitimate merchants often profited by accepting these illegal goods for resale in shops from New England to Virginia. This same practice exists today in some parts of the world.

Pirate Island

The Texas-sized Indian Ocean island of Madagascar became a premiere haven for pirates between the late 1600s and early 1700s. Pirates virtually controlled the island and were able to safely conduct raiding operations from its ports. The natural harbor of St. Mary's Island on Madagascar's northeast coast became a perfect place for pirates to hide out during the early 1690s. At the southern end of Madagascar, another pirate colony was established at Fort Dauphin in 1696.

By the early 1700s, the rough-and-ready pirates of Madagascar had deteriorated to feuding among themselves and fell victim to murder, disease, and poverty. It was estimated that no more than 70 pirates still lived on the island by 1711. However, during Madagascar's prime as a pirate island, highly successful raids were conducted on shipping in the Indian and Pacific Oceans.

The Pirate Life

Despite Hollywood's campy and sanitized view of pirates, they were almost always a ruthless pack of seagoing scum. Despite their criminality and frequent viciousness, necessity prompted pirates to create innovative management methods to keep their criminal operations running smoothly. Rank-and-file input into daily operating decisions and fair methods of employee compensation worked out by the pirates predated similar modern principals that have come into vogue during the last half of the twentieth century.

Words To Treasure

The **articles** amounted to a contract signed by each pirate aboard a ship, spelling out the rate of payment to each as well as a code of conduct and the penalties for failing to adhere to the rules.

Because criminal organizations are often brutal enterprises where ascension is the result of assassination and intrigue, pirates soon realized that such activities aboard a ship would cause more problems than it would solve. Hence the pirate ship captain became a manager working with a crew of partners (the pirates) who had a vote in the use of the ship. Each man was compensated with a percentage of the booty seized from prize ships, and all were expected to abide by the *articles* each man had to sign before being allowed to join the crew.

Democracy and Piracy

Pirate Basil Ringrose was enjoying the pirate's life in 1681 when he and his fellow sea robbers captured a Spanish treasure ship near Chile. Each man received 234 pieces of eight after the successful attack. During the same voyage, the pirates became unhappy with their captain Bartholomew Sharp and voted him out of office. They voted in another pirate named John Watling. After Watling was killed during a shore raid, Sharp was voted back into his captaincy, and the pirates went about their business.

Piratical HMO

Unlike virtually every other worker prior to the twentieth century—when work-related injuries were the individual's own problem—pirates established a system of workmen's compensation for those hurt while plundering, murdering, and kidnapping. Robbing ships at sea could be dangerous work if the crew of the target ship put up a fight.

Many pirate articles plainly stated how much compensation a pirate would get if he were injured in the line of duty. In one documented instance during the late 1600s, pirate articles set the rate for the loss of a right arm at 600 pieces of eight. A right leg was worth only 500 pieces of eight. (Since peg legs seemed so easy to come by for pirates, the loss may have been deemed rather incidental.) Inexplicably, the loss of a left leg was only worth only 400 pieces of eight. Go figure.

What's in a Name?

Pirates have been around so long that their name is rooted in the Greek-Latin word *pìrâta,* but other words have become interchangeable with the word *pirate,* and they deserve some explanation because they represent the regionalism of piracy.

The other most common name for a pirate is *buccaneer,* which is truly a wonderful word, bringing connotations of swashbuckling and close-in sword fights on the decks of contested ships. However, buccaneers gained their name from a Native American word that describes the technique used to barbecue wild oxen and boar on the islands of Hispaniola and Tortuga. The French word *boucan* came from this native word describing a frame for holding a carcass as it was smoked. Apparently the *boucaniers,* or "barbecuers," wielded a steak knife long before they grabbed the hilt of a pirate's cutlass. The true buccaneers were French and English trespassers on Hispaniola who were forced to a life at sea when evicted by Spanish authorities.

Although the word *corsair* can stand for any pirate, it is most often applied to the Muslim pirates who plied what was known as the Barbary Coast off North Africa. These pirates were about as cruel as the rest but often used their religious beliefs as thin justification for raiding the ships of infidels such as the Europeans. The term is French and also came to stand for the name of a fast pirate ship whose captain is armed with official letters of marque. One of the most famous corsairs is the legendary Turk Barbarossa.

Piracy's Garden

Poverty may have been the sterile fertilizer for the garden that grows pirates. Piracy flourished in the Americas and the Caribbean when many turned to robbery at sea as a means of survival. Many escaped the grinding poverty of European cities by turning to a seaborne life of crime. It was not uncommon for penniless sailors—put ashore by pirates who had stolen the sailors' ship—to find the only way to survive was to turn to piracy like their own tormentors.

The so-called golden age of piracy began in the late eighteenth century during a time of poverty, harsh punishment for small crimes, and massive unemployment. Governments tilled this spawning ground for pirates by enlisting men by the thousands for sea duty only to release them at war's end with nowhere to go. Knowing only seamanship as a skill and with little hope of employment, many former sailors of England's Royal Navy turned to piracy. In fact, most of the pirates who sailed the Spanish Main and plundered the Atlantic were either British or American.

To make matters worse, countries such as England blurred the line between military sailors and

Words To Treasure

Pirate, corsair, and **buccaneer** all mean virtually the same thing, although true buccaneers were French and English squatters on Hispaniola, while corsairs were generally Arab pirates.

plundering pirates by making merchant seamen privateers who could legally capture ships and seize cargoes. When the Peace of Utrecht was consummated in 1713, the major European powers drawn into the War of Spanish Succession released thousands of sailors from duty to the cold embrace of unemployment.

Shiver Me Timbers

At least two great periods of piracy involving English pirates came on the heels of peace after long wars. When 50 years of war between England and Spain ended in 1603, scores of unemployed sailors turned to piracy, creating a sizable problem for merchant shipping for the next three decades. When the treaty known as the Peace of Utrecht was signed in 1713 stopping war between all the major European powers, 40,000 Royal Navy sailors were discharged with many going to sea to become pirates. The signing of this treaty is one of the reasons that piracy increased shortly after 1713.

With Spain still hauling tons of treasure from her colonial mines in the Americas to Spain, piracy seemed like a good idea and many decided to serve under the Jolly Roger, an ensign also known as the "black flag." If the treasure ships weren't plentiful enough, a growing amount of ordinary merchant trade between Europe and the Americas also provided rich prey for sea robbers.

Words To Treasure

Walking the plank is perhaps the most famous thing that never happened and reputedly involved blindfolding a victim who was prodded to his death across a plank extending out over the water from the deck of a ship. Although this rather ceremonious event did not occur, it was not uncommon for pirates to simply throw people overboard to their deaths.

Horror, Hype, and Punishment

Although it has long been said that the first casualty of war is the truth, the same might be said about the fate of truth when it comes to the telling and retelling of the history of pirates. Undoubtedly many were murderers and rapists. Pirates also took hostages and demanded ransom for their release, making some pirates kidnappers and extortionists. However, many pirate stories are suspicious and should be viewed with healthy skepticism.

Some pirates tortured their victims, but many of the stories of their misbehavior get a bit farfetched, requiring us to believe that many of these criminals—who often possessed remarkable leadership abilities and sailing skills—were as insane as a person can get. Even some of the most famous punishments supposedly meted out by pirates such as *walking the plank* have no basis in fact.

Many pirates undoubtedly practiced some horrifying punishments, but most were taught by Britain's Royal Navy of the period that used floggings and the practice of dragging a miscreant crewman beneath a ship in a punishment known as keelhauling.

Unbelievable Barbarity

The pirate Blackbeard, also known as Edward Teach, is reputed to have cut the lips from a pirate raid victim, cooked them, and forced the man to eat them under threat of death. The grisly nature of the story seems designed to frighten and disgust. As it turns out, similar stories have circulated about other pirates, making one wonder whether the stories were embellished by storytellers or by the pirates themselves to inflate their reputations for cruelty. This lip-smacking tale about Blackbeard has never been substantiated.

Although Jean Lafitte is sometimes credited with killing every person he and his crews robbed, Lafitte was actually something of a chief operating officer over a piratical enterprise that commanded more than a dozen ships and 1,000 men. When Martha Martin and her husband's boat sank in a storm near Louisiana's coast in 1814, Lafitte ordered one of his own ships to take the couple home. Lafitte even gave one of his own cloaks to Martin's husband to wear in the cold January weather, an occurrence recounted by Mrs. Martin in her diary. This true account portrays odd behavior for an alleged homicidal maniac.

Were Blackbeard and Lafitte psychotic killers or canny businessmen who knew that a vicious reputation was worth a hundred cannon when terrorizing merchant ships? The full truth, which may be lost to history, perhaps lies somewhere in between.

Dastardly Deeds

For every myth of pirate misbehavior, there are probably a dozen true stories of piratical cruelty. If you're going to be an armed robber, then you have to be willing to use deadly force, and the pirates did so. During a 1719 pirate raid upon Captain William Snelgrave's ship off Africa's coast, the pirates were enraged that Snelgrave had ordered his men to fire upon the boarders. When a pirate pressed his pistol into Snelgrave's chest and pulled the trigger, Snelgrave knocked the gun away as it fired. Though slightly wounded, Snelgrave was then pistol-whipped.

During his three weeks as a prisoner, Snelgrave also observed another captured merchant captain hoisted up and down by a rope tied around his neck. A pirate captain was angry with the merchant ship's officer and had decided to torture him. Incredibly, when Snelgrave was released, the very pirates who almost murdered him gave him a ship to replace the one they seized.

Loose Lips

Among the confirmed horrors perpetrated by pirates was the vicious behavior toward a ship's captain taken by pirate Dirk Chivers in the Red Sea in 1695. Because the captive officer complained so bitterly about being attacked by the pirates, Chivers ordered the man's lips sewn up. The tortured man was later marooned off Aden in southern Arabia to die.

Torture as Entertainment

In 1719 a ship under the command of Captain Skinner was attacked and seized by a pirate ship under the command of Edward England. Although England had no quarrel with Skinner, one of England's pirates had. This gave the pirates an excuse to torment Skinner for the fun of it. Skinner was bound to the mast and pelted with broken bottles by pirates. Gashed and bleeding, Skinner was eventually shot in the head, and his body dumped overboard.

Punishing the Pirates

Traditionally, piracy has been a crime punishable by death. In 1573, the German pirate Klein Henszlein and his 33 men were beheaded in a public execution. German officials then dragged out the bodies of the pirates killed while fighting authorities and chopped off their heads also. British authorities were still beheading pirates in the early part of the twentieth century.

Words To Treasure

A **gibbet** is an iron cage used in England to contain the body of an executed criminal that is then suspended in public view.

Perhaps the most horrific public spectacle in terms of punishment for the crime of piracy could be seen in merry olde England, where condemned pirates were hanged and their bodies displayed for months in a suspended cage known as a *gibbet*. To ensure the spectacle lasted as long as possible, authorities would coat the bodies in tar so they would not decompose too quickly. The infamous pirate Captain William Kidd, convicted not for killing innocents but one of his own men, was displayed in this way following his execution on May 23, 1701.

Piracy's Waning Days

Piracy had become a substantial problem by the 1720s with 2,000 pirates raiding ships in the Atlantic. Officials decided to tackle the problem from several directions. Pardons were granted pirates who agreed to halt their raids and sizable rewards were offered for the capture or death of pirates. In addition, the British Royal Navy launched naval expeditions against Caribbean and Atlantic pirates. As a result, pirate attacks dropped from 40 to 50 attacks on merchant shipping in 1718 to a half-dozen attacks in 1726.

The last recorded pirate attack in the open Atlantic occurred September 20, 1832, when an American brig named *Mexican* was attacked and seized by the *Panda*, a pirate schooner commanded by Don Pedro Gilbert. The *Mexican*'s crew was locked below decks, and Gilbert, proclaiming that "dead cats don't mew," ordered the crew burned alive with the ship. The *Mexican*'s crew escaped during the fire as Gilbert's crew sailed away. The crew extinguished the blaze and spent six weeks sailing the damaged ship back to port.

Gilbert was captured by the British in Africa in 1834 and was returned to the United States where he was executed for his piracy. During Gilbert's trial, *Mexican* crewman and prosecution witness Thomas Fuller struck Gilbert in court for the cruel way he treated Fuller and his shipmates.

Shiver Me Timbers

The brig *Mexican* was an ironic final victim of piracy in the Atlantic. Although plundered silver carried from the New World to Spain by treasure galleons did much to spark piracy in the Caribbean and Atlantic following Hernán Cortés's 1521 conquest of Mexico, the *Mexican* was carrying silver to South America. Her cargo of $20,000 in silver was bound for Rio de Janeiro, Brazil, from Salem, Massachusetts.

The Least You Need to Know

➤ The Hollywood depiction of pirates as friendly adventurers, as portrayed by the likes of Errol Flynn, is something less than accurate and also highly sanitized since real pirates were murderous criminals.

➤ Social conditions in Europe, including war, harsh laws, and unemployment, were among the reasons that many decided to choose a life of crime upon the sea rather than to remain at home.

➤ Although considered something from the past, piracy still exists, and in areas of Asia is actually thriving with pirates stealing and selling entire ships after sometimes killing their crews.

➤ Piracy goes back at least 4,000 years, according to recovered historical texts from what is now Iraq.

➤ European governments actually encouraged piracy for centuries by issuing "letters of marque," making private ships and crews "privateers" by giving them the right to seize enemy ships during wartime.

➤ The proliferation of Spanish ships carrying treasure from Spain's New World along with goods made the Caribbean something of a pirate hangout for nearly three centuries until the early nineteenth century.

Sunken Treasure: Spain's Accidental Gift

When you think of sunken treasure, you probably conjure an image of a smashed Spanish galleon with its spilled treasures glinting seductively from the seabed. Sure, there are other types of "treasure" ships in other places, but no fleet of sunken ships can rival the monetary value, the mystique, and the quantity of Spanish wrecks littering what was once known as the Spanish Main.

The Spanish treasure fleet was a constant waterborne stream of silver and gold that traveled from the Americas to Spain for nearly 300 years. Though Spain was enriched with this treasure, bad weather and accidents meant that much of it would be bequeathed to King Neptune and—eventually—to today's treasure hunters.

The accidental discovery of the New World was one of the most important events in history. Its ruthless conquest and enslavement was fueled by Spain's belief in myths about New World treasures—tall tales that eventually came partially true. Spanish greed was rewarded beyond the wildest dreams of any Renaissance tax collector, but the story of New World treasure is also one of accidental discovery, brutality, and cultural annihilation.

Step into the past and see how these complex events unfolded to leave a legacy of both treasure and history beneath the waters of the Spanish Main.

Columbus: The Man with the Plan

A seasoned seaman and navigator born in Genoa around 1451, Christopher Columbus became driven by legendary tales of voyages into the then-mysterious western Atlantic. His goal was to sail west and perhaps find a new route to the Orient. Though he convinced himself he had reached the Indies, Columbus had instead done something even more amazing—he "discovered" an entirely new continent.

Though historians have satisfied themselves that Columbus was not the first European to truly discover the Americas, his voyages resulted in the widespread colonization and exploitation of the New World.

The Salesman

Just as money makes the world go around, it also takes money to go around the world. Knowing this, Columbus embarked on a campaign to get Portugal to finance his discovery of a route to the Indies across the Atlantic.

Unfortunately, the Portuguese showed Columbus the door, but the unstoppable Columbus moved his act to nearby Spain. There, in 1485, the world's most persistent fund-raiser began a seven-year campaign to coax the King of Spain to bankroll the discovery of a shortcut to the Indies. Columbus believed (correctly) that the world was round but determined (incorrectly) that Asia was roughly 3,000 miles to the west.

Words To Treasure

Dead reckoning is one of the earliest forms of navigation and combines the use of a magnetic compass (invented around 1183), measurements of the ship's speed, and timekeeping devices. It was crude but effective, since Columbus made it to the New World and back four times. Celestial navigation simply means using the position of the stars (celestial bodies) for determining one's location. Stars have a position above the horizon at certain times. Determining that position tells the navigator his location with a high degree of accuracy.

Same Pitch, Different Country

For seven years the navigator lobbied Spanish officials for financing, but his efforts seemed be going nowhere. A frustrated Columbus was on the verge of carrying his plan to the French, thinking they might be enlightened enough to pay him some mind as well as some cash. At the last moment, Queen Isabella II convinced her husband King Ferdinand to bankroll the project.

Goodbye, Columbus

With the *Niña*, *Pinta*, and *Santa Maria*, Columbus set sail on August 3, 1492, across the uncharted emptiness of the Atlantic. As if crossing the Atlantic in relatively small boats with nervous crews wasn't bad enough, Columbus had fewer navigational aids than today's average hiker. Without any modern marvels such as a Global Positioning System or even complete maps, Columbus was on his own.

Using *dead reckoning,* one of the earliest forms of navigation, Columbus was able to cross the Atlantic, which was actually easier in a way than navigating the uncharted reefs and shoals surrounding any lands he would approach.

Asia! (Give or Take 10,000 Miles)

In Columbus's mind, the sight of land on October 12, 1492, told him he had accomplished his dream of circling the earth, using a western route to Asia. Actually, Columbus had just discovered a Bahamian Island he would name San Salvador. Encountering friendly natives, Columbus christened them "Indians," believing he'd arrived in India. Never mind that the island already had a name and that the so-called Indians had never heard of India; the famous explorer had arrived.

Know The Ropes

The *Niña* and the *Pinta* were **caravels,** and Columbus's flagship, the *Santa Maria,* was a **nao,** a cargo-type vessel that was larger and less nimble than the other two ships. The caravel used triangular sails called lateens like the Arab ships that served as its model, while the nao used several square sails.

The New World's Newest Shipwreck

Soon after his arrival on San Salvador, Columbus discovered a large island he named La Isla Española, now known as the island containing both Haiti and the Dominican Republic, where his flagship *Santa Maria* was wrecked on a coral reef on Christmas Eve, 1492. It was the first of nine ships Columbus would lose during his New World expeditions and the first of hundreds to be lost by Spain in treacherous Caribbean waters during the next three centuries.

Columbus sailed around the New World a bit longer, planting flags and greeting the Indians before gathering up a tiny amount of gold and some really odd leaves that the Indians seemed totally in love with. Curious about the leaves, the clueless Columbus decided to take some back to Spain. Once the mystery of the tobacco leaves was unraveled, Europe would soon understand the joy of a nicotine buzz and the downside of its effects on their health.

A Few More Pesos, Please

When Columbus pulled back into Spain, Isabella and Ferdinand agreed to finance another expedition, although they were a bit disappointed that he had not managed to return with more gold. Despite their disappointment and even though Columbus's claims of finding Asia didn't seem to add up, the royal couple decided Columbus's idea had been a good gamble.

Spain wanted to do some serious colonizing and treasure hunting, so, for his second expedition, Columbus was given a hefty fleet that included 17 ships and 1,500 men.

Two Strikes and You're Out

Columbus considered himself an explorer first and a conqueror second or third, but Spain wanted treasure and wanted it fast. After returning from his second voyage without finding the tons of treasure legend had placed in the New World, Columbus had a tough time getting anyone to back a third try.

It didn't look like Columbus would return to the New World at all until the news arrived that the Portuguese explorer Vasco Da Gama was headed for India and would be traveling along Africa's west coast. This news prompted Spain to once again back Columbus's attempt to find a faster way to Asia.

It was on this third trip that Columbus hit the big time (geographically) by discovering the mainland of South America, where he landed on August 1, 1498.

Chained but Unbowed

Owing to the twists and turns of Spanish power plays in the New World, Columbus had been stripped of his governorship over the island of Hispaniola. His successor was Francisco de Bobadilla, who sent Columbus back to Spain in irons. Columbus's low standing with the officials of Hispaniola would eventually turn him and two shiploads of men into castaways for nearly a year!

Columbus talked his way out of trouble and into a fourth trip to the New World, only to be denied the use of Santo Domingo's ports by then-governor Nicolás de Ovando, another political rival. Unable to repair his ships that had been badly damaged by shipworms, he sailed on to discover Central America.

The leaking ships were finally abandoned in Jamaica, where Columbus and his crew were marooned for a year because Ovando delayed sending help to his political enemy. Columbus was rescued and returned to Spain in 1504.

Shiver Me Timbers

Being marooned is bad enough but having an official intentionally delay your rescue for a year is pretty vindictive. Columbus, who was considered a political rival to the Hispaniola governor Nicolás de Ovando, found himself stranded in Jamaica for a year after his worm-eaten ships would sail no farther. Ovando, who knew of Columbus' fate, delayed the explorer's rescue for a year. Before he became marooned, Columbus tried to dock his fleet at Hispaniola for repairs but was denied entry to Santo Domingo harbor by Ovando.

Ignored, Revered, and Reviled

By the early 1500s, the court was granting others permission to explore in the New World despite King Ferdinand's claim that Columbus would be the only one granted the right to do so. Columbus died on May 20, 1506, while still fighting to prove that he had reached Asia.

Unfortunately, the explorer's reputation has again fallen on hard times. In 1992, Canada decided not to celebrate the 500th anniversary of Columbus's feat. In that same year, protests were staged around the world demanding that Columbus's hero status be revoked. His recent fall from grace has occurred because critics say his discovery of the New World prompted genocide and slavery against the original cultures of the Americas.

In reality, however, although Columbus did find the New World and opened the door to Spanish conquest, he didn't establish the policies of subjugation toward the Indians. That would be left to the *conquistadors* and then to the entrepreneurs. While Columbus wasn't exactly a defender of the Indians, and perhaps not the first European to sail to the Americas, he's generally regarded as the "discoverer" of the New World.

I guess we will always wonder whether Columbus would have bothered to cross the Atlantic had he known he would be cast as a villain in the age of political correctness.

Words To Treasure

Conquistadors were fearsome adventurers who carried Catholicism to the New World along with a ruthless brand of treasure hunting.

Golden Dreams

Since arriving in the New World, Spanish conquistadors had been aware of Indian legends about El Dorado, a fabled city of gold. Though no such fabled city was ever found, it would nonetheless take hundreds of years for the legend to die.

When the mysterious Spaniard Juan Martinez emerged in 1586 after living 10 years with the Indians of present-day Guyana in South America, he blew more life into the legend by claiming he saw a "city of gold." True or not, he'd said the operative word: gold! Conquistadors spent years combing North and South America for the treasure that never was—the golden city of El Dorado.

Disappointed that gold and silver were not being conveyed by the ton from the New World, Spain encouraged explorers to investigate the Americas and locate what wealth they could. Though gold

Don't Go Overboard!

The peoples of the Americas were often friendly and helpful, but when confronted with aggression and brutality, they fought tenaciously. Not anticipating a friendly reception, Cortés equipped his men with shirts padded against edged weapons, but they were probably ineffective against the dart-firing blowguns carried by some Indians.

and silver and other treasures had been found, the amounts were relatively small. The real treasure, believed the conquistadors, was on the unconquered American mainland in the Aztec Empire now known as Mexico.

Cracking the Treasure Chest: Mexico's Conquest

The conqueror of Mexico was born the same year Columbus began dunning the Spanish monarchy for backing. By 1519, Hernán Cortés would begin the process of turning the Americas into Spain's cash cow in one of the most infamous and clever expeditions in military history.

Cortés, like every other greedy Spaniard blown to the New World by the wind of rumored riches, believed that conquering Mexico was the path to wealth and power. It was widely believed the country was impregnated with fabulous riches of gold and gems.

Know Your Enemy

Before launching his expedition into Mexico, Cortés was able to learn of the internal political drama in Mexico's interior where Montezuma II had alienated much of his population. Cortés learned that the former warrior and stern emperor had withdrawn into the complex religious rituals of Aztec society. The religious and superstitious Montezuma was also anticipating the return of the mythical, fair-haired Aztec god Quetzalcoatl.

Know The Ropes

Quetzalcoatl was to the Aztecs what Jesus of Nazareth was to the Christians, a man converted into a deity who was to someday return to earth.

Cortés seized upon Montezuma's belief and deceitfully held himself out as the deity. Hoodwinked both by Cortés and his own beliefs, Montezuma ignored the advice of his royal advisors and did not destroy Cortés at the water's edge in Cozumel. Had Montezuma not made this fateful mistake, the Aztec Empire might have been saved, if only temporarily.

No Exit

Cortés's clever and ruthless campaign was bringing him closer to personal gain and bringing Spain closer to dreamed-of riches. Aligning himself with the Tlaxcalan tribe, who were known to hate the Aztecs, Cortés set about slaughtering 3,000 Aztecs in the village of Cholula, a two-hour ride southeast of Mexico City. By now, Cortés is said to have ordered his three ships burned, giving his men only two choices: victory or death.

The Stalls of Montezuma

After the mass killing at Cholula, Cortés's Spanish-Indian force marched on to the capital city of Tenochtitlan in November 1519. Surprisingly, Montezuma seemed unfazed by the brutality of "Quetzalcoatl," whom he believed Cortés to be. The Aztec emperor welcomed the Spaniard and then made the biggest mistake of all.

Montezuma offered the conquistador a fabulous gift of gold and jewels—the very thing the Spaniard wanted. Cortés's greed was ignited by the gift, and he decided that taking Montezuma hostage would provide a shortcut to Aztec wealth. The Spaniard demanded and received a ransom of treasure for the life of Montezuma. This event was only the beginning of the plunder of the New World—the Spanish treasure fleets would not be far behind.

Aztec emperor Montezuma greets Spanish conquistador Hernán Cortés in an unsuccessful attempt to persuade the conqueror to leave his nation. (Courtesy ARTTODAY.COM)

Cortés Makes a Bloody Comeback

A revolt by the Aztecs, who were sick of Montezuma's hesitancy to stand up to Cortés, resulted in the death of the emperor either at the hands of stone-throwing Aztecs or his Spanish captors. (Things were a bit confused at the time.) Cortés was driven out with heavy casualties but returned to finish the job of subduing Mexico.

The indefatigable Cortés again waged war against the Aztecs, and by May 1521 he had defeated every corner of the Aztec Empire except for the capital city itself. Finally, on August 13, 1521, Cortés took the city, leaving as many as 40,000 Aztecs dead from combat and an epidemic of *totomonaliztli,* or "smallpox." However, historians say the battle was won more by European-carried illness than by Spanish firepower or tactics.

The rest of Latin America fell like dominoes to the conquistadors, and the treasure stampede was on.

Words To Treasure

Smallpox, carried to the New World by Europeans, was a virus new to the Native Americans, who died from the disease in great numbers. The Aztec word for smallpox was **totomonaliztli,** meaning "blisters."

Spain's Treasure Addiction

Money was always a problem for the government of Spain, which seemed perpetually engaged in expensive wars. Even Spain's European territories, though nominally loyal, were not always so when it came time to pay taxes to the central government. Spain's economic policies were self-defeating, and the government did little to create a viable economy.

Said Count Gaspar de Guzman Olivares, a minister under King Philip IV, of the problem: "… nobody who has any property, nor any man of influence in the place he lives, pays taxes, and when I say nobody, I mean nobody."

Something had to give, and it was going to be the people and the lands of the New World.

Words To Treasure

The term **Spanish Main** stood for the coastal areas of New World but came to also mean the sea routes taken by Spanish treasure fleets when traveling between ports in the Caribbean, the Gulf of Mexico, and South America. **Flotas**, or fleets, were organized by Spain to carry goods to the Americas for sale to colonists and to return with products and treasure, most of which was provided by the slave labor of Indians. Eventually, the highly organized flotas had as many as 100 ships.

A Not-So-Reliable Source of Income

Although the flow of silver and other riches from the New World seemed endless, the amount of treasure coming from the Americas could fluctuate wildly for a variety of reasons. Between 1580 and 1584, an estimated 48 million pesos' worth of treasure sailed from the Americas to Spain. From 1645 to 1648, only 36 million pesos in treasure made its way to Spain. At other times, the treasure fleet brought staggering amounts of riches, with 81.8 million in pesos arriving between 1690 and 1694.

During the 1660s, a series of bankruptcies overwhelmed the debt-ridden Spanish government. The dependence on American treasure took the place of fixing deep-rooted economic problems that would have made Spain stronger. In reality, agricultural goods and other New World products were four times as valuable as the treasure mined with slave labor.

All That Glitters Is Not Gold

Conquistadors and explorers dreamed of finding fabled cities of gold in the New World, but what they eventually discovered was a continent abundant with more silver than gold. While this was not bad news, the gold and silver for the most part was not there for the taking. It had to be mined. Some estimates place the amount of silver loaded aboard the treasure fleets to be 10 times greater than the amount of gold carried to Spain.

Bloodstained Riches

The Indian peoples were the obvious source of labor for New World enterprises. As fate would have it, their populations began to decline drastically at the very moment their labor was most needed. The causes of the population decline were numerous, though the most lethal may have been accidental. Lacking immunity from European diseases such as smallpox, the Indians were decimated by illness brought by European explorers.

Shiver Me Timbers

Beset by disease and exploitation, the Indians may have had their own revenge: A mere four months after Columbus's return to Spain in 1494, the first outbreak of syphilis ravaged Europe. The illness was almost as lethal to Europeans as smallpox was to the Indians. The death rate from syphilis during its initial 40 years in Europe ranged from 20 to 40 percent.

Spanish warfare against the Indians and the general calamity of cultural disruption also contributed to the population drop. Short of labor, the Spanish introduced African slaves into the New World. A legalized slavery program known as ecomienda was established under which American Indians were literally "given" to plantation and silver mine owners who promised to convert them to Catholicism. Harsh working conditions for those under the ecomienda system only exacerbated the Indian mortality rate. As many as 40 percent of such slaves died under Spanish rule.

The Spanish Treasure Fleet

The treasure fleet, or *flota,* served a twofold purpose for the Spanish government. Those living in the New World were proscribed from purchasing anything not delivered by an official Spanish flota. The returning ships were then loaded with confiscated indigenous treasures, products of the Americas, or silver and gold mined by Indian slaves for their Spanish masters.

The Spanish Main

The route of the Spanish treasure fleet originally began at the port city of Seville but later started at the port of Cadiz as warships and merchant ships

Know The Ropes

Spanish fleets included a variety of ships, from the **galleons** that were the warships to the **naos** that were essentially cargo ships. **Refuerzos** were the supply ships needed on the long voyages, while **pataches** were nimble reconnaissance vessels. A single treasure fleet would divide into two fleets upon its arrival in the Americas with the **Nueva Espana** (New Spain) Fleet going to drop off goods and pick up treasure in Mexico while the **Tierra Firme** (Mainland) Fleet would be doing the same at South American ports.

gathered to convoy across the Atlantic to the New World. The *Spanish Main* was actually made up of the several locations that were part of the routes and ports of call of the ships.

The Deadliest Enemy

Despite the plethora of pirates along the Spanish Main, the biggest threat that usually faced the treasure fleet was bad weather, in particular the savage hurricane season that lasted from June to November. Ships caught in such storms could be hurled miles off course to be sunk outright or smashed against coral reefs.

The most spectacular caches of sunken treasure were delivered to Florida's coastal waters by vicious hurricanes. The *Atocha,* whose astounding treasure was reclaimed by Mel Fisher, was one such ship that fell victim to a powerful storm. Hundreds of ships, many with Spanish treasure, still litter the Caribbean and the Gulf of Mexico. Almost all were victims of hurricanes that constantly smash through the region.

The Floating Highway's Dead End

The treasure fleet system reached its apex between 1590 and 1600 when New World silver production was high and Spain's restrictive trade policies were still in force. For the next 100 years, the flotas began to shrink in size and importance, though Spain's dependence on New World treasure never abated.

The average size of the fleets went from 100 ships during the 1590s to half that number by 1610. An average of only 25 ships made up a treasure fleet by 1640. Privateer and pirate attacks made the voyage increasingly treacherous as Spain's navy declined. By 1778, Spain finally decided to allow its colonies to trade freely with any nation. This sealed the fate of the constrictive and counterproductive system controlled by the government's Casa de Contratación (House of Trade). Since 1503, this system specified which merchants could trade with the New World colonies and forbade the colonies from trading outside the system. The Spanish monarchy (of course) had taken a piece of the action.

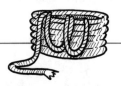

Know The Ropes

Hurricanes and cyclones generate powerful winds and rough seas. They originate off Africa's western coast and travel toward the Caribbean or the eastern seaboard of the United States. They have killed untold numbers of people in the Caribbean and Gulf of Mexico. Even modern mariners don't take them lightly.

The Least You Need to Know

➤ Christopher Columbus convinced himself that he had discovered a portion of the Far East when, in fact, he had discovered the Americas.

➤ The first New World European settlement was wiped out by Indians on Hispaniola when the Spaniards left behind tried to exploit their new neighbors.

➤ The *Santa Maria* was the first of nine ships that Columbus would wreck during his four voyages to the New World.

➤ Conquistador Hernán Cortés pretended to be the Aztec god Quetzalcoatl to make the Aztec emperor afraid to oppose the Spaniard's conquest of the New World.

➤ The native peoples encountered by early explorers like Columbus were usually friendly but reacted negatively when treated cruelly by arrogant European explorers.

➤ Spain's economy was usually in shambles, and the government was consistently unable to collect its taxes, forcing it to depend heavily on riches from the Americas.

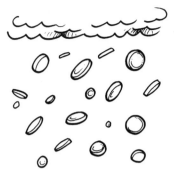

Chapter 28

Pennies from Heaven

In This Chapter

➤ A cool (and wet) $100 billion

➤ Fidel wants his booty

➤ Expeditions beckon

➤ Treacherous investment waters

Can we all agree that treasure is anything of extreme value including precious metals, rare art objects, historic artifacts, and gems? Sure we can. Put all these treasures in a submerged shipwreck and you're now talking about the light that glimmers in the eye of every would-be millionaire dreaming of early retirement—sunken treasure!

However, if a ship is old enough (like thousands of years) or if it's a famous wreck like the *Titanic,* then just about anything recovered from the wreck will have value as a collector's item, even if it's something as common as coal or as banal as a plumbing fixture. Anything recovered from a shipwreck is a hot item these days, especially if it's from a famous shipwreck like the liner *Andréa Doria.*

Although a recovered deck chair is nice, treasure is treasure and all of us would prefer a sixteenth-century Spanish gold ingot instead of a commode off a fishing boat.

Now that we agree on what sunken treasure is and isn't, we can slip into the murky waters of the world of sunken treasure in an attempt to find out what is lying out of sight below, where it's located, and just how much there is. We'll also have a glimpse at how ordinary folks with a few spare dollars and a willingness to toss it into the sea can become treasure hunters.

The good thing about sunken treasure is that it inspires dreams, expeditions, the development of technology, and the investment of millions. The bad thing is that the prospect of sunken treasure also generates hype, tall tales, mythology, and outright lies. Separating fact from fiction is harder than finding a shipwreck by randomly dragging a grappling hook in the middle of the Atlantic.

So even though getting the full picture can be tough, let's at least try to figure out what is probably true about the amount of sunken treasure in the Americas. How much is there, and where are the shipwreck hot spots? There's still plenty of treasure lying around despite the efforts of the best professional treasure hunters in the world.

A Cool (and Wet) $100 Billion

A lot of ships that have been lost through the centuries were carrying valuable cargoes, but if you're interested in sunken treasure in the Western Hemisphere, you're talking about Spanish treasure ships. Some experts estimate that $100 billion in Spanish treasure is still lying along the Spanish Main that curled around the waters off Latin America and the Caribbean islands. Please remember, this amount is just an estimate because we'll never know for sure how much sunken treasure was really lost. Some say it's more, and some say less.

So much of the silver and gold stuff is lying about that an entire American subculture of treasure hunting has developed around this largesse. Participants include everyone from regular folks who become armchair buccaneers to those who actively hunt for lost ships and their treasures. Still others make a good living by conducting research for treasure-hunting operations, and yet another group produces high-technology equipment for treasure searches.

Virtually all the sunken treasure recovery operations have to raise money to finance their searches, meaning, of course, that mixed in with the adventurers, researchers, and remotely operated vehicle technicians are investors. In short, it's a business in which there is not only plenty to gain but lots to lose.

Researchers disagree on how many voyages Spanish ships sailed to and from the New World between the 1500s and the early 1800s, with some estimating as many as 13,000 trips. Consequently, these ships carried billions in precious metals and gems from the places that are now known as Mexico and Peru. It's also generally accepted that one half or one third of these ships—with some containing treasure—may have ended up as accidental underwater attractions around the Gulf of Mexico, the Caribbean, and along Florida's coast.

Know The Ropes

Because the stakes have gotten higher in the search for treasure, companies now hire expert researchers to study records worldwide to help them more accurately pinpoint the location of treasure. Simply going to a bay or a beach at random and looking for treasure isn't good enough. Precision means the difference between success and economic ruin in a treasure hunt.

The Treasure Funnel

Don't think that all the sunken treasure ships originated in the Americas. For hundreds of years, Spain was conducting trade with the Philippines. Much of this wealth, in the form of manufactured goods, also ended up in the Caribbean, as strange as that seems. The reason: geography. Portuguese, Dutch, and English ships coming from Asia had to make the incredibly dangerous voyage around southern Africa to travel between Europe and Asia prior to the construction of the Suez Canal in Egypt.

To avoid Cape of Good Hope—one of the world's most dangerous shipwreck grave-yards—Spanish ships would cross the Pacific to bring their cargo to Mexico's west coast. From there, the cargo would be carted overland to ships on Mexico's east coast where they were loaded aboard ships bound for Cuba. The ships would assemble at Cuba into a treasure fleet for the voyage across the Atlantic back to Spain. Just making it out of the Caribbean was tough enough. These ships had to survive razor-sharp coral reefs, devastating hurricanes, and pirates.

Shiver Me Timbers

Spanish ships headed toward Asia and the Philippines often carried silver coins from the New World with which to purchase trade goods such as silk and porcelain, but they did so at great risk. Vast stretches of ocean lay before these "Manila galleons" that departed from Mexico's west coast. The Pacific versions of Atlantic hurricanes known as typhoons wrecked many ships. Storms caught and separately sank two Manila galleons in 1600 and 1603. Each ship carried 1.5 million silver pieces of eight at the time of its loss. At $250 a coin at today's collector's prices, the booty would be worth $750 million—if it were located and salvaged.

Most Spanish Ships Unfound

Readers of popular newspapers and magazines might gain the impression that Spanish treasure ships are being found at a steady clip, but the truth is that many remain lost despite the best efforts of skilled treasure hunters. Chance discovery of rich treasure ships in the Gulf of Mexico, such as the accidental snagging of the long-lost *Cazador* by a fishing boat crew in 1993, makes this obvious.

Perpetual Treasure Troves

Although Spain tried to salvage many ships soon after they sank (when their locations were known), these efforts were usually only partially successful. Many treasure hunters are still recovering treasure from wrecks that have been picked over for hundreds of years.

A fine example of this phenomenon is the wrecked Spanish Treasure Fleet of 1715. Though Spanish officials immediately located and salvaged many of its sunken ships off what is now Florida's Vero Beach, treasure remains beneath the waters. Despite a massive Spanish recovery effort that lasted from 1715 until 1720, pirates and British privateers plundered the wrecks for years when the Spaniards weren't around. More years of official salvage went on until the wrecks were forgotten.

By the 1950s, treasure hunter Kip Wagner was following a path of silver from the beach near his home to one of the 1715 treasure ships offshore. By the 1960s, Wagner was using modern scuba equipment and other technology to bring up even more silver. He claimed to be a millionaire by the mid-1960s. Despite 250 years of salvage efforts, silver and gold continue to be found near the wrecks today.

A Billion Here, a Billion There

Just what is the estimated value of treasure lounging beneath the waters of the old Spanish Main? A figure frequently bandied about is $100 billion. Of course, this amount is often based not on the actual value of the precious metals and gems aboard, but on the higher value of gemstones, coins, and ingots as rare artifacts.

Know The Ropes

Pieces of eight were also referred to as pesos and represented the value of eight Spanish reales, a coin of lesser denomination. These coins were such a successful form of currency that they became used around the world between the sixteenth and eighteenth centuries. Chinese favored the piece-of-eight coins over their own unstable paper currency, and even Americans continued to use the coins into the nineteenth century.

A brand-new, commemorative gold coin would be worth far less than a Spanish doubloon three centuries older, even if both contained the same amount of gold. If recovered, the gold bars believed to be in a World War II Japanese submarine (18,000 feet beneath the Atlantic) will probably be sold as valuable artifacts and not simply melted down.

Take the relatively common Spanish piece of eight and consider its actual value as opposed to what people are paying for these coins today. An ounce of silver during the late 1990s might go for $4.45 on the world market. A Spanish piece of eight containing an ounce of 93 percent pure silver can sell from $265 to $1,500—that's up to 400 times the original face value of the coin. Public demand has made such coins far more valuable than the currency they represent. Obviously, no treasure hunter is going to melt down the silver and gold recovered from a 300-year-old wreck and sell it based on weight alone.

Fidel Wants His Booty

Cuba, one of the last surviving communist nations, has decided it wants to get into the sunken-treasure business. The treasure ships sunk off its shores contain a staggering volume of wealth that's too hard to ignore right now. Socialism hasn't been very lucrative for flat-broke Cuba, and Spain's plunder of the New World could be the way Castro repays some of the billions owed to Russia and other international creditors.

After years of refusing to plunder the treasures in his country's waters, Fidel faced the hard truth. Owing billions while treasures basked beneath the 750-mile-long communist kingdom's warm waters, Castro had only one choice: Hire a treasure hunter!

The main reason Cuba's sunken treasures have remained intact is timing. Castro seized control of the island nation in 1959, just about the time scuba diving and other effective treasure-hunting and recovery technology entered the scene. Castro was too busy securing his hold on the island and dodging CIA assassination attempts to worry about centuries-old Spanish treasure. As a result, virtually no effort was placed into recovering the hundreds of Spanish treasure ships believed wrecked around Cuba's hundreds of miles of coastline. Now, however, Fidel wants his booty!

Don't Go Overboard!

Ocean explorer Jacques-Yves Cousteau wanted to explore the wrecks in Matanzas Bay in the mid–1980s and was initially given permission to do so. However, Fidel Castro later withdrew the invitation. This instance provides a good lesson for anyone attempting to gain approval for a treasure expedition or an investor in the same, since permission can be withdrawn as easily as it is given by an unpredictable dictator!

Cuba's Gold Coast

Why so many wrecks around Cuba? Havana was the staging area for Spanish treasure ships heading for the New World. Virtually all ships sailed to and from Cuba loaded with silver, gold, and gems. And, of course, any time you have a large amount of maritime traffic, you invariably have a large number of shipwrecks. These wrecks piled up near Cuba and its islands at an amazing rate to become the savings account for Castro's flagging socialist experiment.

Fidel, America's most implacable Cold War foe, may also be the owner of the richest treasure trove in the Americas. The treasure available for recovery could be in the millions, if not the billions.

Castro's Treasure Hunter

Florida treasure hunter Mel Fisher once said he was approached by representatives of Cuba's bearded dictator about locating the island's sunken treasures. Fisher, who was no stranger to controversy, decided this was one hassle he didn't need. The United States has long imposed an economic embargo against Cuba, or more specifically, against Fidel.

However, Canada has not had such rancorous relations with Castro, and Fidel selected Canadian treasure hunter and professional diver Glenn Costello, head of Terrawest Industries. Costello has listed his company on the Vancouver Stock Exchange and is raising money to help him complete his treasure-hunting project that could last 10 years—even though his 1995 contract is only for five years.

Pirate Legacy

The treasure being sought by Costello was contained aboard 11 treasure ships pounced by a fleet of Dutch ships led by freebooter Admiral Piet Heyn. At the time of the ambush, Heyn's piracy was made legal with a letter of marque issued by the Dutch government, making him a Dutch navy representative. Heyn, who had served as a galley slave aboard a Spanish ship for four years, considered the attack sweet vengeance. The Spanish, believing Heyn had returned to Europe, sailed into his naval trap on September 8, 1628.

Unknown to Heyn, the commander of the fleet was Juan de Benavides y Bazan who commanded one of the galleys on which Heyn had been forced to serve. The incompetent and corrupt Benavides wasn't much of a seaman. Panicked by the sight of Heyn's fleet, Benavides ordered his own into Matanzas Bay where many ships were burned and treasure was thrown into the water to prevent capture.

Nevertheless, Heyn's men took a great deal of this treasure, including 90 tons of silver and gold. Also seized were three million pieces of eight. When Castro came to power, he ruled that the remaining treasure was to be untouched, but Cuba's dire economic straits have altered his intentions.

Expeditions Beckon

Want to become a treasure hunter? Just sit down, turn on your computer, and sign on to the Internet. Even though you don't know a galleon from a magnetometer, a single e-mail message and the transfer of your hard-earned money to a professional treasure-hunting expedition could make you a treasure hunter.

Recovery consortiums are springing up like coral growth on sunken Spanish cannon. Many have Internet sites and glossy brochures. A few even have successful track records. However, the discovery and recovery of a fabulous treasure doesn't mean it's time to go to the bank with your earnings. Competing legal claims often follow a treasure discovery. Partners squabble, accounting for the treasure is sometimes problematic, and the government can step in for a last-minute cut. Payday is often far, far away for treasure hunters even when they're holding the recovered gold in their hands.

Who runs these treasure-hunting operations? Well, sometimes they're treasure hunters like the late Mel Fisher, whose own life was a case study of the term "feast or famine." At other times they're commercial divers and salvors. Some are rock-solid entrepreneurs, and a few are scientists and engineers like Tommy Thompson of the Columbus-America Discovery Group that discovered the SS *Central America*'s gold.

A Sure Thing

There are other options for the budding treasure hunter that might provide a bit more than simply treasure or an annual report of success or failure for your investment. Treasure travel has become a very hot commodity. You can even don scuba equipment and go treasure hunting on a shipwreck site with a guide. You may not find a thing, but at least you'll have a nice vacation.

Treacherous Investment Waters

Ready to invest in a treasure hunt and recovery operation? Perhaps you shouldn't count your doubloons before they splash to the surface. There are some things to consider.

Landlubbers usually have no idea how expensive it is to conduct business on the seas. It literally takes a boatload of money to conduct maritime treasure-hunting operations. Fuel is bought by the hundreds of gallons, and divers require equipment and pay. Sometimes ships must be purchased or leased for months on end. Deep-sea wrecks may require specialized, remotely operated vehicles and advanced detection equipment like side-scan sonar that can run into the hundreds of thousands of dollars.

As George Tulloch—the organizer of RMS Titanic, Inc., which is the salvor-in-possession of the *Titanic*'s wreck—has often pointed out, expenses related to shipwreck recovery are counted by the minute and not the hour.

The Long (If Ever) Haul

And don't forget that it might take weeks, months, or even years to finally track down the mother lode of a sunken ship's treasure hiding in the crevices of coral reefs or covered by sand. And all the while, the meter will be running on the previously mentioned expenses.

Most important, bear in mind that the best equipped and most expert search may in fact find absolutely nothing but a spare tire. The research, the equipment, the ability of the divers, and the search methods must all work perfectly to achieve success. Even though the precise area of a shipwreck is found, a diver might not recognize that the large lump of coral contains a dozen gold coins. A lot can go wrong.

On the other hand, if the location search is faulty, the world's most careful diver might spend months digging through silt using sand-blowing mailboxes in an area where no ship ever existed. If treasure hunting were easy, then anyone could be a treasure hunter! There are far safer and surer investments than treasure hunting, but few are as much fun.

Deep Water and Deep Pockets

It's never been cheap to be a treasure hunter searching for sunken ships, but it's getting more expensive as the shallow, easy-to-find wrecks are snapped up. The remaining treasure ships are deeper, better hidden by marine growth, or worst of all, lost without the slightest clue as to their general location. As a rule, shallow-water shipwrecks are easier and cheaper to find and recover. Deep-water wrecks are far more expensive to pursue, though some recent expeditions have provided sizeable returns.

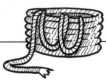

Know The Ropes

Legitimate treasure finders know they must be as frank as possible about the fiscal pitfalls of locating and recovering treasure because a lack of realism can poison the financial well. Disappointed investors can file law-suits, withdraw funds, and scare away potential backers. Florida's Odyssey Marine Exploration's up-front warning to investors is half a page long. The leader of any legitimate expedition wants only the most realistic and stalwart investors he or she can find. And the treasure hunt-ers must reciprocate with professional behavior.

Treasure-Hunting Risks

The Tampa, Florida, firm Odyssey Marine Exploration agrees with this assessment and is touting recovery of deep-ocean treasure ships. However, so much money is required for deep-sea operations that Odyssey provides a lengthy disclaimer warning potential investors of the perils of investing in treasure-hunting ventures.

High Tech: Low Depths

Engineer Tommy Thompson, who long dreamed of salvaging riches from the sea, decided in the early 1980s to become a treasure hunter, but he realized that shallow wrecks were becoming too scarce and their booty inadequate to justify an expedition. Deep-water treasure ships, untouched due to the difficulty in reaching them, seemed to offer the right return.

Thompson set his sights on the steamship SS *Central America* that contained an estimated billion-dollar gold cargo. It sat unmolested beneath 8,000 feet of Atlantic water. Thompson found his ship but only after raising $12.7 million from 160 limited partners. The search went on for five years as incorrect locations were searched, doubts grew, and technology was perfected.

Another expensive deep-ocean search (costing $3.5 million) was one performed by Odyssey Marine Exploration in 1991. Not only did it utilize the robotic abilities of a remotely operated vehicle similar to the effort on the *Central America* expedition, but Odyssey also conducted a complete archaeological study of the ship and its artifacts. The 370-year-old Spanish ship was in 1,500 feet of water between Cuba and the Florida Keys. The depth of the wreck's location kept it undisturbed for nearly four centuries!

Legal Shoals

The efforts and the investment of Thompson's Columbus-America Discovery Group were capped with success in 1989, but a hurricane of lawsuits arrived soon after. No less than 39 insurance companies were seeking 15 percent of the hundreds of millions in gold recovered by the group. The companies claimed that they had insured portions of the SS *Central America*'s shipment.

The courts eventually granted the insurers 8 percent of only 15 percent of the gold aboard the *Central America,* while the Columbus-America Discovery Group was granted the remainder. The lesson is a hard one. Despite their gamble and their success, Columbus-America found itself in court for six years.

Lawsuits are frequent in treasure-hunting ventures. Sometimes workers steal recovered treasure, or partners begin to mistrust one another over the accounting done in a successful treasure search.

Even Thompson, the mastermind of what may have been a recovery of up to three tons of gold from the SS *Central America,* has been criticized by his partners for being secretive and for not allowing them a greater say in how the gold is to be sold.

Bottom Feeders

Although con men and scam artists inhabit every field of business, treasure hunting seems to carry the connotation of something extremely informal, if not downright shady and therefore untrustworthy. The new treasure hunters prefer to be called "commercial explorers" or "shipwreck researchers," but even the name change doesn't completely erase the possibly shady impression.

This game of semantics is based on the fact that no legitimate treasure-hunting operation wants to be lumped in with slipshod treasure hunters or fast-buck artists who are raising money instead of treasure.

The latter are similar to those who make a good living selling oil-exploration ventures. Sure, there's a well and a drilling crew and a lot of expenses, but often there's no oil. Everybody wins except the investors. The same can happen in the treasure business. Boats are leased, divers are paid, and searches are conducted, but the only treasure is the money raised from investors. Some treasure hunters selling partnerships have been known to simply disappear after the money has been raised.

Don't Go Overboard!

When the pitch by a treasure hunter seeking funds is as highly pressurized as an overfilled scuba tank, it might be time to back off and rethink the situation. Although they are financially risky, treasure-hunting operations can sometimes pay off. But if you're made to feel you have to sign on the dotted line that instant, you might want to recall that the Spanish treasure you seek has already been underwater for several centuries. Find someone who is willing to let you take your time.

Researching the Researcher

Approaching a treasure-hunting investment as a business prospect is probably the most important thing to do. You wouldn't put money into an aerospace company if you knew its president didn't know an airplane wing from a chicken wing. Why would you put money into a treasure hunter without checking out that person and his or her associates?

Go to the courthouse and ask a clerk to assist you in discovering whether any lawsuits have been filed against your prospective treasure hunters, their associates, or the company they represent. Anyone can do such checks, though lawyers and investigators often act as if the courthouse is their personal domain. Some Internet databases perform the same type of search for a fee. Find out the result of the litigation because its resolution may have vindicated the treasure hunter! We're not talking distrust here; we're talking caution.

Another way to confirm the sincerity of your treasure hunter (or shipwreck researcher) is to ascertain whether the individual has received permission from the state to conduct a recovery in state waters. Many states require recovery operations to obtain a permit to "work" a wreck site. Don't ask the treasure hunter. Instead, go to the state officials in charge of such permits and see whether the required paperwork has been obtained. And while you're at it, talk to people knowledgeable about treasure-recovery operations. Find out the buzz about the people or organization you're about to invest in.

The Least You Need to Know

➤ Ordinary items such as portholes and plumbing fixtures can command sizable sums when recovered from shipwrecks, but not nearly as much as actual treasure items such as gold or silver coins.

➤ Prior to the construction of the Suez Canal in Egypt, ships traveling from Asia to Europe had to navigate around Africa's dangerous southern cape.

➤ Some treasure ships lost along the Spanish Main contained Asian goods such as silk, porcelain, and artwork. These goods were transported from Asia to Mexico for overland transport to that country's east coast and shipment through the Caribbean back to Spain.

➤ Fidel Castro agreed in 1985 to allow underwater explorer and filmmaker Jacques-Yves Cousteau to dive upon the treasure-laden shipwrecks in Cuba's Matanzas Bay but later reneged on the promise and denied Cousteau permission to do so.

➤ Tommy Thompson, an Ohio native who masterminded the location and discovery of tons of gold from the SS *Central America* wreck that was lost in 1857, was a deep-ocean engineer before becoming a treasure hunter.

Notable Pirates

If pirates hadn't existed in history, writers would have had to invent them. They're far too fascinating, especially those black-hearted buccaneers that terrorized the Atlantic and the Caribbean between the sixteenth and nineteenth centuries. Fictional versions of these seagoing rogues would have undoubtedly been anemic compared to the real thing, since the reality of piracy is arguably stranger than fiction.

Pirates embodied terror, adventure, scorn for society, and a devotion to hedonism. And most important, they conducted their amazing and often vile exploits upon the sea whose environment adds the briny touch of mystique to any enterprise.

Although thousands of pirates have roved the seas looking for plunder and victims, the ones we remember the most are the pirate captains who led the expeditions and set the tone for their operations. Names like Blackbeard, Drake, and Lafitte are still household words in many places, although history now labels them as little more than criminals of the maritime variety.

Pirates like Jean Lafitte, whose life remains shrouded in mystery, seemed to come from nowhere and to then disappear in the same way. Lafitte's business acumen and his willingness to serve authority when it suited his purposes were not unusual traits for pirates.

These pirate captains were often shrewd enough to know the value of political connections. Lafitte's downfall was precipitated not so much by his piracy in itself, but by the challenge he posed to legitimate merchants competing against his open-air bazaar of stolen goods.

Many of these pirate captains were born to respectable families and pursued genteel and law-abiding careers before deciding that plunder and adventure were more to their liking. There were some, however, like Sir Henry Morgan and Sir Francis Drake, who were from humble backgrounds and managed to obtain knighthood because of their officially sanctioned piracy.

Shiver Me Timbers

Although pirates are often depicted as slovenly, vile, and poorly dressed, historians point out that pirates often festooned themselves in colorful clothing to which they added brilliantly dyed silk scarves tied about their necks and arms. Either the pirates were literally making a fashion statement (disposed as they were to revile the conventions of normal society) or they sought to make their appearance even more shocking to their victims whom they wanted to frighten into submission.

For the most part, pirate captains sought to capture ships and their cargo rather than sink them. They also raided cities like their piratical forebears, the Vikings, who terrorized the world from the Atlantic to the Mediterranean between 800 and 1100 A.D. Captain Henry Morgan raided city after city in the Caribbean basin and engaged in protracted land campaigns to do so. During his career, Morgan seized the Panamanian cities of Panama and Portobelo.

Although some were occasional patriots, the pirate's true goal was personal enrichment. They challenged merchant fleets and the navies of sovereign nations to pursue their plunder.

Other pirate captains—like Blackbeard, for example—had frightening reputations and were said to enhance their scary personae by any means at hand. Blackbeard, who commanded a pirate gang of hundreds, supposedly put burning cannon fuses in his hat during pirate attacks. Although a seemingly funny stunt, it may have had the desired effect on a merchant ship's crew. Besides being a robber in command of murderers, Blackbeard was apparently a showman whose antics probably cowed crews into instant surrender.

Let's get up on deck and meet some piratical CEOs who robbed their way across the seas as heroes and villains. Although some ended up swinging from a hangman's noose and others lived out their lives as heroes, all shared an appreciation of a fast ship and a fast buck.

The Queen's Own Pirate

Perhaps the most socially acceptable pirate to ever sail the seas, Sir Francis Drake is today viewed as a hero in his home nation of England and as a *pirata,* or pirate, to the Spanish whose ships and cities he plundered. Born around 1541 to a Protestant clergyman and his wife in the County of Devon, Drake went to sea at a young age. It is assumed that he was influenced by his seagoing uncle William Hawkins and his cousin John Hawkins who was nine years his senior. By age 18, Drake was at sea aboard a Hawkins family ship. At 20 he was in command of his own small vessel. And, by the way, the Hawkins clan had long been in the piracy game.

All in the Family

Piracy was never far from Drake's upbringing. The Hawkins clan had engaged in it for years as privateers with letters of marque issued by English officials. These letters allowed the seizure of Spanish or French ships, since England was usually at war with one or the other. It was during privateer raids to the Caribbean beginning in 1567 with his cousin John Hawkins that Drake first gained experience as a pirate.

Shiver Me Timbers

John Hawkins would become a legendary pirate sacking cities and seizing Spanish ships. Both he and Drake would eventually be knighted for their officially sanctioned piracy. A Spanish defeat of Hawkins at San Juan de Ulúa in Mexico's state of Veracruz in 1568 would galvanize Francis Drake into even more aggressive attacks against the Spanish. The defeat came on the heels of a brilliant ruse by Hawkins that allowed him to bluff his way into a harbor, past Spanish coastal gun batteries, where he forced the local governor to allow him to remain and refit his ships. The governor broke his pledge and attacked Hawkins's ships. Drake's ship made a getaway, but Hawkins had to fight his way out, leaving behind nearly 100 men. Hawkins's allegation of Drake's desertion was a lifelong sore spot between the two men.

A Pirate's Progress

Having learned valuable lessons during his previous New World pirate expeditions, Drake returned to the Caribbean in 1569 on the ships *Dragon* and *Swan* to plunder Spanish shipping. In 1572, Drake again raided Spain's shipping with the *Swan* and the *Pascha* and another ship commanded by James Raunse. During a ground assault on the Panamanian port town of Nombre de Dios, a wound temporarily incapacitated Drake and his attack failed. Raunse later abandoned the operation, and Drake was forced to move south along Panama's wild Atlantic Coast to establish a raiding base on the Gulf of San Blas. From this location, Drake conducted raids on Spanish shipping for nearly a year.

Global Pirate

In 1577, Drake performed his most famous feat by embarking on a voyage that would make him the first English ship's captain to circumnavigate the world (a feat accomplished by Portuguese mariner Ferdinand Magellan in 1521). However, Drake's expedition had to support itself financially, ensuring that piracy would be conducted along with discovery of new peoples and places. A fleet of five ships embarked on the voyage in December 1577.

During the first month of "exploration," Drake managed to capture three Spanish ships and then seized three Portuguese merchant vessels. All were stripped of their goods. Drake's fleet continued around the world, seizing ship after ship.

Words To Treasure

Nombre de Dios is a common name for towns in the Americas, and at least nine cities and towns in Florida and Latin America bear the title, which means "Name of God."

Drake returned to England on September 26, 1580, with an astounding accumulation of treasure seized from mostly Spanish ships during a very lucrative 33 months at sea. The treasure was estimated at two million pesos and included 23,000 pounds of silver and an unknown quantity of gold. The roughly 160 men of Drake's crew may have received as much as 40,000 English pounds' worth of booty as their share. Drake retained control of much of the remainder of the treasure, making him one of the richest men of the era.

Hero or Heel

While some pirates have been portrayed as far worse than they really were, it seems Drake was really a pretty nasty guy who was incorrectly presented as a stainless hero for centuries. Not only was Drake a pirate plain and simple, he was also known as a complete jerk among his contemporaries who found him contemptible for making false boasts about his abilities. His planning was poor, and he was such a penny pincher that his expeditions were seldom properly provisioned. Drake preferred to steal supplies whenever possible. It's also said that he was intolerably arrogant toward his men.

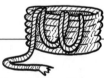

Know The Ropes

During Drake's time, a captain could not order the execution of any crew member without possessing authority from the king or queen of England. Drake never produced such a document, explaining why he depended on Queen Elizabeth to shield him from prosecution for the execution of Thomas Doughty.

Among the many dark chapters of Drake's supposedly heroic circumnavigation was his order to execute accused mutineer Thomas Doughty, who was a partner in the enterprise. Drake did so without proper authority and was protected from prosecution by Queen Elizabeth I. Doughty's brother John (another member of the expedition who later sought Drake's prosecution) was subsequently imprisoned for life after it was alleged he agreed to kill Drake on behalf of Spain.

Good Knight

Queen Elizabeth I knighted Drake in 1581 for his service to England (and to her bank account). The honor seemingly legitimized Drake's piratical actions during his trip around the world. Drake would not be the last pirate knighted by England.

Piracy's Biggest Raid

With the Queen of England's money, Drake was able to mount the biggest privateering expedition in history. With plenty of backing, Drake launched a new expedition to the West Indies in January 1586. Equipped with 20 ships and about 2,300 men, Drake first pillaged Santo Domingo in what is now the Dominican Republic.

On February 19, 1586, Drake and his force did the same thing to Cartagena, sacking the city for nearly two months. On his way back to England, Drake then sacked and burned the Spanish settlement at what is now St. Augustine, Florida.

He would later raid cities in Spain and take a small role in the famous sea fight against the Spanish Armada that unsuccessfully attempted to invade England on July 30, 1588. Drake's raids a year later on the Iberian Peninsula revealed him to be a poor field commander accused of not obeying orders.

Drake's Last Foray

Drake's final pirate raid of 1595 to 1596 was nothing more than a naked example of piracy. Heavily financed by England's Queen Elizabeth I, the expedition was so large the crew could not be paid a salary. Instead they would be given the classic pirate's remuneration of a share of the plunder taken from ships and cities.

Drake's cousin John Hawkins was also a member of the expedition that was jinxed from the start. Recognizing the threat of piracy, Spain had drastically increased its military forces in the New World. Drake realized this when the expedition reached the eastern edge of the Caribbean and Spanish warships quickly captured one of the raiding force's six ships. Drake's expedition took another drubbing when strong resistance repulsed an assault on San Juan, Puerto Rico.

During this unsuccessful action, Hawkins, who had been ill, died on November 11, 1595. Several small Puerto Rican towns were looted, and a subsequent attempt to take the city of Panama was defeated. The entire pirate force was racked by illness, and Drake himself died of dysentery on January 28, 1596. He was buried at sea near Nombre de Dios, Panama, despite his request to be interred on land.

The Bold Henry Morgan

There are pirates and there are pirates, and then there's Henry Morgan. The son of a Welsh farming family who masterminded brilliant and daring operations in the New World, Morgan conquered Spanish colonial cities, murdered Spanish prisoners en masse, and plundered Spanish shipping.

Words To Treasure

One step away from slavery, **indentured servants** were bound by contract for periods ranging from four to seven years in order to obtain passage to the labor-starved English colonies. Once released from their period of servitude, they were granted full rights and property and accepted as citizens.

Not surprisingly, England gave him a knighthood for his loyal service to the crown. He later became an acting governor of Jamaica where he based his own pirate operations for many years. Morgan was a buccaneer who may have actually arrived in Jamaica in the early 1650s as an *indentured servant*.

Sacker of Cities

For all of his exploits, little is known about Morgan, the man. By 1668, Morgan had amassed a sizable force of buccaneers and was successfully seizing Spanish ships and conducting ship-to-shore pirate raids in Spanish-held areas of the Caribbean. In 1668, Morgan mounted a pair of famous assaults by using 12 ships and 700 buccaneers to successfully seize what is now Camaguey, Cuba.

Shiver Me Timbers

In 1669, Morgan staged a big seagoing gathering of his pirate ships where copious amounts of liquor were consumed by his buccaneers. Unfortunately, some extremely drunken pirates fired muskets aboard Morgan's flagship the *Oxford*, an English ship loaned him by the monarchy, and detonated the gunpowder stored in the ship's magazine. The resulting explosion was massive and killed 200 of the *Oxford*'s crew whose mutilated bodies were thrown everywhere. The buccaneers on the surrounding ships were momentarily stunned but soon regained their composure and set about the task of stripping the floating bodies of valuables. Hacking off fingers to obtain a gold ring from a fellow buccaneer wasn't considered bad manners in this group.

The citizens of Camaguey rushed to hide their valuables but were later caught and tortured by Morgan's men. The tormented residents revealed the location of their wealth and Morgan's buccaneers profited handsomely from the expedition. A few months later, Morgan mounted a second raid on the fortified Spanish city of Puerto Bello, Panama.

Morgan's careful planning and daring allowed him to mount brilliant but ruthless attacks on three forts guarding the entrance to Puerto Bello. When soldiers in the first fort refused to surrender, they were locked in a building after their capture and blown to bits with gunpowder. (Morgan had warned them this would be their fate!) After the second fort fell, the third resisted staunchly, prompting Morgan to callously round up Catholic priests and use them as human shields for his assaulting buccaneers. Once taken, Puerto Bello was subjected to days of murder, rape, and looting.

Conqueror of Panama

The Pacific port of Panama City was the largest settlement in the New World in 1670 when Morgan decided it would be the next target of his buccaneers. Morgan landed his invasion force on the Caribbean coastline of Panama and moved 1,400 of his buccaneers up the Chagres River in canoes before continuing on foot.

The men lived off the land but fared badly during the grueling jungle trek and were soon beset with tropical illnesses, including dysentery and fevers. To stave off hunger, some boiled and consumed leather goods. They camped outside the city only to awaken and find themselves facing 2,000 Spanish troops. The buccaneers were charged by 400 Spanish cavalry troops, but Morgan ordered an advance and the cavalry was halted by musket fire and the desperate courage of the pirates. The Spanish infantry then turned and fled for Panama City with Morgan's ragged but gutsy band in pursuit.

The Spanish burned two thirds of the city and virtually all of its warehouses to prevent them from falling into Morgan's hands. Once the city was taken, Morgan and his buccaneers set about torturing the populace to find hidden treasures. Although the sacking of Panama was a great military feat, it provided little treasure and created dissension among the buccaneers. Accused of hoarding most of the treasure, Morgan sailed away unannounced, leaving hundreds of buccaneers to go their separate ways.

Pirate Judge

Morgan's raid made the Spanish so angry that they threatened to declare war on England if the buccaneers were not punished. Morgan was immediately called back to England, where instead of being punished, he was knighted by King Charles II and returned to Jamaica as a judge in the vice-admiralty court where punishment was meted out to pirates. Morgan began dispensing justice against pirates and even returned some to Spanish authorities to face justice in their courts.

> **Know The Ropes**
>
> A legal technicality that saved Morgan was that his expedition against Panama City was supported by Jamaican colonial governor Thomas Modyford who, like Morgan, was ordered to return to England to face the music. Modyford was imprisoned until 1674 to mollify the Spanish, while Morgan was sent back to Jamaica as a hero.

Regardless of his eleventh-hour salvation by the English monarchy, many suspected that Morgan was still conducting pirate business on the side, and for years Morgan was suspected of organizing buccaneers to operate with letters of marque issued by French authorities who then held Hispaniola. Morgan was repeatedly charged with misdeeds but managed to beat the rap each time. Morgan was eventually removed from office on charges of drunkenness.

Words To Treasure

Obeah was a religious belief brought to Jamaica and the West Indies from West Africa and practiced by African slaves and their descendants as a form of sorcery that could be used for good or evil.

Jamaica Farewell

Descending into alcoholism, Morgan's health deteriorated and he exhibited all the symptoms of hepatitis when examined in 1688. Morgan preferred the medical treatment of a man who practiced *obeah,* a form of mystical healing. As part of his treatment, Morgan's body was slathered with clay. Despite the best efforts of the witch doctor, Morgan died August 25, 1688. God had the last word on Morgan. When a massive earthquake struck Port Royal on June 7, 1692, Morgan's grave disappeared beneath the waters of the Caribbean.

Blackbeard: Wild, Weird, and Mean?

No one knows the real origins of the pirate Blackbeard. It's generally accepted that he came to the world of piracy like many pirates of his day—as a crewman aboard a licensed privateer ship from England. Thousands of sailors took part in the wide-ranging naval conflict that accompanied the War of Spanish Succession that raged between 1701 and 1713 between England and the alliance of France and Spain. When Blackbeard decided to enter the piracy game outright in 1716, he signed on with pirate captain Edward Hornigold at the piratical redoubt of New Providence Island in the Bahamas.

The two worked well together and captured several prize ships. Hornigold was so impressed with the tall, powerfully built Blackbeard (so named because of his long, black, braided beard) that the pirate was given command of a ship. Before the two parted after 18 months of cooperative plunder, Hornigold presented Blackbeard with a superb French ship they had captured.

Begging Your Pardon

In January 1718, Blackbeard decided to seek a pardon from English authorities by taking an oath to never again conduct pirate operations. He surrendered to the governor of North Carolina, Charles Eden, who received a portion of Blackbeard's booty. The legendary pirate then began selling stolen goods before deciding to forget his oath and resume piracy on the high seas.

Blackbeard soon met a pudgy, retired English colonial planter named Stede Bonnet who had turned to piracy. The two joined forces, and Blackbeard eventually made the amateur pirate Bonnet his prisoner and placed another pirate in command of Bonnet's ship. When Bonnet was allowed to go ashore to Topsail Inlet on the North Carolina coast to acquire a letter of marque, he returned to find 24 of his own men marooned on a sandbar. Blackbeard had severed their "partnership" and sailed in search of plunder.

Wanted: Dead or Alive

A pair of English colonial governors—one in the Bahamas and another in Virginia— were about to reshape Blackbeard's Atlantic playground into a fatal place for the pirate.

When Woodes Rogers began capturing and executing pirates in the Bahamas in 1718, the governor narrowly missed capturing Blackbeard, who had been one of his prime targets. At nearly the same time, Virginia's colonial governor Alexander Spotswood ordered the Royal Navy to hunt down Blackbeard, who, having been chased from the Bahamas by Rogers, was forced to operate out of the coastal areas of North Carolina.

In his eagerness to get rid of Blackbeard, Spotswood financed the expedition out of his own pocket while Virginia's elected representatives argued over how to raise the money. Spotswood knew North Carolina lacked the resources and the resolve to root out the pirates raiding ships from its coastal waters. A pair of shallow draft sloops— the *Ranger* and *Jane*—were acquired for the assault on Blackbeard who anchored his own sloop *Adventure* in the shallow waters behind North Carolina's Oracoke Island.

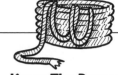

Know The Ropes

The sloops were necessary for an attack on Blackbeard, since the Royal Navy's full-size warships were unable to maneuver in the shallow waters west of Oracoke Island where Blackbeard's sloop was anchored. The larger ships would have run aground, although their added firepower would have been an advantage. The light sloops were armed with only rifles and pistols and the time-tested cutlass.

Fight to the Death

Blackbeard's mythical battle against the Royal Navy was preceded—appropriately enough—by a night of heavy drinking by him and his men. At dawn on November 22, 1718, the *Ranger* and *Jane* slowly made their way toward Blackbeard's sloop but took rifle and cannon fire as they did so. As it turned out, Blackbeard had only 19 men aboard his *Adventure* and was heavily outnumbered by the 62 men aboard the approaching sloops.

The navy's sloops then ran aground, and Blackbeard's own cruised close enough by for him to take a swig from a cup and announce to Royal Navy Lieutenant Robert Maynard: "Damnation seize my soul if I give you Quarters, or take any from you." Maynard, upon whose handwritten account this exchange survives, told Blackbeard to expect the same. Just as the sloops worked themselves free, Blackbeard's sloop fired a lethal broadside into the *Ranger,* knocking it temporarily out of action.

Fatal Mistake

Maynard ordered all but two of his men below decks to protect them from the withering fire from Blackbeard's sloop, unintentionally making the pirate believe there were few men left alive on the *Jane*. When Blackbeard's sloop tied up alongside the *Jane* and he leaped aboard with his men, they were greeted by Maynard's unharmed crew swarming on deck. Blackbeard engaged in a sword fight with Maynard, who pushed his sword into Blackbeard's torso. Incredibly, the pirate's ammunition pouch halted and bent Maynard's blade.

Maynard then drew his pistol and fired once, wounding Blackbeard. A Scottish sailor wielding a broadsword entered the fray and slashed Blackbeard on the neck. Blackbeard reportedly complimented the sailor's handiwork before the Scotsman finished the job by lopping off Blackbeard's head. The fight raged until the decks of the *Jane* were slimy with blood. The arrival of the *Ranger* to assist Maynard's efforts finished the fight. Maynard noted that Blackbeard suffered five bullet wounds and as many as 20 sword wounds before the pirate was decapitated. Legend has it that when thrown overboard, Blackbeard's headless body swam vigorously around the navy sloop.

Words To Treasure

Quarters, or **quarter,** means "mercy shown to an enemy during battle." Bargains were often struck during war in which surrender terms could include the provision of "quarter" or mercy. Those who failed to surrender when offered quarter knew that if captured they would face execution or torture.

Unmatchable Finale

On Blackbeard's orders, one pirate remained below decks to ignite the *Adventure*'s gunpowder if it appeared the Royal Navy was about to gain the upper hand. Blackbeard may have taken everyone with him had the plan worked. A pair of visiting merchants who stayed overnight on Blackbeard's ship and were hiding in the hold during the fight tackled the pirate before the deed could be carried out.

Shiver Me Timbers

During the eighteenth century when Africans were still being bought and sold as slaves and blacks lived without rights in the Americas, slaves were often equal partners aboard pirate ships. Blackbeard's crew at the time of his final fight with the Royal Navy was made up of 13 men of European background and six of African descent. It's no surprise that men of differing backgrounds were so alienated by the harsh laws and brutal poverty of the era that they found common ground in the cruel democracy of a pirate ship. The loyal pirate who stood ready to detonate the *Adventure* was reputedly named "Black Caesar."

Heading Home

Justifiably proud of his victory over one of the Atlantic's most notorious pirates, Maynard had Blackbeard's head mounted on his sloop's *bowsprit*. A skull, reputedly Blackbeard's, belongs to the Peabody Museum in Salem, Massachusetts.

Lafitte: Patriotic Plunderer

To call Lafitte an American patriot would be carrying things a bit far. It appears that this pirate mastermind, who commanded a fleet of pirate ships and then sold plundered goods directly to the public, was loyal to nothing other than his own interests. Nevertheless, this legendary pirate managed to not only operate one of the largest pirate fleets in history, but also to play a pivotal role in defending the United States from the British during the January 8, 1815, Battle of New Orleans.

Words To Treasure

A **bowsprit** is a pole that extends from the prow of a ship, which is used to tie the ropes securing various sails.

Dignified, gentlemanly, shrewd, and possessing a keen sense of humor, Lafitte was a man whose origins are hard to pin down. The historical rumor mill presents him as either a nobleman displaced by the French Revolution or a French buccaneer from Hispaniola who became a pirate powerhouse in southern Louisiana. No one knows where he came from or where he went, but he was one pirate whose actual exploits exceeded the legends of many others.

Baffling Buccaneer

Lafitte's education and eloquence kept him from comfortably fitting into the rough-hewn category of the ordinary buccaneer. Being a cultured pirate of French descent who operated from a North American base placed the mysterious Lafitte in a league of his own. It's likely Lafitte was born on Haiti around 1780, though records indicate that he may have been born in Bordeaux or that his parents came from that French city.

A diary purported to be Lafitte's has the pirate revealing his Jewish heritage and the persecution of his grandfather by the Spanish Inquisition. This trauma was followed by his family's evacuation from Haiti in the aftermath of the 1791 slave revolt. With Lafitte, it seems the more you hear, the less you know. It appears that Lafitte was also once a blacksmith who became the glib godfather of a vast pirate enterprise.

CEO: Corsair Executive Officer

It seems that Lafitte may not have been a cutlass-swinging corsair of the Gulf Coast, but rather an

Words To Treasure

Barataria was a very appropriate name for Lafitte's pirate haunt, since it comes from an old French word meaning "to deceive or swindle." The pirates who inhabited the region were known as Baratarians.

employer of pirates who boosted his profits by cutting out the middleman. Lafitte sold goods stolen by his pirates directly to the public. Barges brought the goods north from the Gulf of Mexico through Barataria Bay and into the secluded bayous. Once at their destination, the goods were loaded into inland warehouses constructed by Lafitte amid the mystical swamplands of South Louisiana.

Lafitte also dealt in the most inhumane of all maritime commodities—slaves—and held slave auctions at Barataria. The entire piracy enterprise came to be detested by some officials but was a mecca for well-heeled bargain hunters from New Orleans.

Lafitte usually stayed one step ahead of the law by claiming his pirates raided only Spanish or British ships under letters of marque issued by either France or one of the emerging Latin American nations angry with Spain. However, as the Americans secured their hold on Louisiana following its 1803 purchase from France, Lafitte began to feel the heat, even though he worked hard to curry favor with his influential customers. In November 1812 he was charged with smuggling but managed to wriggle clear of prosecution with the assistance of the War of 1812.

Saved by War!

While Lafitte considered his legal situation, his brother Pierre Lafitte—who was also charged with smuggling—was jailed. In the summer of 1814, in the third year of the War of 1812, Lafitte learned the British were coming. A British Army officer named Captain McWilliams and Royal Navy Lieutenant Nicholas Lockyer arrived to begin talks with Lafitte. The officers wanted to enlist the pirate leader on the side of the British, who intended to assault the underbelly of the United States through New Orleans.

Lafitte was the recipient of several carrot-and-stick letters from British officials, with some threatening retaliation for his piracy against their ships while others offered protection from the Americans now attempting to prosecute him and his brother Pierre. If this wasn't enough to sway Lafitte, the English kicked in $30,000 to sweeten the deal. During one of the conversations, McWilliams revealed to Lafitte the English plan to split America in two by driving north from New Orleans while inciting a revolt of the slaves in the southern states.

Patriotic Pirates

In an emotional letter to his enemy Claiborne, Lafitte told of the English offer, calling it a temptation "few men would have resisted." The pirate also revealed the British plans as told to him. All he got for his troubles was an assault on Barataria by American naval forces and officials on September 5, 1814. Eighty of the pirates were captured, and Lafitte's enterprise was torched. Six of Lafitte's 13 ships and a half-million dollars in goods were seized.

The pirates—many of whom were Americans—would not fire when they saw the American flag fluttering on the approaching ships. When bombarded by the U.S. Navy, the pirates scattered into the swamps until they could regroup.

Shiver Me Timbers

If you're up around 1 A.M. watching old movies, you might see one of three made about history's most famous buccaneer. Lafitte was portrayed by Fredric March in The Buccaneer (1938), by Paul Henreid in Last of the Buccaneers (1951), and by Yul Brynner in the remake of The Buccaneer (1958).

The Odd Couple

Despite the raid on his redoubt, Lafitte remained ready to defend his adopted nation and met with U.S. Army General Andrew Jackson who reluctantly accepted Lafitte's help. Jackson had foreseen a British assault on New Orleans and rushed to Louisiana from combat with Creek Indians in Mississippi. Jackson—a former judge—was loath to grasp what he considered to be the bloody paw of a cutthroat like Lafitte. However, what Lafitte had to offer Jackson's tired and poorly supplied Army were desperately needed munitions and flints for the rifles of Jackson's exhausted force.

Jackson detested the thought of fighting with Lafitte but eventually recognized that using Lafitte's forces and supplies was a necessary bargain with the devil. The future president and the pirate king were now uneasy comrades-in-arms. On January 8, 1815, a British force of 8,453 troops assaulted the city defended by 3,500 men augmented by Lafitte's Baratarians. Jean Lafitte conducted a maritime patrol to prevent the British from sneaking up on the American defenses.

Shiver Me Timbers

Lafitte and his men, whom Jackson had once called "hellish banditti," conducted themselves so ably during the Battle of New Orleans that he subsequently referred to them as gentlemen. After the battle ended, the British counted 2,000 casualties compared to only eight dead among the American forces. President James Madison pardoned Lafitte and his Baratarians of all past crimes. After Lafitte's magnificent show of patriotism, he inexplicably became a spy for Spain against the United States as he made plans to move his pirates to Galveston. Lafitte's motives remain unclear, although he did seek financial and military support from Spain to set up a base on the Texas coast.

The Vanishing Buccaneer

Lafitte moved his pirate force from Barataria to Galveston, where he set up fortifications and began conducting piracy in the Gulf of Mexico. The abduction of a Karankawa Indian girl by his pirates culminated in a battle between his men and the fierce Indians. Lafitte's battle-hardened pirates killed many of the Karankawas whom it's believed also slaughtered a French settlement in 1689 founded by French explorer Robert Cavelier Sieur de La Salle. La Salle's shipwreck woes are discussed in Chapter 12, "The *Belle* of the Bay."

Lafitte's charm aside, he was still the ringleader of a huge piracy ring, and the seizure of American ships and goods in the Gulf of Mexico and Caribbean meant the end of his operations on Galveston Island. Officials no longer believed he left American shipping unmolested. The final straw came after a new ship being sailed to Galveston by his pirates engaged in a naval battle with the American warship *Alabama*. The *Alabama* caught Lafitte's pirates red-handed as they looted an American merchant ship in December 1819. The pirates were taken into custody, and 17 were eventually executed.

Unable to claim he was a licensed privateer, Lafitte was ordered to abandon Galveston by the U.S. Navy, and the pirate complied. He destroyed his Galveston encampment under Navy supervision and disappeared soon after leaving Galveston in early 1821. The golden age of piracy in the Americas would end four years later.

Shiver Me Timbers

Lafitte may be the only pirate in the world to have a national park named after him! The Jean Lafitte National Historical Park and Preserve contains six different park centers around Louisiana including the Barataria Preserve that protects a portion of the region once inhabited by the pirate and his followers. The Chalmette Battlefield and National Cemetery is at the site of the Battle of New Orleans.

The Least You Need to Know

➤ Sir Francis Drake was the son of a Protestant clergyman but lived much of his life with relatives who owned ships and practiced piracy with the permission of England's government.

➤ Sir Henry Morgan was most likely an indentured servant when he came to live in Jamaica during the mid-1600s, although like most pirates, his precise origins are still subject to debate.

➤ A pirate party at sea in 1669 turned into a real blast when Morgan's flagship, the *Oxford,* was blown to bits by pirates who discharged muskets too close to the ship's gunpowder magazine.

➤ Blackbeard, whose real name may have been Edward Teach, was famous and much feared for his seemingly unbalanced behavior that included wearing a burning cannon fuse in his hat during pirate attacks.

➤ Unwilling to be taken alive by the British Royal Navy when cornered in 1718, Blackbeard ordered a pirate to detonate the gunpowder aboard his own sloop if it appeared that he or the crew was destined for capture and a trip to the gallows.

➤ Lafitte's willingness to order his forces to fight in the January 8, 1815, Battle of New Orleans on the side of the Americans remained strong, even though British officials bribed him for his support and promised him protection from American prosecution for his piracy.

Words to Treasure Glossary

abandoned   The state of a wrecked ship whose ownership has been officially renounced by its owner.

admiralty court   Any court that has the jurisdiction to hear cases involving maritime law, including salvage issues or crimes committed at sea.

adventurer   A person who becomes a soldier of fortune in his own employ and who engages in warfare for the sole purpose of gaining wealth or position.

adze   A long-handled tool with a highly sharpened, curved blade for shaping large pieces of wood.

amber   A transparent substance formed by resin from prehistoric trees that is gathered from the sea or mined on land for use in jewelry.

America   The name applied to what is now known as the United States, which is derived from the name of Italian navigator Amerigo Vespucci and came into use around 1507.

Americas   A region including most of the islands and nations discovered by the Spaniards in the Western Hemisphere, including North and South America.

Amiable   A ship that was part of LaSalle's ill-fated expedition to what is now Texas; the French name means "amiable."

amidships   The middle section of a ship.

Argo   The mythical Greek ship sailed by Jason and his Argonauts in search of the equally mythical Golden Fleece. Also the name of a remotely operated vehicle used in the discovery of the liner RMS *Titanic*.

arrest   The first legal step in obtaining trusteeship and salvage rights to an abandoned wreck by a salvor who intends to save the ship or its cargo under salvage law.

awash   The condition of a ship's deck when a vessel is riding so low in the water that waves are constantly sweeping across its deck.

ballast   The weight placed at the lowest level of a ship's centerline or keel to counterbalance the weight of its upper decks and provide stability to prevent capsizing.

Barataria   An area in southern Louisiana where the pirate leader Jean Lafitte maintained a force of nearly 1,000 men along with a fleet of ships and a bazaar where he sold stolen goods.

bathyscaphe   The first deep-submergence craft to reach the ocean's deepest point. The bathyscaphe contains a spherical crew compartment attached to a cylinder filled with gasoline for buoyancy. The Latin term means "deep ship."

bathysphere   The original deep-submergence system designed as a sphere to hold two men who were lowered deep into the ocean for the first look at how sea life thrived under great sea pressure. Its name is derived from the Greek word *bathy,* meaning "depth," and the word *sphere,* describing its shape.

Battleship Row   The nickname given to an anchorage of massive concrete moorings at the U.S. Naval Base Pearl Harbor where the battleships of the Pacific Fleet were tied at the time of the attack by the Japanese.

becalmed   The state in which a sailing ship is left motionless by a lack of wind.

Belle   A French word meaning "the beautiful one" and the name of a ship owned by the French explorer LaSalle.

below   Refers to any portion of a ship below the main deck, which can include the cargo hold or crew quarters.

blown down   The pressurization of a chamber in which saturation divers become physiologically acclimated to the sea pressure they will work in.

blue water   A term connoting the sailing ability of a ship or a person who ventures far out at sea, with a "blue water sailor" being a capable, deep-ocean mariner.

bosun's chair   A chair attached to a pulley that is used for transferring people and items from ships.

bow   The leading portion of a ship designed to part the water as the vessel moves forward.

bowsprit   The pole extending from the bow of a ship, which is used to tie the ropes securing various sails.

bridge   The command center of a ship, usually located high on its superstructure so officers in charge can maintain a view of the ship and the sea ahead.

brig   A ship equipped with a pair of masts and square sails, although the word can also refer to a compartment of a ship where prisoners are temporarily confined.

choke points   Confined areas of water bounded by land through which maritime traffic is funneled, creating prime hunting grounds for submarines during war.

coaming   A raised portion of the deck around a hatch opening designed to keep water from sloshing into the hold.

cob   A cob is a Spanish coin crudely cut in the New World from a thin strip of silver by Indian slave labor. The term is derived from the Spanish phrase *cabo de barra*, meaning "end of the bar."

collier   A ship used for hauling coal but also the name for a coal miner in England.

conquistadors   Ruthless adventurers who carried Catholicism to the New World while subjugating the Native Americans during the search for treasure.

coureurs de bois   French settlers in seventeenth- and eighteenth-century North America who were extremely adroit at surviving in the wilderness and who obtained the nickname meaning "wood runner."

cubit   An ancient measure of length that corresponds to 1.5 feet.

Davy Jones's locker   The slang term for the bottom of the sea as well as a collective graveyard for all whose bodies were lost at sea. Old mariners believed Davy Jones was a soul-snatching devil.

decapod crustacean   Any of the shelled sea creatures having 10 legs, including shrimp, lobsters, and crabs.

deep-submergence vehicle   Any deep-diving craft, manned or unmanned, that is not a full-duty submarine; it must be transported to a dive site by another ship.

diving bell   A compartment that is open at the bottom, which provides an air-filled space in which divers can be lowered into the water to work.

draft   The depth to which the bottom of a ship's hull extends beneath the water.

dry dock   An enclosed space at shipyards where water is pumped out so a moored ship is left high and dry on blocks to allow repairs.

dynamic positioning   An automated means of keeping a salvage ship directly over an ocean location using a combination of specially built propellers and computerized navigational aids.

East Indies   A collection of land masses in the southwest Pacific, including Indonesia and Malaysia.

Edmund Fitzgerald   The former president of Northwest Mutual Life insurance company that built the bulk cargo carrier *Edmund Fitzgerald*.

electromagnetic field   An area of energy containing both electrical and magnetic components.

417

fathometer   A device that uses sound waves to determine the depth of water beneath a ship's hull.

Florida Keys   A long chain of islands curving down from the southern tip of Florida's peninsula and extending about 150 miles to the west, with its southernmost island city being Key West.

flotas   The Spanish word for fleets organized by Spain to carry goods to the Americas for sale to colonists and to return with products and treasure.

fog of war   The confusion and misunderstanding that accompanies combat.

foundered   To sink either completely or partially beneath the surface.

free diver   One who swims beneath the surface of the water without devices to assist in breathing.

frigate   A relatively small warship.

galleon   A relatively large ship used between the fifteenth and seventeenth centuries, possessing a trio of masts and two or more decks and used by many nations, though most closely identified with Spain.

Grand-Congloué   The name of a large rock in Marseilles Bay that has been the site of numerous shipwrecks throughout history.

gunwales   Walls around the main deck of a ship designed to keep waves from splashing over the deck but also the place where the ship's cannon were traditionally located.

HOMES   An acronym that makes it easy to remember the names of the five Great Lakes; it stands for Huron, Ontario, Michigan, Erie, and Superior.

hot run   An electrical malfunction that activates a submarine's armed torpedo prematurely.

hydrothermal vent   An opening on the seafloor through which magma or water superheated by molten lava is forced to the surface.

hypothermia   The reduction of body temperature due to exposure to cold water or air. This condition can be fatal.

Iberian Peninsula   The land mass protruding from Europe into the Atlantic that contains Portugal and Spain.

icebreaker   A ship with both massive engine power and a powerfully built hull that is designed to break ice to allow the passage of ships.

Iliad   Written by Homer, this epic poem chronicled the Trojan War and gave insight into Bronze Age societies, providing invaluable help to modern archaeologists studying shipwrecks dating back thousands of years.

indentured servant   A mild and impermanent form of slavery in which people coming to British colonies in America worked for four to seven years to repay the cost of their transportation; freedom and a grant of land followed the end of that period.

Isle of Wight   An island close to England's southern coast that serves as a natural fortress protecting Portsmouth Harbor, the traditional anchorage of Britain's Royal Navy.

Kami Kazi   A powerful wind that appeared twice during the thirteenth century to save Japan from two separate Mongol invasions. The term means "Divine Wind."

keel   The spine of a ship running down the center of the hull from bow to stern.

keelhauling   A barbarous punishment occasionally used by Britain's Royal Navy in which a man was tossed over the side of a ship and then hauled by rope under the hull.

Kestner clamp   A large fastener tightened with a heavy bolt for securing hatches tightly over openings on the decks of cargo ships.

ketch   A small sailboat with a main mast at the front and a smaller one at the rear.

kiloton   A kiloton is a measurement equal to 1,000 metric tons of the explosive TNT and is used as a means of quantifying the explosive power of nuclear weapons.

Kriegsmarine   The German name for its navy during World War II meaning "War Navy" in English.

lanyard   A short rope or cord used to secure rigging or for any other purpose necessary on a ship as well as a pull-cord used for the firing of an artillery piece.

letter of marque   An official document from a government granting a private ship and its crew the right to attack and seize enemy shipping during war.

littoral   Waters near shore extending out to where the depth is no more than 200 feet.

LOF   The Lloyd's Open Form, or LOF, was the first standardized contract for salvage and has been used since 1892, with the latest revisions made in 1995.

Lusitania   The ancient Roman name for Portugal given to the liner RMS *Lusitania,* which was sunk by a German U-boat's torpedo in 1915.

magazine   A special storage compartment within the hold of a warship where munitions, shells, and other explosives are stored.

magnetometer   A device identical to a magnetic anomaly detector (MAD) used to sense disruptions in the earth's magnetic field caused by sunken objects and ships containing iron or steel.

mailbox   A steel tube lowered over the propeller of a treasure hunter's boat so sand can be blown from the seafloor to reveal buried treasure and artifacts.

mainsail   The largest sail on a ship, often used to give a sailing ship the greatest amount of speed in conjunction with smaller sails.

Manifest Destiny   A belief among nineteenth-century Americans that the United States should be extended from Canada to Mexico and westward to the Pacific Ocean.

419

Manila galleons   Ships that were part of Spanish fleets carrying beautiful crafts and other items from Asia to Mexico's west coast for eventual shipment to Europe.

Mary Rose   This name was famous during the time of Henry VIII not only because it was the name of his sister but also because it was the name of the English warship that sank with nearly 700 people aboard in 1545.

material condition   The state of repair of the items of a ship related to its structure, its engine, and any other machinery.

molybdenum   A strategically important metal often used as an alloy material to make extremely hard steel or for making heating elements used in superhot furnaces.

neoprene   A synthetic rubberlike material, manufactured to contain insulating bubbles, that is used in wet suits to protect divers from the heat-robbing effects of being submerged.

"no cure, no pay"   A traditional term in salvage law describing how salvors will receive payment for salvaging a ship or its cargo only if they are successful in the endeavor.

Nombre de Dios   At least nine cities and towns in Florida and Latin America bear this name which means "Name of God."

obeah   A religious belief brought to Jamaica and the West Indies from West Africa and practiced by African slaves and their descendants as a form of sorcery that could be used for good or evil.

outfitting   The work done to complete a ship once its hull has been built.

oxhide ingots   Flat, ancient copper ingots cast in the shape of a hide whose four corners provide carrying handles.

patch   A steel plate cut from the pressure hull of a nuclear submarine so components can be repaired or its reactor can be replenished with nuclear fuel.

pay out   The releasing of extra line, chain, or cable on a ship.

periscope   An optical device that extends from inside a submarine to the surface so the crew can observe activities above the water.

Phoenicia   An old Greek word for the coastal areas of Syria and Palestine that became a trading and manufacturing center as early as 2000 B.C.E.

pintle   A type of pin used to attach a rudder to the rear of a ship, ordinarily made out of a corrosion-resistant metal such as bronze.

pirata   The Spanish word for "pirate," which is identical to the original Latin version of the word.

pirate   Someone who commits crimes such as robbery and murder at sea, but a term applied in the twentieth century to those who sell unauthorized music recordings or illegally use the airwaves to operate unlicensed radio stations.

plunder   The theft of goods during war or piracy; it means the same as the term "booty."

privateer   A sailor or ship that has received governmental permission to destroy and capture ships belonging to that nation's enemies.

Procesal   An archaic form of Spanish that is complicated to read and was used extensively to document the history of the Spanish treasure fleets sailing from the New World to Spain from the 1500s until the 1800s.

promenade deck   The upper deck of a ship open to the sun and breeze where passengers can take walks.

propeller   A device with blades arrayed on a hub that pushes water or air to provide propulsion to a ship or aircraft.

purser   An officer aboard a ship who handles financial matters including the storage of passenger valuables.

quarter   The mercy shown to an enemy during battle.

radar   A system that detects the location, speed, and direction of travel of objects by reflected radio waves.

rail   A banister made out of steel cable, metal piping, or wood that serves as a safety fence around the deck and superstructure of a ship.

remotely operated vehicle   Ungainly looking robotic machine controlled from a ship that can be equipped with the capability to descend to great depths to photograph submerged objects, conduct repair work on oil rigs, or recover sunken artifacts and treasure.

researcher   A person with in-depth knowledge of maritime history and insurance records who searches documents to reveal the location of ships and the nature of their cargo.

rudder   A wooden structure attached to the rear of a ship to serve as a control surface so the vessel can be steered.

S5W   This acronym stands for "Westinghouse steam reactor, model number 5," which is a nuclear reactor installed in American nuclear submarines during the late 1950s.

salvage   The act of saving a damaged ship or one that has run aground, or the rescue of its cargo.

salvor   A person other than a member of a ship's crew who assists in the saving of a ship in distress or who salvages a ship and cargo that have been abandoned to the sea.

salvor-in-possession   A salvor who has been granted salvage rights by an admiralty court to a ship and all its artifacts, equipment, and cargo.

scorpion   Although the name of a fish with poisonous spines, it was also the name of the USS *Scorpion* nuclear attack submarine lost with all hands in 1968.

scuba   Stands for self-contained, underwater breathing apparatus, the first successful self-contained underwater diving system.

scupper   A hole built into the base of a ship's gunwale that allows water to drain off the deck during a heavy rain or rough weather.

seine   A fishing net suspended from the surface with floats and weighted below so the lower part drags along the bottom.

shallow draft   A term indicating that the keel of a ship does not extend deeply below the surface of the water.

shipworms   These destructive mollusks, also known as teredos, slowly bore into the wooden hulls of ships until they are no longer watertight.

showboat   A nuclear submarine sent out during the Cold War to foreign and domestic ports to impress and reassure those who were able to view it.

silvermaster   A person charged with the responsibility of accounting for Spanish royal treasure loaded aboard treasure fleet ships for their return to Spain.

siren   A mythical, beautiful woman whose singing lured sailors to their deaths against ship-smashing rocks.

sloop   A low-profile ship with a short bowsprit or prow and a relatively shallow draft that was used on the sea as well as the Great Lakes.

smallpox   An often fatal virus carried to the New World by Europeans; smallpox played a major role in drastically reducing the Native American population.

solent   A strait located behind the Isle of Wight.

sonobuoy   A device usually deployed from an aircraft during antisubmarine operations that picks up the underwater sounds of submarines and then radios them to the aircraft so the submarine can be located and attacked.

Spanish Main   The Atlantic coastal areas once held by Spain from Panama to Venezuela. It is also the term for compilation of sea routes used by Spain's treasure fleets when traveling between ports in the Caribbean, the Gulf of Mexico, and South America.

Spithead   The northern end of the Solent Strait located behind the Isle of Wight, which sits just off Britain's southern coast near Portsmouth.

SS   This abbreviation before the name of an American ship stands for "steamship."

SSN   A prefix used before the hull number of American submarines, which stands for "submarine service, nuclear (powered)." The USS *Scorpion*'s hull number is SSN589, meaning it was the 589th American submarine built.

stern   The rear of a ship where the rudder is located.

strike   To rapidly lower a sail or flag.

stroboscope   A bright light that can flash at extremely short intervals to make fast-moving objects appear motionless or serve as a brilliant light source for high-speed photography.

sweeper   A type of salvor who recovers anchors, anchor chains, and other objects from the bottom of harbors and ports.

swivel gun   A small-caliber cannon, mounted on the railing of a ship, that was used to provide firepower at close range against those attempting to board.

tack   The process of turning a sailing ship to port or starboard, usually to take advantage of the wind.

technical diver   A diver who uses a mixture of gases including oxygen, nitrogen, and helium to allow safer diving at depths below 130 feet. Such divers are also known as "Trimix" divers.

teredo   The Latin and technical term for a form of wood-eating mollusk that can bore holes into the hulls of wooden sailing ships.

territorial waters   The waters around nations that they can claim as their sovereign territory; was traditionally set at three nautical miles but extended to 12 miles through the United Nations Convention on the Law of the Sea in 1982.

tether   A cable or line used to pull or recover a camera sled or a robotic device such as a remotely operated vehicle being controlled from a ship.

Thresher   The name of an American nuclear submarine lost with all hands in 1963, which was named after a type of large shark.

topsail   A topsail is a small sail at the top of a mast.

torpedo   A missile launched by surface ships or submarines that is powered by its own engine and travels swiftly underwater to strike the hulls of surface ships or other submarines.

trench   A geological formation beneath the ocean that is similar to an extremely long and deep gorge on land.

umbilical   A line or bundle of lines carrying electrical power, maneuver commands, or electronic data to and from a remotely operated vehicle; also can carry information and video images back to a support ship.

USS   The prefix before the names of American warships, which means "United States Ship."

vane   A stabilizing control surface usually mounted on an object towed underwater to enable the device to maintain stability, in the same way that feathered vanes stabilize an arrow in flight.

Vasa   A Swedish word meaning "arms"; given as a name to a Swedish warship shortly before it sank on August 10, 1628.

vent   An opening that allows air to enter or escape from ballast tanks as they are filled and emptied to adjust a ship's buoyancy.

vent cover   A mushroom-shaped attachment to the top of a vent on a ship's deck to keep water from entering a vent leading to a ballast tank.

ways   The timbers upon which a ship rests while undergoing construction and the ramp from which it is eventually launched.

West Indies   Nearly 1,000 Caribbean Islands of which a fraction were discovered in 1492 by Christopher Columbus, who incorrectly believed he had reached Asia.

wolfpack   The term given to groups of U-boats that converged on merchant ship convoys in the Atlantic during Nazi Germany's campaign to starve England of food and supplies during World War II.

Deepen Your Knowledge

The subject of shipwrecks and treasure encompasses many disciplines including seafaring, naval engineering, salvage techniques, maritime law, history, and geography. Don't forget to consider the technology of locating and diving to sunken ships as well as the discipline of archaeology. The information sources listed here will provide a good "grounding" in shipwrecks and sunken treasure.

Books and Periodicals

Alden, John D. *Salvage Man: Edward Ellsberg and the U.S. Navy.* Annapolis, MD: Naval Institute Press, 1998.

Bailey, Thomas, and Paul B. Ryan. *The Lusitania Disaster: An Episode in Modern Warfare and Diplomacy.* New York: Free Press, 1975.

Ballard, Robert D. *The Discovery of the Titanic: Exploring the Greatest of All Lost Ships.* New York: Warner/Madison Press Books, 1987.

Ballard, Robert D. "Riddle of the Lusitania." *National Geographic,* April 1994.

Ballard, Robert D., and Rich Archbold. *The Discovery of the Bismarck: Germany's Greatest Battleship Surrenders Her Secrets.* New York: Warner/Madison Press, 1990.

Ballard, Robert D., and Rich Archbold. *Lost Liners: From the Titanic to the Andréa Doria, the Ocean Floor Reveals Its Greatest Lost Ships.* New York: Hyperion, 1998.

Ballard, Robert D., and Spencer Dunmore. *Exploring the Lusitania: Probing the Mysteries of the Sinking That Changed History.* Toronto: Warner/Madison, 1995.

Ballard, Robert D., and Malcolm McConnell. *Explorations: My Quest for Adventure and Discovery Under the Sea.* New York: Hyperion, 1995.

Bartholomew, C.A. *Mud, Muscle, and Miracles: Marine Salvage in the United States Navy.* Washington, D.C.: Department of the Navy, 1990.

Bass, George F. "New Tools for Undersea Archaeology." *National Geographic,* September 1968.

Bass, George F., et al. *A History of Seafaring Based on Underwater Archaeology.* New York: Walker, 1972.

Beavis, Bill, and Richard G. McCloskey. *Salty Dog Talk: The Nautical Origins of Everyday Expressions*. Dobbs Ferry, NY: Sheridan House, Inc., 1995.

Biel, Steven. *Down with the Old Canoe: A Cultural History of the Titanic Disaster*. New York: W.W. Norton and Company, 1997.

Blount, Steve. *Treasure Hunting with a Metal Detector: In, Around and Under the Water*. New York: Pisces Books, 1987.

Botting, Douglas. *The Pirates*. Alexandria, VA: Time-Life Books, 1978.

Bradley, Mark. *Why They Called the Scorpion "Scrapiron."* Proceedings, U.S. Naval Institute, July 1998.

Burgess, Robert. *They Found Treasure*. New York: Dodd, Mead, 1977.

Burgess, Robert F., and Carl J. Clausen. *Florida's Golden Galleons: The Search for the 1715 Spanish Treasure Fleet*. Port Salerno, FL: Florida Classics Library, 1982.

Carpenter, Dorr, and Norman Polmar. *Submarines of the Imperial Japanese Navy*. Annapolis, MD: Naval Institute Press, 1986.

Carr, Arnold, H., and John Perry Fish. *Sound Underwater Images: A Guide to the Generation and Interpretation of Side Scan Sonar Data*. Newton, MA: Horvitz Communications, 1990.

Cohat, Yves. *The Vikings: Lords of the Seas*. New York: Harry N. Abrams, Inc., 1987.

Cordingly, David (consulting ed.). *Pirates: Terror on the High Seas, from the Caribbean to the South China Sea*. Kansas City, MO: Turner Publishing, 1996.

Cordingly, David. *Under the Black Flag: The ROMANCE and the Reality of Life Among the Pirates*. New York: Random House, 1995.

Court of Enquiry. *Report on the Loss of the S.S. Titanic* (Great Britain's official inquiry). Gloucestershire: Alan Sutton Ltd., 1990.

Cousteau, Jacques-Yves, and Philippe Diole. *Diving for Sunken Treasure*. New York: Doubleday, 1971.

Cussler, Clive, and Craig Dirgo. *The Sea Hunters*. New York: Simon & Schuster, 1996.

Daley, Robert. *Treasure*. New York: Pocket Books, 1986.

Darby, Graham. *Spain in the Seventeenth Century: Seminar Studies in History*. New York: Longman, 1994.

Dobie, J. Frank. *Legends of Texas, Volume II: Pirates' Gold and Other Tales*. Gretna, LA: Pelican Publishing Company, 1995.

Earl, Sylvia, and Al Giddings. *Exploring the Deep Frontier: The Adventure of Man in the Sea*. Washington, D.C.: National Geographic Society, 1980.

Eaton, John, and Charles A. Haas. *Titanic: Destination Disaster: The Legends and the Reality*. New York: W.W. Norton and Company, Inc., 1996.

Edgerton, Harold E. *Sonar Images*. Englewood Cliffs, NJ: Prentice-Hall, 1986.

Ellms, Charles. *The Pirates Own Book: Authentic Narratives of the Most Celebrated Sea Robbers*. New York: Dover Publications, Inc., 1993. (Originally published 1837.)

Fernandez-Armesto, Felipe. *Columbus*. New York: Oxford University Press, 1991.

Fish, John Perry. *Unfinished Voyages: A Chronology of Shipwrecks—Maritime Disasters in the Northeast United States from 1606 to 1956.* Orleans, MA: Lower Cape Publishing, 1989.

Friedman, Norman. *U.S. Submarines Since 1945.* Annapolis, MD: Naval Institute Press, 1994.

Hillier, Chris. *The Devil and the Deep: A Guide to Nautical Myths and Superstitions.* Dobbs Ferry, NY: Sheridan House, Inc., 1997.

Hoehling, A., and Mary Hoehling. *The Last Voyage of the Lusitania.* New York: Madison Books, 1996.

Hoffer, William. *Saved! The Story of the Andréa Doria, the Greatest Sea Rescue in History.* New York: Summit Books, 1979.

Horner, Dave. *The Treasure Galleons: Clues to Millions in Sunken Gold and Silver.* Port Salerno, FL: Florida Classics Library, 1990.

Howard, Ed. "Pitcairn Island." *National Geographic,* October 1985.

Jessop, Keith. *Goldfinder: The True Story of One Man's Discovery of the Ocean's Richest Secrets.* London: Simon & Schuster, 1998.

Johnson, Stephen. "A Long and Deep Mystery: Scorpion Crewman Says Sub's '68 Sinking Was Preventable. Navy's Silence on Scorpion Adds Bitterness to Families' Grief." *Houston Chronicle,* May 23, 1993.

Johnson, Stephen. "Sub Sank in 1968 After Skimpy Last Overhaul." *Houston Chronicle,* May 21, 1995.

Johnson, Stephen. "Torpedo Theory Contradicts Findings of USS Scorpion's Wreckage in 1968." *Houston Chronicle,* December 27, 1993.

Keatts, Henry C. *Guide to Shipwreck Diving: New York and New Jersey.* Houston, TX: Gulf Publishing Company, 1992.

Kelsey, Harry. *Sir Francis Drake: The Queen's Pirate.* New Haven: Yale University Press, 1999.

Kinder, Gary. *Ship of Gold in the Deep Blue Sea.* New York: Atlantic Monthly Press, 1998.

Kuntz, Tom. *The Titanic Disaster Hearings: The Official Transcripts of the 1912 Senate Investigation.* New York: Pocket Books, 1998.

Lyon, Eugene. *Search for the Atocha.* Hobe Sound, FL: Florida Classics Library, 1989.

MacGinnis, Joseph. *Fitzgerald's Storm: The Wreck of the Edmund Fitzgerald.* Lansing, MI: Thunder Bay Press, 1997.

Marden, Luis. "HMS Pandora." *National Geographic,* October 1985.

Marden, Luis. "I Found the Bones of the *Bounty.*" *National Geographic,* December 1957.

Marriott, John. *Disaster at Sea.* New York: Hippocrene Books, 1987.

Martin Gaite, Carmen. Translated by Maria G. Tomisch. *Love Customs in Eighteenth-Century Spain.* Berkeley: University of California Press, 1991.

Marx, Robert F. *The History of Underwater Exploration.* New York: Dover Publications, 1990.

Marx, Robert F. *Sunken Treasure: How to Find It.* Dallas, TX: Ram Publishing Company, 1990.

Marx, Robert F., and Jennifer Marx. *The Search for Sunken Treasure: Exploring the World's Great Shipwrecks*. Toronto: Key Porter Books Limited, 1993.

Mathewson III, Duncan. *Treasure of the Atocha*. New York: Dutton, 1986.

McKee, Alexander. *Golden Wreck*. New York: Morrow, 1961.

McKee, Alexander. *History Under the Sea*. New York: Dutton, 1969.

McKee, Alexander. *H.M.S. Bounty*. New York: Morrow, 1962.

Morison, Samuel Eliot. *Admiral of the Ocean Sea: A Life of Christopher Columbus*. Boston: Little, Brown, 1942.

Moscow, Alvin. *Collision Course: The Andréa Doria and the Stockholm*. New York: Putnam, 1959.

Muhlstein, Anka. *Explorer of the North American Frontier*. New York: Arcade Publishing, 1994.

Noble, John. *The Mysterious History of Columbus: An Exploration of the Man, the Myth, the Legacy*. New York: Vintage Books, 1992.

Paasch, H. *Paasch's Illustrated Marine Dictionary*. New York: Lyons and Burford, 1997.

Parry, J. H. *The Spanish Seaborne Empire*. Los Angeles: University of California Press, 1990.

Pickford, Nigel. *The Atlas of Shipwrecks and Treasure*. New York: Dorling Kindersley; Boston: Distributed by Houghton Mifflin, 1994.

Polmar, Norman, and Noot Jurrien. *Submarines of the Russian and Soviet Navies: 1718 to 1990*. Annapolis, MD: Naval Institute Press, 1991.

Ritchie, David. *Shipwrecks: Encyclopedia of the World's Worst Disasters at Sea*. New York: Facts on File, 1996.

Roberts, Nancy. *Blackbeard and Other Pirates of the Atlantic Coast*. Winston-Salem, NC: John F. Blair Publishing, 1993.

Rogozinski, Jan. *Pirates!: Brigands, Buccaneers, and Privateers in Fact, Fiction, and Legend*. New York: Facts on File, 1995.

Rule, Margaret. *The Mary Rose: The Excavation and Raising of Henry VIII's Flagship*. Annapolis, MD: Naval Institute Press, 1984.

Sauer, Carl. *The Early Spanish Main*. Los Angeles: University of California Press, 1966.

Saxon, Lyle. *Lafitte the Pirate*. Gretna, LA: Pelican Publishing Company, 1994.

Simpson, Colin. *Lusitania*. New York: Penguin Books, 1983.

Sontag, Sherry, and Christopher Drew. *Blindman's Bluff: The Untold Story of American Submarine Espionage*. New York: Public Affairs, 1998.

Stenuit, Robert, Peter Throckmorton, et al. *Undersea Treasures*. Washington, D.C.: The National Geographic Society, 1974.

Stonehouse, Frederick. *The Wreck of the Edmund Fitzgerald*. Marquette, MI: Avery Color Studios, 1996.

Throckmorton, Peter. *The Sea Remembers: Shipwrecks and Archaeology—From Homer's Greece to the Rediscovery of the Titanic*. New York: Weidenfeld & Nicolson, 1987.

Villiers, Alan. *Posted Missing: The Story of Ships Lost Without Trace in Recent Years*. New York: Scribner's, 1974.

Wade, Wyn. *The Titanic: End of a Dream*. New York: Penguin Books, 1986.

Walton, Timothy R. *The Spanish Treasure Fleets*. Sarasota, FL: Pineapple Press, 1994.

Ward, Ralph. *Pirates in History*. Baltimore, MD: York Press, 1974.

Weller, Bob. The Dreamweaver: *The Story of Mel Fisher and His Quest for the Treasure of the Spanish Galleon Atocha*. Charleston, SC: Fletcher, 1996.

Wright, John. *Encyclopedia of Sunken Treasure*. London: Michael O'Mara Books Limited, 1995.

CD-ROM

➤ *The Edmund Fitzgerald Interactive Explorer*. Made by International Software Engineers, this CD allows the viewer to inspect the wreck of the *Edmund Fitzgerald* through actual video footages taken during expeditions to the famed wreck. A Web site describing the wreck as well as the CD is at http://www.haja.com/cdrom_products/fitz.html.

Web Sites: Maritime Museum, Shipwreck, and Underwater Archaeology Web Sites

These Web sites contain a wide range of information about shipwrecks, efforts to locate and preserve them, their history, and exhibits of their artifacts. Many of these sites also contain information on where to see these artifacts and shipwrecks in person.

The Andréa Doria

➤ *Andréa Doria:* Tragedy and Rescue at Sea. The site was designed by Anthony Grillo, a survivor of the liner's sinking as an infant passenger. It contains photographs of the ship along with digital sound files of news reports about the disaster.

http://www.andreadoria.org/index.htm

The Belle *and LaSalle*

➤ Texas Historical Commission Web site provides detailed information and images of the excavated *Belle,* a ship sunk near South Texas that belonged to prolific French explorer Rene Robert Cavalier, Sieur de LaSalle.

http://www.thc.state.tx.us/Belle/index.html

El Cazador

➤ *El Cazador* Museum site: Erected by the Grumpy Partnership that discovered the Spanish treasure ship *El Cazador,* this site provides numerous details about the wreck and the treasure of silver discovered accidentally beneath the Gulf of Mexico.

http://www.elcazador.com/

Diving/Shipwreck General Information and History

➤ Bathysphere site describes the cooperative effort between naturalist William Beebe and bathysphere designer Otis Barton to descend to the deepest depths ever attempted by humans beginning in May 1930.

http://hometown.aol.com/chines6930/mw1/beebe9.htm

➤ Florida State University's Program in Underwater Archaeology Web site provides a list of informative links regarding the projects undertaken by the oldest underwater archaeological program in America. The site also provides links to other archaeological information sites.

http://www.adp.fsu.edu/uwarch.html

➤ Great Lakes Shipwreck Files. Researcher and author David Swayze spent years compiling this extraordinary list that covers more than 300 years of shipwrecks on the Great Lakes. The wrecks are listed alphabetically, and the entries contain numerous details about each ship and the circumstances of its loss.

http://www.oakland.edu/boatnerd/swayze/shipwreck/

➤ Great Lakes Shipwreck Museum site.

http://www.shipwreckmuseum.com/

➤ Great Outdoor Recreation Pages. A site devoted to archaeology and culture-related travel.

http://www.gorp.com/gorp/trips/spi_arc.htm

➤ Institute for Nautical Archaeology Web sites showcases its numerous and fascinating projects with links to other undersea archaeology sites.

http://nautarch.tamu.edu/ina/index.htm

http://nautarch.tamu.edu/ina/ub_main.htm

http://www.diveturkey.com/inaturkey/otherlinks.htm

➤ Museum of the Roman Docks site contains information about the only surviving Roman docks in Marseilles, France.

http://www.culture.fr/culture/archeosm/en/docks-m.htm

➤ National Oceanographic and Atmospherics Administration Web site lists the known history of major tropical storms in the Atlantic in the Caribbean and along the East Coast of the United States.

http://www.nhc.noaa.gov/pastdeadlyappnote.html

➤ Nordic Underwater Archaeology Web site provides detailed information and a wreck database for numerous northern European shipwrecks and archaeological projects along with many images.

http://www.abc.se/~m10354/uwa/

➤ Odyssey Marine Exploration, Inc., site provides updates on deep-ocean search operations for shipwrecks and background on a high-tech, commercial shipwreck exploration company including images and downloadable videos of undersea discoveries.

http://www.shipwreck.net/

➤ Overview of all museums, ship exhibits, and schedules at the Royal Naval Base, Portsmouth, United Kingdom.

http://www.stvincent.ac.uk/WfS/Tourism/Portsmouth/HistShips/

➤ Royal Naval Submarine Museum site.

http://www.resort-guide.co.uk/portsmouth/submarine/

➤ The Maritime History Virtual Archives contains links to maritime museums and information regarding maritime history.

http://pc-78-120.udac.se:8001/WWW/Nautica/Nautica.html

➤ Treasure Dive Sites Web site is filled with map coordinates of dozens of shipwreck and treasure locations around the world with many in the Florida area.

http://treasuresites.com/

➤ Underwater Archaeology Branch of the U.S. Naval Historical Center has a Web site that explains the legal issues surrounding military ship and aircraft wrecks as well as information on wreck locations and artifact preservation.

http://www.history.navy.mil/branches/nhcorg12.htm

➤ United Kingdom shipwreck locations and information on shipwreck protection laws.

http://www.st-and.ac.uk/institutes/sims/deswreck.h

➤ National Maritime Museum in Greenwich, England.

http://www.nmm.ac.uk

http://www.nmm.ac.uk/Index.htm

The Edmund Fitzgerald

➤ *Edmund Fitzgerald* page devoted to a fascinating discussion of the weather conditions surrounding the mysterious 1975 loss of the bulk ore carrier. The site was prepared by two University of Wisconsin weather researchers who provide meteorology diagrams and speculation about the cause of the disaster.

http://cimss.ssec.wisc.edu/wxwise/fitz.html

➤ Michigan State University's SS *Edmund Fitzgerald* bell restoration site.

http://www.msu.edu/bell/index.html

The HMS Bounty

➤ HMS *Bounty* History Ring Web site contains a wealth of information about the mutiny aboard the *Bounty* with links to other *Bounty*-related subjects.

http://www.visi.com/~pjlareau//bounty1.html

➤ HMS *Bounty:* The Tall Ship Bounty Foundation's site provides details on how to sail aboard a replica of the *Bounty* built by Hollywood for the 1962 film *Mutiny on the Bounty*. The site also provides pages on the history of the mutiny and links to sites regarding the surviving descendants of the mutineers.

http://www.tallshipbounty.org/

431

The *HMS* Pandora

➤ HMS *Pandora* virtual museum provided by the Queensland Museum in Australia. It contains information about the excavation and recovery of artifacts belonging to the ship sent to capture the mutineers of the HMS *Bounty*.

http://www.qmuseum.qld.gov.au/culture/pandora/pan1.html

The *I-52*

➤ Desert Star Systems site describes the technical challenges of locating and surveying the sunken Japanese treasure submarine *I-52* in 18,000 feet of water. Desert Systems provided underwater tracking and surveying technology for the project.

http://www.desertstar.com/news.htm

The Lusitania

➤ *Lusitania* Web page by North Park University in Chicago. This page provides a brief synopsis of the sinking of the *Lusitania* and the questions surrounding the nature of its cargo.

http://www.npcts.edu/acad/history/WebChron/USA/Lusitania.html

➤ Trenches on the Web: The *Lusitania*. This Web site provides information on the sinking of the liner *Lusitania* in the context of World War I.

http://www.worldwar1.com/arm012.htm#lus

The Mary Rose

➤ *Mary Rose* virtual museum.

http://www.maryrose.org/

Mel Fisher

➤ Mel Fisher Museums and treasure information site.

http://www.melfisher.com/tourfact.html

Spanish Treasure Fleets

➤ 1733 Spanish Treasure Fleet wreck site provided by Florida State University.

http://www.adp.fsu.edu/1733.html

➤ Pirates of the Spanish Main Web site is an omnibus location with links to dozens of sites with information on the pirates and buccaneers who plundered ships and terrorized the Americas. Links for Web sites devoted to children are also available.

http://www.sonic.net/~press/index.html

The Titanic

➤ The official *Titanic* Web site provided by RMS Titanic, Inc., the corporation that owns the *Titanic* and all of its artifacts as salvor-in-possession. The site also contains information about traveling exhibits of actual Titanic artifacts.

http://www.titanic-online.com/index.htm

The USS Scorpion

➤ USS *Scorpion* Web pages contains investigative newspaper articles written by Stephen Johnson for the *Houston Chronicle* regarding the complex story behind the 1968 loss of the submarine with all 99 hands.

http://www.txoilgas.com/589-news.html

http://wavecom.net/~rontini/hc1.htm

Viking Ships

➤ Vasa Museum site where the Swedish warship *Vasa,* which sank on its August 10, 1628, maiden voyage, is on display in this superb virtual museum. Recovered in 1961 from Stockholm's harbor, the well-preserved ship can be seen with many of its artifacts.

http://www.vasamuseet.se/indexeng.html

Notable Shipwrecks

The wrecks listed here are merely a fraction of the thousands of shipwrecks that have occurred around the world. These wrecks are mentioned elsewhere in this book, and this list provides a quick and chronological reference to each wreck along with the suspected cause and the number of deaths that occurred in each.

Twelfth Century, B.C.E.

➤ Uluburun Wreck—Lost: 1200 B.C.E. The wreck of the merchant ship occurred just off Turkey's Uluburun Point in the Aegean. Sponge diver Mehmet Cakir discovered the wreck in 1982. The ancient Phoenicians may have manned the ship whose cargo included not only bronze and glass ingots but also a gold scarab inscribed during the lifetime of the ancient Egyptian queen, Nefertiti. Perhaps the oldest known shipwreck, it has provided a wealth of historical knowledge.

Sixteenth Century

➤ *Mary Rose*—Lost: July 19, 1545. The *Mary Rose,* reputed to be among King Henry VIII's favorite warships, suffered one of the greatest naval disasters in English history. The warship, whose "improvements" may have made it unseaworthy, sank unexpectedly during a battle with the French navy. More than 650 soldiers and sailors drowned in the disaster. It was first located in 1836 at the bottom of the Solent Channel when some of the ship's cannon were recovered, but the location was again forgotten. Although side-scan sonar determined the ship's general location in 1967, the *Mary Rose* was not located positively until a diver found the timbers of the ship protruding from the mud on May 1, 1971. The ship's remains and artifacts have been fully recovered and restored.

Seventeenth Century

➤ 1622 Spanish Treasure Fleet—Lost: September 5, 1622. A destructive hurricane sank eight of 28 ships that were part of a Spanish treasure fleet. Among these ships were the treasure galleons *Atocha* and *Margarita*—two of the richest treasure wrecks ever found. Both ships were located on the southern tip of the Florida Keys by search teams working for treasure-hunting legend Mel Fisher. Another lost ship was discovered by Odyssey Marine Exploration, Inc., in 1989 and became the object of the world's first deep-ocean archaeological excavation. The *Atocha's* remains were first located in 1973, and the *Margarita's* location was discovered in 1980. The treasures from both ships are still being recovered.

➤ *Belle*—**Lost: January 1686.** The *Belle,* the personal ship of French explorer Robert Cavelier, Sieur de LaSalle, sank after running aground during a storm in what is now known as Matagorda Bay in Texas. The ship was discovered in 1995 using a magnetic anomaly detector. Much of its hull and many of its artifacts—including the skeleton of a French sailor—have been recovered. Most of the ship and many of its artifacts were extremely well preserved and may soon be on display following a conservation process.

Eighteenth Century

➤ **1715 Spanish Treasure Fleet—Lost: July 31, 1715.** An estimated 1,200 people died when 11 of 12 ships that were part of the fleet were smashed upon the reefs by a hurricane. Treasure valued at 14 million pesos was torn from the bellies of the ships when the fleet was decimated off Florida's East Coast. Spanish officials recovered some treasure at the time despite frequent raids by pirates. Enough treasure remained to make twentieth-century treasure hunters Kip Wagner and Mel Fisher famous and to begin the modern treasure-hunting craze.

➤ **HMS *Bounty*—Lost: 1789.** Within months following its seizure in a mutiny led by Fletcher Christian on April 28, 1789, the *Bounty* was burned to the waterline and sunk in a bay of Pitcairn Island in the Pacific. *National Geographic* magazine writer Luis Marden discovered its remains in 1957.

➤ **HMS *Pandora*—Lost: August 28, 1791.** The HMS *Pandora*, dispatched to arrest the mutineers of the HMS *Bounty,* was wrecked when it blundered onto the jagged reefs of Australia's Endeavour Reefs. The wreck's death toll included four mutineers and 31 crewmen. The *Pandora* was located in 110 feet of water on November 16, 1977, with the help of a Royal Australian Air Force plane carrying submarine detection equipment.

Nineteenth Century

➤ **SS *Central America*—Lost: September 11, 1857.** Carrying passengers and a huge amount of gold from the California gold rush to New York, the *Central America* ran smack into a hurricane off North Carolina's coast. During a 36-hour fight to save the sinking ship, 154 people—mostly women and children—were taken aboard two other ships. When the *Central America* sank, it took 426 men to their deaths and plunged an estimated $1 billion in gold 8,000 feet beneath the Atlantic. Much of the gold was recovered with the help of a remotely operated vehicle during operations that began in 1988.

➤ *Royal Charter*—**Lost: October 26, 1859.** The *Royal Charter* was a propeller-driven steamer also equipped with sails. It was famous for making the long trip from Australia to England in record time. As it neared Liverpool, a massive storm drove the ship onto the rocks of the Welsh island of Anglesey where 447 men, women, and children died within shouting distance of the shore. Waves smashed the ship to pieces as families clung together on the disintegrating deck. The *Royal Charter*'s hold was filled with gold from the Australian gold rush, and while much of it was salvaged, treasure hunters still report finding gold coins.

Twentieth Century

➤ RMS *Titanic*—**Lost: April 15, 1912.** The *Titanic*'s loss after striking an iceberg while traveling at high speed during its maiden voyage became the stuff of legend. A high percentage of the 1,517 who died in the disaster were among the richest people in the world. Though many still debate what caused the "unsinkable" ship to end up 13,000 feet beneath the Atlantic, most agree that the iceberg and bad judgment are to blame.

➤ RMS *Lusitania*—**Lost: May 7, 1915.** When a German Imperial Navy submarine torpedoed the *Lusitania* in the third year of World War I, the world was outraged. The ship sank rapidly, killing 1,198. It has long been suspected that the *Lusitania* carried a sizable cargo of munitions. Since many Americans were killed in the attack, it played a role in America's entering the war against Germany in 1917.

➤ *Bismarck*—**Lost: May 27, 1941.** The World War II Nazi battleship made a desperate dash into the Atlantic where it was engaged in a historic naval battle and sunk after a fight with British warships and torpedo planes. Although Britain's Royal Navy has long claimed that the *Bismarck* was sunk by British shelling and torpedoes, results from a 1989 expedition organized by researcher Robert Ballard revealed it may have been scuttled by the ship's own crew to prevent capture.

➤ HMS *Edinburgh*—**Lost: May 2, 1942.** The cruiser *Edinburgh* was transporting 5.5 tons of Soviet gold to Great Britain when struck by three German torpedoes in an attack by a submarine and surface ships. A Royal Navy destroyer had to sink the *Edinburgh* with a final torpedo to prevent its capture by the Germans. Most of the gold aboard the ship was removed during a five-week salvage operation using saturation diving that began September 2, 1981. Divers descended to an amazing 800 feet to cut their way into the ship and remove the gold bars.

➤ *I-52*—**Lost: June 24, 1944.** The aircraft carrier USS *Bogue* executed a fatal mid-ocean ambush against the Japanese submarine *I-52* while it carried crucial war materials bound for Nazi Germany—including two tons of gold—in the South Atlantic. The *I-52* was attacked during a nighttime rainstorm. The *I-52* was done in by planes dropping a then-secret torpedo that pursued a submarine's sounds. An estimated 100 died aboard the submarine including a small number of Japanese war technology experts and a pair of German navy radar technicians. The *I-52* was discovered by an expedition organized by sunken-ship researcher Paul Tidwell in 1995. Tidwell hopes to raise the *I-52* intact and recover its gold.

437

➤ *Andréa Doria*—**Lost: July 26, 1956.** The Swedish-American liner *Stockholm* and the Italian liner *Andréa Doria* collided during a foggy night despite the use of radar and extensive "Rules of the Road" set down by the shipping industry. A total of 51 people died with 46 casualties being aboard the *Andréa Doria* and five aboard the *Stockholm*. The specially strengthened bow of the *Stockholm* knifed into the *Andréa Doria*'s side, causing the beautiful Italian ship to flood and eventually sink. The *Stockholm* remained afloat and helped rescue some of the *Andréa Doria*'s 1,706 passengers.

➤ USS *Scorpion*—**Lost: May 22, 1968.** The nuclear attack submarine *Scorpion* was 400 miles southwest of the Atlantic's Azores Islands when it was stricken by a problem investigators have yet to unravel. The nuclear-armed submarine went down with 99 men in nearly 12,000 feet of water and was not discovered until five months after its loss. Though theories abound, no one yet knows why the submarine was lost.

➤ *Edmund Fitzgerald*—**Lost: November 10, 1975.** The Great Lakes ore carrier *Edmund Fitzgerald* was famous as one of the largest such ships operating on the Great Lakes. It was lost in a powerful storm with all 29 hands on Lake Michigan in 530 feet of water. The ship was located soon after the wreck. Although its loss was officially blamed on poorly fitting hatch covers that allowed storm-driven water inside the *Fitzgerald*'s hold, controversy still rages over what caused the ship to sink.

Index

T